Investigating RELIGIOUS TERRORISM and RITUALISTIC CRIMES

Investigating
RELIGIOUS
TERRORISM
and
RITUALISTIC
CRIMES

DAWN PERLMUTTER

CRC PRESS

Boca Raton London New York Washington, D.C.

Editorial Production Note: At the author's request, editing of this work has been minimal, and the text largely reflects the original manuscript. Any comments or questions regarding word usage and style should not be directed to CRC Press, which abrogates responsibility.

Library of Congress Cataloging-in-Publication Data

Perlmutter, Dawn, 1959-
    Investigating religious terrorism and ritualistic crimes / by Dawn Perlmutter
       p. cm.
    Includes bibliographical references and index.
    ISBN 0-8493-1034-2
    1. Occult crime. 2. Ritual abuse. 3. Terrorism–Religious aspects. I. Title.

HV8079.O25P47 2003
364.1–dc21   2003046210

Visit the CRC Press Web site at www.crcpress.com

© 2004 by CRC Press LLC

No claim to original U.S. Government works
International Standard Book Number 0-8493-1034-2
Library of Congress Card Number 2003046210
Printed in the United States of America 1 2 3 4 5 6 7 8 9 0
Printed on acid-free paper

2001 was a year of both national and personal loss.
This book is dedicated to two American heroes.
In loving memory of my brother and father:

Lance Elliot Perlmutter
Abraham David Perlmutter

Author

Dawn Perlmutter, director of the Institute for the Research of Organized & Ritual Violence, LLC, is considered one of the leading experts in the areas of religious violence and ritualistic crimes. She regularly consults for and trains local, state and federal law enforcement agencies throughout the United States on identifying and investigating ritualistic crimes and terrorism perpetrated by extremist religious groups. She is the author of two books and numerous publications on ritual violence in contemporary culture.

Dr. Perlmutter is a philosophy professor in the Pennsylvania State System of Higher Education. She holds a Doctor of Philosophy from New York University and a master's degree from The American University, Washington, D.C.

Contents

10 Symbolic Analysis: Ritual Homicide Typology 349

Contemporary Religious Violence

1

Regardless of how heinous, irrational or inexplicable, religious violence is always justified and never considered terrorism by the religious groups that practice it. Throughout history and across cultures, sacred violence has been sanctioned, condoned and deemed necessary for religious principles. Today sacred violence is still sanctioned, condoned and deemed necessary for religious principles, only now man has the technology to at best terrorize the world and at worst completely destroy it. Understanding the religious beliefs, ethics and ritual practices of unfamiliar religions is imperative to preventing future acts of terrorism. Some religions not only justify violence but specific acts of bloodshed are often ritually required for proper worship. Analyzing religious practices from each individual group's theological perspective provides insights into the nature of these seemingly inexplicable acts of violence.

The purpose of this book is to provide law enforcement investigators, academic scholars, forensic scientists and criminal justice professionals with a resource guide to assist in intelligence gathering, criminal investigation, crime scene identification, prevention and understanding of religious violence and ritualistic crimes.

Defining Religious Terrorism

Definitions of religious terrorism are problematic because it is a relative concept that essentially is determined by the theological, moral, political, sociological and legal perspectives of each group. Hence, religious terrorism is most often attributed to groups designated as "cults," a pejorative term ascribed to unfamiliar religions. The problem can be summed up in two basic concepts: "One man's God is another man's devil" and "One man's terrorist is another man's freedom fighter."

Relative Concepts

- One man's god is another man's devil.

- One man's terrorist is another man's freedom fighter.

There are many contrary definitions of religion and terrorism that are dependent upon the perspective of the author. While religious scholars debate where to draw the line for religious freedom, political philosophers and legal scholars attempt to distinguish between political freedoms, terrorism, anarchy and justice. The concept of violence or more specifically force is intrinsic to the definition of terrorism but that only further complicates the issue because not all acts of violence are considered negative. One political view will deem an action terrorism and another political view will deem it justifiable retribution. Furthermore, the distinction between terrorism and retribution is dependent upon the perception of who was violated first. Hence, religious terrorism is a culturally relative construct that varies in place and in time and is intrinsically intertwined with issues of political and religious freedom even if that freedom entails the subjugation and harm of others.

Building upon both the Federal Bureau of Investigation's and the State Department's definitions of terrorism, the following operational concept of religious terrorism is posited: religious terrorism is defined as any act of violence or threatened use of violence by a group or individual with the intent of intimidating individuals, citizens or governments in the furtherance of religious objectives. Religious terrorism is frequently characterized by the

Definition of Religious Terrorism

- Religious terrorism is defined as any act of violence or threatened use of violence by a group or individual with the intent of intimidating individuals, citizens or governments in the furtherance of religious objectives. Religious terrorism is frequently characterized by the imposed or self-imposed infliction of either physical, psychological, symbolic or spiritual assaults in order to achieve the group's and/or individual's objectives.

imposed or self-imposed infliction of physical, psychological, symbolic or spiritual assaults in order to achieve the group's and/or individual's objectives.

Defining Ritualistic Crimes

Ritualistic crime not only encompasses particular manifestations of religious terrorism but also entails a wide variety of both sacred and secular violent acts perpetrated by groups and individuals. Ritualistic crimes are most often attributed to practitioners of occult ideologies such as Satanism, Palo Mayombe, Brujeria, etc., or to serial killers and sexual sadists who ritually murder their victims. Similar to religious terrorism, ritualistic crimes have no agreed-upon definition.

Building upon a 1989 California Law Enforcement study of occult crime, ritualistic crime is defined as any act of violence characterized by a series of repeated physical, sexual and/or psychological actions/assaults combined with a systematic use of symbols, ceremonies and/or machinations. The need to repeat such acts can be cultural, sexual, economic, psychological and/or spiritual.[1] Crimes entailing ritual violence are generally referred to as cult or occult crime. It is significant to note that religious terrorism and ritualistic crimes are not mutually exclusive and frequently manifest aspects of both.

Definition of Ritualistic Crime

- Ritualistic crime encompasses ceremonial actions and/or ritualistic acts, and often involves occult-related behavior patterns, and is frequently motivated by a belief in some occult ideology.

Palo Mayombe crime scene. (Photo courtesy of Ocean County Sheriff's Department, Criminalistics Investigative Unit, Detective William Pozanlante, Toms River, NJ.)

Since the ritual practices of alternative religions are generally unknown and contrary to traditional Western beliefs, investigating a crime that is the result of unfamiliar religious practices can be disturbing, problematic and often overlooked. The phenomenon of ritual activity can be comprehended when situated in sacred rituals of initiation, sacrifice, healing, protection and worship of gods and ancestors. Due to the many legal, practical and ethical controversies that surround the investigation of spiritual practices the study of contemporary religious violence is in its infancy. There have been no serious empirical studies of occult crimes or classifications that adequately distinguish ritual homicides committed for sacred versus secular motivations. In the final chapter of this book, a ritual homicide classification system based on forensics and symbolic evidence found at crime scenes is put forth in an attempt to standardize the identification, investigation and analysis of ritual murder.

This book will help you distinguish religiously motivated ritualistic crime from other motivations, recognize the rituals, symbols and practices of distinct groups, differentiate legal religious practices from criminal activity and objectively identify organizations whose religious ideologies pose a potential terrorist threat.

Religion

In addition to the hundreds of established major religions of the world, there are literally thousands of unrecognized and new religious movements. The textbooks about world religions can only briefly describe some of the better known beliefs. For law enforcement purposes, it is necessary to understand the complexity of religious differences and the enormity of the problems to which they give rise. The significance of religious belief is astounding when you appreciate that it determines ethics, morality, politics, laws, manners, etc.

For many societies, religious belief also determines significant daily activities such as what their members can wear, eat, drink, read, listen to, and whom they can marry. Additionally, religion is intrinsic to political conflicts and justifies violence, war and terrorism. Knowledge of specific religions is essential to understanding the motivations, justifications and prevention of terrorism. To comprehend the enormity of the variety of religions, a few terms will be clarified. The corresponding simplistic chart (see next page) illustrates them. The chart is by no means inclusive; categorizing religions is problematic because (1) the concept of religion is not easily defined, (2) many religions are absolutist, which means they only acknowledge their own doctrines and often do not recognize other religions as valid, and (3) the chart reflects a traditional Western perspective.

Categories of Religious Groups

Occult Religions	**Cults (non-mainstream or new religions)**
• Satanism	• Millennial groups (apocalyptic beliefs)
• Neo-Pagan/Witchcraft	• White Supremacist (Militia/Patriot)
• Syncretic beliefs: Santeria, Voodoo, Palo Mayombe, Brujeria	• UFO Religions
• Goth, Vampire, Fetish	
Traditional Religions	**Extreme Orthodox**
• Christianity	• Fundamental extremists
• Judaism	• Sects (branched off from traditional religions)
• Islam	

Traditional Western religions refer to Judaism, Christianity and Islam, all of which are monotheistic (believe in one god), highly organized and well established. A sect usually refers to a dissident group that has separated from another usually mainstream religion, often proclaiming its intent to recover principles and practices from an earlier time that the mainstream religion abandoned. For example, the Protestant Reformation split Christianity into Roman Catholicism and Protestantism, which further divided into many churches and sects. Sects can evolve into recognized religions such as the Lutheran, Baptist and Methodist churches or they may dissipate for lack of support. Most new religious movements aspire to become recognized as valid churches.

Fundamental extremist religions or fundamentalism are also considered sects and can branch off from any religion but most often derive from Christianity and Islam. Fundamentalist theology usually entails a return to what is considered a purer or truer form of the original religion. Fundamentalist world views are consistently duelist with the world being sharply divided between the forces of good and evil. Unfortunately, many fundamentalist religious groups have become actively militant in the form of domestic and international terrorists and will be the subject of Chapters 3 and 4.

New Religious Movements, sometimes called New Age Religions, can either be new sects that have branched off from more established religions or entirely new religions. For example, the Branch Davidians were a Christian sect of the Seventh Day Adventists that derived from the 19th century Millerites established by Baptist leader William Miller. Christian Identity is a new religion based on British Israelism, which was not originally a racist religion. Bonnie Lu Nettles and Marshall Herff Applewhite, the leaders of Heaven's Gate, combined Christian and Theosophical doctrines with a belief in unidentified flying objects (UFOs) to create a monastic community of followers. Although they have entirely unrelated and distinct doctrines, these

---

Cult vs. Occult

Cult	Occult
• Any group with a shared ideology (belief system) and usually a charismatic leader.	• Any group with a shared ideology whose members believe they can magically intervene in the universe through specific rituals. Individuals can also practice occult beliefs.

---

groups are all considered New Religious Movements or more commonly referred to as cults.

In academia, *cult* is not only a politically incorrect term; it is viewed as a method of stigmatizing entire groups of people. The term is used to designate religious groups as aberrant and dangerous. According to religious scholars, *cult* is a word that expresses prejudice. It portrays an oversimplified and bigoted stereotype that dehumanizes the religion's members and their children and labels them subhuman. Religious scholars maintain this position even if a group has been proven to be dangerous and has committed heinous acts of violence. Their arguments against stigmatizing unfamiliar religions certainly have merit, but simply eliminating the term will not eliminate violent religious groups. *New Religious Movement* is the current politically correct term for non-mainstream religions, although many of them are not new and are derived from established religions. *Alternative Religion* is another expression, but *alternative* implies *other* and retains pejorative connotations. The most accurate and neutral expression is *unfamiliar religions*.

Essentially, a New Religious Movement is a group with a shared ideology, a charismatic leader and little else in common. The movements differ in their theologies, structures, practices and attitudes toward the government. This is why assorted millennial religions, white supremacists and UFO believers can all be designated as New Religious Movements.

Another important distinction is the difference between New Religious Movements and occult religions. This can be very confusing because they are often grouped together and are not mutually exclusive. *Occult* literally means *hidden* and refers to various methods of developing hidden powers through extensive training and discipline of the will. *Occult* also refers to any matter concerned with the supernatural and encompasses a variety of religions with occult beliefs. Essentially an occult religion is any group with a shared ideology whose members believe they can magically intervene in the universe through specific rituals. Individuals also practice occult beliefs.

While there are literally thousands of different religions, it is important to note that only a small percentage actively engage in illegal activities. Finally, it is important to note that although religious differences are fundamental to cultural conflicts; knowledge, consideration and respect for unfamiliar religions constitute a basic strategy for preventing violence.

Religious Concepts

To successfully investigate religious violence, it is advantageous to have a basic understanding of relevant religious concepts that are fundamental to the theologies of violent and potentially violent groups. Many violent ritual practices of nontraditional religions are initially incomprehensible because they are exceedingly different from traditional Western doctrines found in

Understanding relevant religious concepts and terminology is requisite to successfully investigating religious violence. The above bumper stickers advocating religious freedom and goddess worship are on display at an occult religious supply store.

Judaism and Christianity. For example, contemporary religious terrorism inspires, condones and advocates inexplicable acts of violence such as mass suicide, mass murder and suicide bombings. These acts can only be comprehended by understanding the theologies of religious terrorist groups.

Ritualistic crimes are even more difficult to comprehend because they entail inconceivable crimes such as ritual abuse, torture and ritual homicide based on ancient religious concepts such as idol worship, divination and sacrifice. Clarifying religious concepts and terms is requisite to understanding unfamiliar religious beliefs and their corresponding criminal acts. In addition to the complete glossary of terms provided at the end of this book, the following brief descriptions of religious freedom, ritual and sacrifice, pertinent religious concepts will clarify the motivations and justifications for sacred violence described throughout the book.

Religious Freedom

A thin line separates legally protected spiritual activity and illegal criminal activity. Occult groups and practices are protected by the First Amendment of the Constitution which guarantees Americans freedom of religious choice. It is especially important when investigating religious violence that accurate distinctions are made between legal and illegal activities. For example, animal slaughter for religious purposes has been the subject of both state and federal law suits. The severity, symbolism, place and date of animal mutilation can easily determine not only the legalities, but also the degree of danger a group may pose.

Another aspect of the law enforcement role in regard to the First Amendment is that officers may be placed in the position of protecting religious groups from being harassed or intimidated by other citizens. The protection role most frequently occurs with Neo-Pagan (witches) and white supremacist

Religious Freedom

- Occult groups and practices are protected by the First Amendment of the Constitution, which guarantees Americans freedom of religious choice.

- Many alternative religious groups are recognized as religions by the U.S. government.

- Law enforcement officers are often placed in the protection role during group rallies, festivals and marches.

- Many nontraditional religious groups are campaigning for recognition as genuine religions.

groups who openly hold festivals, rallies and marches in communities where citizens are radically opposed to their beliefs. Many nontraditional religious groups such as Wicca actively campaign for recognition as genuine religions. Conversely, many white supremacist groups deliberately hold provocative marches for recruitment purposes and to reinforce their claims of government persecution in the minds of their followers.

Although the beliefs of nontraditional religious groups may be highly offensive it is significant to realize that many are recognized as religions by the U.S. government. If investigations or arrests are conducted, it is imperative to have sufficient evidence of illegal or potential terrorist activities. Examples of applicable evidence will be demonstrated throughout the book.

Ritual

The concept of ritual has many meanings ranging from specific required religious rites to a diverse range of human activities inclusive of daily habits and manners. Definitions are dependent upon the theoretical perspectives of a variety of academic disciplines. For example, from an anthropological perspective, a ritual is any formal action following a set pattern that expresses shared meanings through symbols — typically the practical aspects of a religious system that express sacred values.[2] In sociology, *ritual* often refers to a regular pattern of interaction via routine events like eating meals the same time each day.

In psychological terms, a ritual is viewed as a form of compulsion, a repetitive ritualistic behavior such as handwashing or a mental act such as praying or repeating words silently in order to prevent some dreaded event or situation. A person feels driven to perform ritualistic actions in response to an obsession or according to rules that must be applied rigidly, even though the behaviors are recognized as excessive or unreasonable.[3] In religion, ritual represents community rites or ceremonies that can be simple or

---

Ritual

- Ritual has many meanings ranging from specific, required religious rites to a diverse range of human activities such as daily habits.
- In religion, ritual represents the rites or ceremonies of a community.
- Ritual behavior provides valuable insights into the motivations for religious terrorism and ritualistic crimes.

highly complex, brief or performed several times a day and required for proper worship.

Theories concerning the function and purpose of ritual are so diverse that an entire academic discipline is dedicated to ritual studies. Theoretical conceptions of ritual behavior are observable in specific types of criminal activities that provide valuable insights into the motivations for religious terrorism and ritualistic crimes. When forensic and symbolic information found at crime scenes is analyzed in regard to theories of ritual, subtle but clear distinctions become evident, for example, whether a ritualistic crime is committed for secular or sacred motivations, as part of a shared group belief system or as an individual expression of psychopathology. These distinctions also apply to the theoretical views of expert witnesses. For example, a psychiatric perspective may deem all acts of ritual murder as a form of psychopathology regardless of a perpetrator's strong religious beliefs. In regard to prosecution, ritual theory is extremely pertinent because it establishes both the foundations for arguments for diminished capacity, coercion, and mental defect and arguments for rational choice, premeditation and murder. In brief, the interpretation of how an individual or group ritually expresses what they believe distinguishes between true believers, true criminals, psychopaths and dabblers, all of whom may be terrorists.

Sacrifice

Across cultures and throughout history, the one practice common to all religions is sacrifice and the most potent form is achieved through blood rituals. Whether animal or human, blood historically is the mandatory substance for religious ritual, and sacrifice is the ultimate religious experience. Symbolically, blood represents both purity and impurity, the sacred and the profane, life and death. Blood is extremely significant in religious ideology. There are specific rituals, attitudes and prohibitions on blood in almost every society.

Blood Ritual / Sacrifice

- Historically and today, blood is the mandatory substance for religious ritual.
- In nonviolent occult religions such as Santeria, Voodoo etc., sacrificial offerings are an intrinsic part of religious belief.
- Perpetrators of ritualistic crimes use sacrifice as a method to achieve personal goals.
- The use of blood in ritualistic crimes is more revealing than any other form of evidence.

Rituals entailing blood sacrifice existed at least 20,000 years ago, until Biblical prohibitions on idol worship abolished communal blood rites and made human and animal sacrifice morally repugnant. The use of blood in ritualistic crimes (not to be confused with blood stain pattern analysis) is more revealing than any other form of evidence. In occult crime the physical pattern is not as important as the symbolic meaning of blood. Additionally, the level of experience of the perpetrator is immediately evident in the cleanliness of the crime scene or victim. For example, it takes a high level of experience to remove blood from a person or animal without soiling the scene. A juvenile dabbler would not be able to remove blood in the same manner as an experienced high priest who might have the skills of a surgeon. Additionally, juveniles do not always treat a scene with the proper regard for sacred space as true believers would. In ancient times and today, the role of the sacrificer is an honored and privileged position and he will most likely be the leader of the group.

The term *sacrifice* derives from the Latin *sacrificium* (*sacer*, holy, and *facere*, to make) meaning *to make holy*. It carries the connotation of a religious act in the highest or fullest sense; it can also be understood as an act of sanctifying or consecrating an object.[4] Historically, theologians have proposed four purposes of sacrifice: (1) homage or praise — a form of pure adoration, (2) thanksgiving — giving thanks for a favor granted, (3) supplication — asking for anything from material goods to divine intervention and (4) expiation — placating or requesting forgiveness or the removal or prevention of evil and misfortune. Traditionally, the recipients of sacrifice are divine beings such as gods, spirits, demonic beings and sometimes humans who are either worshipped or feared, although sacrifice in the proper sense is offered to humans only after they die and are considered to possess superhuman power.[5]

In nonviolent occult religions such as Santeria, Voodoo, Candomble and others, sacrificial offerings are intrinsic parts of religious belief and are equivalent to the Judeo-Christian concept of prayer. However, perpetrators of ritualistic crimes consciously use sacrifice as a method to achieve personal goals and embrace the malevolent side of religions such as Satanism, Palo Mayombe, and Brujeria to cause harm, personal gratification, achieve power and protection from enemies. Ritualistic crimes committed as sacred acts of sacrifice are described in detail in Chapters 5 and 7.

Human sacrifice that entails the killing of humans or the use of the flesh, blood or bones of the human body for ritual purposes has been a widespread and complex phenomenon throughout history. Ritual homicide for the purposes of religious sacrifice occurs, and there are recent cases described in this book. Religious scholars have proposed nine basic purposes of human sacrifice. In addition to the four previously cited reasons for sacrifice, they include a form of transformation, communion, regeneration, divine assimilation and a method of achieving immortality.

The significant ideology behind sacrificial ritual is that blood consists of life force energy constituting the highest offering to the gods or ancestors. In malevolent occult worship, bloodletting or imbibing blood from a victim represents the assimilation of raw power. Additionally, the longer a victim is tortured and the pain is prolonged, the more life energy/power is emitted. In this manner, ritual torture, cannibalism and ritual homicide are contemporary acts of human sacrifice that represent sacred communion meals for the perpetrators in which the power of life is assimilated and regenerated. Ritual homicide is also a method for the perpetrator to achieve immortality and/or become a god by unifying the divine and the mortal.

The theology of many contemporary occult groups describes their most sacred rituals in sacrificial terms. For example, The Temple of the Vampire, an acknowledged religion, claims that genuine Vampirism is the exchange of energy between living Vampires and Undead Gods in a holy ritual that the temple calls Vampiric Communion. Through this communion, a practitioner becomes closer to the gods, develops higher levels of Vampiric skills and ultimately achieves immortality by becoming an Undead God.

Rod Ferrel, the youngest person on Florida's death row, convicted of the brutal murders of two people, started his own vampire cult and was described by his followers as wanting to be a god. Many occult groups have specific rituals and degrees of initiation that culminate in achieving some level above human such as godlike or superior beings. At best, this superior attitude contributes to lack of regard for others and at worst it leads to justifying genocide. Vampirism, the latest popular manifestation of occult religions and corresponding crimes, is described in Chapter 6.

Research into historical acts of sacrifice is remarkably pertinent to contemporary ritual killings. Applying academic theories of ritual murder and blood rites to contemporary ritualistic crimes and religious terrorism reveals similar motivations, goals and justifications. The classical works on sacrifice posit specific questions about common elements of sacrifice: Who offers the sacrifice? What is offered? What external forms belong to the act of offering? In what places and at what times are sacrifices offered? Who is the recipient of the sacrifice? For what reasons are sacrifices offered?[6]

Answers to these questions are not only relevant to a classification system of historical acts of sacrifice but to a contemporary typology that can contribute to solving and preventing religious terrorism and ritualistic crimes. A ritual homicide typology based on the phenomenon of sacrifice is the subject of Chapter 10.

Crimes Typically Associated with
Ritual Violence

Common:	Controversial:
• Trespassing	• Suicide
• Vandalism	• Kidnapping
• Church Desecration	• Ritual Homicide
• Theft	• Ritual Abuse
• Graffiti	
• Arson	
• Animal Mutilation	
• Extortion	

The popular secular conception of sacrifice is viewed as forfeiture of something of value for an idea or a cause, for example, when soldiers are willing to commit the ultimate sacrifice for their countries. Although this common concept of sacrifice may initially be applicable to suicide bombers, it does not encompass the very significant religious sphere. Religious terrorism is sanctioned by severe interpretations of sacred texts and intrinsically intertwined in fundamentalist religious beliefs.

Crimes Typically Associated with Ritual Violence

Crimes entailing ritual violence are generally perpetrated by practitioners of occult belief systems including Satanism, syncretic belief systems (Santeria, Palo Mayombe, Brujeria) and the Vampire/Goth scene. Examples of the types of crimes associated with ritual violence are shown in the chart above. It is important to note that other motivations for these crimes should not be ruled out. Forensic evidence such as occult writings and specific use of symbols and objects are common indicators of ritual crimes. These and additional ritualistic crime scene clues are discussed in Chapter 8.

The following typology was compiled from excerpts of *Occult Crime: A Law Enforcement Primer* published by the State of California's Office of Criminal Justice Planning in Sacramento.

Trespassing related to ritual violence or, more specifically, occult activity usually involves persons entering private areas such as wooded and forested lands, barns and other old or abandoned buildings. Their purpose is to worship either in the area as it is naturally arranged or to arrange the area so it becomes a place of worship with the appropriate altars and symbols. Occult-related trespassing of this nature is committed by persons who seek private and isolated places to worship.

Vandalism most often associated with ritualistic crime includes cemetery and church desecration. The most common types of cemetery desecration attributed to occult groups are overturning, breaking and/or stealing headstones, digging up graves, grave robbing and tampering with human corpses or skeletons. Such crimes are frequently motivated by religious beliefs that require cemetery desecrations and human bones to fulfill certain rituals.

Church Desecration frequently includes the destruction of Bibles, urinating and defecating on holy objects and furniture, tearing crucifixes off walls and destroying rosaries and crucifixes. It is important to note that the motivations behind such vandalism can also be attributed to hate crimes.

Theft from Christian churches, Jewish synagogues, hospitals, morgues, medical schools and funeral homes are often linked with ritual violence. Items stolen most often include cadavers, skeletal remains, blood and religious artifacts that are considered sacred, crucifixes, communion wafers, wine, chalices, and other items. Frequent motivations for these thefts are that particular groups require actual holy artifacts or human organs, bones and other materials for their rituals.

Graffiti is one of the most common offenses related to ritualistic crime. While a small amount of graffiti can be attributed to other occult groups, the vast majority is directly related to involvement in Satanic groups. Nearly all instances of Satanic-related graffiti, which frequently depicts Satanic symbolism, are committed by juveniles and young adults, most of whom dabble in the occult.

Arson (occult-related) is almost always attributed to Satanists, especially juveniles and young adults. Among the most common places for juveniles to commit arson are churches and synagogues where particularly holy sections or artifacts are burned, and houses or buildings where damaging evidence could be uncovered by investigators. Additionally, law enforcement officers have found Satanic graffiti at some arson scenes. It is important to note that the motivations behind the arsons of churches and synagogues can also be attributed to hate crimes.

Animal Sacrifice is primarily practiced by believers in Afro-Caribbean religions, principally practitioners of Santeria who sacrifice animals as part of rituals designed as offerings to their gods to intervene in the universe through magic. However, animal sacrifice can also be attributed to practitioners of Satanism. The symbolic objects at the crime scene, type of mutilation and other forensic evidence generally indicate the belief system practiced.

Extortion — Although group practice of extortion is not a known activity of any occult group, individual practitioners of some occult belief systems use their religious involvement to extort money and information. Investigators have noted such crimes are especially difficult to prosecute because the victims will not come forward. More often than not, the victims do not perceive themselves as victims because they trust the Santero (Priest) and believe their economic sacrifices will be used to protect them.

Suicide (occult-related) appears to be the primary domain of juveniles and young adults involved in Satanism who are often true believers but may be dabblers. Satanic-related teenage suicide is a major concern among many criminal justice practitioners and therapists.

Kidnapping — Although extremely difficult to prove, kidnapping people of all ages, but especially children, is thought to be a prevalent crime among some occult practitioners, particularly traditional/cult Satanists who are said to kidnap victims needed for ritual sacrifice, self-styled juvenile Satanists whose dabbling has taken them "to the point of no return" and Mayomberos (Palo Mayombe priests) whose rituals require human skulls, often with the brains still attached, to add to their ngangas (sacred cauldrons).

Ritual Homicide — Probably the most controversial crime allegedly committed for occult purposes is murder perpetrated for spiritual reasons and sometimes as a human sacrifice. Sacrificing of human beings has occurred in almost every culture throughout history and contemporary incidents have been documented. Currently, both Palo Mayombe practitioners and Satanists are often linked to human sacrifice. Evidence indicates that juvenile and young adult Satanists who have become true believers commit murder for sacrificial reasons based on their spiritual beliefs.

Ritual Abuse — This is a particularly heinous and controversial crime, which is known as ritual abuse, ritual child abuse or more specifically Satanic ritual abuse. The alleged perpetrators of such abuse are most often Satanists. In the broadest sense, ritual abuse of children, adolescents and adults involves repeated physical, sexual, psychological and/or spiritual abuse which utilizes rituals. Probably no issue is more divisive within the criminal justice community than Satanic ritual abuse. While no one disputes the existence or increase of ritualistic abuse, few agree about several other aspects: the extent of ritualistic crimes committed specifically by cult Satanists, the motivations of perpetrators and the veracity of the victims who claim to have survived ritual abuse at the hands of Satanists.

Crimes Typically Associated with Religious Terrorism

Crimes entailing religious violence are generally perpetrated by practitioners of alternative religions, commonly referred to as cults, extremist groups and terrorists. The chart on the following page shows typical examples of crimes associated with religious terrorism. It is important to note that other motivations for these crimes should not be ruled out. Forensic evidence such as manifestos,

Crimes Typically Associated with:
Religious Terrorism

• Hate Crimes	***Current Trends in***
• Tax Evasion	***Terrorist Weapons***
• Weapons Violations	• Weapons of Mass
• Vandalism	Destruction
• Arson	• Bioterrorism
• Robbery	• Cyberterrorism
• Torture/Coercion	• Dirty Bombs
• Mass Murder/Suicide/	• Suicide Bombers
Homicide	• Suicide Shooters
• Terrorism	

religious doctrines, specific use of symbols, objects, and language are common indicators of religious group violence. It is also significant that groups engaging in religious terrorism often simultaneously practice forms of ritual violence.

Hate Crimes are criminal offenses committed against persons, property or society that are motivated in whole or in part by an offender's bias against an individual's or group's race, religion, ethnic or national origin, gender, age, disability or sexual orientation. All crimes designated religious terrorism are fundamentally hate crimes although legal definitions of hate crimes vary according to state statutes and most frequently refer to arson, vandalism and homicides in which the victim or property was selected due to the perpetrator's bias against a race, religion or ethnicity.

Tax Evasion — Many organized religious groups own large businesses in which the members/followers work for little or no pay or their salaries are turned over to the charismatic leader or prophet of the group. Financial arrangements are often illegal. Additionally, members of right-wing extremist organizations whose political ideologies are characterized by their embracement of anti-government and anti-regulatory beliefs openly do not pay taxes.

Weapons Violations — Many organized groups stockpile weapons due to their millennial religious ideologies that entail beliefs of an apocalyptic war in the near future. Additionally, right-wing extremist groups stockpile weapons based on their beliefs in a future race and/or civil war.

Vandalism — Many organized right-wing extremist groups are characterized by their adherence to the principles of racial supremacy and their embracement of anti-government/anti-regulatory beliefs. They often commit acts of vandalism to synagogues and churches, frequently using symbols such as swastikas.

Arson — Right-wing extremist groups also commit acts of arson such as burning churches and synagogues to intimidate citizens based on their racist ideologies.

Robbery — Militia and white supremacist organizations have financed their operations by robbing banks. The goals of these groups are to create social and political chaos, thereby forcing the U.S. government to declare martial law — an act they believe will lead to a violent overthrow of the American government.

Torture/Coercion — Many religious group doctrines include extreme forms of asceticism as a method of indoctrinating members. These can involve sleep deprivation, diet restrictions, immersion in extreme hot or cold water, physical beatings, silence and other forms of physical and psychological abuse. Members often voluntarily submit to these actions in order to attain the spiritual goals of the group.

Mass Murder/Mass Suicide are responses to a belief in collective salvation or actual or perceived threats of persecution that would prevent the group from achieving salvation. During mass suicides, children are murdered, often by their own parents. Mass murders and mass suicides involving large numbers of members of new religious movements have occurred several times in the past few years. Examples include Jonestown, the Branch Davidians, Heaven's Gate, Solar Temple and The Movement for the Restoration of the Ten Commandments of God.

Homicide in an alternative religious group frequently occurs when a member decides to leave the group. This person is viewed as a traitor and a potential threat because he may inform authorities of ongoing illegal activities in the group. Homicides also occur during power struggles within a group, accidentally by overexposure to the group's violent rituals, or murders of persons outside the group who pose a threat to the group. Finally, individuals who symbolically represent opposition to fundamental group beliefs (e.g., abortion doctors, homosexuals, interracial couples) are often targeted and murdered.

Terrorism — No single agreed-upon definition of terrorism exists because the concept is determined by the theological, moral, political, sociological and legal perspectives of each group. However, for the purposes of describing criminal acts the State Department provides a concise definition of terrorism: premeditated, politically motivated violence perpetrated against noncombatant targets by sub-national groups or clandestine agents, usually intended to influence an audience.

Current Trends in Terrorist Weapons

The Federal Bureau of Investigation's (FBI) typology of terrorist groups includes current trends in modern terrorism that fall into two categories: weapons of mass destruction (including what is currently referred to as bio-

Weapons of Mass Destruction

B-NICE
- Biological
- Nuclear
- Incendiary
- Chemical
- Explosive

- **Overt Release**
  An announced release of an agent.

- **Covert Release**
  Not discovered until individuals
  report symptoms.

Biological Incidents

Four Common Types of Biological Agents
- **Bacteria:** Anthrax, cholera, plague, tularemia
- **Rickettsia:** Q fever (*Coxiella burnetii*)
- **Virus:** Smallpox, Venezuelan equine encephalitis,
  viral hemorrhagic fevers (Ebola and Marburg viruses,
  Lasa fever)
- **Toxins:** Botulism, SEB, Ricin, Mycotoxins

terrorism) and the use of the Internet to commit acts of terrorism (including what is currently known as cyberterrorism).

Weapons of Mass Destruction/Bioterrorism include chemical, biological and radiological agents. A *1999 Emergency Response to Terrorism Self-Study Manual* published by the Federal Emergency Management Agency (FEMA) for training fire, medical and hazardous materials first responders lists five categories of terrorist incidents and uses the acronym B-NICE as a simple way to remember them (biological, nuclear, incendiary, chemical, and explosive). FEMA also lists four routes of entry (inhalation, absorption, ingestion and injection) and four common types of biological agents (bacteria, viruses, rickettsiae and toxins). The FEMA manual also describes handling of biological, nuclear, incendiary and chemical incidents. Chemical agents fall into five classes: nerve agents, blister agents, blood agents, choking agents and irritating agents which are described in horrifying detail in the manual.[7]

Statistics listed in a congressional statement dated May 10, 2001 claim that between 1997 and 2000 the FBI investigated 779 weapons-of-mass-destruction reports generally involving individuals or small groups. In spite of the fact that the vast majority of these cases were found to be false, the two agents most frequently involved in the investigations were ricin, a bio-

Nuclear Incidents

Types of Nuclear Threats

- The threatened use or detonation of a nuclear bomb
- The threatened use or detonation of a conventional explosive incorporating nuclear materials.
- Detonation of a large device near a nuclear plant or radiological cargo in transport.

Incendiary Incidents

- Any mechanical, electrical or chemical device intentionally used to initiate combustion and start a fire.
- These elements may be used singly or in combination.
- Devices may be simple or elaborate.
- Each device consists of three basic components: an igniter or fuse, a container or body, and an incendiary material or filler.

Chemical Incidents

Chemical Agents Fall into Five Categories

- **Nerve Agents** (toxic, and small drops are fatal): Sarin, Soman, Tabun, V agent
- **Blister Agents** (causes severe burns; corrosive and toxic): Mustard, Lewisite
- **Blood Agents** (interferes with blood oxygen): Hydrogen cyanide, cyanogen chloride
- **Choking Agents** (interferes with respiratory tract): Chlorine, phosgene
- **Irritating Agents** (non-lethal, designed to incapacitate): Chloropicrin, MACE, tear gas, pepper spray, dibenzoxazepine

---

Explosive Incidents

Two Categories of Explosives

1. Any substance or article, including a device, designed to function by explosion.

2. Any substance or article, including a device, which by chemical reaction within itself can function in a similar manner even if not designed to function by explosion.

70% of all terrorist attacks worldwide involve explosives.

---

logical toxin, and anthrax, a bacteriological agent. Surprisingly, although ricin toxin had been involved in some cases, no anthrax agents had been uncovered in a law enforcement investigation in the U.S. even though in 2000 90 of the 115 biological threats investigated involved the use of anthrax.

A more recent congressional statement (November 6, 2001) specifically concerning bioterrorism noted that since the events of September 11, which included the tragic deaths of five persons from anthrax, the FBI responded to approximately 7089 suspicious anthrax letters, 950 incidents involving weapons of mass destruction and an estimated 29,331 telephone calls from the public about suspicious packages. The statement on bioterrorism classifies potential threats into the categories of overt and covert releases, based on the manner by which the biological agent is released into the community and the nature of the response. An overt scenario involves the announced release of an agent; a covert release may not be discovered until individuals report symptoms. An example of an act of religious terrorism using weapons of mass destruction occurred in 1995 when the Japanese group Aum Shinrikyo released sarin gas into the Tokyo subway because their apocalyptic religious ideology stated that they had to destroy the world to save it. Aum Shinrikyo is discussed in detail in Chapter 2.

Cyberterrorism — Terrorists are increasingly using the Internet to recruit members, communicate between cells and members, raise funds and spread propaganda. Other terrorist uses of the Internet include attacks on government websites and e-mail servers and attempts to inundate systems with e-mail messages. Cyberterrorism is the use of cyber tools to shut down or degrade national infrastructures such as energy, transportation, communications or government services for the purpose of coercing or intimidating a government or civilian population. Clearly, we have reached new levels of insecurity.

Cyberterrorism

Criminal Threats
- Theft of National Security information
- Interruption of electrical power to metropolitan area
- Potential attacks on water reservoirs, dams, uranium storage sites, nuclear and gas facilities
- Attacks on e-commerce websites

Terrorist Use of the Internet
- Formulate plans
- Raise funds
- Spread propaganda
- Engage in secure communications
- Intelligence gathering

Radiological Weapons (commonly referred to as dirty bombs) came to public attention in June 2002 with the arrest of Jose Padilla, an American operative for the al-Qaeda network. Padilla converted to Islam while serving time in prison in the early 1990s for his activities as a Chicago gang member. Subsequent to his release from prison, he changed his name to Abdullah Al Muhajir and in 2001 traveled to Afghanistan and Pakistan on several occasions where he met senior al-Qaeda officials. While in Afghanistan and Pakistan, he trained with al-Quaeda, learning the skills to wire explosive devices and researching radiological dispersion devices. He was arrested on May 8, 2002 at O'Hare International Airport upon his return from Pakistan as an "enemy combatant" who posed a serious threat to the American people and our national security for exploring a plan to build and explode a radioactive dirty bomb. A radioactive dirty bomb involves exploding a conventional bomb that not only kills victims in the immediate vicinity but also spreads radioactive material that is highly toxic to humans and can cause mass deaths, radioactive sickness and injury. Essentially, radiological dispersion devices are conventional bombs wrapped in radioactive waste that can readily be found in hospitals and industrial plants. Unfortunately, radioactive waste materials are much more widely available than weapons-grade materials and are kept in conditions that are not highly secure. Dirty bombs can be miniature devices or as big as truck bombs. Al Muhajir is currently in the custody of the U.S. military in a navy brig in South Carolina.

Suicide Bombers — One of the most difficult types of weapons to comprehend is the suicide bomber. Although several historical precedents exist, it is almost incomprehensible that suicide bombings occur on a regular basis in the 21st century. The only method of truly understanding these acts of violence is to view them from the perspective of a religious tradition that encompasses an extreme dualistic belief in good versus evil, the ability to

Dirty Bomb/Radiological Weapon

- A "dirty bomb" is a conventional explosive such as dynamite that has been packaged with radioactive material, which scatters when the bomb goes off.
- A dirty bomb kills or injures through the initial blast of the conventional explosive and by airborne radiation and contamination — hence the term *dirty*.
- Such bombs can be miniature devices or as big as a truck bomb.

Suicide vs. Homicide Bomber

- Homicide bomber is inaccurate and diminishes the seriousness of the group's religious beliefs and the seriousness of the threat.
- Suicide bomber implies a true believer, someone who will **deliberately** die for the cause, and who is much more dangerous (martyr).

achieve martyrdom and a real and immediate expectation of reaching paradise. Actual economic and psychological factors such as the bombers' lack of future expectations and the receipt by their families of large amounts of money after their terrorist attacks are also pertinent motivations for committing suicide. However, these motivations would not be sufficient without the entire community's unwavering respect, support and devout religious beliefs. Interpretations of Islamic religious concepts that justify suicide bombers are described in detail in Chapter 4.

In early April 2002, the Bush administration started using the phrase *homicide bomber* rather than *suicide bomber* in an attempt to emphasize the brutal consequences of such actions. Subsequently, the media had to make individual decisions whether to retain the suicide bomber terminology or use the new expression. With regard to religious terrorism and the intent of the crime, *homicide bomber* is an inaccurate term because homicide intrinsically implies that the perpetrator wants to survive after committing the crime. The expression *homicide bomber* diminishes the commitment of true believers to their religious theology, political cause and, more significantly, the severity of their threat.

Potential targets substantially increase in numbers when the perpetrator does not have to find an escape route, the bomb does not have to be planted and the perpetrators show no regard for civilians or consideration of specific targets. Law enforcement agents must understand that a true believer who is willing to die cannot be investigated, negotiated with or interrogated in the same manner as typical perpetrators.

In addition to the obvious deaths and injuries caused by the standard explosives the bombers wear around their chests or waists, the bombs have a more insidious aspect. Nails, bolts, spikes and steel balls are routinely added by terrorists to the explosive charges to increase the number of fatalities. If the thought of projectiles shooting into your body is not disturbing enough, the latest trend in terrorism is to first saturate the nails and bolts with rat poison to create chemical weapons. This technique was first used by a Hamas suicide bomber on December 1, 2001 in a Jerusalem pedestrian mall. Interrogations of members of the Hamas underground network captured during Israel's Defensive Shield Operation revealed that Hamas was in the process of turning standard explosives into a mix of chemical weapons. Hamas detainees claimed that different networks of both Fatah and Hamas were testing a variety of combinations ranging from regular rat poison to improvised versions of nerve gas. It is difficult enough for victims to survive projectiles embedded in their spines, necks, hearts and brains without suffering physical or mental damage for life. However, the effect of the added rat poison in the human body prevents blood from coagulating so that when physicians attempt to operate they cannot stop the bleeding. The addition of chemical weapons to suicide bombers' explosive belts clearly maximizes the terror.

A photograph of what is now known as the "Baby Bomber" has come to represent the epitome of the high esteem in which suicide bombers are held in Palestinian culture. In June 2002, the Israeli army released a photo of a Palestinian baby dressed like a suicide bomber with ammunition belts and explosives strapped to its body and a headband of the Islamic militant group Hamas. The picture was found in the family album of a senior member of Hamas during a search of his home in the West Bank city of Hebron. Although it is not unusual to see older children dressed as bombers, the photo of the baby bomber emphasized the deeply rooted hatred toward Israel and the acceptance of martyrdom in Palestinian culture.

Suicide Shooters — At the time of this writing, the only suicide bombings to occur thus far on American soil were the tragic events of September 11. Although the bombs were in the form of commercial airliners, they were still suicide bombers. However, on the fourth of July 2002, Independence Day, America witnessed its first suicide shooting. Egyptian immigrant Hesham Mohamed Hadayet went to Israel's El Al ticket counter at Los Angeles airport armed with a 45-caliber semiautomatic Glock pistol, a 9-mm handgun, a 6-inch knife and extra ammunition. He killed two people and injured several others before he was fatally shot by an El Al guard. American authorities were reluctant to call this incident an act of terrorism in an apparent attempt to distinguish an isolated incident that may legally be designated a hate crime from an al-Qaeda-planned operation. However, Israeli authorities immediately recognized it for what it was — an act of terrorism.

Whatever reasons the FBI have for not designating this a terrorist incident, possibly to avoid panic and violence against American Muslims or simply to protect the integrity of the investigation, the evidence is quite compelling that Hadayet committed a suicidal act of religious terrorism. Hadayet sent his wife and two sons back to Egypt a few weeks prior to the shooting. He selected El Al Airlines, killed two Jews, was heavily armed and was an Egyptian national. He placed a "read the Koran" bumper sticker on his front door before leaving for the airport. His neighbors stated that he frequently denounced Israel and U.S. support of Israel. He was once slated for deportation by the U.S. Immigration and Naturalization Service and was angry at a neighbor for flying large American and marine corps flags from a balcony above his door after September 11. Whether Hesham Mohamed Hadayet was a "sleeper" for Egyptian Jihad or simply a terrorist sympathizer overcome with hatred for Israel and the U.S., there is no doubt that he was on a suicide mission and the July 4, 2002 incident was the first of what will inevitably be many more individual suicide terrorist attacks.

References

1 . State of California Office of Criminal Justice, *Occult Crime: A Law Enforcement Primer,* Sacramento; see definition of ritualism, 1989, p. 25.

2. Abercrombe, N., Hill, S., and Turner, B.S., *The Penguin Dictionary of Sociology,* New York, Penguin Books, 1988, p. 209.

3. Abess, J., Glossary of Psychiatric Terminology, www.abess.com/glossary.html July 2002.

4. Eliade, M., Ed., *The Encyclopedia of Religion,* New York, Macmillan, 1987, p. 544.

5. Eliade, M., Ed., *The Encyclopedia of Religion,* New York, Macmillan, 1987, p. 549.

6. Eliade, M., Ed., *The Encyclopedia of Religion,* New York, Macmillan, 1987, p. 545.

7. FEMA, *Emergency Response to Terrorism Self Study Manual,* Washington, D.C., U.S. Department of Justice, 1999, p. 7.

Millennial Religions and Terrorism

2

Millennialism is often confused with *millennium*, a Latin word meaning a 1000-year time span. In religious terms, Millennialism, also known as millennarianism, is defined as the belief in an imminent transition to a collective condition consisting of total well-being (salvation) that may be heavenly or earthly. This collective salvation is often called the millennial kingdom.

Chiliasm, a related concept derived from the Greek word *chilia* (meaning 1000), is defined as the belief that the rewards of the saved will be enjoyed on this Earth — the idea that collective salvation will come in this world. Chiliasm sees the current system as hopelessly riddled with evil that must be radically transformed and encourages political activism. In Christianity, Millennialism refers to the Biblical concept of Christ's 1000-year kingdom on Earth and the belief in the complete transformation of the world into a golden age of peace and justice. Additional related concepts include the apocalypse — the belief that the end of the world as we know it is imminent.

In Biblical literature, *apocalypse* refers to the catastrophic events that will occur at end times. Armageddon is the location in the Holy Land where the great battle between good and evil will occur. In a popular sense, Armageddon simply refers to the final great battle between good and evil.

Messianism is the belief that a chosen individual will bring about the millennial period and is one of the most common ways that millennial beliefs manifest themselves socially in the form of new religious movements.[1] The chosen individuals are variously designated as charismatic leaders, prophets and messiahs. The distinctions between the terms are subtle but significant. The phrase charismatic leader is based on *charisma*, a term used by religion scholars to designate access to a divine or superhuman source of authority that is not shared with many others. Hence, a charismatic leader is believed by the group to have received special revelation from unseen

Millennialism

- Millennialism is a group belief in a collective salvation (total well-being).
- The end of the world is going to occur in the near future.
- Salvation can be earthly or heavenly.
- Salvation will only occur for true believers.
- Frequently the world has to be destroyed in order for salvation occur.

Millennialism and apocalyptic beliefs were the subject of many news articles in 1999. (From *Time Magazine* cover January 18, 1999, digital photomontage by Aaron Goodman. With permission.)

sources that could be God, angels, or even extraterrestrials. A charismatic leader can be a prophet or a messiah. A prophet may announce the arrival of the millennial kingdom or the arrival of the messiah but does not have the power to create the millenial kingdom whereas a messiah is an individual believed to be empowered by God or a superhuman agent to create the millennial kingdom. A messiah is always a prophet but a prophet is not always a messiah and both have charisma; thus, their followers believe they have access to divine authority.

Millennial Religious Groups and Law Enforcement

The concepts of millennialism, apocalypticism and messianism have substantial implications for investigating religious terrorism. Of primary importance, millennial, apocalyptic and messianic groups' beliefs and allegiances are to a higher power that may conflict with the authority of civil law. When people enter apocalyptic time as a result of a religious or secular prophecy, their beliefs lead them to dramatic changes in behavior. Believers may become violent in order to preserve their religious goals, especially when there are internal power struggles or perceived or actual persecution from outsiders.

Millennial religions have existed throughout history because they address authentic human religious concerns. It is significant to acknowledge that numerous millennialists and their respective groups peacefully await divine intervention to achieve salvation and never become involved in violence.

Millennial Religious Groups: Law Enforcement Issues

- Millennial groups' beliefs and allegiances are to a "higher power," which may conflict with the authority of civil law.
- Believers may become violent in order to preserve their religious goals, especially when there are internal power struggles or perceived or actual persecution from outsiders.
- Some believers are armed for self-protection, initiate violence and have revolutionary theologies.

Catherine Wessinger's

Millennial Classification System

Assaulted Groups
- Perceived by outsiders to be dangerous.

Fragile Groups
- Initiate violence to preserve their religious goal.

Revolutionary Groups
- Possess ideologies and theologies that legitimate violence.

Progressive Millennialism
- Optimistic view that humans under the guidance of a divine plan can peacefully build the millennial kingdom.

Catastrophic Millennialism
- Pessimistic view that the millennial kingdom can only be accomplished by the world being destroyed and created anew.

However, others are armed for self-protection, initiate violence and have revolutionary theologies. Many white supremacist groups, some of which are designated by the government as domestic terrorists, adhere to millennial religious doctrines. In the past 30 years, violence, mass murder and suicide have occurred in a variety of new religions including the Peoples' Temple, Branch Davidians, Solar Temple, Aum Shinrikyo and Heaven's Gate. Additionally, new religious movements are not the only contemporary active millennialists. A variety of Christian and Islamic fundamental extremists are also preparing for end times. The difficult role for law enforcement is distinguishing which groups are nonviolent, potentially violent and actively violent. Unfortunately, the dynamics of religious groups change, depending upon new leaders, interpretations of sacred texts and threats of both real or imagined persecution. Hence, all millennial religions are potentially violent.

Acknowledging that cases of violence involving millennial groups are not all the same, religious scholar Catherine Wessinger devised a typology that distinguishes between millennial groups that are assaulted because they are perceived by outsiders to be dangerous, fragile millennial groups that initiate violence to preserve their religious goals and revolutionary millennial groups possessing ideologies or theologies that legitimize violence.[2]

Wessinger also proposed two terms to indicate two major patterns of belief about how the millennial kingdom is expected to be accomplished. Progressive millennialism is an optimistic view of humanity and includes the belief that humans working in harmony with a divine plan can progressively build the millennial kingdom. Catastrophic millennialism involves a pessimistic view of humanity and society that essentially claims that the world must be destroyed and then created anew. The millennial kingdom can only be accomplished after the violent destruction of the current evil world. This will be accomplished by God or by superhuman agents such as extraterrestrials or ascended masters. There are different views about the role humans play in the destruction of the world. Some believe they can prepare themselves by being faithful and living ethically; others believe they must be armed for self-defense and fight if attacked by enemies. Finally, some are revolutionaries who believe that the divine plan calls for them to participate in overthrowing the evil government. This group has the greatest potential for committing acts of religious terrorism.

Another substantial aspect of millennialism that is significant to law enforcement is that many leaders of millennial groups prophesy a date in the near future when Armageddon is supposed to occur. This date is purportedly chosen through the leaders' interpretations of the groups' sacred

---

Apocalyptic Beliefs:
Law Enforcement Issues

- The apocalyptic date represents a critical point in time for the group because the leader may claim that religious doctrine instructs followers to commit suicide to achieve salvation before the entire destruction of the world.
- When people enter apocalyptic time their belief leads them to dramatic changes in behavior.
- Many leaders of millennial groups prophesy a date in the near future on which Armageddon is supposed to occur.
- This date is purportedly chosen through the leader's interpretations of the group's sacred text.
- When the end of the world does not occur on the chosen date, the leader's credibility may come into question effecting drastic changes.

Mass Suicides / Homicide

- **2000:** Movement for the Restoration of the Ten Commandments of God, Uganda, *over 1000 deaths*
- **1997:** Marshall Herff Applewhite, Heaven's Gate, *39 deaths*
- **1994, 1995, 1997:** Order of the Solar Temple, *74 deaths*
- **1993:** David Koresh, Branch Davidians, *approximately 90 deaths*
- **1978:** Reverend Jim Jones, The People's Temple, *over 900 deaths*

texts; however, it can coincide with internal struggles, the deterioration of a leader's physical or mental health or the leader's loss of control over his followers. When the end of the world does not occur on the chosen date, the leader's credibility as a prophet may come into question, effecting a situation in which an ambitious member can also claim divine revelation and vie for leadership.

The apocalyptic date represents a critical point in time for the group because the leader may claim that religious doctrine instructs followers to commit suicide to achieve salvation before the destruction of the entire world. David Koresh predicted that Armageddon would occur in 1995. The 1993 siege at Waco following Koresh's prophecy served to validate his position and enhance his status in the eyes of his followers. Koresh continued to interpret scripture during the 51-day siege.

Each and every action taken by the government held symbolic value for the Branch Davidians who literally believed that Satan was knocking at their door. It is significant to mention that in 1987 David Koresh had been in a power struggle for leadership of the group with George Roden, the son of the former Branch Davidian prophets. Roden, who also claimed divine revelation, lost both legal and spiritual battles to Koresh who ended up not only as the Branch Davidians' messiah but also obtained the rights to Mount Carmel while Roden was imprisoned for violating restraining orders barring him from Mount Carmel. This indicates that David Koresh fully understood the implications of failed prophecy. The decisions he made during the stand-off essentially resulted in a self-fulfilling apocalyptic prophecy. He was able to die as a prophet rather than return to the status of a mere mortal facing murder charges.

Shoko Asahara, leader of Aum Supreme Truth, predicted the end times would occur in 1999. Based on his prophecies in 1995, he attempted to begin destroying the world with weapons of mass destruction. In 1997, Heaven's Gate believers opted to exit planet Earth, which they thought was going to be destroyed, by leaving their bodies via suicide and beaming up to the mother ship behind the Hale–Bopp comet. Similarly, members of the Solar Temple chose to avoid the destruction of the world and decided to make transits — mystical voyages using group murder and suicide on three separate occasions in 1994, 1995 and 1997. The leaders of both Heaven's Gate and Solar Temple were experiencing health problems in addition to facing disconfirmed prophecies. The very nature of millennial beliefs is that they fundamentally entail death, deception, destruction and disease culminating in the end of the world. Ordinary events and typical economic and social pressures are viewed as signs of the apocalypse and believers maintain a heightened anticipation of immediate future violence. Unfortunately, salvation is not achieved until their world comes to an end. Some groups simply get tired of waiting and theologically justify suicide, murder and terrorism.

Consulting Religious Scholars

Religious scholars have recognized the dilemma involving the roles of law enforcement and new religious movements. Particularly after the incident with the Branch Davidians, a number of excellent papers and books were published both criticizing what happened and offering solutions to the very real problem of investigating millennial groups without persecuting them. The books and papers provide valuable insights into the dynamics of millennial groups and much of their research is cited in this book. Religious

Consulting Religious Scholars

- Consulting with religious scholars is advisable and they may provide valuable insights into the dynamics of millennial groups. However, it is imperative to understand that some academics misinterpret the true intentions of a new religious movement.

- Religious scholars optimistically study new religions and nobly advocate for religious freedom and civil rights, but they are not trained to recognize duplicity and charismatic leaders are often masters of deception.

- Scholars are not trained in negotiations and should not personally interact with the group.

scholars repeatedly emphasize that negative attention from the authorities or the media can easily be religiously interpreted as a sign of the end times and provoke fragile groups to acts of violence.

Some religious scholars argue against prevalent stereotypes that depict members of new religions as irrational, brainwashed and violence prone, and emphasize that violence involving millennarians is a complex phenomenon. Finally, some suggest that law enforcement agents consult them in order to avoid unnecessarily assaulting a group, initiating a siege or making a group feel persecuted. They specifically suggest that they be used as intermediaries (translators) of the religious worldview and goals of the group. Consulting with academic religious scholars is advisable, but it is imperative to understand that some academics are either unknowingly deceived while studying and interviewing members of a group or may misinterpret the true intentions of a new religious movement.

For example, two well-known American religious scholars went to Japan and held news conferences suggesting that the Aum Shinrikyo sect was innocent of criminal charges and its members were victims of excessive police pressure. The Americans were invited to Japan by the religious group after they expressed concern to Aum's New York branch about religious freedom in Japan. It was later proven that Aum Shinrikyo had not only perpetrated dozens of individual murders, but operated factories where they manufactured weapons of mass destruction which they released, among other places, in the Tokyo subway. Religious scholars optimistically study new religions and nobly advocate for religious freedom and civil rights, but they are not trained to recognize duplicity and charismatic leaders are often masters of deception.

Recent catastrophic events such as the September 11, 2001 attack on the U.S., the war in Israel and natural disasters are all viewed as signs of the apocalypse by numerous traditional and new religious groups, causing memberships to increase in a variety of millennial religions. For example, many people believed they saw the face of Satan in the smoke of the World Trade Center and interpreted it as a sign of the apocalypse. Furthermore, increased numbers of believers are viewed as another sign of end times and have the effect of giving more credence to the believers. The mere fact that violence is a necessary component of apocalyptic ideologies increases the potential for violence that can rapidly erupt into various forms of religious terrorism.

A Case Study in Religious Terrorism

Aum Shinrikyo, translated into English as Aum Supreme Truth, is a new religious movement that was founded in 1987 in Japan by Shoko Asahara.

Aum Shinrikyo

- Aum Shinrikyo, translated Supreme Truth, is a Japanese new religious movement that was founded in 1987 by Shoko Asahara.
- In only 7 years it became the paradigm of a religious terrorist group.
- Developed, manufactured and used a variety of weapons of mass destruction.
- Responsible for approximately 32 individual murders and thousands of injuries.
- Violence based on religious ideology.
- Added to U.S. Department of State's list of terrorists and groups identified under Order 13224 on November 2, 2001.

Tokyo subway, March 20, 1995, after Sarin gas was released by Aum Shinrikyo. (From Desmond E. and Kunii, I.M., Prophet of Poison, *Time Magazine*, April, 3, 1995, p. 29, Asahi Shimbun Publishing, Tokyo. With permission.)

In only 7 years, it became the paradigm of a religious terrorist group. Aum Shinrikyo which reached a peak of about 40,000 members worldwide was officially registered with the Japanese government under the Religious Corporations Law, Shukyo Hojin Ho, in August 1989. Aum Shinrikyo combines elements of Buddhism, a variety of Asian traditions, and Christianity and evolved into an apocalyptic movement. It is best known for the degree of violence enacted by members including detention, coercion, torture, murder and, most notably, the development and use of weapons of mass destruction.

Shoko Asahara was born in 1955 as Chizuo Matsumoto and was partially blind at birth. He attended a school for the blind from the age of five. After graduating in 1977, he moved to Tokyo where he failed to gain admission to

Tokyo University and turned to studying acupuncture and traditional Chinese medicine. He married in 1978 and in the early 1980s opened a folk medicine shop and established a school for yogis with his wife. During that time, he joined Agonshu, a "new new religion" that stressed liberation from bad karma via meditation. In 1986, while alone in the Himalayan mountains, he claims to have received enlightenment. Upon his return to Japan in 1987, he changed his name from Chizuo Matsumoto to the holy Shoko Asahara. This inspired him to organize his religion, which he named Aum Shinrikyo. The name of the religion includes the sacred symbol *Om* used by Hindus and Buddhists, which Asahara taught refers to the creation, preservation and destruction of the universe. *Shinrikyo* is translated as *teaching of the supreme truth*. Therefore, Aum Shinrikyo is a religion that teaches the supreme truth about creation and destruction.

Aum Shinrikyo Theology

The fundamental religious belief is that Aum Shinrikyo offers liberation from suffering and illness. The religion includes Hindu motifs and practices. The primary deity of Aum is Shiva, the Hindu god of destruction. Shiva embodies Aum's main focus on the creation and destruction of the universe. The Buddhist ideas incorporated in Aum include transmigration and rebirth, the world of suffering and the goal of better rebirth and enlightenment through meditation.

Asahara initially taught that "members must work to transfer evil energy into positive energy and avoid mass destruction via nuclear war."[3]

Aum Shinrikyo Theology

- The fundamental religious belief is that Aum Shinrikyo offers liberation from suffering and illness.
- Full of Hindu motifs and practices, the primary deity in Aum is Shiva, the god of destruction. This deity embodies Aum's main focus: the creation and destruction of the universe.
- Buddhist ideas are incorporated, including transmigration and rebirth, the world of suffering and the goal of better rebirths and enlightenment through meditation.
- Aum members are taught that enemies identified as the United States military, Freemasons, the Japanese government and Jews were conspiring to destroy them.

Asahara claimed he was the savior who would establish the perfect Shambhala kingdom on earth. The aim was to make Japan into Shambhala, and then to make the whole world into Shambhala ... In Asahara's 1987 book *Initiation*, he predicted that a nuclear war would occur between 1999 and 2003, but could be averted if Aum established centers overseas and gained 30,000 renunciants. Even if Armageddon occurred, Aum devotees would be saved because they would have the ability to consciously abandon their physical bodies for existence in the astral world.[4]

With this theology, Asahara began what was called the Lotus Village Plan, which was the building of small communes in order to be self-sufficient and rebuild civilization after Armageddon. However,

Asahara's thoughts began to take a more pessimistic turn as he studied the New Testament Book of Revelation on which he produced two commentaries, *Doomsday 1989* and *From Destruction to Emptiness: A Sequel to Doomsday 1989*. By 1990, the Lotus Villages need to be equipped with shelter for protection from nuclear, chemical and bacterial weapons ... In 1989 to 1990 his focus shifted to a catastrophic millennialism involving a pessimistic evaluation of society and unredeemable humanity, corresponding with Aum's increasing conflicts with the world outside its communes.[5]

In 1990, Asahara and a number of other top ranking members of the group announced their candidacies as Supreme Truth Party representatives for the House of Representatives. They were severely disillusioned when they lost because they believed they were serious contenders. The loss of the election combined with many negative news articles significantly affected the future ideology of Aum Shinrikyo and they now viewed the world as persecuting them and no longer attempted to save the world, only Aum members. In addition, Aum members were being taught that enemies identified as the U.S. military, the Freemasons, the Japanese government and the Jews were conspiring to destroy them. Asahara started preaching Armageddon by utilizing the predictions of Nostradamus, the New Testament Book of Revelation, Hitler's statements about a 1000-year reich and Asahara's own psychic powers.[6] In 1992, Asahara wrote *The Ideal Society: Shambhala*, and in 1993, compiled a collection of his public talks entitled *The Frightening Prophecies of Asahara Shoko*.

Shoko Asahara / The Messiah

- Asahara claimed he was the savior who would establish the perfect Shambhala kingdom on earth. The aim was to make Japan into Shambhala, and then to make the whole world into Shambhala.
- Shoko Asahara not only identified himself as the Buddha of the current age and the reincarnation of the god Shiva but in 1992 he claimed to be the lamb of God.
- Asahara's role as the messiah was to enable persons to attain a superhuman condition.
- In 1994 Aum scientists began producing drugs such as LSD, sodium thiopental, mescaline, methamphetamine and PCP for use in religious initiations. Chemically induced mystical experiences were attributed by Aum believers to the Shakti, the spiritual power, the energy of the guru.

The Messiah Shoko Asahara

In the years after founding the religion, Shoko Asahara claimed that he was a Buddha who possessed psychic powers and further claimed to have the power to levitate, to soul-travel out of his body, and to have an infallible power of prophecy. In *Initiation* in 1987;

> Asahara claimed that shaktipat given by himself to the devotee was necessary to awaken the kundalini. In 1994 Aum scientists began producing drugs, LSD, sodium thiopental, mescaline, methamphetamine, and PCP, for use in religious initiations. Even those chemically induced mystical experiences were attributed by Aum believers to the Shakti, the spiritual power, energy of the guru.[7]

Aum members believed that their enlightenment would come if they submitted to Asahara as the guru. In fact, they were encouraged to repeat 20 times a day, "I pledge faithfulness to Aum, the Guru and the god Shiva. Please lead me [name] quickly to enlightenment."[8]

Shoko Asahara not only identified himself as the Buddha of the current age and the reincarnation of the god Shiva, but in 1992 he published a book entitled *Declaring Myself the Christ* in which he also claimed to be the lamb of God who absorbed the bad karma of his disciples even though it made him ill. Asahara taught that people who rejected him as the guru were destined for rebirth in the lower realms of animals, hungry ghosts and the

Aum Shinrikyo Rituals

- Rituals include the Initiation of Blood, a secret Tantric rite where the blood of the guru is taken into one's body so vials of Asahara's blood were sold so that devotees could absorb his special DNA by drinking his blood.
- Special caps called PSI (perfect salvation initiation) were rented and worn by members to bring their thoughts into harmony with the guru.
- Asceticism included fasting or living on a meager diet, being lowered into scalding or near freezing water, being hung upside down or given drugs such as LSD to stimulate altered consciousness.

hells due to their bad karma. Acceptance of Asahara as the incarnation of Shiva as the guru was necessary to attain good karma and salvation.[9] Asahara's role as the messiah was to enable persons to attain a superhuman condition. Aum Shinrikyo was intended to be an organization of superhumans who would survive Armageddon and then establish Shambhala on earth, which would be a 1000-year kingdom.[10]

Aum Shinrikyo Religious Rituals

Shinrikyo rituals included the Initiation of Blood, a secret Tantric rite where the blood of the guru is taken into one's body. Vials of Asahara's blood were sold so that devotees could absorb his special DNA by drinking his blood. Special caps called PSI (perfect salvation initiation) were rented and worn by members to bring their thoughts into harmony with the guru.

Asahara insisted that his devotees practice an extreme form of asceticism or else they would not achieve salvation in the Shambhala millennial kingdom. His practice of asceticism, in order to achieve salvation, was so important to the group that it was necessary for everyone to undergo. It included fasting or living on a meager diet, being lowered into scalding or near-freezing water, being hung upside down or being given drugs such as LSD to stimulate altered consciousness.

> Every member was encouraged to meditate and practice a variety of yogic disciplines, and the most committed disciples became shukkesha, renunciants. Becoming a renunciant meant cutting off all contact with one's family, turning over all property and assets to Aum, pledg-

ing devotion to Asahara, living communally and practicing rigorous asceticism. By these means, shukkesha believed they would develop superhuman powers of clairvoyance, levitation, and the ability to travel through the spiritual realms. The shukkesha aimed to become superhuman beings, the only ones who would not be destroyed in Armageddon.[11]

Aum Shinrikyo Community

Aum Shinrikyo reportedly was worth over $1 billion from real estate, stocks, sales of Ashara's blood and headgear and donations from members. Asahara also maintained a number of small businesses. Aum attracted highly educated young men and women who felt that Japanese society had become too commercialized. Men who became Aum leaders were highly educated scientists who researched and developed a variety of weapons of mass destruction. There were also a significant number of female leaders who were involved in diverse fields such as medicine, nursing and bookkeeping and also oversaw the administration of the communes and factory work.

Asahara had sex with a number of Aum women with the intention of impregnating them. He explained this by claiming that the guru knew how to catch the good souls floating in the air and bring them into physical incarnation. Little is known about the children except that they were generally neglected.

Members were convinced that society outside the Aum compound was under the influence of evil mind control and that Aum counteracted society's

Aum Shinrikyo Community

- Aum Shinrikyo was worth over a billion dollars from real estate, stocks, selling Shoko Asahara's blood and headgear and donations from members. He also had a number of small businesses.
- Aum attracted highly educated young men and women who felt that Japanese society had become too commercialized.
- The men who became the Aum leaders were highly educated scientists who researched and developed a variety of weapons of mass destruction. A significant number of female leaders were also involved in diverse fields.
- Members were convinced that society outside the Aum compound was under the influence of evil mind control and that Aum counteracted society's brainwashing with good mind control that taught supreme truth.

brainwashing with good mind control that taught supreme truth. Aum members would listen for hours to audio taped affirmations that said they should not doubt Aum because doubt was an illusion caused by earthly desire. In brief, members were severed from contact with their families and the outside world and systematically indoctrinated into worshipping Asahara via the use of standard mind control techniques such as drugs, sleep and food deprivation, fear, physical beatings, isolation and constant reinforcement of new beliefs. Once inculcated into Aum Shinrikyo under orders of Shoko Asahara, its members attempted to destroy the world in order to recreate it.

Religious Terrorism of Aum Shinrikyo

The violence associated with Aum Shinrikyo ranged from the extreme ascetic practices of the members to individual murders and attempts to annihilate thousands of people. In 1988, a member died while being subjected to cold water immersion. In 1989, several parents of members hired Tsutsumi Sakamato, a Yokohama lawyer who represented the Aum Shinrikyo Victims Society, which was made up of the families of members of the group. He was interviewed in 1989 by the Tokyo Broadcasting System where he revealed details of the group's illegal activities. The interview was never broadcast because Tsutsumi, his wife and 14-month-old child were kidnapped from their Yokohama apartment and murdered by Aum members who later confessed to the killings.

In June 1993, Aum scientists tested their first weapon of mass destruction by using a fan on a rooftop of a Tokyo building to spray anthrax across the city. Birds, pets and plants died, people got sick and cars and clothing were stained. In June 1994, sarin gas was released by Aum devotees from a truck in the central Japanese city of Matsumoto, killing seven people and injuring 600.

In January 1994, two former members attempted to rescue one of their mothers who was still in the commune. They were captured and brought in front of Asahara and his wife and one was forced to murder the other and then report to family members outside the commune that everyone was fine. In September 1994, a lethal gas used in World War I was released into the apartment of a journalist who had written two anti-Aum books and critical articles. She was hospitalized but survived. In December of 1994, a Tokyo parking attendant who had provided shelter for five defectors was injected with VX nerve agent. He was hospitalized but survived. In the same month, a man believed to be an undercover police agent was killed on the street when an Aum member injected him with VX nerve agent.

In January 1995, the head of the Aum Shinrikyo Victims Society was sprayed with VX as he walked across a parking lot. He was in a coma for

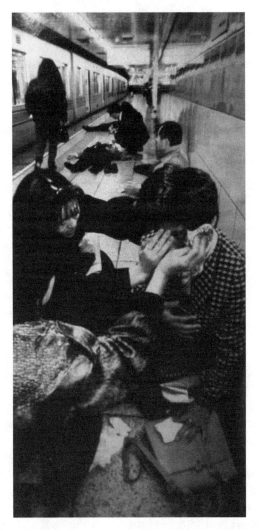

After the release of sarin on the Tokyo subway passengers on cars farther from the poison gas tried to help those who had been more severely affected. (From Desmond, E. and Kunii, I.M., Prophet of Poison, *Time Magazine*, April 3, 1995, p. 28. With permission from Asahi Shimbun Publishing, Tokyo.)

several weeks but recovered. In February 1995, a businessman who was hiding his sister after she defected was abducted from a Tokyo street and injected with sodium thiopental. He died during interrogation and an industrial-size microwave oven was used to incinerate his body. His sister had donated about $600,000 to Aum.

Aum also ran a hospital in Tokyo where they treated dissenting and disruptive members by incarcerating and drugging them. The hospital had an unusually high death rate. Japanese police concluded that Aum members killed

Aum Shinrikyo Violence

- **1988:** member died while being subjected to cold water immersion.
- **1989:** members kidnapped and murdered opposing attorney, wife and infant.
- **1993:** sprayed anthrax from a Tokyo rooftop, wildlife died and people became ill.
- **January 1994:** two former members attempting to rescue a member get caught and one is forced to murder the other.
- **June 1994:** released sarin gas from a truck, killing seven and injuring 600.
- **September 1994:** lethal gas is released into the apartment of a journalist; she survived.
- **December 1994:** an undercover police agent is injected with VX nerve agent on the street and is killed.
- **December 1994:** a person providing shelter for five defectors is injected with VX nerve agent; he survives.
- **January 1995:** head of the Aum victims' society is sprayed with VX and is in a coma for weeks.
- **February 1995:** a man hiding his sister who defected is injected with sodium thiopental and dies during interrogation.
- **March 20, 1995:** sarin gas is released in five Tokyo subway cars, killing 12 and injuring over 5000.

approximately 32 people between October 1988 and March 1995; at least 8 died from the ascetic practices and others were killed for wanting to defect.

On March 20, 1995, five members of Aum Shinrikyo boarded five subway cars at different stations in Tokyo at 8:00 A.M. They deposited plastic bags containing sarin gas on the floor, punctured the bags and immediately disembarked. The fumes of the deadly nerve gas injured over 5000 people and 12 people died. Two days later, a videotaped message from Shoko Asahara was broadcast in Japan and motivated members to more violent actions.

On March 30, 1995, the head of the National Police was shot outside his residence as he left for work. Two hours later, an anonymous call to the media warned that more police officers would be assassinated if the investigation was not stopped. The official was seriously injured but not killed. Asahara predicted that on April 15, 1995 a huge catastrophe would occur in Tokyo. It caused the closing of two shopping complexes, quieted the normally bustling Shinjuku station and caused deployment of 20,000 police. On May 5, 1995, an attempt to release hydrogen cyanide at Tokyo's busiest station failed when the device burst into flames.

Aum Shinrikyo Violence

- **March 30, 1995:** head of the national police is shot outside his residence; seriously injured but he survives. Two hours later an anonymous call warns more officers will be assassinated if the investigation is not stopped.
- **April 1995:** two huge shopping complexes are closed down and 20,000 police deployed because Asahara predicts a huge catastrophe.
- **May 5,1995:** an attempt to release hydrogen cyanide at Tokyo's busiest station fails when the device bursts into flames.
- **May 16, 1995:** the day of Asahara's arrest a letter bomb arrives at the Tokyo governor's office and explodes in a secretary's hands.

(Left): Police confiscate containers from Aum Shinrikyo property in the village of Kamikuishiki, west of Tokyo. (Right): A police officer with gas mask and canary; the bird's collapse would warn of the poison gas. (From Desmond, E. and Kunii, I.M., Prophet of Poison, *Time Magazine*, April 3, 1995, pp. 32–33, Asahi Shimbun, Tokyo. With permission.)

The intensive police hunt led to the arrest of over 200 Aum members, but Asahara remained at large until May 16, 1995 when he was found hiding at Aum headquarters. He was charged with murder in relation to the Tokyo subway gas attack, the Matsumoto gas release, the murders of the Sakamoto family and Kariya and the production of illegal drugs. On the same day as his arrest, Aum devotees sent a letter bomb to the Tokyo governor's office. It exploded in the hands of a secretary. The bombing was attributed to the governor's announcement of his intention to revoke Aum Shinrikyo's status as a registered religion.[12]

Shoko Asahara went to trial on 17 criminal charges in April 1996. In October 1998, an Aum member was sentenced to death for the murders of four people. Two other members were sentenced to death in September 1999 and June 2000 for releasing sarin gas in the subway. Many members received long prison sentences.

Asahara maintains his innocence although many followers confessed their involvement in these crimes and claimed they acted under his direct orders. On June 22, 2001 Asahara's trial reached its 200th hearing, if the trial proceeds as scheduled a verdict should finally be handed down in February 2004, nearly 9 years after the event shocked the nation. Prosecutors have demanded the death penalty for Shoko Asahara over the sarin nerve gas attack that killed 12 people and harmed more than 5000 in 1995. Asahara, now 48, still faces 12 other charges, including the masterminding of a nerve gas attack in the central Japanese city of Matsumoto in July 1994 that killed 7 people and hurt 144.

In January 2000, the cult, still in existence, changed its name to Aleph (meaning to start anew). Although the group publicly renounced their founding leader, Asahara, police have found instructions for making nerve gas in a member's car. Aum's every move is now monitored by authorities under a new law passed in December 1999 that allows police to conduct raids and demand information without a warrant. In the aftermath of September 11, the U.S. government updated its list of foreign terrorist organizations on October 5, 2001 to include Aum Shinrikyo/Aleph.

References

1. Center for Millennial Studies at Boston University, web site glossary, www.mille.org/scholarship,index.html, July 2002.

2. Wessinger, C., Ed., *Millennialism, Persecution, and Violence*, Syracuse, NY, Syracuse University Press, 2000, pp. 3–4.

3. Religious Movements Homepage, University of Virginia, p. 6, *Aum Shinrikyo: Beliefs of Group* (http://religiousmovements.lib.virginia.edu/nrms/aums.html).

4. Wessinger, C., *How the Millennium Comes Violently*, New York, Seven Bridges Press, 2000, pp. 135–136.

5. Wessinger, C., *How the Millennium Comes Violently*, New York, Seven Bridges Press, 2000, p. 136.

6. Wessinger, C., *How the Millennium Comes Violently*, New York, Seven Bridges Press, 2000, p. 137.

7. Wessinger, C., *How the Millennium Comes Violently*, New York, Seven Bridges Press, 2000, p. 128.

8. Wessinger, C., *How the Millennium Comes Violently*, New York, Seven Bridges Press, 2000, p. 129.

9. Wessinger, C., *How the Millennium Comes Violently*, New York, Seven Bridges Press, 2000, p. 129.

10. Wessinger, C., *How the Millennium Comes Violently*, New York, Seven Bridges Press, 2000, p. 137.

11. Wessinger, C., *How the Millennium Comes Violently*, New York, Seven Bridges Press, 2000, p. 134.

12. Wessinger, C., *How the Millennium Comes Violently*, New York, Seven Bridges Press, 2000, pp. 121–126.

Domestic Terrorist Religions

3

Terrorism exists and is present in American culture as a religion, as a genre in film, music and art, as a political ideal and as a popular subject in the media. Terrorism is enacted by millennial religious groups that maintain doctrines of ethical tenets, specific rituals and true believers. Often referred to as cults, militias or cells, these religions are widely practiced individually and communally throughout the world. Similar to other organized religions, beliefs vary among different groups and according to church leaders. They range from a form of devout purism as a return to original strict interpretations of sacred text to the worship of a leader as a deity. Similarities are found in elitist ideologies advocating violence, terrorism and genocide, and viewing every other group as Satanic or the evil Babylon. Religious terrorists maintain a dualistic worldview where the world is seen as a battleground between good and evil, God and Satan, "us" and "them." This millennial worldview that identifies the enemy as evil is how terrorists theologically justify their violence.

Modern Terrorism

The FBI has two general categories of terrorism: domestic and international. Domestic terrorism is defined as "the unlawful use, or threatened use, of violence by a group or individual that is based entirely within the United States or its territories without foreign direction and which is committed against persons or property with the intent of intimidating or coercing a government or its population in furtherance of political or social objectives."[1] The FBI's definition of international terrorism involves "violent acts, or acts dangerous to human life, that are a violation of the criminal laws of the

FBI's Categories of Terrorism

Domestic Terrorism
- Right-Wing
  Terrorist Groups
- Left-Wing
  Terrorist Groups
- Special Interest
  Terrorist Groups

International Terrorism
- Radical International
  Jihad Movement (prior
  to 9/11, loosely
  affiliated extremists)
- Formalized Terrorism
  Organizations
- State Sponsors of
  International Terrorism

United States or any state, or that would be a criminal violation if committed within the jurisdiction of the United States or any state, and which are intended to intimidate or coerce a civilian population, influence the police of a government, or affect the conduct of a government."[2]

Typologies of terrorism are just as problematic as definitions for similar reasons. Terrorism is a culturally relative construct that is fundamentally defined by antithetical ideologies. The most relevant source for categories of terrorism from the ideological perspective of the U.S. government can be found in a Congressional Statement made to the Senate Committee on Appropriations dated May 10, 2001 by Louis J. Freeh, Director of the Federal Bureau of Investigation, entitled "On the Threat of Terrorism to the United States." This pre-September 11 statement accurately foreshadowed terrorist incidents by describing recent trends, statistics, arrests and investigations into acts of terrorism. The FBI classifies terrorism as international or domestic based essentially on geography and not the ultimate goal of the behavior.

Domestic Terrorism

Domestic terrorism has three subcategories based on the ideologies of various groups which are designated as right-wing extremist groups, left-wing extremist groups and special interest extremists. The right-wing extremist groups are characterized by their adherence to the principles of racial supremacy and their embrace of anti-government and anti-regulatory beliefs.

Formal right-wing hate groups that represent continuing terrorist threats on a national level include the World Church of the Creator (WCOTC) and the Aryan Nations. Racism-based hatred remains an integral component of these groups' core orientations. Another example of a right-wing extremist group is the Southeastern States Alliance, an umbrella organization of militias in Florida, Georgia, South Carolina, Alabama and other southern states who

---

Domestic Terrorism:

Right-Wing Extremist Groups

Characteristics

- Adhere to principles of racial supremacy.
- Embrace antigovernment antiregulatory beliefs.
- Potentially large-scale, high-casuality attacks.

Formal Hate Groups

Representing a continuing terrorist threat:

- National Alliance
- World Church of the Creator (WCOTC)
- Aryan Nations

Domestic Terrorism:

Left-Wing Extremist Groups

Characteristics

- Revolutionary socialist doctrines
- Protectors of the people from dehumanizing effects of capitalism and imperialism
- Bombings to bring attention to cause

Active Left-Wing Groups

Generally, Puerto Rican separatist groups seeking independence from U.S.

- FALN (Fuerzas Armadas de Liberación Nacional Puertorriqueña)
- Los Macheteros

---

were prevented from attacking National Guard armories. The goal of this group was to create social and political chaos thereby forcing the U.S. government to declare martial law — an act they believe would lead to a violent overthrow of the government of the American people. Two of the seven planned acts of terrorism prevented in 1999 were potentially large-scale, high-casuality attacks planned by organized right-wing extremists. Many right-wing extremist groups have created their own religions and will be the main focus of this chapter.

The second category of domestic terrorism is left-wing and Puerto Rican extremist groups who generally profess a revolutionary socialist doctrine and view themselves as protectors of the people against the dehumanizing effects of capitalism and imperialism. Their method of bringing about change is through revolution rather than the political process. Several of these groups seek to secure full Puerto Rican independence from the U.S. Extremist Puerto Rican separatist groups include the Armed Forces for Puerto Rican National

Domestic Terrorism:

Special Interest Extremists

Characteristics	Active Special Extremists
• Seek to resolve specific issues	Individuals and Groups
• Politically motivated violence to bring attention to their causes	• Animal Liberation Front (ALF)
	• Earth Liberation Front (ELF)
• Vandalism (millions in damages)	• Pro-Life Extremists
	• Anarchists
	• Extremist Socialists

Liberation also known as Fuerzas Armadas de Liberacion Nacional Puertor-riqueña (FALN) and Los Macheteros. FALN carried out bombings in the U.S. mainland, primarily in and around New York. Los Macheteros is suspected of three bombings in Puerto Rico.

The third category of domestic terrorism consists of special interest extremists. They differ from right-wing and left-wing terrorists in that they seek to resolve specific issues rather than overthrowing the entire political system. They conduct acts of politically motivated violence to bring public attention to their specific causes. These groups occupy the extreme fringes of animal rights, pro-life, environmental, anti-nuclear and other political and social movements. The groups most noted for acts of vandalism and terrorist activities are the Animal Liberation Front (ALF) and the Earth Liberation Front (ELF). They have caused millions of dollars in damages to businesses they consider hostile to the environment or to animal rights. Many pro-life extremists identify with right-wing extremists' religious ideologies.

Domestic Terrorist Religions

Just as many varieties of Christianity are manifested in a number of diverse Christian religions there are many varieties of unfamiliar religions and religious sects pejoratively designated as terrorist religions or cults. Practitioners of these non-recognized religions vehemently disavow the designations of terrorist and cult. Common characteristics of the major non-recognized religions designated as terrorist groups/cults include hierarchical structures, opposition to mainstream Christian tenets and the acquisition of personal and political power.

Similar to other religious denominations, individual religious sects profess spiritual superiority over each other and claim that they are practicing

White Supremacist Religions

Nativist Millennial Movements
- Consist of individuals who feel oppressed by a foreign colonizing government, believing that the government is removing the natives from their land and eradicating their traditional way of life.

- **British Israelism**
  Evolved into Christian Identity
- **Christian Identity**
  Extremist fundamentalists Patriot, militia groups
- **Creativity**
  World Church of the Creator
- **Odinists**
  Racist neo-pagans

the one true faith. It is impossible to describe all the terrorist religions, sects and pertinent churches in this brief chapter so the focus will be on groups and religions that have either been identified as domestic terrorists by the U.S. government or have inspired individual acts of murder and homicide.

Domestic terrorist religions are more commonly known as white supremacist religions. Although they appear to have a number of significant differences, they can all be classified as Nativist Millennial Movements. Nativist Millenial Movements consist of individuals who feel oppressed by foreign colonizing governments, believing that the government removes natives from their land and eradicates their traditional way of life, their religion and takes away their means of survival. They long to return to their past, which they view as an idealized golden age, and believe that divine intervention will eliminate their oppressors.

The movement is a response to colonization either by an outside culture or a ruling bureaucratic class. The colonized people are economically oppressed, pressured by government law enforcement agents and tax collectors and are systematically removed from their land. Historically, these movements typically referred to third world people who were reacting to colonization by Europeans who threatened their way of life with technology and developed economies. The contemporary Euro-American nativist movement in the U.S. is a movement of white Americans who possess education and advanced technology but believe the Aryan white race is being subjected to genocide, and systematically deprived of their land by an illegitimate government controlled by foreign and Satanic beings identified as Jews.

The contemporary Euro-American nativist movement in the U.S. includes the Freemen, Identity Christians (believers in Christian Identity), neo-Nazis, Odinists, the Ku Klux Klan and many other white supremacists. They refer to the government as ZOG, Zionist Occupation Government, and

Common Religious Beliefs

- White race is superior.
- Genocide (eventually destroying all other races).
- Jewish conspiracy, ZOG (Zionist occupation government).
- RAHOWA (racial holy war).
- Future Aryan race (apocalyptic or through war).

think a vast Jewish conspiracy controls the media, Hollywood, the nation's schools and universities, the economy, the Federal Reserve System and the international banking industry; the goal of the conspiracy is to enslave and eliminate the white race. This is consistent with Christian Identity theology that preaches that the Jews descended from Satan.

The nativist millennial movement has strong roots in the economic crisis that affects rural America. During the 1970s, farmers were encouraged by bankers and representatives of the Farm Home Administration to take out large loans to increase their farming operations. Then, in 1979, the Federal Reserve Chairman in an attempt to curb inflation raised interest rates and property values dropped while interest rates on loans increased. Unable to make profits on their crops, farmers could not pay high taxes and multinational corporations bought their repossessed farms. This resulted in a high suicide rate among farmers who lost homes that had been in their families for generations. It also made them ripe for recruitment into right-wing extremist groups whose ideologies blame a Jewish conspiracy of international bankers and the government for the loss of their land and their way of life.

In addition to disillusioned farmers, the contemporary Euro-American Nativist Millennial Movement includes the Christian Patriot Movement, as well as the Christian Constitutionalist and Common Law Movements, militia groups, a variety of Christian Identity churches and tax protesters. This white nativist movement also includes non-Christian groups such as Odinists, neo-Nazis and other neo-pagan white supremacist groups.[3]

Christian Identity

The Christian Identity movement is comprised of many radical fundamentalist Christian churches, extreme right-wing political groups and survival groups. It is a complex, highly varied and loosely organized movement whose fundamental teachings are based on the ideology that Anglo-Saxons are the direct descendents of the Ten Lost Tribes of Israel and thus are the true chosen

Christian Identity Movement

- Complex, varied, loosely organized.
- Unifying theology for diverse groups.
- Groups include radical fundamental Christian churches, extreme right-wing political groups, paramilitary and survival groups.
- Preaches hate, racism, genocide.
- Condones violence toward minorities and Jews.
- *Same description fits Islamic extremists.*

Christian Identity Groups

Groups (no national organizational structure [yet])
- Aryan Nations
- American Nazi Party
- Confederate Hammerskins
- Posse Commitatus
- National Association for the Advancement of White People
- White Aryan Resistance
- Many more

Churches
- Church of Jesus Christ Christian
- Kingdom Identity Ministries
- Christian Research Scriptures for America
- Laporte Christian Church
- Church of Israel
- Many more

people of God. Current groups that practice Christian Identity are associated with preaching hate, racism, genocide and condoning violence toward minorities, especially Jews.

However, the original movement evolved from the British Israelism movement of the mid-19th century, which did not start as a hate group nor did its leaders preach violence. Christian Identity took shape in early 20th century America when it was influenced by American nativism, the Ku Klux Klan (KKK) and various strands of anti-Semitism. By the 1970s and 1980s, Christian Identity ideology merged with anti-tax and paramilitary movements and its rhetoric and actions became even more violent. In its current form, Christian Identity is the most unifying theology for a number of diverse groups. Its ideology provides its members with a religious basis for racism

Christian Identity Common Beliefs

- Christian Bible is sacred text.
- Bible is interpreted to hate homosexuals, other religions and races.
- White race (***Adamic race or True Israelite***) is superior to all others.
- Non-whites are subhuman, beasts, mistakes, were already on earth before Adam and Eve.
- Commandment that forbids adultery refers to racial adultery and interracial marriage (10th commandment already bans adultery).
- Jews are descended from Satan and Eve.

and a religious doctrine that allows believers to fuse religion with hate, conspiracy theories and apocalyptic fear of the future.

There is no single founder of the Christian Identity movement because it developed over a period of 70 years and is still changing. Three people who were significant to its evolvement were John Wilson, Edward Hine and Howard Rand. Reverend Wilson and Edward Hine began the movement as British Israelism in 1840. It developed into the Christian Identity movement when Howard Rand founded the Anglo-Saxon Federation of America in 1930 with the help of Wesley Swift, a member of the KKK. Later Swift founded his own church called the Church of Jesus Christ Christian which developed into the Aryan Nations.

The following beliefs are held in common by most Christian Identity groups:

1. A very conservative interpretation of the Christian Bible, which is their main sacred text. This interpretation includes hatred of homosexuality and homosexuals and strict rejection of followers of other religions.
2. A view of the white race, sometimes referred to as the Adamic race or True Israelites, as superior to all others. The view that other races are the Satanic spawn of Cain, which leads to a hatred of African Americans, Native Americans and all persons from non-Aryan countries.
3. The belief that other pre-Adamic and non-white people were already in existence when Adam was created and that Adam and Eve were white. This directly leads to the belief that Anglo-Saxon Protestants are the true identity of God's chosen people of the Hebrew Scriptures, hence the term Christian Identity.

Christian Identity: Two Seed Line Doctrine

- Adam was preceded by other races (identified as the beasts of the field).
- Eve was seduced by Satan and gave birth to two seed lines.
  - Cain descended from Satan and Eve.
  - Abel descended from Adam and Eve.
- Cain became the progenitor of the Jews by mating with non-Adamic races.
- Abel is good Aryan stock through Adam.
- Jews carry on a conspiracy against the Adamic seed line to control the earth.

4. The commandment that forbids adultery does not refer to extramarital affairs, but refers to racial adultery and interracial marriages. The tenth commandment in their view already bans adultery.
5. They consider themselves the direct descendants of God's chosen people and regard the Jewish people as having descended from Cain, which has led to extreme anti-Semitism within the movement.

The previously mentioned beliefs can be summed up in what is referred to as the Two Seed Line doctrine. Christian Identity followers assert that Adam was preceded by other, lesser races, identified as "the beasts of the field" (Gen. 1:25). Eve was seduced by the snake (Satan) and gave birth to two seed lines: Cain, the direct descendant of Satan and Eve, and Abel, who was of good Aryan stock, descended through Adam. Cain then became the progenitor of the Jews in his subsequent matings with the non-Adamic races.

Christian Identity adherents believe the Jews are predisposed to carry on a conspiracy against the Adamic seed line and today have achieved almost complete control of the earth.[4]

Christian Identity does not have a national organizational structure. Rather, it is a grouping of churches throughout the country that follow its basic ideology. Some of these churches can be as small as a dozen people and some have memberships in the thousands. The Southern Poverty Law Center currently lists 602 active hate groups of which 32 are specifically identified as Christian Identity groups. Some of the better known organizations that follow Christian Identity beliefs include the American Nazi Party, Church of Jesus Christ Christian, Confederate Hammerskins, National Association for the Advancement of White People, Kingdom Identity Ministries, Posse Com-

---

Christian Identity: Apocalyptic Beliefs

- Inevitable end of the world, Christ's return.
- Part of a cleansing process before Christ's Kingdom can be established on earth.
- During end times, Jews and allies will attempt to destroy the white race.
- Violent and bloody war between good (Aryans) and evil (everyone else).
- Different views of end time, race war, Jews will take over world.

---

itatus, Christian Research, Scriptures for America, White Aryan Resistance (WAR), White Separatists Banner and many more.

Church of Jesus Christ Christian

The Church of Jesus Christ Christian, more commonly known as Aryan Nations, is a particularly violent organization that adheres to Christian Identity and espouses hatred toward Jews, the federal government, African-Americans and other minorities. Their ultimate goal is to forcibly take over five northwestern states (Oregon, Idaho, Wyoming, Washington and Montana) from the U.S. government to establish an Aryan homeland. Until 2001, Aryan Nations was headquartered in Hayden Lake, ID and continues to have a large number of state and international chapters. Its annual world congress attracts a number of different factions from right-wing groups and has furthered its base of support.

Aryan Nations and similar groups' activities led to a study conducted by the FBI announced on October 20, 1999 as Project Megiddo. This study was intended to alert U.S. law enforcement to what was described as "the potential for extremist criminal activity in the United States by individuals or domestic groups who attach special significance to the year 2000." An accompanying FBI statement mentioned that the "threat posed by extremists as a result of perceived events associated with the year 2000 is real. The volatile mix of apocalyptic religious and New World Order conspiracy theories may produce violent acts aimed at precipitating the end of the world as prophesized in the Bible."[5] The data for the report was collected over 9 months by the FBI's domestic terrorism unit and was not supposed to be made public. However, the Center for the Study of New Religious Movements (CESNUR), a cult apologist organization, obtained a copy and placed it on the the the center's website.

The Christian Identity movement was discussed at length in the Project Megiddo report because of its apocalyptic beliefs:

> Christian Identity also believes in the inevitability of the end of the world and the Second Coming of Christ. It is believed that these events are part of a cleansing process that is needed before Christ's kingdom can be established on earth. During this time, Jews and their allies will attempt to destroy the white race by any means available. The result will be a violent and bloody struggle, a war, in effect between God's forces, the white race, and the forces of evil, the Jews and nonwhites. The view of what Armageddon will be varies among Christian Identity believers. Some contend there will be a race war in which millions die; others believe that the United Nations, backed by Jewish representatives of the antichrist, will take over the country and promote a new world order.... After the final battle is ended and God's kingdom is established on earth, only then will the Aryan people be recognized as the one true Israel.... Christian Identity adherents believe that God will use his chosen race as his weapons to battle the forces of evil. Christian Identity followers believe they are among those chosen by God to wage this battle during Armageddon and they will be the last line of defense for the white race and Christian America. To prepare for these events, they engage in survivalist and paramilitary training, storing foodstuffs and supplies, and caching weapons and ammunition. They often reside on compounds in remote areas.[6]

The Megiddo report also identified potential violent threats from groups and individuals whose mission is to bring about a race war. Some of their stated reasons for potential violence include (1) the lack of structure in Christian Identity that creates a greater potential for violence from lone offenders and/or leaderless cells, (2) it is easy for persons to move from one group to another until they find a more radical one, (3) the increased cooperation between different groups that pair up with militias and receive paramilitary training, and finally (4) the formation of splinter groups or state chapters in which the leaders have diminished control.

Unfortunately, there are many examples of violence committed by practitioners of Christian Identity. A subgroup of the Aryan Nations called The Order headed by Bob Matthews committed a number of violent crimes including murder. Their mission was to bring about a race war and they inspired several other groups to pursue their goal. Dennis McGiffen formed a cell called The New Order and the members were arrested before they could follow through on their plan. Chevie Kehoe, another person who spent time at the Aryan compound, was convicted of three homicides, conspiracy and interstate transportation of stolen property. A few of the incidents perpetrated by Christian Identity members include bombings at a Birmingham, AL abortion clinic and at the Atlanta Olympics, torching of three synagogues in Sacramento, CA in July 1999 and the murder of a gay couple near Redding, CA. Christian Identity is a religion that fundamentally advocates racism, hatred, violence, genocide and terrorism.

World Church of the Creator

The World Church of the Creator (WCOTC) is a highly organized, sophisticated white supremacist new religious movement that practices a religion known as Creativity. Practitioners are referred to as Creators. Ben Klassen founded the religion in 1973 with the publication of *Nature's Eternal Religion*. He subsequently authored ten books including *The White Man's Bible, Salubrious Living, On the Brink of a Bloody Racial War, Expanding Creativity, Building a Whiter and Brighter World, The Little White Book* and more.

The first three of Klassen's books are considered the holy texts of Creativity. He emphasizes that Creativity is based on the eternal laws of nature as revealed through science, history, logic and common sense. Creativity is significantly different from Christian Identity in that the theology does not include belief in God. It differs from Odinism in that it does not believe in any gods or supreme beings. Essentially, Creativity is a form of Social Darwinism whose fundamental belief is the survival, expansion and advancement of the white race. Its basic creed (considered its golden rule) is, "What is good for the white race is the highest virtue; what is bad for the white race is the ultimate sin."

Creativity has 5 fundamental beliefs, 16 commandments and specific rituals. One of the sacred rituals is to repeat the five fundamental beliefs five times a day:

1. We believe that our race is our religion.
2. We believe that the white race is nature's finest.
3. We believe that racial loyalty is the highest of all honors and racial treason is the worst of all crimes.

WCOTC Theology: Basic Beliefs

Do Not Believe in:
- God
- Any gods or supreme beings
- Afterlife

Believe in:
- Nature (religion is a form of Social Darwinism).
- Survival of the fittest.
- White race is the fittest (superior).
- Culling out the weak is natural.
- Race is their religion.
- Terrorism; anything threatening their race is a primal threat endangering their species; fear of annihilation.
- Eugenics (genetic upgrading).

WCOTC Five Fundamental Beliefs

1. We believe that our Race is our Religion.
2. We believe that the White Race is Nature's Finest.
3. We believe that racial loyalty is the highest of all honors, and racial treason is the worst of all crimes.
4. We believe that what is good for the White Race is the highest virtue, and what is bad for the White Race is the ultimate sin.
5. We believe that the one and only, true and revolutionary White Racial Religion — Creativity — is the only salvation for the White Race.

4. We believe that what is good for the white race is the highest virtue and what is bad for the white race is the ultimate sin.
5. We believe that the one and only, true and revolutionary White Racial Religion — Creativity — is the only salvation for the white race.

The 16 commandments illustrate the basic tenets of the religion including beliefs in the survival of the fittest, culling out the weak is natural and anything threatening the white race is a primal threat endangering the species. The commandments also emphasize that the inferior colored races are their deadly enemies and Jews are the most dangerous. Commandments include being fruitful and multiplying, showing preferential treatment in business dealings to members of their own race and keeping the race pure. Prohibitions include banishing and destroying all Jewish thought and influence.

The current leader of the WCOTC is 33-year-old Reverend Matt Hale who is referred to as Pontifex Maximus (Latin for *highest priest*) or supreme leader. Hale was officially confirmed as head of the church on July 27, 1996. His predecessor was Rick McCarty who replaced the original Pontifex Maximus, Ben Klassen, who committed suicide in 1993. McCarty stepped down after a brief time, which left the church leaderless for a time and resulted in fractionalization and a decrease in support.

Hale's goal is to promote Klassen's religion and to honor his memory. Hale has been very successful at bringing attention to the World Church of the Creator. He has spread Creativity through the media, seldom receiving good publicity, but getting publicity nonetheless. He has given interviews on radio, national television and in newspapers, runs a very active website that includes a children's page and created a public access television show called "White Revolution."

Hale attended law school at Southern Illinois University while serving as head of the church and graduated in 1998. He successfully passed the Illinois bar examination but has been denied his law license due to the church's anti-government beliefs. He is fighting this decision, claiming that his license was denied because of his religious beliefs. He regularly holds speaking engagements in public libraries and other venues and protests and controversies ensue at most of his lectures. Reverand Hale also has political aspirations. In April 1995, he ran for East Peoria City Council. WCOTC is headquartered in Peoria and Hale received 14% of the vote. As of January 2003 he was running for City Commissioner of East Peoria. However, on January 8, 2003 Hale was arrested as he arrived in court for a hearing concerning a legal battle for the name of the church. Hale was charged with solicitation to murder a federal judge and obstruction of justice. As of this writing Hale is still in prison awaiting trial. What Matt Hale lacks in charisma he makes up for in determination and he is committed to building this church and spreading the white racialist religion even if he has to accomplish it from his prison cell.

According to its website, the WCOTC has member chapters in all 50 states and 24 countries. The organizational structure of the church is that each group has city, county, state and national directors and each state has its own authority. Giving each group autonomy prevents power struggles for leadership. The primary group is the basic organizational cell and consists of two to ten members. The church manual suggests that five is the best number to keep the group closely knit, maintain trust and make the group difficult for enemy agents to penetrate. The WCOTC also has what it refers to as security legions consisting of White Rangers and White Berets.

As described in the church manual, White Rangers, as the name implies, draw their inspiration from the tradition of the heroic white conquerors of the North American continent — pioneers, frontier fighters, cowboys and Texas Rangers. Their official uniform features a white cowboy hat (with the church logo) and cowboy boots. White Berets, as implied by their name, draw their inspiration mainly from the heroic white military tradition, especially as exemplified by elite commando units (such as paratroopers). Their official uniform features a white military beret (with the church logo) and paratrooper boots.

The primary mission of the White Berets and White Rangers is to provide security services for members and church property. Their secondary mission is to prepare members for active and effective self-defense. Commanders of the security legions (White Berets and White Rangers) have jurisdiction over all those in their legions and are responsible only to the Pontifex Maximus. The security legions provide excellent recruitment incentives for disillusioned young men who want to feel like they are respected and belong. Other recruitment techniques include a children's website, prison outreach program to gather what they call members behind bars and advertising campaigns with posters, pamphlets and other items. The children's website has cute pictures and games such as racial crossword puzzles and word scrabbles.

The church did not waste any time responding to the tragedy of September 11th for recruitment purposes. A variety of posters available online included graphic photos of the airplanes crashing into the World Trade Center and captions that read, "Friendship with Israel leads to this," and "Are you prepared to fight the Arab holy war on American soil?" The World Church of the Creator preyed on people's fears when they were most vulnerable and felt a need to understand the tragic events. It took the opportunity to suggest that blame be placed on America's Zionist Occupation Government (ZOG).

WCOTC also provides specific detailed advice on how to deal with law enforcement and cites ten specific points if any of its members are questioned by police. As stated in the manual:[7]

1. Never trust police, FBI or other agents of the ZOG. However, retain a friendly, positive, respectful and professional attitude at all times. Do not assume a belligerent attitude for this will inspire belligerence on the part of the officer.
2. Never allow them inside your home or your car without a search warrant. Always demand to see the warrant.
3. If unwillingly detained, demand to know if you are under arrest and under what charge.
4. If under arrest, refuse to answer any questions and demand to see a lawyer. However, never trust your lawyer if he advises you to break any of these basic legal self-defense principles.

5. When questioned by law enforcement in an attempt which you believe is calculated to form evidence against you, silence is your best defense.
6. Be silent, suppress the urge to tell your side of the story.
7. Never plead guilty and never waive any of your legal rights.
8. Never make any deals.
9. Never betray your comrades or the World Church of the Creator.
10. Remember, nothing great is won without great sacrifices. Persecution and suffering are the inevitable obstacles on our path to victory. We must overcome them through dedication and perseverance. Let the great vision of a Whiter and Brighter World inspire and lead you through all trials, sufferings and deprivations.

The National Alliance offers similar information with the additional advantage of being able to print out an on-line card that can be handed to police and eliminate any verbal contact.

Due to his provocative lectures and choice of venues, Matt Hale has need of security. A highly publicized event occurred on January 12, 2002 when Hale organized a march and held a public meeting in the York, PA library with the support of many other racist organizations including members of his WCOTC, the National Alliance, Aryan Nations and the Eastern Hammer-skins. Hale chose York because it is a racially mixed city of 41,000, has a history of severe race riots and, specifically, because nine white men including its mayor had recently been prosecuted for complicity in the murder of Lillie Belle Allen, a black preacher's daughter who was shot and killed while driving through a white neighborhood in 1969. At the time of the crime, Mayor Robertson was an officer on the York police force and was accused of encouraging children to kill as many blacks as possible and providing ammunition for them to do so.

The white supremacist organizations wanted to show their support for a racist who not only shared their violent ideological views, but also managed to become mayor of the city. They saw value in publicly expressing their support for racist murderers and agreed to join forces to hold their conference in York. More than 200 anti-racist militants from a variety of organizations showed up to violently protest the event. Many of the protesters wore bandanas over their faces for fear that they would be photographed by white supremacists who at prior rallies threatened to post their photos on Nazi websites and hunt them down when they were alone. Many of the masked protestors were angry white women, one of whom was arrested for throwing a snowball at the Hammerskins.

White supremacist religions are exceptionally patriarchal, anti-feminist and relegate women to very specific roles. Although they allow women to train as soldiers, women are never involved in politics and never hold

---

WCOTC Suggestions for Dealing with Law Enforcement

I. Never trust the police, FBI, or other agents of the ZOG. However, retain a friendly, positive, respectful, and professional attitude at all times. Do not assume a belligerent attitude for this will inspire belligerence on the part of the officer.

II. Never allow them inside your home or your car without a search warrant. Always demand to see the warrant.

III. If unwillingly detained, demand to know if you are under arrest and under what charge.

IV. If under arrest, refuse to answer any questions and demand to see a lawyer. However, never trust your lawyer if he advises you to break any of these basic legal self-defense principles.

V. When questioned by law enforcement in an attempt which you believe is calculated to form evidence against you, silence is your best defense.

---

positions of authority. When the Anti-Racist-Action group members began distributing flyers for the York counter-demonstration, they urged protesters to bring rocks to drive the racists out of town. Organizers of the conference immediately contacted the FBI and claimed that they were being intimidated by protesters who were trying to take away their right to free speech.[8] As a result, the city, state and federal authorities provided security inclusive of hundreds of police in riot gear, rooftop snipers, police on horseback and a hovering police helicopter. The police blocked off the streets around the library where Hale was speaking and frisked people for weapons. At one point, police in riot gear had to form a human barrier between the protesters and the marchers who traded insults and taunted each other. Police made 25 arrests, mostly for disorderly conduct, and several guns were confiscated. Witnesses reported seeing cars vandalized and minor confrontations in the streets.

Matt Hale holds many of his appearances in libraries and they often erupt into violence. In 2000, two of his Illinois lectures entailed arrests of protestors. Hale, surrounded by his security forces, arrived and left in an unmarked police van. Unfortunately, the library conference room was reserved in November by Michael Cook, director of the WCOTC York area chapter who simply told the library that his church would be meeting there. Not until a week before the speech did library officials realize the room was reserved by a white supremacist group. It is quite common for white supremacist churches to deliberately choose names that appear to be benign Christian

WCOTC Views on Terrorism

- The theology of the World Church of the Creator advocates overthrowing the government through acts of terrorism.
- The *White Man's Bible*, their holy text, has an entire section, Creative Credo No. 64, entitled Law and Order vs. Violence, Terrorism and Self-Preservation which clearly identifies the U.S. government as their enemy and promotes violence and terrorism.

White Man's Bible **Quote:** "There is an ultimate weapon that such a beleaguered people can resort to against its "own" government that has been utilized for thousands of years when the situation has become desperate and intolerable. That weapon is terrorism and violence, taking the law into our own hands."

churches and reside in communities without people realizing that hate is being preached. The York rally provided exactly the kind of attention that Matt Hale thrives on. Violent public protests only serve to bring more attention to his cause and reinforce white supremacists' beliefs that they are persecuted by the government. Such protests also place law enforcement officers in the unpleasant role of protecting racist groups.

There is no doubt that Creativity, the theology of the World Church of the Creator, advocates overthrowing the government through acts of terrorism. The church is a millennial religious group that believes that a racial holy war will occur in the near future. This is such a significant part of WCOTC ideology that the expression RAHOWA (RAcial HOly WAr) is used as a common expression of greeting that functions as hello, goodbye and amen. *The White Man's Bible*, the church's holy text, contains an entire section titled "Creative Credo No. 64, Law and Order vs. Violence, Terrorism and Self-Preservation" that clearly identifies the government as a church enemy and promotes violence and terrorism. It reads:

> We must decide. The issue we must resolve is this: if our survival is at stake, is so-called "illegal" terrorism justified? And the answer overwhelmingly is — hell yes! …. Criminals are the Government. This is not a theoretical question. It is as real today as life and death itself. In the United States the Jew-controlled government is waging a secret but sinister war of destruction against the noble White Race, the race that built this country

in the first place. It is very real not only in America but throughout the world wherever the White Man resides. In America, as elsewhere an alien hostile race, the tribe of Judah, is in full control, making and breaking "the laws of the land" at its whim and caprice. It is a vicious criminal government that is obsessed with the destruction of the White Race at any cost and will stop at nothing to reach its goal.... The Ultimate Defense. There is an ultimate weapon that such a beleaguered people can resort to against its "own" government that has been utilized for thousands of years when the situation has become desperate and intolerable. That weapon is terrorism and violence, taking the law into our own hands. There are basically two ways to direct the behavior of other people, including tyrants who would destroy you. One is persuasion and reason, and the other is terrorism. When persuasion and reason fail, the only recourse is violence, legal or illegal. As we shall see, the only difference between "legal" and "illegal" is only a matter of whose point of view — namely who is on top and who is at the bottom.[9]

Even more disturbing than the anti-government beliefs is that the *White Man's Bible* also advocates genocide, which they describe in detail in what they call their eugenics program whose goals include being white and cleansed of all traces of any of the "mud races"; becoming increasingly intelligent, raising the IQ level to an average of 150, with outstanding geniuses having IQs as high as 250; being mentally healthy, devoid of neurosis and other ailments of the mind; having physically healthy bodies; producing future generations of children free from hereditary defects, as near 100% as possible, so they will grow into strong, healthy, beautiful and athletic specimens of their fine race, becoming aesthetically finer as each generation progresses — the men more handsome and virile, the women more beautiful and feminine.[10] In addition to these extreme objectives, the World Church of the Creator also has a program for genetic upgrading whose specific goals include, first and foremost, physically removing the "alien mud races" from their midst, encouraging the more desirable specimens of their own race to have more children, inducing the less desirable members of the white race to have smaller families, and finally sterilization of individuals the church deems incurable misfits, idiots, and genetically diseased.[11]

Taking into consideration the sophisticated organizational structure of the World Church of the Creator, its appeal to American citizens who are disillusioned with the federal government, its recruitment and publicity campaigns, and its theological justifications for overthrowing the government and implementing a eugenics program, there is no doubt that this religious group constitutes a serious threat to public safety. Fortunately, the World Church of the Creator has been designated a domestic terrorist group by the Federal Bureau of Investigation.

Odinism

Odinism or Asatru (its Icelandic name) is an ancient pre-Christian tradition that is now interpreted and practiced as a racist religion. All pre-Christian religions are designated Pagan, a Biblical expression for religions that worship more than one god (polytheism) or gods other than the one true God. Neo-paganism consists of hundreds of new religious movements that have revived ancient traditions. Neo-pagan groups include Wicca who trace their roots back to the pre-Celtic era in Europe, Druids who base their faith and practices on the ancient Celtic professional class, followers of Odinism/Asatru who adhere to the ancient pre-Christian Norse religion, and many other neo-pagan religions that follow Roman, Greek, Egyptian and other traditions.

The non-racist version of Odinism, more commonly referred to as Asatru, at its peak encompassed all of Northern Europe. The Norse pantheon includes three races of deities and all are regarded as living beings who are involved with human life. The Aesir are the gods of the tribe representing kingship, the Vanir represent the fertility of the earth and forces of nature, and the Jotnar are giants who are in a constant state of war with the Asir and represent chaos and destruction. Asatru is an apocalyptic religion where in the final battle of Ragnarok, many of the gods will die, the world will come to an end and be reborn. Some of the specific gods are Thor, Frey and Odin, Odin is the one-eyed god who gave up his eye to drink from the fountain of wisdom; he is a magician and wise man and understands the secrets of the runes (northern European alphabet symbols). Odin is the god for whom the religion is named. Some of the important goddesses are Freya, Frigg (Odin's Wife), Skadi and Ostara.

Asatru ethical values include the nine noble virtues: courage, truth, honor, fidelity, discipline, hospitality, industriousness, self-reliance and perseverance. The view of the afterlife is that those who die in battle will go to Valhalla and live with the gods. Those who are evil will go to Hifhel, a place of torment, and the remainder will go to a place of calmness and peace. Local religious communities are called kindreds, hearths or garths; priests are called Gothi; priestesses are Gythia.

Like other religious sects, racist Odinism retains many of the same fundamental beliefs as the non-racist religion, e.g., worshipping the same gods,

Odinism: Racist Pagans

- Fastest growing religion for under-30 neo-Nazis, skinheads.
- Popular in prisons.
- Extremely violent.
- Odinism shares the Social Darwinian philosophy of the survival of a pure white race.
- Attractive to younger racists who consider Christian Identity to be too weak.

- A theology that is rooted in pre-Christian warrior traditions that appeal to young racists who reject what they consider Jewish-influenced Christianity.
- An indigenous faith rooted in pre-Christian Anglo-Saxon warrior cultures and the oneness of the Aryan race with nature.

nine noble virtues, and its view of the afterlife. However, it interprets doctrines to authenticate white supremacist ideals. It is easy to see how Asatru easily lends itself to a religion based on creating an Aryan race. Its origins in Northern Europe are consistent with racist ideologies and the desire to return to what they perceive was a purer time.

Racist Odinism is the fastest growing religion among under-30 right-wing extremists, neo-Nazis and skinheads. It is a theology rooted in pre-Christian warrior traditions that appeal to young racists who reject what they consider Jewish-influenced Christianity. They want to embrace an indigenous faith rooted in pre-Christian Anglo-Saxon warrior cultures and the oneness of the Aryan race with nature. Additionally, National Socialism appeals to many neo-Nazi Odinists who point out that many prominent Nazis practiced a form of Odinism in Nazi Germany.

Neo-paganism is extremely appealing to young persons who are disillusioned with traditional beliefs so it is not surprising that white supremacy would emerge in a pagan new religious movement. The racist version of Odinism shares the Social Darwinian philosophy of the survival of a pure white race as a goal to be achieved at all costs and embraces the Nazi concept of might is right. It is attractive to younger racists who consider Christian Identity to be too weak. The pantheon of gods including Odin, the warlike father of all gods and men, Freya, his wife, and Thor, their rugged hammer-wielding son, who are a part of a theology rooted in a glorious past are also appealing to young racists. An intelligence report published in Spring 2000 by the Southern Poverty Law Center titled *Pagans and Prison* concludes:

> Today, the growth of racist neo-paganism is remarkable. Oklahoma Skinhead recruiter Dennis Mahon has

become a devout Odinist. Long-time Alabama Klansman and four time felon Bill Riccio, who has also energetically organized skinheads, says Odinism is the true religion of the Aryans, and one of his former followers now heads the Sonnenkinder Kindred, an Alabama racist pagan outfit. John William King, the convicted ringleader in the truck dragging murder of James Byrd Jr., became an Odinist in prison before the infamous Texas slaying. Nathan Thill, a neo-Nazi skinhead who boasted to television cameras about murdering a black man in Denver, bears Odinist tattoos of Celtic warriors on his right hand and wrist. And true to form, Ferris Wolf recently congratulated Thill for his grisly handiwork. "Special Thanks" the magazine exclaimed and "Blood Regards."[12]

One of the better known racist Odinist groups is the White Order of Thule created in the mid-1990s and headed by Nathan Pett, also known as Nathan Zorn, a skinhead tattoo artist who operated two websites, published a newsletter titled *Crossing the Abyss* and a journal *Ferris Wolf Press,* all advocating white supremacy. The group lists its world headquarters in Deer Park, WA and also maintains a post office box in Richmond, VA. According to one of its publications, the order's name derives from the ancient Greek word *Thule* (pronounced Too-lee) designating the place of origin of the Aryan race. Ideologically, the group mixes racist Odinism, Satanism and occult neo-Nazism and calls itself "the foremost occult Aryan pagan order in the World." Their literature states that the "soul which was unified in the people of Thule must now be reunited in a new experience of spirituality in order to manifest the next great Aryan race."[13]

The White Order of Thule consists of a loosely knit group of individuals who believe in the superiority of the Aryan race as represented by Norse, Viking and other Nordic cultures. They interpret Odinism as a spiritual way of life, based on the Nordic ancestral mythos or the collective beliefs and folk consciousness of the Aryan people. Thule members must advance through degrees of membership by studying required readings by philosopher Friedrich Nietzsche and Adolph Hitler.

The group also glorifies the 1980s group known as The Order founded by Bob Matthews in Metaline Falls, WA. The Order carried out racist murders, robberies, bombings and counterfeiting to fund its race war in 1983 and 1984. It was inspired by the fictional group described in William Pierce's *Turner Diaries*. Members of the White Order of Thule are also required to read *Bruder Schweigen* written by Bob Matthews. Although Matthews was killed in a shoot-

White Order of Thule

- One of the more well-known racist Odinist groups is the White Order of Thule created in the mid 1990s.
- Ideologically it mixes racist Odinism, Satanism and occult neo-Nazism and it calls itself "the foremost occult Aryan pagan order in the World."
- Members consist of a loosely knit group of individuals who interpret Odinism as a spiritual way of life, based on the Nordic ancestral mythos or the collective beliefs and folk consciousness of the Aryan people.
- Thule members must advance through degrees of membership by studying required readings by philosopher Friedrich Nietzsche and Adolph Hitler.

out with the FBI, David Lane, Richard Scutari and other members of The Order are confined in high-security prison facilities. This has not prevented them from contributing articles to a number of white supremacist publications including Pett's. Lane and Scutari were already heroes to the radical right for serving life sentences for their crimes as members of The Order and both are very influential in advocating Odinism. Racist Odinism is very popular in prisons and practitioners are feared by other white supremacists. Prison officials around the country claim that it is the fastest growing religion behind prison walls and that practitioners of Odinism are especially violent. The violence caught up to Nathan Pett in early 2001 when he was beaten into a coma by rival skinheads. Although Pett survived, Joe Roy, the director of the intelligence project, said Pett can barely feed himself with a spoon.

In June 2001, Leo V. Felton, 31, a member of the White Order of Thule, was arrested with his girlfriend, Erica Chase, 22, for attempting to bomb a Jewish or black landmark in Boston. Felton and Chase were originally arrested in April for passing a counterfeit $20 bill, and authorities soon uncovered a potentially disastrous conspiracy. Prosecutors charged Felton and Chase with belonging to a white supremacist cell that sought to finance terrorist attacks by printing fake money and robbing banks. This is consistent with the White Order of Thule's glorification of The Order which committed both crimes. Authorities found a 50-pound bag of ammonium nitrate in Felton's home, the same chemical fertilizer used by Timothy McVeigh to blow up the federal building in Oklahoma City, a calendar with Hitler's birthday (April 20) circled, books on terrorism and subterfuge, newspaper clippings about a planned event at the New England Holocaust Memorial and notes on bomb making. Felton and Chase were officially charged with conspiring to make a destructive device, firearms violations, making and passing counterfeit currency and conspiracy to obstruct justice. Felton was charged with attempting to receive explosive materials in interstate commerce with intent to use the materials in an explosive device to kill and injure people and destroy property.

Felton had been released from a New Jersey state prison in January 2001 after serving 11 years for attempting to murder a black taxi driver in New York City with a crowbar. While serving his sentence the 6-foot, 7-inch, 225-pound Felton tried to slit the throats of two black inmates. He has many neo-Nazi and white supremacist tattoos and it is possible he became a member of the White Order of Thule behind bars. Felton is pointing a gun at the camera in a court exhibit photo that he mailed to Chase.

Chase, whose body also has neo-Nazi tattoos, is a member of the World Church of the Creator and the Indiana chapter of the Outlaw Hammerskins. She allegedly began writing Felton in March 2000 while he was in prison. Prison outreach is one of the roles carried out by the Sisterhood, a branch of the WCOTC specifically designated for women.[14] During the trial in July 2002, a friend testified that Chase joined Felton in Boston with ambitious plans: "They were going to burn off their fingerprints with hot oil and assume the identities of missing children; they were going to go around and be terrorists."[15] In case there is any doubt about how seriously dangerous practitioners of Racist Odinism are, the Odin's Rage website provides the complete texts of *The Terrorist Handbook, System Breakdown: A Guide to Disrupting the System, In Praise of War* and *A Practical Guide to the Strategy and Tactics of Revolution*.

Lone Wolves and the Phineas Priesthood

Sacred violence has manifested in the Christian Identity movement in a concept known as the Phineas Priesthood. This relatively new tenet justifies the use of violence if it is perpetrated in order to punish violators of God's law as found in an extreme interpretation of the 25th chapter of the Book of Numbers. These priests are initiated by committing violent acts such as murder, referred to as Phineas acts, against non-whites, Jews, abortion doctors and homosexuals. Unfortunately, the concept is very appealing to Christian Identity extremists who believe they are being persecuted by the Jewish-controlled U.S. government and are eagerly preparing for Armageddon. The Phineas Priesthood is viewed as a call to action or a badge of honor.

The concept of the Phineas Priesthood in Christian Identity originated in an obscure 1990 book titled *Vigilantes of Christendom: The Story of the*

Phineas Priests

- Phineas Priests are initiated by committing violent acts such as murder, referred to as Phineas Acts, against non-whites, Jews, abortion doctors and homosexuals.
- Based on an extreme interpretation of the Bible (25th chapter of the Book of Numbers).
- The Phineas Priesthood is viewed as a call to action or a badge of honor among white supremacists.
- The concept of the Phineas Priesthood originated in an obscure book entitled *Vigilantes of Christendom: The Story of the Phineas Priesthood* by Richard Kelly Hoskins.
- One form of "lone wolf activism" and "leaderless resistance."

Phineas Priesthood by Richard Kelly Hoskins.[16] According to Hoskins, history is seen as a series of ongoing judgments meted out by God and responded to by believers. This response takes the form of murdering those who transgress against the law. For Hoskins, the Phineas priest — the embodiment of Christian Identity belief and obedience to God — is not one who prepares for impending race war; but one who commits racist, anti-Semitic or homophobic murder to stave off God's ongoing judgment of white people for failing to uphold the "law." For Hoskins this includes such "crimes" as interracial marriage and allowing homosexuals to live.[17]

The concept of the Phineas Priesthood was further advocated in a gathering in Estes Park, CO that included Reverend Pete Peters of the Church of Christ based in La Porte, CO, Identity followers, members of the neo-Nazi movement, and the Ku Klux Klan. They met shortly after the murders of Vicki and Samuel Weaver in 1992 during an armed standoff with federal agents near Naples, ID; the result of which was a report that many observers claim to be the impetus for the armed wing of the Patriot movement, the militias and the Phineas Priesthood. The Estes Park report, initially called the "Special Report on the Meeting of Christian Men held in Estes Park, Colorado, October 23, 24 and 25, 1992, Concerning the Killing of Vickie and Samuel Weaver by the United States Government" clearly advocates vigilante violence:

> As was the case with our Founding Fathers, the establishment of a Christian civil body politic should be a primary goal for Christian men across the nation, for

it is the chief means for carrying out the judgments of God. It has the authority to punish the evildoer as mandated in Romans 13. This country's existing government does not fit the description of the 'governing authorities' in Romans 13. The current situation in America is one in which the established government does not punish evildoers, but rather is increasingly using its power to punish the righteous. It is a tyrannical government. Therefore, it is not a Christian civil body politic.... The means for Christian men to bring about Divine judgment is not limited in certain cases to the actions of the body politic. In such cases, God's Word also provides precedent for what is today termed 'vigilante action'. Vigilante action is Scriptural, but any such action must be in conformity with Bible precedents and directives. Vigilante action is the exception, not the rule. It should be noted that the action of Phineas (Numbers 25:1–9) is considered by many not to be true vigilante action, but was in fact the carrying out of directives of God through the civil body politic.[18]

Reverend Peters' writings have made him one of the foremost leaders of the Christian Identity movement. The Estes Park Report also included a text by Louis Beam Jr., Ambassador-at-Large for the Aryan Nations and former Grand Dragon of the Ku Klux Klan. The text is titled *Leaderless Resistance* and it was used as a model by the paramilitary right for the creation of phantom cells, decentralized gangs of terrorists that carry out special operations in militia groupings.

Christian Identity ideology has inspired many individuals to commit a number of heinous crimes. In only 2 months, July and August 1999, subsequently known as the Summer of Hate, there were three unrelated incidents of hate crimes involving murder. Benjamin Smith, a 21-year-old student at the University of Indiana, went on a weekend shooting rampage in Illinois and Indiana, killing two people and wounding nine before he committed suicide. He specifically targeted minorities. On July 2, 1999, he first murdered Ricky Birdsong, the well-known college basketball coach, then wounded six orthodox Jews in Chicago. The next day, Smith opened fire on two African-American and six Asian men in the Illinois towns of Springfield and Champagne–Urbana. On July 4, Smith killed a Korean man outside a church in Bloomington, IN, then shot himself as police closed in. Smith was a member of the World Church of the Creator headed by Reverend Matthew Hale and was named Creator of the Year in March 1998.

Lone Wolf Activism	Leaderless Resistance
• Through his Internet magazine the *Nationalist Observer* and telephone hotlines, Alex Curtis promoted an ideology called Lone Wolf Activism where he encouraged white supremacists to act alone in violent ways.	• "Leaderless Resistance" is advocated in a text by Louis Beam Jr., Ambassador-at-Large for the Aryan Nations and former Grand Dragon of the Ku Klux Klan that is used as a model by domestic terrorists for the creation of "phantom cells," decentralized gangs of terrorists that carry out special operations in militia groupings.
• Lone wolves are racist combatants acting alone or in small groups who chip away at the government's infrastructure by daily anonymous acts.	

Dr. William Pierce, head of the National Alliance, author of the *Turner Diaries* and a leading figure in the white supremacist movement, commented on the Benjamin Smith shooting spree in an article titled "Knowledge and Discipline." Pierce said:

> I don't know anything about Smith except what was on the television news and the Internet, but I cannot help but feel sympathy for him. Smith, according to those who knew him, was intelligent, quiet, and serious. He was a student of criminal justice at the University of Indiana. Most, notable, however, he was racially conscious. He was unhappy about the destruction of our White society in America and the perversion of our European culture by the program of Multiculturalism promoted by the government and the media. He distributed leaflets on the University of Indiana campus in Bloomington, expressing his views, and the university administration harassed him for it. He distributed leaflets off the campus in Bloomington and in the Chicago suburb of Wilmette, Illinois, where he grew up. Leftists, feminists, and Jews organized a public demonstration against him in Bloomington in an effort to stop his leaflet distribution, and the police in Wilmette arrested him. Blacks repeatedly smashed the windows of his apartment in Bloomington to show their

disagreement with Smiths "racist" views. It must have been very stressful for Smith, trying to exercise his freedom of speech in a society which pays lip service to our Bill of Rights but which actually tries its best to make life difficult for anyone who doesn't tow the party line.[19]

This is a clear example of how white supremacist ideology justifies violent acts and praises the perpetrator as a hero.

Fortunately, this incident inspired legislation called the Hate Crimes Prevention Act, a bill that amends the existing federal hate crimes law to expand the government's role in investigation and also expands the definition of *hate crime* to include sexual orientation, gender and disability. Unfortunately, one day before the bill went to Congress, another hate crime occurred. On July 21, 1999, two brothers, Benjamin Matthew Williams and James Tyler Williams, broke into a gay couple's home in northern California and shot them to death. During Benjamin Williams' confession, he said his only regret about the murders was that they did not inspire others to emulate him. He insisted that his actions did not constitute a crime. The Williams brothers are practicing members of Christian Identity. Benjamin Williams stated, "You obey a government of man until there is a conflict, then you obey a higher law…." He added, "It's part of the faith. So many people claim to be Christians and complain about all these things their religion says are a sin, but they're not willing to do anything about it. They do not have the guts."[20] Williams is revered in jail by his fellow white supremacists and receives considerable media attention. Both brothers were also suspected of three Sacramento area synagogue arsons and were recently given lengthy prison sentences. Benjamin Williams received 30 years and James Williams received 21 years for the synagogue fires. Police discovered one other notable item, a letter from Benjamin Williams to National Alliance leader William Pierce in which he allegedly asked the white supremacist for assignments and suggested he could bring other recruits aboard.[21] While awaiting trial for murder charges, on November 15, 2002 Benjamin Matthew Williams mailed a signed confession to his brother's attorney, taking full responsibility for the 1999 murders of Gary Matson and Winfield Mowder. Two days later, on November 17, Benjamin Williams bled to death in his Shasta County Jail cell after using a homemade razor knife to slash his legs, arms and neck. Tyler Williams subsequently pleaded guilty to the murders on February 25, and on March 27 Superior Court Judge William Gallagher sentenced him to 29 years to life in prison. Benjamin William's suicide will be hailed by Identity Christians as an honorable act of martyrdom that not only demonstrated loyalty to his brother but also his commitment to the cause.

Summer of Hate

In July and August 1999, subsequently known as the
Summer of Hate, there were three unrelated incidents
of hate crimes involving murder. All of the perpetrators
were affiliated with white supremacist organizations.

- Benjamin Smith, a 21-year-old student at the University
  of Indiana,went on a weekend shooting rampage in Illinois
  and Indiana killing two people and wounding nine before
  he committed suicide. He specifically targeted minorities.

- Two brothers, Benjamin Matthew Williams and James
  Tyler Williams, broke into a gay couple's home in northern
  California and tortured and shot them to death. The two
  brothers were also responsible for three Sacramento area
  synagogue arsons.

- Buford Oneal Furrow, Jr. walked into the North Valley
  Jewish Community Center in suburban Granada Hills,
  California and opened fire, wounding five including one
  5-year-old and two 6-year-old boys. Shortly afterward
  he murdered a Filipino-American postman.

The third major incident in the Summer of Hate occurred on August 10,
1999. Buford Oneal Furrow, Jr. walked into the North Valley Jewish Community Center in suburban Granada Hills, CA and opened fire, wounding
five including a 5-year-old boy and two 6-year-old boys. Shortly afterward,
he murdered a Filipino-American postman. In the early 1990s, Furrow joined
the Aryan Nations and was influenced by the Christian Identity concept of
the Phineas Priesthood. *War Cycles. Peace Cycles*, another book by Richard
Kelly Hoskins was found in Furrow's possession. According to the indictment,
Furrow expressed no regrets over the killing of Joseph Santos Ileto and the
wounding of five people at the Jewish Community Center. In the 61-page
indictment, Furrow said he would not have killed the postal worker if the
worker had been white. He also said he targeted the center because of his
hatred for Jews. At the time of his arrest, Furrow admitted the crimes and
said "it was a wake-up call" to anti-Semitic and hate groups.

One of the major influences for these crimes can be found in Reverend
Pete Peters' book titled *The Bible: Handbook for Survivalists, Racists Tax
Protesters, Militants and Right-Wing Extremists* in which he reinterprets the
Biblical story of Phineas for his racist believers:

> Perhaps there was an organization in Phineas' day
> known as the NAACP (National Association for the
> Advancement of Canaanite People), who took excep-
> tion with this teaching of segregation. Perhaps there
> were pulpits proclaiming a more tolerant and socially

accepted view and government agency crusading for affirmative action. We really do not know; but we do know from the Bible story in Numbers Chapter 25 that the Israel people began to disobey God's law, accepted integration, cultural exchange and a type of interracial marriage, and thus were struck collectively by a plague. Phineas was the man who courageously fought against the racial treason to the point of bloodshed, and he too was honored by God.[22]

Another radical and influential voice of the racist right is Alex Curtis who, through his Internet magazine the *Nationalist Observer* and telephone hotlines, promoted a new ideology called Lone Wolf Activism where he encourages white supremacists to act alone in violent ways. He advocates a two-tiered revolutionary hate movement. The first tier is above ground and spreads subversive propaganda that guides the underground. The second (underground) tier consists of lone wolves — racist combatants who act alone or in small groups to chip away at the government's infrastructure by daily anonymous acts.[23] Curtis also copied a chart from Louis Beams' book titled *Essays of a Klansman* that assigns point values to various targets and titled the chart the Lone Wolf Point System, part of which states:

> Policy Formulation and Decision Making Leaders of International satanic anti-Christ Conspiracy for control of the world are each worth one full point. Members of Congress are each valued at one-fifth of one point. The Director of the FBI carries a reward of one-sixth of one point and lone wolves earn half of one point for each national leader of the NAACP. A racist who collects one full point earns the designation Aryan Warrior, one-third of one point merits the title Commando and so on.[24]

Curtis was the target of a joint FBI and San Diego Police Department investigation dubbed Operation Lone Wolf. The investigation revealed that Curtis led a cell of various white supremacist associates to commit criminal acts and target public figures who spoke out against hate crimes. The investigation led to an indictment charging Curtis with conspiracy to violate civil rights by targeting prominent members of the community.

Special interest extremists, described in the third category of the FBI's typology of domestic terrorists, can also be described as Lone Wolves and occasionally Phineas Priests, many of whom specifically target abortion doc-

Lone Wolf Point System

One Full Point:
- Policy formulation and decision-making leaders of international satanic anti-Christ conspiracy for control of the world

One Fifth of One Point:
- Members of Congress

One Sixth of One Point:
- Director of the FBI

Half of One Point
- Each national leader of the NAACP

Aryan Warrior
- A white supremacist who collects one full point

Commando
- A white supremacist who collects one third of one point
- Etc.

tors. Vandalism, arson and murder are advocated by an extremely violent religious group who call themselves the Army of God. Their website contains photos of mutilated infants, presumably actual images of third trimester abortions. The group even provides a free e-mail service urging people to "send a baby murdered by an abortion postcard" showing an image of a dead baby and allowing selection from two dozen phrases such as, "What part of *Thou Shalt not Kill* don't you understand?" and "Who broke the baby?" The website also has tributes glorifying what they call soldiers in the Army of

Army of God

- The Army of God is an extremely violent anti-abortion religious group.
- Their website contains photos of mutilated infants.
- Their website also has tributes glorifying what they call soldiers in the Army of God who either murdered abortion doctors, blew up clinics or perpetrated a variety of other violent illegal activities in the name of God.

Army of God Manual
- Published in its entirety on their website.
- The manual contains 99 covert ways to stop abortion including everything from methods of vandalizing clinics and doctors' property, sabotaging the construction of clinics, to burning down buildings.
- Found in the possession of anti-abortionists who targeted and murdered doctors.

God who murdered abortion doctors, blew up clinics and performed a variety of other violent illegal activities in the name of God.

Finally, their website also publishes the enire text of the *Army of God Manual* found in the possession of anti-abortionists who targeted and murdered doctors. The manual contains 99 covert ways to stop abortion including methods of vandalizing clinics and doctors' property, sabotaging clinic construction and burning down buildings. Evidence indicates that Reverend Paul Hill who shot and killed Dr. James Britton on July 29, 1994 in front of a Pensacola, FL abortion clinic considered himself a Phineas Priest. Hill quoted relevant passages from the Old Testament Book of Numbers, describing the murderous zeal of Phineas from a treatise he wrote entitled "Should We Defend Born and Unborn Children with Force?" justifying the murders of abortion providers. Hill's interpretation of the Old Testament allowed him to conclude that acts of vigilante murder and terror are approved by God. He inspired a dramatic change in anti-abortion rhetoric and transformed the movement into a fundamentalist Army of God. Hill's evocation of Phineas aligned him with the vigilante violence of Armed Patriotism Freemen and white supremacists. His utilization of the Phineas story is evident in similar actions taken by Smith, the Williams brothers and Furrow.[25]

Not only have white supremacist and Christian Identity ideologies influenced Phineas Priests and Lone Wolves but also a number of other violent hate crimes. Two particularly disturbing examples include the 1998 sadistic dragging death of James Byrd Jr. in Jasper, TX. During the savagery, the three white supremacists who tortured and murdered Byrd made reference to William Pierce's *Turner Diaries*, and Timothy McVeigh's 1995 Oklahoma City bombing of the Murrah Federal Building that killed 168 people. McVeigh referred to the dead children as "collateral damage" and his only regret was that their deaths became a public relations nightmare that detracted from his cause of avenging the incidents at Waco and Ruby Ridge. Other crimes committed in the cause of white supremacy are too numerous to mention but significantly not a single perpetrator felt any remorse for his crimes because violence in the name of religion is always justified.

Recent Trends in Domestic Terrorist Groups

This is an extremely critical time for domestic terrorism. Many of the original leaders of important groups have recently retired or died and the next generation has taken over and is beginning to implement more dangerous ideas and programs. On July 23, 2002, William Pierce, leader of the National Alliance and author of the *Turner Diaries, Hunter* and numerous articles that influenced bombings, assassinations and robberies, died at the age of 68. His death

Recent Trends in Domestic Terrorism

- The merging of White Supremacy with Satanism and Paganism (racist Odinist and others).
- Many of the original leaders of important groups have recently retired or died and the next generation has taken over and is beginning to implement more dangerous ideas and programs.
- There have been recent attempts to organize all of the white supremacy groups under one umbrella organization similar to al-Qaeda.
- White Supremacists are publicly sympathizing with Islamic terrorists and are reaching out to gain support for each other to overthrow the U.S. government and annihilate Jews. Their current philosophy is "the enemy of my enemy is my friend."

will most likely have widespread ramifications. Because there is currently no clear leader to succeed him, members may vie for leadership or other white supremacy groups may target National Alliance members for recruitment.

According to the Anti-Defamation League, Pierce's death will most likely increase the stature of Matt Hale, leader of the World Church of the Creator, among white supremacists since Aryan Nations founder Richard Butler is in poor health and former neo-Nazi David Duke is self-exiled in Europe. Hale is the highest profile white supremacist in the U.S. Both WCOTC and the Aryan Nations websites acknowledged Pierce's death with tributes of respect.

In addition to major changes that will take place in the National Alliance, there have already been very pertinent changes in the Aryan Nations. In July 2000, at the Aryan Nations' National Congress in Hayden Lake, ID, Neuman Britton of Escondido, CA was appointed the group's new leader; however, in August 2002 he died of cancer and in October 2002, Harold Ray Redfaerin of Ohio's White Supremacist Church of the Sons of YHVH was named leader.

Redfaerin served 6 years in prison for aggravated robbery and attempted aggravated murder in the shooting of a Dayton police officer in 1985. The officer was shot five times but survived because he was wearing a bullet proof vest. Aryan Nations founder Richard Butler, 83, named Redfaerin his successor and says that he will continue to remain the rock and spiritual leader of the group but will be less involved in everyday affairs. Redfaerin, 49, known as Pastor Ray, has already publicly stated that he will not renounce violence as a form of defense. He moved the compound from Idaho to Ulysses, a farming town in North Central Pennsylvania about 90 miles northeast of Pittsburgh. This was necessitated by a lawsuit spearheaded by Morris Dees that resulted in the confiscation of Aryan Nations' historic church grounds in Idaho.

The move inspired questions concerning Redfaerin's leadership, so he stepped down as national director and appointed a three-man high council that included Charles John Juba, Pastor August B. Kreis, III, and Redfaerin. Juba was formerly associated with the Invisible Empire Knights of the Ku Klux Klan, and later was the minister of the Aryan Nations' Youth Action Corps and served as its Pennsylvania state leader. Pastor Kreis was influential in the Sheriff's Posse Comitatus and was a former klansman in the Invisible Empire.

Sharing leadership encourages loyalties among typically divergent groups and lessens the infighting. However, the most disturbing aspect of Redfaerin's new influence in Aryan Nations is his sympathies for Islamic terrorists. In a statement that he wrote on June 6, 2001 in reference to a suicide bombing in Israel that killed 17 teenagers, he stated, "I do not see the Tel Aviv bomber as a terrorist, but as a patriot defending his home and his people. In this case I would say Vive Hamas, Viva Islamic Jihad."[26] On the revised Aryan Nations' website, Redfaerin does not hide his support of terrorism in Israel and his questioning of who was responsible for the September 11 attacks on America.

> In the midst of the mass confusion and fear in America following the successful destruction of the World Trade Centers in New York City (allegedly committed by members of an extremely anti-Jewish Middle Eastern terrorist group known as al-Qaeda), Pastor Redfaerin forged ahead with a strong vision of Aryan Nations as an up-and-coming white elite in a darkening world:

> Aryan Nations continues to step up its work of exposing the vile nature of the Jew and unyieldingly holds high the truth of racial Covenant Identity. Rather than join the sheep in disguising misplaced patriotism to the United States government (which has turned this country into a rogue state) — Aryan Nations supports loyalty to our race. Aryan Nations supports loyalty and service to our white kinsmen who are the genetic seedline of Our Heavenly Father, YHVH who is Our Yahshua.[27]

Finally, in their commitment to destroying all Jews and the Zionist Occupation Government, they have added a sector of Aryan Nations which they refer to as the Ministry of Islamic Liaison and clearly state:

> Aryan Nations' Ministry of Islamic Liaison is an outreach of Identity believers who work to establish fur-

ther discourse and working relationship with the Muslim world (who we believe are Ishmaelites, our cousins through Nahor). As the worldwide attack against the Yehudi-Shataan intensifies we, the watchers on the wall, know full well that the "enemy of our enemy is our friend" and any cause which further undermines the United States government (ZOG) is a worthy cause.[28]

It seems incomprehensible that American citizens are actually reaching out to Islamic terrorists with the express goal of overthrowing our government. This is extremely frightening and creates a situation in which law enforcement must defend against the combined forces of domestic and international terrorists. A precedent for international and domestic terrorists combining operations may have already occurred.

Disturbing connections between al-Qaeda and domestic terrorists have recently been reported. Jose Padilla, the man accused of plotting to set off a dirty bomb, looks remarkably similar to the mysterious John Doe No. 2 of the Oklahoma City bombing. Numerous witnesses described a man resembling Padilla seen with Timothy McVeigh in the weeks leading up to the bombing. Padilla's whereabouts at the time were unknown. Furthermore, McVeigh's accomplice, Terry Nichols' ex-wife, is named Lena Padilla and Nichols had ties to the Philippine Islands, a known outpost for al-Qaeda operatives. Nichols visited the Philippines a few months before the Oklahoma City attack.

Finally, Stephen R. Jones, McVeigh's attorney, argued that his client was part of a broader conspiracy, although McVeigh himself denied it. While preparing their case, members of Jones' team traveled several times to the Philippines, where Mr. Nichols had visited, to research possible contacts Nichols may have had with foreign terrorists, including associates of Osama bin Laden. McVeigh was executed on June 11, 2001. Nichols is serving a life sentence in prison without the possibility of parole and Padilla is currently being held in a military Navy brig.

Although there is clear evidence that Islamic fundamentalists were responsible for the 9/11 attacks on the U.S., coincidentally a similar plan of attack was described in detail in William Pierce's *Turner Diaries*. As previously mentioned the *Turner Diaries* was the blueprint for numerous acts of terrorism inclusive of Bob Matthews' group, The Order, which was based on the identical activities of the fictional group in the book and the inspiration for the construction of the truck bomb used by Timothy McVeigh for the Oklahoma City bombing that was described in explicit detail in Pierce's book. The *Turner Diaries* has also been responsible for inspiring many individual acts of violence and terrorism. Finally, the last entry in this fictional diary is dated 11/9. The main character, Earl Turner, a member of The Order, writes his last entry:

> It's still three hours until first light, and all systems are "go." I'll use the time to write a few pages — my last diary entry. Then it's a one-way trip to the Pentagon for me. The warhead is strapped into the front seat of the old Stearman and rigged to detonate either on impact or when I flip a switch in the back seat. Hopefully, I'll be able to manage a low level air burst directly over the center of the Pentagon. Failing that, I'll at least try to fly as close as I can before I'm shot down.[29]

In light of the Aryan Nations' mission of overthrowing the government which they perceive as being run by a conspiracy of Jews, their new leader Redfaerin publicly announcing his sympathies for Islamic Jihad in June 2001 currently advocating that "an enemy of our enemy is our friend," and the reports connecting al-Qaeda to the Oklahoma City bombing beg the question of whether there was not already complicity among domestic and international terrorists.

References

1. Freeh, L.J., Statement on the threat of terrorism to the United States, presented before the U.S. Senate Committees on Appropriations and Armed Services and the Select Committee on Intelligence, May 10, 2001, p. 3. http://www.fbi.gov/congress/congress01/freeh051001.html

2. Freeh, L.J., Statement on the threat of terrorism to the United States, presented before the U.S. Senate Committees on Appropriations and Armed Services and the Select Committee on Intelligence, May 10, 2001, p. 2. http://www.fbi.gov/congress/congress01/freeh051001.html

3. Wessinger, C., *How the Millennium Comes Violently*, Seven Bridges Press, New York, 2000, pp. 172–175.

4. Federal Bureau of Investigation, Project Megiddo, Center for Studies on New Religious Movements website, October 20, 1999, p. 1.

5. Ontario Consultants on Religious Tolerance website, Project Megiddo, p. 1. http://www.religioustolerance.org/megiddo.html

6. Federal Bureau of Investigation, Project Megiddo, Center for Studies on New Religious Movements website, October 20, 1999, p. 2.

7. Klassen, B. and Hale, M., The Creator Membership Manual, 3rd ed., The World of the Creator, East Peoria, IL, 2002, pp. ix–x.

8. Bennett, H., *Insubordination Magazine*, http://awol.objector.org/recentnews-andevents/york.html

9. Klassen, B., *The White Man's Bible*, Milwaukee Church of the Creator, Milwaukee, WI, 1981, pp. 424–426.

10. Klassen, B., *The White Man's Bible*, Milwaukee Church of the Creator, Milwaukee, WI, 1981, p.168.

11. Klassen, B., *The White Man's Bible*, Milwaukee Church of the Creator, Milwaukee, WI, 1981, pp. 171–172.

12. Southern Poverty Law Center, *Pagans and Prison*, Intelligence Report, Spring 2000. www.splcenter.org/intelligenceproject/ip-4n3.html

13. Suspect may have joined racist group in prison, *Boston Herald*, June 22 , 2001. www.gospelcom.net/apologeticsindex/news1/an010623-05.html

14. Anti-Defamation League, Two with ties to white supremacy suspected in plot to bomb Boston sites. www.adl.org/learn/felton/felton_print.asp

15. Cambanis, T., On-line race plot fictional, defense contends, *Boston Globe*, July 25, 2002.

16. Hoskins, R.K., Vigilantes of Christendom, The Story of the Phineas Priesthood, Virginia Publishing co., Lynchburg, VA, 1990.

17. Burghardt, T., *Paul Hill: a Phineas Priest?*, *Arm the Spirit*, July 3, 1995, p. 5. http://burn.ucsd.edu/archives/ats-1/1995.Jul/0015.html

18. Burghardt, T., *Paul Hill: a Phineas Priest?*, *Arm the Spirit*, July 3, 1995, pp. 6–7. http://burn.ucsd.edu/archives/ats-1/1995.Jul/0015.html

19. Pierce, W., Knowledge and discipline, *Free Speech*, Vol. V, No. 7, July 1999, p. 1. http://www.natvan.com/free-speech/fs997d.html

20. Delsohn, G. and Stanton, S., I'm guilty of obeying the laws of the creator, November 8, 1999, p. 2. http://www.salon.com/news/feature/1999/11/08/hate

21. Lum, R.R., Feds in Sacramento probe national conspiracy, *Jewish Bulletin*, August 6, 1999, p. 1. http://www.jewishsf.com/bk990806/1afeds.shtml

22. Burghardt, T., *Paul Hill: a Phineas Priest?*, *Arm the Spirit*, July 3, 1995, p. 7. http://burn.ucsd.edu/archives/ats-1/1995.Jul/0015.html

23. Curtis, A., 'Lone Wolf' of hate prowls the Internet, Anti-Defamation League, p. 1. http://www.adl.org/curtis/default.htm

24. Curtis, A., By whatever means necessary, Anti-Defamation League, p. 1. http://www.adl.org/curtis/by whatever means.html

25. Burghart, T., *Paul Hill: a Phineas priest?*, *Arm The Spirit*, July 3, 1995. www.burn.ucsd.edu/archives/ats-1/1995.Jul/0015.html

26. Redfaerin, R., Death in Tel Aviv, Church of True Israel. www.churchoftrue israel.com/red/red2.html

27. Aryan Nations website July 13, 2002, www.aryan-nations.org

28. Aryan Nations website July 13, 2002, www.aryan-nations.org
29. Macdonald, A. (also known as William Pierce), *Turner Diaries*, 2nd ed., National Vanguard Books, Hillsboro, WV, 1980, p. 202.

International Terrorist Religions

4

According to the FBI typology, international terrorism has three subcategories based on the structural organizations of the various groups. The categories are Loosely Affiliated Extremists, Formal Terrorist Organizations and State Sponsors of Terrorism.

The first category of international terrorism, Loosely Affiliated Extremists, are designated as Sunni Islamic extremists including Osama bin Laden and individuals affiliated with his al-Qaeda organization and individuals of varying nationalities, ethnic groups, tribes, races and terrorist groups who support extremist Sunni goals. The common elements among the diverse individuals is that they are motivated by political or religious beliefs and committed to the radical international jihad movement whose ideology includes promoting violence against the "enemies of Islam" in order to overthrow all governments not ruled by conservative Islamic law. Foreshadowing the American tragedy on September 11th, a congressional statement dated May 10, 2001 noted that loosely affiliated extremists were considered the most urgent threat to the U.S. because their goals consist of carrying out large-scale, high-profile, high-casualty, terrorist attacks against U.S. interests and citizens. It is not surprising that subsequent investigations led to changing the designation of Loosely Affiliated Extremists to the Radical International Jihad Movement — signifying that they are no longer loosely affiliated but are exceptionally well organized.

The second category of international terrorism is Formal Terrorist Organizations designated as extremist groups. Examples are the Palestinian Hamas, the Irish Republican Army, the Egyptian Al-Gama Al-Islamiyya and the Lebanese Hizballah. They are characterized as autonomous, generally transnational organizations that have their own infrastructures, personnel,

---

International Terrorism:
Radical International Jihad Movement

Characteristics	Groups and Networks
• Commitment to radical jihad movement	• Al-Qaeda (The Base)
• Radical ideology against the enemies of Islam	• Al-Jihad (Islamic Jihad)
	• Al-Gamma Al-Islamiyya
• Overthrow all governments not ruled by Islamic Law	• Egyptian Islamic Jihad
	• Number of jihad groups in other countries
• Large-scale, high-profile, high-casualty attacks	• Individuals of varying ethnicities who support extremist Sunni goals
• Removal of the U.S. military from the Persian Gulf	

---

financial arrangements and training facilities. They have a presence in the U.S. with members who are engaged in fund-raising, recruiting and intelligence gathering. They also maintain operations and support networks in the U.S. Prior to the September 11th events, the Hizballah were responsible for the deaths of more Americans than any other terrorist group.

The third category of international terrorism is State Sponsors of Terrorism that consists of countries that view terrorism as a tool of foreign policy. At the time of the May 10, 2001 congressional statement, the U.S. Department of State listed seven countries as state sponsors of terrorism: Iran, Iraq, Sudan, Libya, Syria, Cuba and North Korea. Iran represented the greatest threat to the U.S. because it financially and logistically supports anti-Western acts of terrorism by others.

International Terrorism:
Formal Terrorist Organizations

Characteristics	Groups
• Autonomous transnational groups, U.S.-based cells	• Palestinian Hamas
• Their own personnel, finances, infrastructures, training facilities	• Lebanese Hizballah
	• Irish Republican Army
• Ability to mount terrorist campaigns on an international basis	• Egyptian Al-Gamma Al-Islamiyya
• Active support of terrorist activities.	

```
┌─────────────────────────────────────────────────┐
│  International Terrorism:                         │
│  State Sponsors of Terrorism                      │
│  ─────────────────────────────────────            │
│  Characteristics            Countries             │
│  • View terrorism as a      • Iran                │
│    tool of foreign policy   • Iraq                │
│  • Provide safe havens                            │
│    to international terrorist • Sudan              │
│    groups                   • Libya               │
│  • Support anti-Western     • Syria               │
│    terrorism both financially • North Korea       │
│    and logistically         • Cuba                │
│                                                   │
└─────────────────────────────────────────────────┘
```

Islamic Beliefs

To fully comprehend Islamic fundamental beliefs, it is necessary to review the essential tenets of Islam and understand how fundamentalism differs from other contemporary sects. Islam is the youngest of the world's three major monotheistic religions. It is also one of the largest, with over one billion adherents and is the dominant religion in the developing nations of the Middle East, Africa and Asia. The fundamental belief of Islam is that there is only one God (Allah); He is the same God that is worshipped by Jews and Christians and He is the sole and sovereign ruler of the universe.

Although Allah has made himself known to other prophets at other times, his most significant and final revelation was made in the seventh century to the Prophet Muhammad. Adherents to the religion are called Muslims, which means "those who submit to God" because believers must submit to the will of Allah. Islam teaches that believers only have one life to live and how they live it determines how they will spend their eternal existence. The sacred text of Islam is called the Quran, which literally means reading or recitation and indicates the basic beliefs that Muslims hold about the Quran, that it is a recitation of an eternal scripture written in heaven and revealed chapter by chapter to Muhammad. The Quran is believed to be God's last word to humanity and it is eternal, absolute and irrevocable.

Although Islam respects the scriptures of the Jews and Christians, the Quran is understood to be God's complete message. It was literally revealed to Muhammad who acted as a speaker for Allah and it has been virtually unchanged since the days of the prophet. An important ritual act is the recitation of the Quran as it is a source of Allah's blessing because it reproduces his divine speech. The sources of legal authority are the Quran and traditions known as the Hadith. There are thousands of Hadith, which

Islam

- Youngest of the world's three monotheistic religions (other two are Judaism and Christianity)
- Over one billion adherents referred to as Muslims (second largest religion in the world)
- Dominant religion in developing nations of Middle East, Africa and Asia

Traditional Islamic Beliefs

- **God** (Allah)
- **Muhammad** (Prophet)
- **Quran** (Sacred Text
- **Sharia** (Islamic Law)
- **Hadith and Sunna** (interpretations of Quran)
- **Five Pillars of Islam** (ritual obligations)
- **Six Pillars of Faith** (religious obligations)

Islamic Beliefs: God

- Only one God, referred to as Allah.
- Same god worshipped by Jews and Christians.
- Sole sovereign ruler of the universe.
- Muslim means "those who submit to God."
- Believers must submit to the will of Allah.

Muhammad

- Revelation made to prophet Muhammad in the 7th century.
- Muhammad speaks for God.
- The last in a line of Prophets, Abraham, David, Moses and Jesus.
- His role as the last of the prophets was to formalize and clarify the faith and to purify it by removing foreign ideas that had been added in error.

Koran/Quran/Qur'an

- Koran is the English spelling (offensive).
- Sacred text literally means reading recitation.
- Contains the word of God revealed to Muhammad by the archangel Gabriel.
- Virtually unchanged since day of prophet.
- Respects Old and New Testament but Quran is God's complete message.

Quran

- The principal source of Islamic law
- Contains the rules by which the Muslim world is governed (or should govern itself).
- Forms the basis for relations between man and God, between individuals, whether Muslim or non-Muslim, as well as between man and things which are part of creation.

Sharia — Islamic Law

- The Sharia contains the rules by which a Muslim society is organized and governed.
- The Sharia is the complete legal system that governs every aspect of individual and social life.
- The Quran is the basis of the Sharia.
- How the Sharia is interpreted for modern times is a significant point of contention among different sects.

Hadith and Sunnah

- The Hadith and Sunna are complementary sources to the Quran.
- They consist of the sayings of Muhammad and accounts of his deeds.
- The Sunna helps to explain the Quran, but it may not be interpreted or applied in any way that is inconsistent with the Quran.
- Not the same status as the Holy Quran, which is God's word.

expand on the basic teachings of the Quran. They have been used by Muslim scholars to answer legal questions as well as to clarify the ritual duties of Islam.

The study of the Quran and Hadith form the basics of religious education in Muslim societies. Islam is essentially a religion that is based on surrender to God. In order for Muslims to submit themselves to Allah and to reassert their faith in Islam, there are various practices and beliefs that each Muslim should follow. Significantly, Islam is not only a belief; it is a way of life and what Muslims believe dictates how they should live for Allah. The five pillars of Islam are the ritual obligations required of a good Muslim. They include (1) shahadah or the declaration of the faith by repetition of the creed, "There is no God but Allah and Muhammad is the messenger of Allah;" (2) Salaht is the name for obligatory prayers, Muslims are expected to pray five times daily; (3) Zakat represents an important principle of Islam — all things belong to God and Muslims are expected to share their possessions with the poor,

Five Pillars of Islam

- **Shahadah:** The declaration of the faith by repetition of the Creed, *"There is no God but Allah, Muhammad is the messenger of Allah."*
- **Salaht** obligatory prayers: Muslims are expected to pray five times daily.
- **Zakat:** Represents charity, which is obligatory according to Islamic law.
- **Sawm** (or fasting): Required every year in the month of Ramadan.
- **Hajj:** The pilgrimage to Mecca. Every Muslim is ritually obligated to make the pilgrimage to Mecca at least once in his lifetime.

Six Pillars of Faith

- Belief in **Allah** (one God)
- Belief in His **Angels**
- Belief in the **Divine Revelations** (Torah, the Psalms, the rest of the Bible and the Quran)
- Belief in **His Messengers** (Adam, Noah, Abraham, Moses, David, Jesus and Muhammad)
- Belief in **the Hereafter** (the day of judgment)
- Belief in the **Divine Will**

widows or orphans — charity is obligatory according to Islamic law; (4) Sawm or fasting is required every year in the month of Ramadan. It is regarded as a principle of self-purification and is held in remembrance of the month when the prophet received his first revelation; and (5) Hajj is the pilgrimage to Mecca. Every Muslim who can afford the trip is ritually obligated to make the pilgrimage to Mecca at least once in a lifetime.

There are also six pillars of faith consisting of (1) belief in Allah; (2) belief in His Angels, (3) belief in the divine revelations, (4) belief in His messengers (5) belief in the hereafter and (6) belief in the Divine will. The combination of the five pillars of Islam and the six pillars of faith outline the Islamic faith and the religious obligations for a practicing Muslim.

Significance of Islamic Beliefs to Terrorism

The significance of fundamental Islamic beliefs to justifying terrorism can be found in the basic tenets of Islam, although this by no means implies that all Muslims interpret their beliefs this way. One basic tenet of Islam is that

Islamic Beliefs:
Significance to Terrorism

- Originally there was no separation between religious and civil law, no separation between church and state.
- Muhammad and his successors were both religious and political leaders.
- Islamic fundamentalists also do not distinguish between religious and civil law.
- Their interpretation of Islam is how they justify acts of terrorism.
- Each person has one life to live, and it determines how one spends his eternal existence.
- Interpretations of the Quran are the sources of laws.
- Islam is a religious belief based on surrender to God.
- Islam is not just a religion, it is a way of life.
- Essentially, what Muslims believe determines how they live their lives.

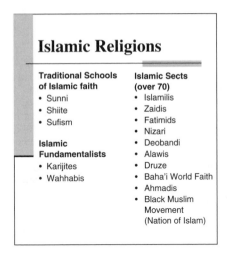

Islamic Religions

Traditional Schools of Islamic faith
- Sunni
- Shiite
- Sufism

Islamic Fundamentalists
- Karijites
- Wahhabis

Islamic Sects (over 70)
- Islamilis
- Zaidis
- Fatimids
- Nizari
- Deobandi
- Alawis
- Druze
- Baha'i World Faith
- Ahmadis
- Black Muslim Movement (Nation of Islam)

an individual has one life to live and how he lives it determines how he spends his eternal existence. Other tenets include: Islam is a religious belief based on surrender to God; it is not just a religion but a way of life and interpretations of the Quran are the sources of laws. In effect, what Muslims believe determines how they live their lives. If this belief entails viewing other people and nations as evil, then extremists can theologically justify their terrorist attacks against the Great Satan, who appears in the form of the United States.

Terrorism becomes not only a political choice, but a religious imperative that is crucial in determining their eternal destiny. It is difficult for Americans to comprehend this perspective because we hold a secular world view and for the most part American religious beliefs concerning the afterlife are not considerations unless an individual faces a tragedy involving death. Fortunately, most Muslims do not view the U.S. as the personification of evil and abide by international law; however, Islamic fundamentalists do not distinguish between religious and civil law. This is vital to understanding the seriousness of the danger posed. Islamic extremists interpret the Quran in such a way as to designate anyone who is not a devout Muslim as an infidel who must be annihilated. Infidels include other Muslims who do not practice their extreme version of Islam.

Islamic Religious Sects

Due to the long history of Islam and the immense populations of believers over the centuries, beliefs have been interpreted differently and have led to sects, factions and subgroups. The first initial division dates back to Muhammad's death when followers debated over who would succeed him as the spiritual leader.

Sunni

- Sunnis are the most dominant sect of Islam comprising about 85% of Muslims worldwide.
- There are four different schools of Sunni faith varying in their strictness of interpreting how the Prophet lived.
- All Sunnis agree in their belief in the legitimacy of the first three successors to Muhammad.
- The four Sunni groups are the Hanabalites, Malikhites, Hanafites and Shafites.

Shiites

- Shiite literally translates as "partisan of the faith."
- The original conflict between the Sunnis and the Shiites was about who should succeed the Prophet.
- Shiites account for less than 15% of all Muslims.
- The fundamental belief of this sect is that the first successor to Muhammad should have been Ali, the husband of Muhammad's only surviving daughter.
- There are two subgroups of Shiites called the Seveners and the Twelvers.

Sufis

- Sufism is a mystical sect of Islam.
- Sufis are considered a heretical sect because of their mystical beliefs.
- Some argue that Sufis are actually the most orthodox believers of Islam.
- Where Sufis diverge from other sects is their belief in saints and martyrs, which mainstream Islam considers a form of idolatry.

Islam initially divided into two groups: the Sunnis and the Shiites. Sunnis are the most dominant sect of Islam, comprising about 85% of Muslims worldwide. The Sunnis are divided into four different schools of faith, varying in the strictness of interpreting how the Prophet lived. All Sunnis agree in their belief in the legitimacy of the first three successors to Muhammad (Abu Bakr, Umar and Uthman) and their strict adherence to the Sunna (a combination of the Hadith and the Quran). The four Sunni groups are the Hanabalites, Malikhites, Hanafites and Shafites. The Shiites comprise the other initial sect of Islam. *Shiite* literally translates to *partisan of the faith*. The original conflict between the Sunnis and the Shiites was over who should succeed the Prophet. Shiites account for less than 15% of all Muslims. Their fundamental belief is that the first successor to Muhammad should have been

Islamic Fundamentalists

Although there are a number of Islamic fundamentalist religious sects, two of the better known sects are the:

- **Kharijites**
- **Wahhabis**

Ali, the husband of Muhammad's only surviving daughter. The two sub-groups of the Shiites are the Seveners and the Twelvers.

Sufism is a mystical sect of Islam. The Sufis are considered a heretical sect due to their mystical beliefs although some argue that they are the most orthodox believers of Islam. Where they diverge from other sects is in their belief of saints and martyrs, considered by mainstream Islam as a form of idolatry.

Islamic Fundamentalist Sects

The primary concern of this chapter is the additional sects of Islam referred to as Islamic fundamentalists that emerged as a powerful ideology in the 18th

Kharijites

- The oldest religious sect of Islam.
- The name means seceders.
- Less than 1% of all Muslims.
- Extremely violent, and responsible for the assassination of the fourth caliph Ali.
- Considered strict fundamentalists and Quranic literalists.
- Believe that the succession of the Prophet was open to anyone of true faith and not just the Sunni and Shiites.

century as a reaction to what they saw as the weakness of Muslims due to Western influences. Fundamentalists believe that the law of Allah revealed by the Prophet is just as relevant today as it was then and they seek to establish the ideal society that Allah proposed. It is important to note that most practitioners of Islam are non-violent, peaceful people and although Islamic fundamentalists may adhere to the previously described basic principles of Islam, their political interpretation is significantly different.

This is most evidenced in the fundamentalist application of the concept of Sharia — the sacred law that guides Muslims in all times and all places. Where the Quran can be viewed as the constitution of Islam, the Sharia is the revealed and canonical laws of the religion. It is the core of how to be a Muslim regardless of sect and essentially is what unites all the diverse communities of Islam. In brief, Sharia is Islamic law, held by Muslims to be a complete legal system that governs every aspect of individual and social life and is derived directly from the Quran. How the Sharia has been interpreted to adapt to current times is a major point of contention among the different sects. Islamic fundamentalists attempt to live by a strict interpretation of the Sharia and view the lifestyle of the West as a threat and the antithesis of what the Sharia represents.

Although a number of Islamic fundamentalist religious sects exist, two of the better known are the Kharijites and Wahhabis. Kharijites are reputedly the oldest religious sect of Islam and the name means *seceders.* They are extremely violent and are responsible for the assassination of the fourth caliph Ali. They are considered strict fundamentalists and Quranic literalists. They believe that the succession of the prophet was open to anyone of true faith and not only Sunnis and Shiites.

The Wahhabi movement is considered the most reactionary of all Muslim sects. Wahhabis refuse to accept any revision of Quranic Law. Their goal is to return to the ideal fundamental form of Islam as it was in the era of the first four caliphs following the Prophet. Many Islamic scholars and organizations through various publications have denounced Wahhabism as a particularly rigid minority Islamic sect that is intolerant of other forms of Islam.

Wahhabism

The Wahhabi view of Islam asserts that all who do not adhere to its beliefs are infidels, including Sunni and Shiite Muslims. Wahhabis practice an extreme form of puritanism inclusive of simple short prayers, undecorated mosques, and they do not permit the name of the Prophet to be inscribed on mosques nor do they celebrate his birthday. In fact, any form of ostentatious spirituality is considered a form of idolatry. The Wahhabis' strict interpretation of the Sharia sanctions extreme laws and corresponding forms of punishment.

Wahhabism	Wahhabism: Beliefs and Practices

• Religion of Osama bin Laden and prevalent in Saudi Arabia.
• The most reactionary of all Muslim sects.
• Refuse to accept any revision of Quranic Law.
• Goal is to return to the ideal fundamental form of Islam as in the era of the first four caliphs following the Prophet.
• The Wahhabi view of Islam asserts that all who do not adhere to its beliefs are infidels, including Sunni and Shiite Muslims.
	• Wahhabis practice an extreme form of puritanism including:
	  • Simple short prayers.
	  • Undecorated mosques.
	  • No drinking.
	  • No sexual transgressions.
	  • Any form of ostentatious spirituality is considered a form of idolatry.
	• The Wahhabis' strict interpretation of the Sharia is what sanctioned extreme laws and corresponding forms of punishment.

There are thousands of current practitioners of Wahhabism. Most citizens of Saudi Arabia, including hundreds of members of the royal family, practice Wahhabism. According to Stephen Schwartz in an October 6, 2001 *Spectator* article, all recent acts of terrorism were enacted by Wahhabis:

> Bin Laden is a Wahhabi. So are the suicide bombers in Israel. So are his [bin Laden's] Egyptian allies, who exulted as they stabbed foreign tourists to death at Luxor not many years ago, bathing in blood up to their elbows and emitting blasphemous cries of ecstasy. So are the Algerian Islamist terrorists whose contribution to the purification of the world consisted of murdering people for such sins as running a movie projector or reading secular newspapers. So are the Taliban-style guerrillas in Kashmir who murder Hindus.[1]

According to some sources, the Taliban do not practice Wahhabism, but belong to what is known as the Deobandi movement, named after a small town in the Indian Himalayas where it was founded in 1860 during British rule. Similar to Wahhabism, it is an unusually strict form of Sunni Islam. The followers of both the Deobandi and Wahhabi movements make sharp distinctions between revealed sacred knowledge and human knowledge and thus exclude any learning that does not appear sacred.

Deobandi philosophy helped spawn many fundamentalist groups in the Muslim world including the Taliban in Afghanistan, although the Afghans have been part of the Deobandi movement since its beginning. Over time, Deobandi philosophy has changed toward more orthodoxy and militant fundamentalism.

Deobandi Movement

- Religion of the Taliban.
- Named after the small town of Deobandi in the Indian Himalayas where the movement was founded in 1860 during the period of British rule in India.
- Similar to Wahhabism it is an unusually strict form of Sunni Islam. The followers of both movements exclude any learning that does not appear sacred.
- Over time, Deobandi philosophy moved toward more orthodoxy and militant fundamentalism.

The Wahhabi movement was founded by Muhammad ibn Abd al-Wahab in the 18th century. It is essentially a purification of the Sunni sect and regards the veneration of images, any ostentatious worship and luxurious living as evil. Basically, Wahhabism teaches that all additions to Islam after the third century of the Muslim era are false and should be removed. Members describe themselves as Muwahhidun (Unitarians) who firmly uphold the doctrine that God is one, the only one, Wahid. In 1744, the founder of the Wahhabi sect, Abd al-Wahhad, was exiled from his native city, Uyayna, because of his controversial preaching from his book, *Kitab al-Tawid* (*Book of Unity*). During his exile he traveled to the northeast Nejd and converted the Saudi tribe. Once the Saudi sheik was convinced that it was his religious mission to wage holy war, jihad, against all other forms of Islam, he began the conquest of his neighbors in 1763. By 1811, the Wahhabis ruled all of Arabia except Yemen from their capital at Riyadh.

The Ottoman sultan attempted to crush them by sending out expeditions but to no avail. However, the Sultan met with success when he called on Muhammad Ali of Egypt and by 1818, the Wahhabis were driven into the desert. In the Nejd, they regained their power and from 1821 to 1833, gained control over the Persian Gulf coast of Arabia. Their subsequent domain steadily weakened; nonetheless a third triumph came for the Wahhabi movement when Ibn Saud advanced from his capture of Riyadh in 1902 to the reconstitution in 1932 of nearly all his ancestral domain as Saudi Arabia, where Wahhabism remains dominant to this day. Members of the Wahab family continue to hold prominent positions in Saudi Arabia because their ancestors helped the Saudi ruling family unify its kingdom in 1932. Wahhabism also served as an inspiration to other Islamic reform movements from India and Sumatra to North Africa and the Sudan.[2]

Taliban Punishments

- Flogging (whipped).
- Amputation of hands and feet (thieves).
- Execution by hanging or shooting in the head (by family members)
- Stoned to death (adultery)
- Carried out in public sports stadiums

Wahhabi theology and jurisprudence are based, respectively, on the teachings of Ibn Taymiyah and on the legal school of Ahmad ibn Hanbal. They stress literal belief in the Quran and Hadith and the establishment of a Muslim state based only on Islamic Law. The contemporary Wahhabi movement is flourishing in every Muslim country. In Lebanon alone, the movement is estimated by officials to have about 4000 members. The sect has far more members in Egypt, Saudi Arabia and Pakistan. It goes by many names including Ikhwan, Wahhabi, Salifiyya, Mowahabin and the well-known Taliban. Anti-Wahhabi Muslims refer to Wahhabism as *fitna an Najdiyyah* or the *trouble out of Nejd*. Wahhabis have in common a militant view of Sunni Islam and financial support at the highest levels of the Saudi Arabian government.[3] Wahhabi religious schools, referred to as madrassas, belong to a worldwide network of Muslim extremist organizations. Beginning at the ages of 7 to 15, young men are indoctrinated into the fundamentals of strict Islam, religious obligations and radical militancy at Wahhabi schools. Between the ages of 15 and 25, the young men are prepared for jihad or holy war and are trained to fight for the conquest of Wahhabi Islam. Not all young men who attend Wahhabi schools turn to violence. Some become religious teachers and the vast majority of Wahhabi communities do not openly maintain armed militias although they engage in paramilitary training. The exception is the Taliban, whose followers do not conceal weapons or other arms.[4] Obviously, the term *Wahhabi* has pejorative connotations and Saudis do not use it, preferring to call themselves Unitarians — believers in one indivisible deity.[5]

The violence inflicted because of Deobandi and Wahhabi religious ideology is substantial, to say the least. Among the thousands of quotes given and articles written about Islamic fundamentalism after September 11th, one particular statement sums up the religious connection:

> Not all Muslims are suicide bombers, but all Muslim
> suicide bombers are Wahhabis.[6]

No one can dispute the violence that this belief system has inspired and continues to inspire. Unfortunately, we have all become familiar with the names of terrorist organizations such as al-Qaeda, Islamic Movement of Uzbekistan, Egyptian Islamic Jihad, Armed Islamic Group, Harakat ul-Muja-hidin (Pakistan) and Abu Sayyaf (Philippines), all of which were linked to bin Laden. The violence perpetrated by these groups includes many incidents of suicide bombings, kidnappings, hijackings and murders.

Islamic Fundamentalist Extremist Groups and Beliefs

In 1998, Osama bin Laden announced the formation of the International Front for Fighting Jews and Crusades, an alliance bent on killing Americans and destroying U.S. interests around the world. Member groups include Al-Qaeda, Egyptian Jihad, Pakistani Society of Ulemas, Ansar Movement, Bangladesh Jihad and Islamic Army for the Liberation of the Holy Sites. Much of the following information on terrorist groups was obtained from CBS news.com's interactive website called The Terror Network. CBS news.com is an excellent resource on terrorism and provides information on a variety of related and current events.

International Front

- Al-Qaeda (Afghanistan)
- Egyptian Jihad (Egypt)
- Pakistani Society of Ulemas
- Ansar Movement (Indian)
- Bangladesh Jihad
- Islamic Army for the Liberation of the Holy Sites

Al-Qaeda

Name means:	The Base
Reportedly has operations in:	Afghanistan, Algeria, Egypt, Morocco, Turkey, Jordan, Tajikistan, Uzbekistan, Syria, Xinjiang in China, Pakistan, Bangladesh, Malaysia, Myanmar, Indonesia, Mindanao in the Philippines, Lebanon, Iraq, Saudi Arabia, Kuwait, Bahrain, Yemen, Libya, Tunisia, Bosnia, Kosovo, Chechnya, Dagestan, Kashmir, Sudan, Somalia, Kenya, Tanzania, Azerbaijan, Eritrea, Uganda, Ethiopia and the West Bank and Gaza in Palestinian areas of Israel
Goal:	To establish a worldwide Islamic regime by routing out non-Islamic governments and expelling Westerners and non-Muslims from Muslim countries
Strength:	May have hundreds to thousands of members; extremist groups such as Egyptian Islamic Jihad and parts of al-Gama'at al-Islamiyya, the Islamic movement of Uzbekistan and the Harakat ul-Mujahidin also fall under its umbrella
History:	Developed in the 1980s when rebels in Afghanistan drew international support and funding from countries including the U.S. that did not support the U.S.S.R.'s occupation of Afghanistan
Finances:	Receives money from donations and profitable front organizations, and by laundering money from legitimate Muslim organizations
Other information:	Has organized thousands of Islamic fighters worldwide; is backed by Islamic leaders and groups in authoritarian states, particularly those in the Arabian Gulf region; has a humanitarian facet, drawing financial support from powerful Muslim groups and communities to aid needy Muslims; also uses contributions to fund its operations; uses terrorist acts such as bombing, assassination, kidnapping and extortion to advance its mission of a worldwide religious regime

Osama bin Laden.   Osama bin Laden is the head of al-Qaeda; his top men usually are based in Afghanistan. His title is Emir General and he oversees military, finance, religious, legal and media committees. He became head of the organization in 1989 after the withdrawal of Soviet forces. His father was a wealthy contractor who renovated the Muslim holy cities of Mecca and Medina. Some estimates place bin Laden's worth around $300 million, but the U.S. has frozen a large portion of his money. Many claim he is a billionaire.

Osama bin Laden uses marriage as a strategic tool. He has four wives and more than ten children (Muslims are limited traditionally to four wives). His wives are from four different countries. Thus, bin Laden has symbolically and literally planted his seed. He married one of his daughters to Taliban leader Mullah Mohammed Omar. His eldest son, Mohammed, wed the daughter of Lieutenant Mohammed Atef.

Hamas/Islamic Jihad

Name means:	Islamic Resistance Movement (HAMAS)
Reportedly has operations in:	Syria, Palestinian autonomous areas, Israel and Lebanon
Goal:	A relatively moderate faction of HAMAS seeks to create a Palestinian Islamic state and accepts some kind of agreement with Israel; the goal of a second faction is to create a Palestinian Islamic state and destroy Israel; the military goal of Hamas is to terrorize Israelis through the use of random violence
Strength:	Although it has tens of thousands of supporters, the number of HAMAS members remains unknown
History:	Developed in 1987 from the Palestinian Muslim Brotherhood, the radical Sunni Muslim HAMAS organization was formed to further the interests of the Palestinian people
Finances:	The organization is funded mainly through wealthy supporters living in other countries including Iran and the Gulf States and donations through a web of non-profit organizations based in London
Other information:	Performs some humanitarian acts and provides food, education and social aid for Palestinians in autonomous areas and refugee camps; HAMAS is a large group that organizes its efforts for political, social, religious and rebellious ends; HAMAS and Islamic Jihad are thought of as sister groups, but some analysts believe Islamic Jihad is a part of HAMAS, both have ties to Hizballah through Syria and Iran; HAMAS' front organizations and main military operations are Izz el-Din al-Qassem and Disciples of Yehya Ayyash; HAMAS operates small rebel cells that are anonymous to one another; suicide bombings are not always controlled by the top leadership of HAMAS; Islamic Jihad has been involved in almost every suicide bombing in the Middle East

Hizballah

Name means:	Party of God
Reportedly has operations in:	Middle East, Europe, Latin America and the U.S.
Goal:	To create a revolutionary Shi'a Islamic state similar to Iran in Lebanon and eradicate non-Islamic influences and interests
Strength:	Membership in the thousands, about 500 members are active in Islamic Jihad
History:	Created in 1983, it is a diverse organization organized into political, business, military and social welfare groups

Finances: Partially self-funded, receives financial support from Iran
Other information: Capable of devastating acts of international terrorism;
                               military faction is Islamic Resistance — a small, highly
                               effective guerrilla organization trained and directed by
                               Iranian revolutionary guards; attacks in small, highly
                               mobile units and shrouds its operatives in secrecy, even
                               from Hizballah leaders; Islamic Resistance uses suicide
                               bombers effectively; overseas cells remain mysterious; an
                               international network of cells exists and Iranian embassies
                               are often involved

Groupe Islamique Arme (GIA)

Name means: Armed Islamic Group
Reportedly has operations in: Algeria and France
Goal: To create a radical Islamic GIA-led government in Algeria
Strength: As of 1999, membership was believed to be slightly fewer
                               than 2000 guerrillas; one of the most deadly organizations
                               in the world
History: Organized as a radical Sunni Muslim group in 1992; later
                               split into several rival factions
Other information: The primary faction retains the name and puts much effort
                               into fighting the Army of Islamic Salvation (AIS), a
                               relatively moderate group associated with the government;
                               that affiliation and the practice of attacking civilians caused
                               GIA to part ways with other terrorist groups for ideological
                               reasons; some members broke away in 1998 to form the
                               Appeal and Struggle Group that opposes the civilian killings
                               but continues attacks against military and law enforcement;
                               other breakaway groups include the Salafi Group for Call
                               and Combat (GSPC), the Islamic League for Call and
                               Djihad (LIDD) and the Islamic Front for Armed Djihad;
                               referred to as the "Green Khmer," a reference to Cambodia's
                               ruthless Khmer Rouge regime, due to use of similar terrorist
                               methods; infamous for targeting politicians, military and
                               police, journalists, feminists, scholars, French speakers and
                               anyone who may remotely be considered un-Islamic; with
                               intent to terrify rural communities, the eradicator faction
                               has carried out massacres of entire villages since 1996

Acts of Terrorism against America, 1982–2002

The following is a selected list of documented Islamic fundamentalist terrorist crimes against U.S. citizens abroad and at home in the past 20 years:

April 18, 1983 — Bombing by Islamic Jihad of the U.S. embassy in
Beirut, killing 63 people including the CIA's Middle East director and injuring 120.

October 23, 1983 — Bombing by Islamic Jihad of marine barracks in Beirut, killing 242 Americans.

March 16, 1984 — Kidnapping and murder of Beirut embassy political officer William Buckley by Islamic Jihad.

April 12, 1984 — Bombing of a restaurant near a U.S. Air Force base in Torrejon, Spain by Hizballah; killed 18 U.S. servicemen and injured 83 others.

June 14, 1985 — Hijacking of a TWA flight by Lebanese Hizballah; 145 passengers were held for 17 days and a U.S. Navy sailor was killed.

October 7, 1985 — Hijacking of the *Achille Lauro*, an Italian cruise liner, by the Palestine Liberation Front; one U.S. passenger killed.

February 17, 1988 — Kidnapping and murder of U.S. Marine Corps Lt. Col. William Higgins by the Hizballah in Lebanon.

February 26, 1993 — First World Trade Center bombing by Islamic terrorists, leaving 6 dead and injuring 1000.

February 23, 1997 — Empire State Building sniper attack by a Palestinian gunman killing one and wounding four.

November 17, 1997 — Killing of 58 tourists in Egypt by Al-Gama'at al Islamiyya; 26 were wounded.

August 7, 1998 — U.S. Embassy bombings in east Africa attributed to Osama bin Laden; killed 91 and wounded over 5000.

October 12, 2000 — Attack on the *U.S.S. Cole* attributed to Osama bin Laden; killed 17 sailors and injured 39.

September 11, 2001 — Hijackings of four commercial airliners, destruction of the World Trade Center towers and an attack on the Pentagon attributed to Osama bin Laden; approximately 3000 dead and an undetermined number injured.

Taliban Views on Women

- Cannot be in public without male relative
- Must be completely covered
- No education
- Not permitted to work
- Can only receive medical care from a woman, but women cannot work

Taliban Abuses of Women

- Public beatings
- Rape
- Mutilation
- Murder
- Forced into prostitution
- Slavery

Religious Justifications for Violence

- Satan
- Jihad
- Sharia
- Fatwah
- Idolatry
- Istishhad martyrdom

Satan

- Fundamentalists view history as a cosmic struggle between God's forces of good and Satan's forces of evil.
- God vs. Satan, truth vs. falsehood, light vs. darkness and good vs. evil.
- Humanity is divided into two opposing camps of believers and unbelievers with no neutrality possible.

In addition to the previously mentioned forms of terrorism it is important to remember that the treatment of women under the Taliban regime in Afghanistan constituted a heinous form of physical, psychological, symbolic and spiritual violence that exceeded even the most extreme interpretations of patriarchal religious tenets. Women had no rights under the Taliban regime and were regularly beaten, raped, mutilated, burned, and denied the most basic necessities of life. They were kept prisoners in their homes, denied education, healthcare and the freedom to leave even if they had the means. Before the Taliban took control of the villages, women were educated, worked outside their homes and were aware of freedoms afforded women in other parts of the world.

Jihad / Holy War

Islamic fundamentalists justify sacred violence through various interpretations of the religious doctrine of jihad. The term *jihad*, which does not

Jihad

- Islamic fundamentalists justify sacred violence through various interpretations of the religious doctrine of jihad.
- The term *jihad*, which does not literally translate into holy war, is very controversial and Islamic scholars have continually been divided on how it should be interpreted.
- Similar to other concepts in the Quran, the interpretation of jihad is dependent upon the religious and political views of individual Islamic sects.
- Even contemporary definitions are contradictory.
- For some, jihad means to struggle to maintain one's faith.
- For others, it represents the duty of Muslims to preserve Islam by ridding the world of Western influences.
- The concept of jihad for militant Islamic fundamentalists, including Osama bin Laden, is clearly a holy war to rid the Muslim Holy Land of infidels and as a justification to wage war against all enemies in their struggle for an Islamic state.
- In fact, some consider jihad the sixth pillar of Islam, the missing or forgotten obligation.

literally translate to holy war, is very controversial and Islamic scholars have continually been divided on how it should be interpreted. Similar to other concepts in the Quran, the interpretation of jihad is dependent upon the religious and political views of individual Islamic sects. Even contemporary definitions are contradictory.

According to the *Islamic Glossary* of the Muslim Students Association at the University of Southern California, *jihad*, sometimes spelled *jihaad*, is an Arabic word the root of which is *jahada*, which means *to strive for a better way of life*. The nouns are *juhd, mujahid, jihad* and *ijtihad*. Other meanings are *endeavor, strain, exertion, effort, diligence* and *fighting to defend one's life, land and religion*. Jihad should not be confused with holy war; Islam does not allow its followers to be involved in a holy war. References to holy war are to the holy war of the crusaders.[7]

The *Encyclopedia of Politics and Religion* states, "The Islamic idea of Jihad, which is derived from the Arabic root meaning to strive or to make an effort, connotes a wide range of meanings, from an inward spiritual struggle to attain perfect faith to an outward material struggle to promote justice and the Islamic social system."[8] T.P. Hughes' *Dictionary of Islam* presents a different definition, "Jihad, An effort, or a striving. A religious war with those who are unbelievers in the mission of Muhammad. It is an incumbent religious duty, established in the Quran and in the traditions as a divine institution, and enjoined specially for the purpose of advancing Islam and of repelling evil from Muslims."[9] For some, jihad means to struggle to maintain one's faith. For others, it represents the duty of Muslims to preserve Islam by ridding the world of Western influences.

The concept of jihad for militant Islamic fundamentalists, including Osama bin Laden, is clearly holy war to rid the Muslim Holy Land of infidels. It is also a justification for waging war against all enemies in their struggle to achieve an Islamic state. In fact, some consider jihad the sixth pillar of Islam —the missing or forgotten obligation.

The origins of bin Laden's concept of jihad date back to early 20th century Pakistan and Egypt. Two leading figures, Hassan al-Bann and Syed Abul Maududi, sought to restore the Islamic ideal of the unity of religion and state which they believed could only be achieved by restoring Islam to a traditional society governed by a strict interpretation of Islamic law. Al-Bann and Maududi emphasized the concept of jihad as holy war in order to end foreign occupation of Muslim lands. Maududi viewed true Islam as a modern revolutionary party:

> Islam is a revolutionary ideology which seeks to alter the social order of the entire world and rebuild it in conformity with its own tenets and ideals.... Jihad refers to that revolutionary struggle and utmost exertion which the Islamic Nation/Party brings into play in order to achieve this objective.[10]

In the 1950s, Sayed Qutb, a prominent member of Egypt's Muslim Brotherhood, took the arguments of Al-Bann and Maududi much further and proclaimed that all non-Muslims, even the so-called people of the Book (Christians and Jews) were infidels. Qutb predicted a future conflict between Islam and the West:

> Islamists emphasize the battle against jahiliyya. Traditionally understood as the pagan state of ignorance in pre-Islamic Arabia. But reinterpreted by Qutb to mean any contemporary system not based on the original holy sources of Quran and Hadith and not operating under Sharia. Qutb also reinterpreted jihad to mean permanent conflict between the Islamic system and all con-

temporary jahili paradigms. The concepts of the two
systems are totally incompatible, so there is no possibility of compromise or coexistence between them.[11]

After Egyptian President Abdel Nasser executed Qutb, Qutb's writings
gained even wider acceptance in the Arab world, especially after the defeat
of the Arabs in the 1967 war with Israel. Qutb's writings shaped the militant
view of Islam and contributed to the fundamentalist designation of the U.S.
as the Great Satan. "Qutb divides the world into two camps: God's party
versus Satan's. Man faces a moral choice he cannot evade, and he must
voluntarily submit to God's moral laws in Sharia. There is only one God and
one truth. All else is error. There is only one law, Sharia. All other law is mere
human caprice."[12]

The writings of Qutb and Maududi influenced many younger Arabs
including Palestine scholar Abdullah Azzam who fought with the PLO in the
1970s. While studying Islamic law in Cairo, Azzam met the family of Sayed
Qutb and eventually taught at the university in Saudi Arabia where one of
his students was Osama bin Laden. The battle to liberate Afghanistan from
Soviet occupation in 1979 provided Azzam with an opportunity to put his
revolutionary ideals into practice. He was dubbed the "Emir of Jihad"
because he was one of the first Arabs to join the Afghan fight along with
Osama bin Laden.

They worked together to recruit Arabs to fight in the holy war and Azzam
published books and magazines advocating the moral duty of every Muslim
to undertake jihad. Azzam's assassination in a car bomb in 1989 contributed
to a more radical fundamentalism led by Ayman al-Zawahri, an Egyptian,
whose cause was again furthered by the 1991 Gulf War that brought U.S.
troops to Saudi Arabia.

Bin Laden and his Muslim soldiers were extremely disturbed to see land
they regarded as sacred occupied by infidel soldiers. It was Zawahri's influence
over bin Laden and the al-Qaeda organization that paved the way for the
famous February 23, 1998 Declaration of War against the United States and
the beginning of the terrorist attacks on American targets.[13] The declaration
of war titled "Jihad against Jews and Crusaders" has now become evidence
that links the bin Laden network to the September 11th attacks.

Bin Laden justifies his declaration of war against the U.S. and his terrorist
actions as a defensive struggle against enemies who attack and occupy Muslim lands:

> Usama bin-Laden does not theorize about jihad, but
> simply claims that it is part of the Islamic religion,
> especially relevant in the case of repelling infidel in-

Sharia

- Sharia or Islamic Law is the complete legal system that governs every aspect of individual and social life.
- How the Sharia has been interpreted to adapt to current times is a major point of contention among different Islamic sects.
- Islamic fundamentalists attempt to live by a strict interpretation of the Sharia and view the lifestyle of the West as a threat and the antithesis of what the Sharia represents.

Fatwah

- A legal verdict given on a religious basis.
- On February 23, 1998 Osama bin Laden declared war against the U.S. in a document entitled "Jihad against Jews and Crusaders."
- Osama bin Laden justifies fatwah against the U.S. and his terrorist actions as a defensive struggle against enemies who attack and occupy Muslim lands.

Jahiliyya / Idolatry

- Traditionally understood as the pagan state of ignorance in pre-Islamic Arabia.
- Reinterpreted to mean any contemporary system not based on the original holy sources of Quran and Hadith and not operating under Sharia.
- Jahli systems are a deviation from the worship of one God and the divinely ordained way of life.

vaders. The stationing of Western military bases on the soil of Muslim states constitutes an occupation by infidels, a clear cause for jihad. In his notorious "ladinese epistle" in which he declared jihad against America, he bases himself on Ibn-Taymiyya who stressed the importance of dealing with the greater kurf before dealing with other, lesser kurfs based on the principle of necessity. It is a religious duty to repel the greatest danger even if it means ignoring smaller enemies for a while. He identifies the greater kurf as America, because of its occupation of the Arabian Peninsula and its support of Israel.[14]

Istishhad / Martyrdom

- Killing oneself for the glory of Islam is considered by extremist fundamentalists to be a supreme form of jihad and a type of terrorism that is allowed by the Sharia.
- It is not suicide (intihar), but martyrdom (istishhad) that will procure a special place in Paradise.
- Martyrdom is being actively encouraged and glorified by fundamentalists, and its rewards in the afterlife stressed to induce many to court it.
- Extreme fundamentalists have revived the khariji and assassin traditions of suicide-killings as a legitimate weapon in their contemporary jihad.

Istishhad/Martyrdom

The suicide attacks on the World Trade Center and the Pentagon are a form of jihad as are all the other acts of terrorism attributed to Islamic fundamentalists. Since suicide is religiously prohibited by Islam, suicide attacks must be viewed as a form of sacred violence. Suicide in the cause of holy war is not only legitimate, but represents one of the highest forms of self-sacrifice. Killing oneself for the glory of Islam is considered by extremist fundamentalists to be a supreme form of jihad and a type of terrorism that is allowed by the Sharia. It is not suicide (intihar), but martyrdom (istishhad), one that will procure a special place in Paradise.

> Active martyrdom is another area of reinterpretation and implementation. Martyrdom is being actively encouraged and glorified by fundamentalists, and its rewards in the afterlife stressed to induce many to court it. Extreme fundamentalists have revived the khariji and assassin traditions of suicide-killings as a legitimate weapon in their contemporary jihad.... Most radicals agree that suicide is a major sin forbidden in Islam. However, they use Quranic verses, Hadith and cases from the early history of Islam to prove either that the voluntary sacrifice of oneself in the cause of Islam (including blowing oneself up as a living bomb) with the objective of defending Muslims and hurting their enemies, is not considered suicide but is a legitimate fight to the death.[15]

Christian Identity groups and Islamic fundamentalists may be surprised to discover that they have many ideological views in common. Both view history as a fundamental cosmic struggle between good and evil. Both justify sacred violence in remarkably similar interpretations of their views of man's relationship to God. They both consider the U.S. government to be Satanic. They both share in their anti-Semitism, justifications for terrorism, suicidal missions and racial supremacist views so it is not surprising that white supremacist groups are still high on the list of suspects for the anthrax attacks. They also have in common with Islamic fundamentalists the ability to recruit individuals for their religious cause and their willingness to break government laws in the name of a higher sacred law.

Modern terrorists fundamentally understand the nature of sacred violence and how to manipulate the political situation so that ordinarily peaceful people will engage in violence as a necessary religious obligation. Trapped in a cycle of righteous revenge, there is no remorse because religious terrorism is always justified by true believers.

References

1. Schwartz, S., Ground zero and the Saudi connection, *The Spectator*, London, October 6, 2001, p. 4. http://www.spectator.co.uk/article.php3?table=old&section=current&issue=2002-01-05&id=1104&searchText=

2. Encyclopedia.com, Wahhabi (electronic library). http://www.encyclopedia.com/printablenew/13580.html

3. Lackey, S., *The 'new Wahhabi' movement*, MSNBC, October 17, 2001. http://www.msnbc.com/news/643005.asp?cp1=1 p. 3.

4. Lackey, S., *The 'new Wahhabi' movement*, MSNBC, October 17, 2001. http://www.msnbc.com/news/643005.asp?cp1=1 p. 2.

5. Hardy, R., Analysis: inside Wahhabi Islam, BBC News, September 30, 2001. http://news.bbc.co.uk/hi/english/world/middle_east/newsid_1571000/1571144.stm

6. Schwartz, S., Ground zero and the Saudi connection, *The Spectator*, London, October 6, 2001, p. 3. http://www.spectator.co.uk/article.php3?table=old&section=current&issue=2002-01-05&id=1104&searchText=

7. Muslim Students Association at University of Southern California, *Islamic Glossary, Jihad*. http://www.usc.edu/dept/MSA/reference/glossary/term.JIHAD.html

8. Wuthnow, R., Ed., *Encyclopedia of Politics and Religion*, Congressional Quarterly, Inc., Washington, D.C., 1998, p. 425.

9. Hughes, T.P., *Dictionary of Islam*. http://www.answering-islam.org/Index/Hughes/jihad.htm), p. 243.

10. Zeidan, D., The Islamic fundamentalist view of life as a perennial battle, Middle East Rev. Int. Affairs, 5, December 2001, p. 4. http:/meria.idc.ac.il/journal/2001/issue4/jv5n4a2.htm

11. Zeidan, D., The Islamic fundamentalist view of life as a perennial battle, Middle East Rev. Int. Affairs, 5, December 2001, p. 3. http:/meria.idc.ac.il/journal/2001/issue4/jv5n4a2.htm

12. Zeidan, D., The Islamic fundamentalist view of life as a perennial battle, Middle East Rev. Int. Affairs, 5, December 2001, p. 4. http:/meria.idc.ac.il/journal/2001/issue4/jv5n4a2.htm

13. Symon, F., Analysis: the roots of jihad, BBC News, October 16, 2001. http://news.bbc.co.uk/hi/english/world/middle_east/newsid_1603000/1603178.stm

14. Zeidan, D., The Islamic fundamentalist view of life as a perennial battle, Middle East Rev. Int. Affairs, 5, December 2001, p. 19. http:/meria.idc.ac.il/journal/2001/issue4/jv5n4a2.htm

15. Zeidan, D., The Islamic fundamentalist view of life as a perennial battle, Middle East Rev. Int. Affairs, 5, December 2001, pp. 19, 20. http:/meria.idc.ac.il/journal/2001/issue4/jv5n4a2.htm

Satanism

5

Satanism exists and is present in American culture as a religion, as a genre in film, music and art, as a political ideal and as a popular subject in the media. Satanism is acknowledged as a religion by the U.S. government and maintains a doctrine of ethical tenets, specific rituals and true believers. It is widely practiced in Western society, both individually and communally through Satanic churches, covens and grottoes. Similar to other organized religions, beliefs vary among different sects and according to church leaders, ranging from a form of ethical egoism through worshipping a particular deity. In most sects, Satanism is a reversal of Christianity and similarities are found in the symbolism and ritual practices of each group.

Defining Satanism

Definitions of Satanism are problematic because it is a relative concept that essentially is determined by the theological, moral, political, sociological and legal perspectives of each group. Basically, one man's god is another man's devil. From a fundamental Christian theological perspective, any practice other than Christianity is considered Satanic just as from a fundamental Islamic perspective any practice other than Islam is considered Satanic. This is based on strict interpretation of identical prohibitions found in both the Bible and the Quran.

The Quran (28.70) states, "And He is Allah, there is no god but He."[1] The Book of Exodus in the Bible (20.2–20.3) states, "I am the Lord your God. You shall have no other gods before Me." One result of these prohibitions has been a history of holy wars. Another result has been people denouncing God and embracing Satanism. Modern Satanists clearly admit that their religion is anti-God and it is irrelevant to them whether it is the God of the Christian Bible or Allah of the Quran; however, that does not necessarily mean that all modern Satanists are devil worshippers. Contemporary Satanism entails either wor-

Modern Satanism

- Satanism is an acknowledged religion by the U.S. federal government.
- Satanic religions maintain doctrines of ethical tenets, specific rituals and true believers.
- Satanism is widely practiced in Western society both individually and communally through Satanic churches, covens and grottoes.
- Similar to other organized religions; beliefs vary among different sects.

shipping Satan as a personified evil being or glorifying what he represents. Other characteristics of Satanism include beliefs based on a form of hedonism (pleasure seeking) or egoism (putting oneself above all others). Many contemporary Satanists also identify with pagan premonotheistic beliefs.

Historically, Satanism was attributed to all designated heretical groups simply because they deviated from strict Christian or Islamic practices. Today, many nontraditional religions, especially those that entail occult practices, for example, Santeria, Voodoo, Wicca and Druidism, are often categorized as Satanic. This controversy is evident in a vehement debate among new religious movement scholars. The scholars usually fall into three general groups: anticult scholars who emphasize potential harms among new religious groups, cult apologists who emphasize religious freedom and countercult organizations who oppose religious groups based on theological arguments. This debate is complicated and ongoing.

The anticult position on Satanism is that it exists in a variety of individual and group religions, some of which are responsible for serious crimes. The cult apologist position on Satanism is that it is a benign new religious movement and that allegations of crimes are based on Satanic panics and urban legends. The countercult position on Satanism was described earlier; from an orthodox perspective, any group other than the fundamental religion is heretical and/or Satanic. Hence, Satanism is a culturally relative construct that varies in place and in time and is intrinsically intertwined with issues of religious freedom even if that freedom entails the subjugation and harm of others.

Categories of Satanism

Classifications of Satanism are just as problematic as definitions, for similar reasons. Satanism is a culturally relative construct that is fundamentally defined by antithetical ideologies. There are additional controversies con-

Defining Satanism

- Defining Satanism is a problem because it is a relative concept, meaning that it is determined by the different perspectives and beliefs of each group.
- Experts cannot agree on a specific definition.

- From a fundamental Christian religious perspective, any practice other than Christianity is considered Satanic.
- Basically, one man's god is another man's devil.

When the Baphomet symbol is tattood on a person it indicates a Satanic High Priest.

cerning the very existence of some Satanic groups. Due to these debates it is especially difficult to present an agreed-upon typology. It is significant to note that the study of Satanism is in its infancy; basic demographic and ethnological data have yet to be compiled and it is problematic whether it is possible to accumulate accurate information.

However, after reviewing proposed typologies from a variety of sources common categories emerged, although they may be referred to by different names or only for the purposes of criticism.[2] The four general categories of Satanism are Religious/Organized Satanists, Traditional/Intergenerational Satanists, Self-Styled Satanists and Youth Subculture Satanists. These classifications are generalized and are not mutually exclusive.

In addition to the four major categories, another classification is sometimes used to differentiate Satanists. Satanic groups can be characterized as

Categories of Experts

- **Anticult:** Emphasize potential harm of cult groups, argue that Satanism exists and is practiced by individuals and groups that are responsible for serious crimes.
- **Cult Apologists:** Emphasize religious freedom, argue that Satanism is a benign new religion and that allegations of crimes are "Satanic panics."
- **Countercult:** Oppose groups based on their theology, argue that any group other than theirs is Satanic and that crimes and conspiracies exist.

Two General Classifications

Theistic Satanism
- A traditional form of Satanism. Worshipping Satan as a personified evil being, or other evil deities as the incarnation of an evil being.

Atheistic Satanism
- Glorifies what they imagine Satan represents, which includes indulgence, vengeance and engaging in all sins as long as they lead to self-gratification.

either atheistic or theistic. Atheistic Satanists glorify what they imagine Satan represents. Theistic Satanists worship Satan or other deities as the incarnation of an evil being. Finally, there are many other occult organizations including many Vampire religions and racist pagans which, even though they are not specifically Satanic, have similar practices and rituals.

Religious / Organized Satanists

Religious Satanism consists of organized groups and churches that practice a diverse variety of Satanic beliefs. Religious Satanists are subclassified as True Believers, individuals who have seriously committed themselves to the beliefs, tenets, rituals, and ideologies of a Satanic religion. Some Satanic

Four Major Categories

- **Religious Satanists**
- **Traditional Satanists**
- **Self-Styled Satanists**
- **Youth Subculture Satanists**

Sabbatic goat candles for sale at a Botanica (religious supply store) in the Bronx, New York. Used in a variety of rituals.

churches in the U.S. are recognized by the government as religions. Hence, they are not only protected by the first amendment, but also receive tax-exempt status. There are many American Satanic churches and a variety of other religious organizations that openly practice Satanism. Most maintain web pages on the Internet to provide information on their beliefs, practices and membership applications.

Religious Satanists

- True Believers
- Variety of organized groups and churches
- Sacred texts, specific beliefs, ideologies, holy rituals and doctrines
- Recognized as religions by the U.S. federal government.
- Highly visible, web sites, chat rooms.
- Claim to be nonviolent, however, allegations from victims that some of the churches are not what they appear to be

Satanism is often also referred to as the Left Hand Path, Occultism, Black Magick or the Dark Arts, although not exclusively. Similar groups use the same designations.

The two most established and well-known American Satanic churches are The Church of Satan (CoS) and The Temple of Set (ToS). It is worth noting that most Satanic religious organizations are often referred to by the first initials of their names but significantly these initials are not read as acronyms. Some Satanic organizations include the First Church of Satan (FCoS), Cult of Mastema (CoM), Ordo Templi Satanis (OTS), Church of Lucifer (COL), Ordo Sinistra Vivendi (OSV) and many others. There are many orders, grottoes, pylons, and covens of the main churches and a significant number of individual, unrelated less well-known groups, many of whom also have web pages on the Internet.

Although it is difficult to establish numbers and geographical locations of members, most are in the United States, Europe and Australia, but members can be found on every continent except Antarctica. It is significant to point out that on the African and South American continents, occult dark magic is practiced in relation to their indigenous religions. This accounts for fewer members of Western Satanic traditions in those countries. In many countries organized Satanic groups are not tolerated and they remain underground. Although the ideologies of these groups may be highly offensive in relation to more traditional religions, religious Satanists are generally law-abiding citizens whose known practices rarely constitute illegal activities. However, this has been questioned due to statements of the many survivors and victims of occult-related crimes who claim that these groups are simply covers for larger criminal acts.

Traditional / Intergenerational Satanists

Traditional Satanists are proposed to be a highly organized, international, secret cult network that is actively engaged in a variety of criminal activities incluive of arson, ritual abuse, sexual abuse, incest, kidnapping, child pornography and ritual murder involving mutilation, dismemberment and sometimes cannibalism. Similar to Religious Satanists, Traditional Satanists are also subclassified as True Believers; however, they are exceptionally devoted to their beliefs and represent the equivalent of extremist fundamental versions of Satanic religions. Also referred to as generational or intergenerational Satanists, many members contend that they were raised in this belief system going back several generations.

Ideologically, Traditional Satanists worship Satan as the evil deity described in the New Testament. Their religious practices include blood rit-

---

Traditional Satanists

- True Believers, called intergenerational because they are born into the religion.
- Thought to be a highly organized international secret network; some smaller groups operate.
- Exceptionally devoted to their beliefs, equivalent to the extremist version of other religions.
- Crimes include arson, ritual abuse, sexual abuse, kidnapping, child pornography, ritual murder involving mutilation and cannibalism.
- Underground organizations, will not be found on the Internet.

---

uals, animal and human sacrifice and a variety of sexual sadistic ritual practices for the glorification of Satan. The Religious Satanists described above all vehemently present disclaimers that they do not engage in these activities and even consider the allegation a form of defamation. Due to a lack of empirical evidence, many scholars, Satanic church members, mental health professionals and a large portion of the general public consider these assertions to be urban myths, false memories or a form of Satanic panic. Although empirical studies have not been conducted to determine the frequency that this occurs, factual evidence indicates that the practice of Traditional Satanism exists.

Examples of criminal cases involving alleged Traditional Satanists include the infamous McMartin preschool trial that lasted 6 years and was the first multi-victim/multi-offender child abuse case. Beginning in March 1984, 208 counts of child abuse involving 40 children were directed against 7 adults (2 owners of the school, one owner's son and 4 teachers). By January 1986, a new district attorney dropped all charges against 5 of the adults and retained 52 charges against Ray Buckey and 21 counts against Peggy Buckey including one count of conspiracy. Several years later, in August 1990, another jury was hung and the prosecution gave up trying to obtain a conviction. This case spurred many other similar prosecutions, which were referred to as witch hunts by people who argue that this type of abuse does not occur. This trial also was a national media event and became the subject of many books, studies and films.

Other famous controversial descriptions of victims of Satanic ritual abuse and entire Satanic communities practicing Traditional Satanism are described in the classic nonfiction (although some claim they are fictional) books titled *Michelle Remembers* and *Satan's High Priest*. Both books describe in detail heinous ritual practices of Traditional Satanists. The religioustolerance.org

> ## Self-Styled Satanists
>
> - Dabblers or True Criminals.
> - Individuals or members of small loosely organized groups.
> - Belief systems are either self-invented or a mixture of traditions and media depictions.
> - Criminal activities include child molestation, animal mutilation, homicide and others.
> - Crimes conform to their invented beliefs.
> - Crimes are difficult to distinguish from serial murder or sexual sadism.

website lists 41 multi-victim/multi-offender court cases involving allegations of ritual abuse.

Self-Styled Satanists

Self-Styled Satanists are either individually involved with Satanism or belong to small loosely organized groups. They are either subclassified as dabblers (people who are intermittently and experientially involved in occult activities) and/or true criminals (people who use the occult as an excuse to justify or rationalize criminal behavior and who are committed not to the belief system but to the criminal action).

The rituals and belief systems of dabblers and true criminals are either completely self-invented, combinations of a variety of traditions or are emulated from media/cultural images of Satanic practices. Self-Styled Satanists are not viewed as true believers because their primary interests usually entail the acquisition of personal power, material gains or gratification through criminal interests and not Satanic worship. Religious Satanists are offended by the claims and actions of Self-Styled Satanists who bring negative publicity to their already controversial religion.

Some Self-Styled Satanists engage in criminal activities ranging from child molestation, animal mutilation to homicide, and their crimes conform to their self-invented ideologies. It is this category of Satanism that most ritualistic crimes are placed in; hence, Satanic ritual abuse is often viewed as a form of sexual sadism or serial murder instead of actual Satanic worship. A classic example of a Self-Styled Satanist is Richard Ramirez. Dubbed the Night Stalker, Ramirez terrorized Los Angeles in 1985 by breaking into homes, raping, torturing, mutilating and murdering his victims and, most

> ## Youth Subculture Satanists
>
> - True dabblers, juveniles and young adults.
> - Interest in Satanism is transitory and may not evolve into criminal activity.
> - Interest in Satanism is influenced by music, film, Internet and other media.
> - Often have a deep sense of alienation from mainstream culture and spiritual traditions.
> - Crimes include vandalism, arson, grave desecration, animal mutilation, school violence and sometimes murder.
> - Ritual crimes escalate the longer they are involved.

notably, forcing them to declare their love for Satan. In the spring and summer of 1985, Ramirez committed over 20 attacks. He was found guilty in 1989 of 13 counts of murder. In an infamous gesture during the trial he raised his hand to show a pentagram on it and said, "Hail Satan." Currently awaiting execution at San Quentin prison, he continues to be completely devoted to Satan. On October 3, 1996 in the San Quentin Prison waiting room Ramirez married Doreen Lioy, a long time fan since his arrest. Doreen was one of many women who regularly visited Ramirez in prison.

Youth Subculture Satanists

Youth Subculture Satanists are similar to Self-Styled Satanists; however, their interest in Satanism is usually transitory and may not evolve into criminal activities. Youth Subculture Satanists are subcategorized as true dabblers, teenagers and young adults who are usually introduced to Satanism via music, film, the Internet and other media influences. Most often, they turn to the occult because of a deep sense of alienation from mainstream culture and spiritual traditions. They either eventually return to more traditional beliefs or may easily be recruited into one of the many Satanic religious organizations.

Their rituals usually escalate, depending upon the length of time they are involved in Satanism. Rituals begin with simple magical incantations progressing to animal and human sacrifice. Common crimes of Youth Subculture Satanists include vandalism, arson, grave desecration, animal mutilation, school violence and sometimes murder. Depending upon their level of seriousness at the time of their involvement, they can also be considered momentary true believers.

There are numerous examples of the more serious crimes of homicide and mass murder committed by Self-Styled Satanists, including the case of 16-year-old Luke Woodham who, on October 1, 1997, in Pearl, MS, stabbed his mother to death, then went to school and opened fire with a rifle. He killed two classmates and wounded seven. Woodham was part of a larger group of teenagers who had embraced Satanism. His new peers belonged to a group known as the Kroth which sought to destroy its enemies and practice Satanic worship. They instructed Luke that murder was a viable means of accomplishing the purposes and goals of their shared belief system. Another example occurred in Chiavenna, Italy on June 6, 2000. Three teenage girls brutally murdered a nun, Sister Mary Laura Manetti, after they formed a Satanic group which they said was influenced by the lyrics of heavy metal musician Marilyn Manson. Numerous murders and suicides have been attributed to media and cultural influences of Satanism.

Anti-Satanism

A typology of Satanism would be incomplete without mentioning opposing organizations specifically established to abolish Satanism. These organizations are chiefly responsible for assigning Satanism into the categories described earlier. The organizations are variously referred to as anticult organizations, countercult organizations and watch groups. Their goal is to abolish the practice of Satanism.

One countercult organization is Apologetics Index whose website contains a vast archive of articles, newspapers, commentaries and resources. Apologetics Index clearly states that it "provides research resources on religious cults, sects, new religious movements, alternative religions, apologetics, anticult, and countercult organizations, doctrines, religious practices and world views. These resources reflect a variety of theological and/or sociological perspectives."[3] Albeit a self-proclaimed Christian countercult organization, it provides surprisingly objective perspectives on most pages.

A few of the better known anticult groups included the Cult Awareness Network (CAN), which was a clearinghouse for information about cults; its mission was to educate the public and to provide support to victims of cults and their families. CAN was subjected to a huge scandal when it was sued by the Church of Scientology who eventually forced them to close down. Scientology obtained all CAN records, bought all its logos, trademarks and other property through a bankruptcy and currently operates its own version of CAN.

The American Family Foundation founded in 1979 is a research center and educational organization whose mission is to study psychological manipulation and cultic groups, educate the public and assist those who have been adversely affected by a cult-related experience. The Watchman Fellowship is considered the foremost Christian countercult ministry. Its resources include over 9000 files and a 35,000-volume library focused on abusive religious groups, cults and the occult. These are just a few of the countercult and anticult organizations.

The primary goals of anticult organizations are to protect their people from external violence and to preserve their way of life. As we examine the religions of modern Satanists, it will become evident that their primary goals are identical to those of their rivals. Significantly, all of the previously mentioned models of Satanism are not categorized by the groups themselves, but by organizations external to the groups, often in direct opposition to their ideologies.

Modern Religious Satanic Groups

Just as there are many varieties of Christianity manifested in a number of diverse Christian religions, there are many varieties of Satanism and Satanic sects pejoratively designated as cults. Most practitioners of Satanism proudly acknowledge the Satanist designation. Others admit that their religion entails occultism, magick and worshipping specific deities but are not specifically Satanic. However, all Satanic religions vehemently disavow the cult designation.

Commonalities among the major Satanic churches include hierarchical structures, opposition to Christian tenets, magical ideologies, advocating ethical egoism and the acquisition of personal and political power. Similar

---

Religious Satanism: Common Beliefs

- Symbolism
- Hierarchical structures
- Opposition to Christian tenets
- Magical ideologies
- Advocate the acquisition of personal and political power
- "Do what thou wilt" philosophy
- Put oneself above all others

to other religious denominations individual Satanic churches profess spiritual superiority over each other and claim that they practice the one true faith. Most of these groups do not practice Theistic Satanism (worshipping Satan as a personified evil being) but practice Atheistic Satanism glorifying what they imagine Satan represents, which includes among other things, indulgence, vengeance, and all other sins as long as they lead to self-gratification or self-deification.

Since it is impossible to describe all the Satanic religions in this chapter, examples are limited to three pertinent active groups that best exemplify the religious practices of Modern Satanists: the Church of Satan, the Temple of Set and Ordo Templi Orientis (O.T.O.). The latter group earnestly claims that it is not a Satanic organization. All three groups have large memberships in countries throughout the world, degrees of initiation, sophisticated websites translated into many languages and are recognized as religions by the U.S. government.

Scholars generally agree that modern Religious Satanism evolved from two specific traditions and the writings of their influential leaders, Aleister Crowley and Anton LaVey. However, there is debate about whether the origin of modern Satanism began with the work of Aleister Crowley in the early 20th century or with the founding of the Church of Satan by Anton LaVey in 1966. It is important to note that contemporary Self-Styled Satanists, Youth Subculture Satanists and Traditional Satanists may follow different unrelated philosophical and mystical traditions.

Ordo Templi Orientis

Aleister Crowley, who never considered himself a Satanist although he was a member of many secret occult societies, founded the Abbey of Thelema and proclaimed himself the antichrist in 1904. Crowley's writings on magick influenced many contemporary Satanic groups, most notably the Ordo Templi Orientis or O.T.O. The O.T.O. was incorporated in California as a not-for-profit religious organization with state and national tax exemptions under Section 501 (c)(3) of the Internal Revenue Code. O.T.O. currently operates in 40 countries and has approximately 3000 active members.[4]

According to its website, "O.T.O. functions as a fraternal, initiatory, social and educational organization of a religious nature."[5] Although officially founded at the beginning of the 20th century, O.T.O. draws from a variety of traditions of esoteric wisdom such as the Freemasonic, Rosicrucian and Illuminist movements of the 18th and 19th centuries, the Knights Templars of the Middle Ages, early Christian Gnosticism and the pagan mystery schools. O.T.O. was founded in 1895 by Karl Kellner and Theodor Reuss, both of whom were high level Freemasons. Reuss brought Crowley into O.T.O. in 1910 and admitted him to the level of three degrees. In 1912,

Ordo Templi Orientis (O.T.O.)

- Claims not to be a Satanic organization.
- Registered religion.
- Operates in 40 countries with approximately 3000 members.
- Founded in 1895 by former high-level Freemasons Karl Kellner and Theodor Reuss.
- Aleister Crowley was Grand Master from 1912 until his death in 1947.
- Crowley became the prophet of the group and his writings became the holy texts.

Thelema (O.T.O. Religion)

- Followers are referred to as Thelemites.
- The heart of Thelemic Doctrine is "Do what thou wilt."
- Draws on a variety of esoteric wisdom traditions: Freemason, Rosicrucian, Illuminist movement, Knights Templar, Christian Gnosticism and Pagan Mystery schools.
- Liturgical Branch is called Ecclesia, Gnostica, Catholica (Gnostic Catholic Church).
- Thelemic Calendar has specific holy days.
- Follows specific holy rituals.

Crowley was appointed National Grand Master General X for Great Britain and Ireland. He subsequently revised rituals and moved O.T.O. away from Freemasonry and toward Thelema. Crowley was appointed to the highest level (Outer Head of the Order) in 1922 and retained this position until his death in 1947. His writings became the cornerstone of the contemporary O.T.O. Current members practice Crowley's religion known as Thelema and Crowley is regarded as its prophet. Followers are referred to as Thelemites.

Religious texts are referred to as the Holy Books of Thelema, all authored by Aleister Crowley, forming the canon of Thelemic Holy Scripture. The most important text is *Liber Al vel Legis, sub figura CCXX*, commonly referred to as *The Book of the Law*. Another significant text that is part of the Thelemic canon but not one of the Holy Books is *Liber XXX Aerum vel Saeculi, sub figura CDXVIII*, commonly called *The Vision and the Voice*.

O.T.O. Holy Books and Rituals

- Religious texts are called *The Holy Books of Thelema*, all authored by Aleister Crowley.
- The most important is the *Liber Al vel Legis, sub figura CCXX, The Book of the Law.*
- Thelemites keep a record of their personal practices in a magical diary.
- A particular prayer is recited four times a day.
- Followers take mystical names for themselves.
- Three rites of passage are observed for each person: birth, puberty and death.

The theology of Thelema postulates all manifested existence arising from the interaction of two cosmic principles: the infinitely extended, all-pervading Space–Time continuum; and the atomic, individually expressed Principle of Life and Wisdom.... The Thelemic theological system utilizes the divinities of various cultures and religions as personifications of specific divine, archetypal and cosmic forces. Thelemic doctrine holds that all the diverse religions of Humanity are grounded in universal truths.... History is considered to be divided into a series of Aeons, each with its own dominant concept of divinity and its own formula of redemption and advancement. The current aeon is termed the Aeon of Horus.... According to Thelemic doctrine, the expression of Divine Law in the Aeon of Horus is "Do what thou wilt."[6]

Thelemites keep a record of their personal practices in a magical diary, practice a particular form of prayer four times a day and often take mystical names as a sign of commitment. They customarily greet each other with the phrase, "Do what thou wilt shall be the whole of the law," to which the customary response is, "Love is the law, love under will."[7]

O.T.O. has a liturgical arm called Ecclesia Gnostica Catholica (E.G.C.), the Gnostic Catholic Church. The principal ritual of the E.G.C. is called the Gnostic Mass. The Thelemic calendar begins in 1904 EV (the year *Liber Al* was received) and each Thelemic year starts on March 20 of the civil calendar at the vernal equinox. Specific holy days are observed as set forth in *The Book of the Law* and include the equinoxes, solstices and dates important to Crow-

---

O.T.O. Organizational Structure

- Religious structure is similar to Freemasonry.
- A series of initiations are conferred ceremonially.
- System of 21 initiate degrees.
- Membership has two categories: associate and initiate.
- Liturgical branch involves baptism and confirmation.
- Specific hierarchal structure, highest level being Grand Master General.
- International headquarters is in Berlin.

---

ley's life. Three rites of passage are observed in each Thelemite's life: birth, puberty and death.

The religious structure of O.T.O. is similar to Freemasonry and the ancient mystery schools based on a series of initiations that are conferred ceremonially in a very sophisticated system involving 21 initiate degrees (13 numbered degrees and 8 unnumbered intermediate or subdegrees). Membership is divided into two primary categories: associate and initiate. Associate members have access to publications and can attend activities but do not enter into the degree ceremonies. Ecclesia Gnostica Catholica is conferred through ceremonies of baptism and confirmation. The O.T.O. U.S. Grand Lodge hierarchical structure includes a Grand Master General, Grand Secretary General, Grand Treasurer General, Initiation Secretary, Electoral College, Quartermasters and Internet Secretary. The international headquarters is in Berlin, Germany. As of this writing, there are 96 separate websites listing branches throughout the world. These branches are referred to as Camps, Oases, Encampments or Lodges, with identifying names preceding them.

Membership information and detailed accounts of the religion are readily available through its many websites. O.T.O. does not consider itself a Satanic religion or a Freemason practice although the theology and ritual practices have significant elements of both. O.T.O. is listed as a Satanic religion in most reference books and websites.

There are no recorded incidents of violence; however, litigation involving different factions of O.T.O. asserting claims to copyrights of Aleister Crowley works, intellectual property issues and control for leadership is documented in U.S. courts. There are also conspiracy theories surrounding high-ranking members' activities during the World Wars. Although O.T.O vehemently claims not to be a Satanic religion, Aleister Crowley, its prophet, variously known as

O.T.O. Potential Violence

- No recorded incidents of violence.
- Crowley is infamous as the antichrist and the wickedest man that ever lived.
- Crowley inspired the basic principles of many modern Satanic groups.
- Holy texts are extremely violent.
- Incidents of members being coerced away from families.
- Thelema theology glorifies all acts of self-gratification.

The Great Beast 666, the antichrist and the wickedest man who ever lived, inspired the basic principles of many contemporary Satanic groups.

Church of Satan

The beginning of religious Satanism in the U.S. was clearly the establishment of the Church of Satan (CoS). The Church of Satan was founded on April 30, 1966, Walpurgisnacht on the occult calendar, by Anton Szandor LaVey who declared himself the High Priest of the Church, the Black Pope, and announced that a new era of "I Anno Satanas" had begun. The church was officially formalized on September 20, 1971 as a California non-profit religious corporation. Conflicting information surrounds its application for tax-exempt status. One claim states that the church was denied tax exempt status

The Church of Satan (CoS)

- Founded April 30, 1966 by Anton Szandor LaVey, who announced new era "I Anno Satanas."
- LaVey, High Priest of the Church, Black Pope until his death in 1997.
- Official religion September 20, 1971.
- Membership is confidential, no available data.
- Current leader is Magister Peter Gilmore.
- Membership is available through its website.
- Very influential to modern Satanism.

Church of Satan Theology

- Hedonistic religion that glorifies what Satan represents as a defiance against Christianity.
- Doctrine advocating that feelings such as greed, lust and hatred are natural instincts and denial of these feelings is wrong.
- Members strive to be in tune with the carnal nature of humanity.
- Incorporates magical ideologies and occult symbolism.

by the Internal Revenue Service and the California Franchise Tax Board while current leaders claim that they oppose government assistance and the church never applied for tax-exempt status. However, there is no doubt that the Church of Satan received nationwide attention as the first publicly self-proclaimed Satanic religion. Because membership information is kept private, there is no available data listing the number of current members.

LaVey worked at a number of unusual jobs before founding the Church of Satan inclusive of lion tamer for a circus, carnival hypnotist, organ player at a burlesque club and photographer for the San Francisco police. In 1950, in San Francisco, LaVey started a group known as the Magic Circle, an occult club that started to attract attention and led to the founding of the Church of Satan in 1966. In 1967, the church received tremendous publicity when LaVey presided over a Satanic wedding, a Satanic funeral for a church member and the Satanic baptism of his 3-year old daughter, Zeena. LaVey was also an actor and consultant on several Hollywood films and played the role of the devil in "Rosemary's Baby." Many celebrities are purported to have had connections with the church including Sammy Davis, Jr., Jayne Mansfield and Kim Novak. More controversial connections were with Marilyn Manson and one of the murderers in the Charles Manson family.

Although almost every aspect of Anton LaVey's history has been scrutinized and several allegations indicate that his personal history was fabricated, there is no doubt that he authored the *Satanic Bible* in 1969.[8] It has sold over one million copies and is still in print and widely distributed throughout the world. It contains the core beliefs of the Church of Satan. Additional texts by LaVey include *The Compleat Witch* in 1970, later titled *The Satanic Witch*, and *The Satanic Rituals* in 1972. LaVey died on October 29, 1997 leaving a legacy of controversy and inspiring thousands to embrace modern Satanism.

Nine Satanic Statements

(1) Satan represents indulgence, instead of abstinence.

(2) Satan represents vital existence, instead of spiritual pipe dreams.

(3) Satan represents undefiled wisdom, instead of hypocritical self-deceit.

(4) Satan represents kindness to those who deserve it, instead of love wasted on ingrates.

(5) Satan represents vengeance, instead of turning the other cheek.

(6) Satan represents responsibility to the responsible, instead of concern for psychic Vampires.

(7) Satan represents man as just another animal, more often worse than those that walk on all fours, who, because of his divine spiritual and intellectual development, has become the most vicious animal of all.

(8) Satan represents all of the so-called sins, as they lead to physical, mental or emotional gratification.

(9) Satan has been the best friend the church has ever had, as he has kept it in business all these years.

The Church of Satan is a hedonistic religion that does not worship Satan as a supernatural being but as a symbol of defiance against Christianity. The main doctrine is summarized in the nine Satanic statements in the *Satanic Bible*:

> (1) Satan represents indulgence, instead of abstinence;
> (2) Satan represents vital existence, instead of spiritual
> pipe dreams; (3) Satan represents undefiled wisdom,
> instead of hypocritical self-deceit; (4) Satan represents
> kindness to those who deserve it, instead of love wasted
> on ingrates; (5) Satan represents vengeance, instead of
> turning the other cheek; (6) Satan represents responsi-
> bility to the responsible, instead of concern for psychic
> vampires; (7) Satan represents man as just another an-
> imal, more often worse than those that walk on all
> fours, who, because of his divine spiritual and intellec-
> tual development, has become the most vicious animal
> of all; (8) Satan represents all of the so-called sins, as
> they all lead to physical, mental or emotional gratifica-
> tion; and (9) Satan has been the best friend the church
> has ever had, as he has kept it in business all these years.[8]

There are also nine Satanic sins: stupidity, pretentiousness, solipsism, self-deceit, herd conformity, lack of perspective, forgetfulness of past orthodoxies, counterproductive pride and lack of aesthetics. Additionally, the church has eleven Satanic rules of the Earth and a 1988 treatise titled "Pentagonal Revisionism: a Five-Point Program." The theology of the Church of Satan proposes that emotions such as greed, lust and hatred are natural instincts and the denial of these feelings is incorrect. Members consider themselves in tune with the carnal nature of humanity. Their religion incorporates magical ideologies, occult symbolism and three main types of rituals: sexual rituals to aid in attaining physical ecstasy, healing or happiness rituals to help loved ones and destructive rituals to release anger and hatred. Ceremonies are pageants in which male members wear full-length black robes and female members wear sexually suggestive clothing. Amulets are often worn and the most distinguishing symbol is the Sigl of Baphomet, a goat's head drawn within an inverted pentagram. Candle magic is employed, the language is Enochian, and in the church's early days, a nude woman was used as the altar.

The hierarchical structure of the church includes a grotto system. Individuals in geographic proximity form a grotto for ritualization, socialization and the pursuit of various projects. Grottos are run by individuals called Grotto Masters, many grottos remain underground, while others have Internet sites. The official representatives of the philosophy of the church are found in the higher levels which include the Priesthood of Mendes who are given titles of Priest/Priestess or Magister/Magistra. Members of the priesthood make up the Council of Nine, the ruling body of the organization responsible to the High Priest/Priestess.

CoS Organizational Structure

- Grotto system consisting of individuals in geographic areas, many remain underground; others have web sites.
- Each grotto has a Grotto Master.
- Priesthood of Mendes called Priest/Priestess or Magister/Magistra.
- Council of Nine formed by members of the priesthood, ruling body of the church.
- High Priest/Priestess.
- Order of the Trapezoid assists in the administration of the church.

CoS Potential Violence

- No recorded incidents of violence.
- Many legal disputes surrounding LaVey's life, including claims to succession.
- *Satanic Bible* has been found in the possession of and/or cited as the influence for many Self-Styled Satanists who have committed a variety of crimes.
- Religion advocates indulgence, self-gratification and vengeance.

The Order of the Trapezoid consists of individuals who assist in the administration of the church. Membership in the priesthood is by invitation only. As of April 31, 2001, Magister Peter Gilmore and High Priestess Blanche Barton, who was LaVey's most recent lover, mother of his son, Xerxes, and partner until his death, are High Priest and Priestess of the Church of Satan.

Registered membership is available through the church's website by submitting legal name, address, writing "Please enroll me as a registered member of the Church of Satan," signing the request and submitting a one-time registration fee of $100 in U.S. currency. Registered members receive an embossed crimson card declaring that they are members of the Church of Satan. To become an active member, an individual must complete a detailed application that requires specific personal information inclusive of 40 questions about preferences, personality and philosophy.

The Church of Satan has no recorded incidents of violence; however, its *Satanic Bible* has been in the possession of and/or cited as an influence by many Self-Styled Satanists who have committed heinous crimes. The Church of Satan has been involved in many legal disputes and controversies surrounding LaVey's life, inclusive of his daughter, Zeena, becoming a Priestess in the rival Temple of Set, divorce proceedings, financial problems and finally claims to succession being fought between Barton and LaVey's daughter Karla. Notwithstanding the controversies, the influence of the Church of Satan has had an irrefutable impact on the establishment of Satanic churches and on advancing Satanism as a contemporary religion.

Temple of Set

The Temple of Set (ToS) was founded in 1975 by Michael Aquino, a former High Priest of the Church of Satan. The same year it was recognized as a

Temple of Set (ToS)

- Founded in 1975 by Michael Aquino, former High Priest in the Church of Satan.
- Recognized as a religion in 1975.
- Membership is confidential; no data available.
- Highly sophisticated, intellectual religion.
- Members refer to themselves as Setians because they identify with the Egyptian God Set.
- Michael Aquino is a former lieutenant in an army intelligence unit that specialized in psychological warfare.

Statues of a variety of Egyptian gods for sale at an occult store in New York City.

non-profit church and subsequently received exemption from federal and state taxes. ToS is a highly sophisticated intellectual religion whose philosophy is comprised of the acquisition of self-knowledge and power through magic, responsibility and will.

Aquino, the head of ToS, is a former lieutenant in an Army intelligence unit that specialized in psychological warfare. His secular vitae available on the ToS website is impressive and lists among his accomplishments a Ph.D. in political science. His dissertation was titled "The Neutron Bomb." He received many distinguished service awards and military decorations including a Bronze Star, Meritorious Service Medal, Air Medal and Vietnam Service Medal for three campaigns. Aquino was trained in special forces and military intelligence.

Aquino joined the Church of Satan in 1969 while he was in the Army. He became a priest in 1970 and was promoted to the level of Magister IV, the highest ranking below High Priest, then held by Anton LaVey. In 1975,

Aquino felt that LaVey used the church for his own personal gain. In addition to philosophical differences, Aquino left the Church of Satan with many members to found the Temple of Set.

Historically, the Temple of Set can be considered a sect of the Church of Satan. Unlike LaVey's hedonistic philosophy expressed in the Church of Satan, Setian philosophy aspires to ultimate self-control and power through magic. Members refer to themselves as Setians because they identify the Egyptian god Set as a much more complex role model than the figure of the Judeo-Christian Satan. However, they still consider their religion to be Satanic in that it is a Left Hand Path that opposes traditional Judeo-Christian beliefs.

Temple of Set Theology

- ToS philosophy is the acquisition of self-knowledge and power through magic, responsibility and will.
- The ultimate goal of Setians is to reach a higher spiritual consciousness called Xeper.
- Xeper is an Egyptian term meaning 'come into being.'
- Setians want to create a tradition of self-deification.
- Followers do not pray to Set; they emulate him.

Temple of Set Holy Books

- Sacred text is *The Book of Coming Forth by Night* written by Michael Aquino, supposedly with the help of Set.
- The Temple also maintains a set of encyclopedias entitled *The Jeweled Tablets of Set*.
- Website has information in seven different languages.

The Temple of Set rejects spiritual traditions of society including programing from advertising to superstition, nihilism and mindless hedonism. Its Being is Knowing concept is the opposite of the Buddhist Right Hand Path philosophy of Being is Suffering. Even though Setians believe in a literal deity, they "do not worship Set in the same way that Christians worship God. Rather they honor Set for representing a deeper consciousness and individual strength — thus worshipping Set is analogous to worshipping the individual. The ultimate goal of Setians is to reach this higher spiritual consciousness and understanding of the self — the process of self-actualization is called Xeper, the Egyptian term meaning 'to come into being.'"[9] Their goal is to recreate a tradition of self-deification. In brief, they do not pray to Set; they emulate him. The *Book of Coming Forth By Night* written by Michael Aquino, supposedly with help from Set, can be considered a sacred text of the ToS. The temple also maintains a series of encyclopedias titled the *Jeweled Tablets of Set* and publishes a regular newsletter called the *Scroll of Set*.

The ToS religious hierarchy has six degrees of initiation: (1) Setian I, (2) Adept II, (3) Priest/Priestess of Set III, (4) Magister/Magistra Templi IV, (5) Magus/Maga V and (6) Ipsissimus/Ipsissima VI. New members start out at Setian I, and advance to Adept II only after mastering the essential principles of black magic. If new members do not advance to Adept II within 2 years, their membership is discontinued. Most members stay at the second degree level throughout their time in the Temple. Executive authority is held by the Council of Nine and the council appoints both the High Priest of Set and the Executive Director. ToS is highly organized and has members worldwide. Because it avoids publicity and keeps its membership information private, there is no available data indicating the number of members.

ToS Religious Structure

Religious hierarchy entails six degrees of initiation:

1. Setian I
2. Adept II
3. Priest/Priestess of Set III
4. Magister/Magistra Templi VI
5. Magus/Maga V
6. Ipsissimus/Ipsissima VI

ToS Organizational Structure

- Executive authority is the Council of Nine, which appoints the High Priest of Set and the executive director.
- Pylons are member chapters that are geographically localized.
- Sentinels are leaders of pylons.
- Orders specialize in particular fields of magic. Each member reaching Adept II must affiliate with an order.
- ToS currently has 11 pylons and 9 orders.

ToS' website, which is referred to as The Official Temple of Set World Wide Website, provides information in seven languages. The organizational structure consists of Pylons, named after the unique gates of ancient Egyptian temples. Pylons are geographically localized and are under the trust and responsibility of a designated officer called a Sentinel. Divisions called orders specialize in one or more particular fields of the magical arts and sciences. Each member who reaches Adept II status must affiliate with an order reflective of his or her personal interests and aptitudes within 1 year. The collective knowledge of all of the Orders is available to the Temple membership. ToS currently lists 11 pylons and 9 orders, each with its own corresponding web page.

Membership is discouraged by lengthy disclaimers on the website that emphasize the serious nature of entering the temple. However, instructions are provided for those who wish to submit an application via one of two methods: (1) sponsorship by a current member, which upon verification approval is automatic, or (2) by writing a letter of introduction to the Executive Director, summarizing your background and reasons for application. Both methods require a $70 application fee (refunded if a candidate is not accepted) which must be submitted along with legal name, sex, mailing address, phone numbers, photocopy of an identity card such as a driver's license that shows date of birth and a list of present organizational affiliations. Members must be 18 years of age or older. If an application is approved, a candidate receives a membership identification card, a certificate, a copy of the *Crystal Tablet of Set*, recent issues of the *Scroll of Set* and a Setian I pendant medallion.

The Temple of Set has no recorded incidents of violence. However, it has been plagued by legal issues involving Aquino over the years. A 1986 scandal

Temple of Set Violence

- No recorded incidents of violence.
- In 1986 Michel Aquino faced allegations of child molestation at the day care center at Presidio Army Base where he was assigned; the case was later dismissed.
- In 1994, Aquino sued Linda Blood, a former member, for libel because of how she depicted him in her book *The New Satanists*; the case was settled out of court.
- In 1997, Aquino brought a lawsuit against an Internet provider because a person named Curio posted over 500 messages defaming Aquino; the case was thrown out of court.

involved allegations of child molestation at a day care center at Presidio Army Base where Aquino was assigned:

> Gary Hambright, a daycare worker, was charged with 12 counts of sodomy, oral copulation, and lewd conduct. Aquino along with his wife Lilith were identified by some of the children as possibly being another who had participated in the molestations. However, no formal charges were ever brought against Aquino and the case against Hambright was later dismissed. In 1994, Aquino sued Linda Blood, a former member of the Temple of Set, for libel in her book *The New Satanists*. The book, Aquino's attorneys said, depicted him and his fellow Setians as pedophiles, child abusers, murderers, and the masterminds behind a nationwide Satanic conspiracy. This was settled out of court, with details of the settlement kept confidential. The latest lawsuit, in 1997, was brought against an internet provider for failing to block defamatory posts from an anonymous user. A person using the name 'Curio' had posted over 500 messages that accused Aquino of having participated in heinous crimes, sexual perversions and acts of moral turpitude, according to Aquino's lawyers. The case against the internet company ElectriCiti was thrown out of court.[10]

Notwithstanding the controversies and ToS' position on keeping the details of its development as a religious movement private, there can be no

Satanic Violence

Violent Scripture
- Violence is explicitly expressed in the writings of some sacred scriptures.

Vengeance
- The law of retaliation is one of the fundamental guiding principles of Satanic religions.

Sacrifice
- Traditional Satanic group doctrines require sacrifice (holy offerings); these have led to crimes from animal mutilation to murder.

doubt that the Temple of Set is a highly organized, sophisticated, influential and flourishing Satanic religion.

Violent Scripture

Violence is not blatantly evident in the rituals of the Church of Satan, Temple of Set or Ordo Temple Orientis (O.T.O.); however, sacred violence is explicitly expressed in several verses of the revered holy scriptures of the O.T.O. In Chapter III of *Liber Al vel Legis*, also known as *The Book of the Law*, Crowley, the Thelemite prophet, states:

> III, 11: Worship me with fire and blood; worship me with swords and with spears. Let the woman be girt with a sword before me; let blood flow to my name. Trample down the Heathen; be upon them, O warrior, I will give you of their flesh to eat!
>
> III, 12: sacrifice cattle, little and big; after a child.
>
> III, 18: mercy let be off; damn them who pity! Kill and torture; spare not; be upon them!
>
> III, 24: The best blood is of the moon, monthly; then the fresh blood of a child, or dropping from the host of heaven; then of enemies; then of the priest or of the worshippers; last of some beast, no matter what.
>
> III, 34: Another prophet shall arise, and bring fresh fever from the skies; another woman shall awake the lust and worship of the Snake; another soul of God and beast shall mingle in the globed priest; another sacrifice shall stain the tomb; another king shall reign.

> III, 51: With my hawk's head I peck at the eyes of Jesus as he hangs
> upon the cross.
> III, 52: I flap my wings in the face of Mohammed and blind him.
> III, 53: With my claws I tear out the flesh of the Indian and the
> Buddhist, Mongol and Din.
> III, 55: Let Mary inviolate be torn upon wheels; for her sake let all
> chaste women be utterly despised among you![11]

It is quite apparent from only these few verses that *The Book of the Law* is the antithesis of Christianity. Crowley's final comments at the end of the text mandate that Thelemites interpret the holy scripture of *The Book of the Law* for themselves. It is possible that the book could be interpreted as some form of allegory, however, there can be no doubt that Thelemite holy scripture advocates violence, is anti-Christian, anti-Islamic and thoroughly Satanic. Although Thelemite rituals do not explicitly contain violence, it is highly probable that violence could arise from a general philosophy of "Do what thou wilt shall be the whole of the Law."

Vengeance

The *Lex Talionis*, 'law of retaliation,' is a common form of sacred violence and one of the fundamental guiding principles of Satanic religions. *Lex Talionis* is also the basis for retributivist justifications for punishment, such as the death penalty in the U.S. It is associated with the Old Testament maxim of an eye for an eye and a tooth for a tooth.

Essentially, retributivist accounts of punishment are viewed as a 'paying back,' retribution for past offenses. A person has been wronged and the state is justified in inflicting the same degree of harm that the perpetrator inflicted on the victim. Essentially, retribution is legal revenge administered by designated authorities to prevent vigilantism from leading to a cycle of mutual revenge. Satanic churches not only promote the Roman legal dictum of *Lex Talionis* (the punishment must fit the crime), but they also argue that it requires stricter and swifter enforcement. This concept is so important to Satanism that Satanic churches refer to *Lex Talionis* as *Lex Satanicus*.

This law of retaliation is one of the fundamental principles of the Church of Satan and is found in several of its tenets. It is the fifth of the nine Satanic Statements found in the *Satanic Bible*, "Satan represents vengeance instead of turning the other cheek." The *Book of Satan* portion of the *Satanic Bible* is quite clear on this issue:

> 7. Hate your enemies with a whole heart, and if a man
> smite you on one cheek, smash him on the other!;

smite him hip and thigh, for self-preservation is the highest law!

9. Give blow for blow, scorn for scorn, doom for doom — with compound interest liberally added thereunto! Eye for eye, tooth for tooth, aye four-fold, a hundred-fold![12]

Finally, the application of the *Lex Talionis* is found in the third point of the Church of Satan's Pentagonal Revisionism's five-point program:

We call for the re-establishment of Lex Talionis throughout human society. The Judeo-Christian tradition which exists secularly under the guise of liberal humanism has exalted the criminal over the victim, taking responsibility away from the wrongdoer with their doctrine of forgiveness. Such thinking is a disgrace towards the ideal of justice…. Satanists are particularly disgusted by the extraordinary level of criminal activity which abounds today and advocate a return to the Roman "Lex Talionis"; let the punishment fit in kind and degree to the crime. To achieve this, we would be pleased to see the institution of an elite police force, of men and women in peak physical and mental condition, trained in advance techniques of crime fighting who would be truly equipped to handle the vermin that make so many of our cities into little more than concrete jungles. Man is by nature a social creature and makes his social contract with his fellows, thus rules of conduct are established to allow maximum freedom for individuals to interact. Disobey those rules and punishment should be swift and sure, and most probably public as well.[13]

The Satanic concept of Lex Talionis is consistent with Satanism's political Social Darwinian philosophy and its promotion of eugenics. Eugenics is advocated in the first point of Pentagonal Revisionism and is referred to as *stratification*, by which each member of society reaches a level commensurate with his own development based on the principle of survival of the strongest.

In the first chapter of Rene Girard's classic text titled *Violence and the Sacred*, he addresses the concept of retribution. He demonstrates that the institution of sacrifice and the judicial system share the same functions: to subdue violence, stifle the impulse to vengeance and stop it from escalating into an endless cycle of uncontrolled reciprocal violence. "The procedures that keep men's violence in bounds have one thing in common: they are no strangers to the ways of violence. There is reason to believe that they are all rooted in religion.... Whether it be through sacrificial killing or legal punishment, the problem is to forestall a series of reprisals."[14]

Modern Satanists hold the same fundamental premise of violence and human nature as put forth in Girardian theory. Satanists maintain that humans are violent by nature; they recognize mimetic desire and consider rituals of sacrifice to be sacred and necessary to defer violence. The significant difference is that Satanists embrace these attributes and manipulate them for their own agendas. They are completely cognizant of mimetic rivalries and not only welcome them but instigate them, which of course is what makes them authentically Satanic. Since Satanists advocate indulgence in human desires, it logically follows that they recognize the need for strict punishments. The *Lex Talionis* is attractive to Satanists because it provides them with a cultural mechanism for dealing with what they deem to be unacceptable behavior, indulging in the emotion of revenge and as a method of enforcing their Darwinian ideology.

The Satanic emphasis on revenge also serves as an excellent recruiting device because revenge is exactly what alienated teenagers often seek. Whether it is referred to as the *Lex Talionis*, retribution, retaliation or vengeance, it is one of the most significant manifestations of sacred violence because, without some system of conflict resolution regardless of whether it is in the form of religious sacrifice or the secular death penalty, there is always the threat of a cycle of uncontrolled reciprocal violence.

Satanic Responses to September 11, 2001

There were a variety of responses to September 11 from different Satanic groups, most of whom expressed their condolences, informed their members if anyone was injured, and provided hyperlinks to donate blood or money. Of course, their acknowledgment of the tragedy had a particularly Satanic perspective. For example, Grand Magister Blackwood of the Worldwide Order of Satanists posted on his website, "September 11, 2001, a day to which the stupidity of those who believe in god crap and their stupid holy war shit has taken lives. As Satanists we can not let the screwballs win this war. I plead with every Satanist out there to donate blood and save a life. We know that god does not exist and it is up to real people to step in and save someone who may need it."[15]

Satanic Priests, like other American clergy, wrote sermons concerning the tragic events and interpreted the theological implications for their followers. Obviously *Lex Satanicus/Lex Talionis* was explicitly expressed in many

Satanic Responses to Sept. 11th

Worldwide Order of Satanists

- I plead with every Satanist out there to donate blood and save a life. We know that god does not exist and it is up to real people to step in and save someone who may need it.

Church of Satan

- The Fifth Satanic Statement from the Satanic Bible says, "Satan represents vengeance, instead of turning the other cheek..." They call us The Great Satan. It is time for our nation to play that role with grim purpose.

Satanic responses to the events of September 11. Peter Gilmore, High Priest of the Church of Satan, wrote on the website:

> Moving among my fellow New Yorkers, it was heartening to hear residents of this city calling-out for the blood of those who are the cause of these acts of war, as well as for the punishment of those who shield, support, or otherwise sympathize with terrorists. The philosophy of Satanism is clear on such issues: the Fifth Satanic Statement from the Satanic Bible says "Satan represents vengeance instead of turning the other cheek …." Many of the people of this nation now share this point of view. Yesterday, Americans saw things they hold as precious being shattered by those who view our society as being the adversary of the theocracy they wish to establish. They call us The Great Satan. It is time for our nation to play that role with grim purpose.[16]

Lord Egan, the High Priest of the First Church of Satan, discussed his church's position on the attacks on its website:

> On September 11, in the Year One, commercial airliners were highjacked by a group of Islamic fundamentalists who perceived the United States as 'the Great Satan'…. On behalf of the First Church of Satan, I wish to express our profound sorrow and grief for the tragic loss of life and suffering…. Rather than shun evil, we should strive to understand it, for without darkness

there can be no light. We must strive to close the gap
which separates God from Satan because, if we don't,
millions more will die. The split mind theology is part
of our national heritage, an international psychosis.
Good and evil cannot be divided as quintessential ab-
solutes, for certainly there are strengths and weaknesses
in everyone. Furthermore, spiritual salvation does not
require blind obedience to the will of a messiah. Satanists speak of a process where by we continue to
challenge ourselves and strip away the layers of blind-
ness which separate us from our own humanity.... I
am understandably opposed to rhetoric used by leaders
who refer to these terrorists as "evil".... However, I am
not opposed to the use of force against those who initiate force, therefore we support U.S. President George
W. Bush, British Prime Minister Tony Blair and others
who have called for military action.[17]

Patriotism is not lost on Satanists; some added American flags to their
websites in recognition of their support. However, since it is obviously
against their beliefs to write statements such as "God bless America," Grand
Magister Blackwood of the Temples of Satan wrote "Hail America" as in
"Hail Satan" under the image of the American flag. A European Satanic
organization called the Black Order of the Trapezoid wrote "God hates U.S.
All!" under an American flag. The Black Order of the Trapezoid, similar to
many other Satanic groups, openly advocates neo-Nazism and merged it
with Satanism. The Order's response to September 11 was that the U.S.
provoked the attack with its foreign policy and took the opportunity to curse
the U.S. government.

Unfortunately, many Satanic groups used the tragic events of September
11 as an opportunity to recruit young Americans by appealing to their fresh
emotions of revenge, disillusionment and insecurity. Modern Satanists fundamentally understand the nature of sacred violence and how to manipulate
a political situation so that ordinarily peaceful people will engage in violence
as a necessary religious obligation. Trapped in a cycle of righteous revenge,
they have no remorse because sacred violence is always justified.

Sacrifice (Ritual Homicide)

Satanic sacred violence is manifested in both overt and covert ways. The most
obvious example of Satanic sacred violence is sacrifice, deriving from the
Latin *sacrificare*, literally meaning *to make holy*. One modern Satanic concept

Order of the Nine Angles

- Traditional Satanic group.
- Satanism mixed with Social Darwinism (white supremacy).
- Based in Britain, claims to be a secret society.
- Website has "Guide to Human Sacrifice."
- Describes in detail targeting a victim, ritually murdering and disposing of the body.
- Justifies sacrifice as "culling out the weak," those who are a liability to evolution; an act of natural justice.

of sacrifice is based on an ancient one that entails a religious offering or gift to a supreme being in which the offering is consecrated through its destruction. This practice is very controversial, and all the Satanic religions discussed (Ordo Templi Orientis, the Church of Satan and the Temple of Set) have issued disclaimers vehemently stating that they do not engage in Satanic ritual abuse, blood rituals or any form of animal or human sacrifice.

However, one traditional Satanic group openly promotes sacrifice, a British-based organization called the Order of the Nine Angles or ONA. Its website provides a guide to human sacrifice, which advocates both voluntary and involuntary sacrifice (murder). The ONA have three methods of involuntary sacrifice: (1) by magical means, (2) by what they call the death ritual or direct killing of a person chosen as a sacrifice or (3) by assassination. The ONA describes ritual death as a powerful form of magick that has two purposes: it releases energy that can be directed or stored and it draws down dark forces which then can be used for specific goals. Their sacrificial rituals are described in detail on the ONA's web page. The ONA refers to human sacrifice as simply just another way of furthering the work of Satan:

> Voluntary sacrifice occurs every seventeen years as part of the Ceremony of Recalling: the one chosen becomes Immortal.... An involuntary sacrifice is when an individual or individuals are chosen by a group, Temple or Order. Such sacrifices are usually sacrificed on the Spring Equinox.... There are no restrictions concerning involuntary sacrifices other than that they are usually in some way opponents of Satanism or the satanic way of living.... Candidates are zealous interfering Nazarenes, those (e.g. journalists) attempting to disrupt in

some way established Satanists, Groups or Orders, political/business individuals whose activities are detrimental to the Satanist spirit, and those whose removal will aid the sinister dialectic and/or improve the human stock…. The victim or victims are brought or enticed to the area chosen for the Ritual, bound by the Guardian of the Temple and at the appropriate point in the Ritual sacrificed either by the Master or the Mistress using the sacrificial knife. The body or bodies are then buried or otherwise disposed of…. Those who participate in the Ritual of Sacrifice must revel in the deaths.[18]

In addition to groups such as the ONA, there are many examples of teenagers and young adult Youth Subculture Satanists who regularly kill animals in attempts to develop their magical skills. In fact, when examining a mutilated animal carcass, the most effective way to identify the perpetrator is by the level of skill evidenced in the attempted ritual sacrifice. Unfortunately, animal sacrifice can easily escalate to human sacrifice, especially when teenage dabblers can get detailed instructions instantaneously on the Internet.

Satanism on the Internet

Due to the provocative nature of this religion, the Internet has become the primary source for the substantial growth of the Satanic community. The World Wide Web provides a significant forum for recruiting new members, disseminating information and exchanging ideas. Satanic organizations, churches, support groups, occult suppliers and other organizations related to the Left Hand Path maintain hundreds of websites. In addition to individual websites, libraries, chat rooms, message boards and resource sites also appear on the Internet.

A few of the more active resource websites include the Satanic Network, the Australian Satanic Council, Devil Spawn and the 600 Club whose name is a deliberate parody of the Christian 700 club. There are so many Satanic websites that several awards are given to the best, including Lucifer's Top List and the Tomb of Darkness. Some hosts of the Satanic awards have their own websites listing the winners and including convenient hyperlinks. They include The Fire Within Top 100, The Best Satanic Sites on the Internet and Blacklist Top 100. The latter is truly disturbing because it has links to violent pornography, torture and images of actual murders.

Finally, as unimaginable as it may seem, there is Radio Free Satan, available 24 hours a day, advertised as the voice of Satan on the Internet. The Church of Satan recently announced the premiere of Satanism Today, another

Internet radio station, whose stated goals are to publicize the philosophy of the church and its membership. Topics include news from the Satanic perspective, applications of Satanic theory to daily life and practical applications of greater and lesser magic featuring a new guest each week and much more.

Similarities of Terrorists and Satanic Religions

There are many similarities between millennial religions, fundamental extremists and Satanists. First and foremost, they all claim that they are the chosen people, superior to other humans and frequently claim to be genetically different. In fact, in all my years of research, I have yet to come across a new religious movement that claimed to be inferior to others. Although the criteria determining who fits into their group differs according to individuals theologies, their hierarchal structures, group dynamics, and potential for violence are alike.

The most fundamental differences are determined by the criteria for followers which may be based on physical attributes especially race, intellectual abilities, commitment to the cause, being born into the group or any combination of the above characteristics. The significance for law enforcement is that many of these groups also have in common a theology that entails eugenics, culling out the weak and ideological programs to cultivate the perfect superhuman race. This is evident in the World Church of the Creator's program for genetic upgrading whose specific goals include, first and foremost, physically removing the alien mud races from their midst and sterilization of whomever they deem incurable misfits, idiots and the genetically diseased, the Church of Satan's Pentagonal Revisionism, referred to as 'stratification,' where each member of society reaches a level commensurate with his own development based on the principle of survival of the strongest and the Order of the Nine Angles guide to human sacrifice.

Just as the Aryan Nations is reaching out to Islamic fundamentalists, many white supremacists are merging with Satanic groups or blending ideologies. One example is the White Order of Thule, which incorporated Satanism into racist Odinism. The reason these differing religions can merge is because their fundamental beliefs are based on superiority and hatred for others. The violent consequences of having organizations such as white supremacists and Satanists merge is that in addition to acts of terrorism for religious political power, victims could also literally be sacrificed which entails torture, mutilation, etc. so the perpetrator can accumulate magical power. Although it is impossible to predict whether this trend of combining religious beliefs will continue, one thing is certain: individually or collectively, not one of these religions preaches tolerance.

References

1. *The Quran* (translated by Shakir, M.H.), Tahrike Tarsile, Elmhurst, NY, 1988, p. 259; *New American Standard Bible*, Moody, Press, Chicago, 1977, p. 61.

2. Miller, T., *America's Alternative Religions*, SUNY Press, Albany, 1995, p. 405; Mather, G. and Nichols, L., Eds., *Dictionary of Cults, Sects, Religions and the Occult*, Zondervan Publ., Grand Rapids, MI, 1993, p. 245; State of California Office of Criminal Justice Planning, *Occult Crime: A Law Enforcement Primer*, Sacramento, 1989, pp. 18–19.

3. *Apologetics Index*, 2001. http://www.gospelcom.net/apologeticsindex/c09c.html

4. Ordo Templi Orientis U.S. Grand Lodge website, History, p. 15. http://www.O.T.O.org/history.html

5. Ordo Templi Orientis U.S. Grand Lodge website, Intro to Thelema, p. 4. http://www.O.T.O.-usa.org/O.T.O./thelema.html

6. Ordo Templi Orientis U.S. Grand Lodge website, Intro to Thelema, pp. 1–2. http://www.O.T.O.-usa.org/O.T.O./thelema.html

7. Ordo Templi Orientis U.S. Grand Lodge website, Intro to Thelema, p. 4. http://www.O.T.O.-usa.org/O.T.O./thelema.html

8. LaVey, A.S., *The Satanic Bible*, Avon Books, New York, 1969, p. 25.

9. The Official Temple of Set World Wide Web Site. http://www.xeper.org/pub/tos/welcome.html

10. University of Virginia Religious Movements Homepage, Temple of Set Legal Problems, p. 4. http://religiousmovements.lib.virginia.edu/nrms/satanism/tempset.html

11. Ordo Templi Orientis U.S. Grand Lodge website, *The Book of the Law*, pp. 1, 2, 4. http://www.O.T.O.hq.org/O.T.O./1220.html

12. LaVey, A.S., *The Satanic Bible*, Avon Books, New York, 1969, p. 33.

13. Gilmore, P.H., *Satanism: The Feared Religion* (Church of Satan website), pp. 5, 6. http://www.churchofsatan.com/Pages/Feared.html

14. Girard, R., *Violence and the Sacred*, John Hopkins University Press, Baltimore, 1977, pp. 23, 25.

15. Blackwood, The Temples of Satan (formerly Worldwide Order of Satanists) website. http://www.geocities.com/thesatanic/blooddonate.html

16. Gilmore, P.H., *Satanic News on the March*, (Church of Satan website), pp. 3, 4. http://www.churchofsatan.com/Pages/News.html

17. Egan, L., *Confronting the Great Satan*, (First Church of Satan website) pp. 1–3. http://www.churchofsatan.org/main.html

18. Order of the White Wolf website, Order of the Nine Angles, *A Gift for the Prince: A Guide to Human Sacrifice*. http://members.easyspace.com/oww/satan/Satanism/Ona/Odoc10htm

Vampirism

6

Vampirism, like other religions, is practiced by people who commit themselves to an ideology, maintain ethical tenets within a hierarchical system and participate in rituals specific to their clans. Practitioners of Vampirism are referred to as Vampires and form part of an extensive subculture that includes Goths, Modern Primitives, Vampire Role Players and the Body Modification and Fetish Scenes. There are many facets to Vampire Culture and members range from dabblers, such as participants in Role-Playing Games, to the extremely devoted who are referred to as Real Vampires within the Vampire community. Vampire belief systems are dependent upon the person's or group's interpretation of a Vampire and may manifest simply as an aesthetic choice or an entire lifestyle based on a sophisticated Vampire philosophy.

Currently, there is a prevailing phenomenon of Modern Vampires whose serious commitment to their beliefs, community and culture meet the criteria for designation as a new religious movement. Vampirism is specific to Real Vampires and is practiced in Western society both individually and communally through many different organized Vampire groups variously referred to as clans, churches, covens, orders, houses and circles. There are many subgroups of the main clans and a significant number of individual unrelated, less known groups. Similar to other new religious movements, it is difficult to establish an accurate number of followers. Estimates range from 1000 to 100,000 self-identified Vampires throughout the world.

Vampire Culture, the most recent manifestation of the occult, has led to many crimes ranging from vandalism to murder. In addition to obvious criminal activity, Vampire Culture is relevant to law enforcement because many juveniles and young adults dabbling in the Goth movement are seduced into the more serious levels of the subculture — the Vampire and Fetish Scenes where blood rituals, sexual sadomasochism and bondage/discipline are regular occurrences.

Modern Vampires

- Vampires are real (but not immortal).
- Vampirism is a recognized religion by the U.S. federal government.
- Practitioners of Vampirism are called Vampires.
- There are a variety of Vampire religious groups referred to as clans, churches, covens, orders, houses and circles.
- Vampires are part of an extensive subculture that also includes Goths, Modern Primitives and the Body Modification and Fetish Scenes.

The Sanguinarium Ankh, the symbol of the largest Vampire group in America.

The dangers implicit in drinking and exchanging blood and violent sexual activities are more insidious when they are viewed as sacred rituals that are required for initiation, membership and status in the group. Many aspects of Vampire groups parallel gang dynamics, for example, specific identifying dress codes, symbols, language, and members sharing a sense of belonging in the group and alienation from mainstream society. Vampire Role-Playing Games such as "Vampire: The Masquerade" are also analogous to gangs in that players take on the persona of game characters who are members of enemy clans and engaged in brutal rivalries. The combination of Role-Playing Games, Vampire clubs and occult ideologies seduce young adults who unknowingly are entering a violent subculture.

Vampire Culture

Vampire Culture, more commonly called the Vampire Scene, refers to individuals, organizations, events, and businesses that share an interest in the Vampire lifestyle. There are many significant distinctions within Vampire Culture inclusive of Real Vampires, Vampire Role Players, Vampire Lifestylers, Goths, Modern Primitives and participants in the Body Modification and

Vampire Culture

- **Real Vampires:** seriously committed to the culture and members of clans
- **Vampire Lifestylers:** identify with the culture but have not yet committed
- **Vampire Role Players:** entry level, participate in vampire role-playing games
- **Goth Scene:** entry level through music, clothes, style
- **Body Modification Scene:** tattooing, piercing, cutting,
- **Modern Primitives:** body mutilation for spiritual reasons
- **Fetish Scene:** hardcore sadomasochism

Law Enforcement Issues

- **Blood Rituals:** drinking and exchanging blood, mutilation and self-mutilation
- **Sadomasochism:** bondage/ discipline, violent sexual activities
- **Role-Playing Games:** leading to violence, suicide, homicide
- **Vampire Cults:** blood rituals escalating to murder

Fetish Scenes. Participation in these movements is not mutually exclusive and members of the various groups interact in scene nightclubs.

Real Vampires engage in blood rituals, are often members of organized religious groups and are seriously committed to the lifestyle. Vampire Role Players pretend to be Vampires in Role-Playing Games but do not identify themselves as Vampires. Lifestylers identify with Real Vampires but have not completely committed to the culture. Vampire Role Players and Lifestylers frequently escalate to the more serious level of Real Vampires. Vampires also distinguish themselves from Goths and the Gothic Scene, although their aesthetic styles are similar and many times they attend the same clubs. The differentiating criterion is that Goths do not become members of clans or adopt a Vampire ideology; however, they are prime candidates for recruitment into the hard-core groups.

The Modern Primitive, Body Modification and Fetish Movements all entail similar activities fundamental to Vampire Culture. The Modern Primitive Movement is a term that is used in the *avant-garde* art world to describe visual artists who distort, manipulate, mutilate and mark their bodies as a form of ritual performance. The expression *primitive* is a deliberate reference to the pejorative anthropological term denoting pre-modern indigenous societies whose customs included tattooing, piercing and endurance rituals. The Modern Primitive Movement blends tribal traditions with technology to combine magic and science. The Body Modification Movement includes people who are involved in piercing, tattooing, branding, implants and extreme body modification but do not have a unifying ideology. They differ

Vampire Style

- Clothing referred to as "Garb" reflects the Victorian or Edwardian eras.
- Bondage jewelry and clothing, chains, leather, corsets, masks, restraints.
- Vampire names derived from literature.
- Name prefixes such as Lord/Lady, Master/ Mistress, Marquise/ Marquette denote status in a clan.
- Fangs (real teeth).
- Piercings, tattoos, scarring, implants.
- Theatrical contact lens.

"Garb," Vampire style clothing for sale at a Vampire Scene store in New York City.

from Modern Primitives who claim their performances are spiritual experiences of transformation.

Finally, the Fetish Scene entails nightclubs where members of all of the Vampire-related movements come together to engage in all manner of sado-masochism, sexual bondage and blood rituals. Vampire Culture is a serious and growing phenomenon that holds gatherings where thousands of Vampires attend. The largest gathering, called Endless Night, is held in New Orleans throughout Halloween. Equivalent European gatherings include Vampyria and the Whitby Vampire Festival.

Vampire Culture has an extremely unique style that has observable recognizable characteristics. The most obvious identifying feature of the culture is clothing, referred to as garb. Clothing usually reflects a historical era such as Victorian or Edwardian, and entails black capes, top hats, long dresses with low bodices and an assortment of chains, corsets, whips and a variety of other bondage fetish-style accessories. Preferred colors are usually red, black and purple.

Another truly unique trait of Vampire Culture is the use of fangs, both real and fake. When a follower decides to have real fangs implanted in his mouth it symbolizes a serious commitment to the culture and can be viewed as the equivalent of a confirmation ritual. Other characteristics of the subculture include use of language and etiquette intrinsic to the Vampire Scene in that it imbues religious customs, ethical behavior and instills a feeling of community. Some Modern Vampires signify themselves by spelling Vampire with a *y* which distinguishes them from Hollywood, mythological and fictional references.

Common conventions and expressions include "The awakening," which alludes to initial attraction to the Vampire scene, and is also referred to as "the birth to darkness" or "the becoming." A Sire is a Vampire parent, which can be a parent and child, lovers, or friends — anyone who guides a fledging to his Vampire nature. The fledgling or childe is an initiate until he moves up to the next level. Mundanes signify non-Vampires and people who do not support the lifestyle. Swans refer to those who are aware of the culture but choose not to partake. Black Swans are tolerant of the lifestyle while White Swans disapprove and try to persuade family members or friends to leave the scene. Fittingly, *black* is a positive term and *white* is a negative term in Vampire Culture.

Other conventions include Vampire or Scene names which are aliases derived from various historical, mythological and biblical sources. Prefixes such as Lord, Lady, Marquis, Marquise, Mistress, and Master denote status in a clan. Distinctive Vampire greetings entail variations of the joining of hands and kissing of hands and cheeks. Music is dominated by Gothic; other music genres include industrial, classical, punk, techno and a variety of other forms. Some of the more popular Vampire bands are Inkubus Sukkubus, Type O Negative, Nosferatu and Malkador. Wine is the drink of choice and some Vampires will partake of absinthe although it is illegal in the U.S. and most European countries.

The above-mentioned characteristics expressed in clothing, language, etiquette and music are specific to Vampire Culture and are what distinguish followers from both traditional and a variety of other occult religious movements. Many people are introduced to the Vampire scene through the Role-Playing Game "Vampire: The Masquerade." Others are introduced through the erotic nature of the lifestyle and many more through popular literature such as Anne Rice's series of books, *The Vampire Chronicles*. However, similar to Satanic groups, the most renowned source for reaching new members, disseminating information and gathering is the Internet, which contains thousands of websites for Vampire organizations, churches, support groups, suppliers, etc. Vampires pride themselves on their use of graphics and technology to create the most distinguished and intricate websites.

Real Vampires

Since there is no agreed-upon definition of what constitutes a Vampire, the modern Vampire is an amalgamation of characteristics derived from a variety of historical and cross-cultural archetypes. The subculture, like the Vampire, evolved from a combination of folktales, cultural myths, legends and even-

Real Vampires

- The modern Vampire is a combination of characteristics derived from a variety of historical and cross-cultural folktales, cultural myths and legends.

Characteristics:

- **"Feeding":** acquiring energy from others either through blood or the psychic energy of others
- **Blood:** drinking and bloodletting (feeding circles)
- **Sadomasochism:** bondage/discipline, vampire as predator, hunter

tually the romanticized images found in Hollywood films and popular novels. An essential unique attribute specific to practitioners of Vampirism is the inherent ability to acquire strength and energy from either empathic capability, imbibing blood or drawing from the psychic energy of others. The latter practice is referred to as Psychic Vampirism, which has its origins in ancient folktales that identified Vampires as evil gods or demons and in medieval legends as incubus/succubus entities.

In the 19th century when science started studying the paranormal through psychical research, the Psychic Vampire was viewed as a ghost-like figure as opposed to the contemporary conception of a Vampire who acquires immortality as a resuscitated body. One of the two primary forms of Psychic Vampirism relates to the concept of the astral body and maintains that there is a second invisible body that can separate from the physical body, usually at the moment of death. Astral Vampirism is the ability to send one's astral body to attack others.

The second more common form of Psychic Vampirism is sometimes termed Magnetic Vampirism and refers to the ability to drain the life force of another person simply by being in his presence. Most contemporary Vampire religious philosophies entail one or both forms of Psychic Vampirism. The ability to acquire energy from others, called *feeding* in the Vampire community, is considered intrinsic to Vampire predatory nature. A dispute among Vampire churches concerns whether it is ethical to feed off of the blood or psyche of an unwilling donor. Since the acquisition of human life force is the fundamental core of all Vampiric teachings, distinctive methods of assimilating life energy distinguish the individual rituals, fundamental principles and philosophy of each Vampire church.

The practice most readily identified with Vampirism is blood drinking and bloodletting. A group of members who imbibe blood are referred to as a *feeding circle*. Unlike media depictions, Vampires rarely bite each other on the neck. They usually use razor blades to make cuts into each other's bodies and suck the blood from those cuts. It is important to clarify that not all Vampires engage in this practice. Each church has an official position concerning blood drinking/letting, ranging from a neutral view of simply recognizing that it exists without encouraging it to treating the practice as the highest sacred act of Vampire worship. All churches post disclaimers concerning the high risk of contracting bloodborne diseases and emphasize that blood play should only be practiced by consenting adults who have had blood testing and are aware of each other's status. Even with official disclaimers, blood drinking/letting is sanctioned, extremely prevalent in the Vampire community and often engaged in publicly at nightclubs, private havens and churches.

Another characteristic immediately associated with the Vampire and related to blood drinking is immortality or more specifically life after death. More than any other attribute, the conception of immortality held by Real Vampires differs from mythological and fictional accounts that portray a person rising from the grave and maintaining mortality by drinking the blood of living people. For Real Vampires, immortality is achieved in similar ways to other religious traditions. In some instances the Vampire God(s) will rise again to restore faithful Vampires to their original state. For other groups, immortality is a form of reincarnation. Additionally, some Vampires already consider themselves immortal by virtue of their ability to consciously connect to their incarnations and walk in both the spiritual and physical realms. None of the Vampire religious groups claim to achieve immortality exclusively or instantaneously through the imbibing of blood.

A custom frequently affiliated with the Vampire Scene includes bondage/discipline sexual activity, fetishism and sadomasochism. This is related to the characteristic of the Vampire as predator/hunter and is a mandatory ritual in some religious groups to achieve higher levels of spirituality. Participants are referred to as regnant (master) and thrall (slave). This involves an aspect of Vampire magic termed "True Name" which is a variation on the sadomasochism safety word. In Vampire religion, sadomasochism is theologically one form of feeding because according to the *Vampire Codex*, a spiritual interpretation of Vampirism, energy coupled with strong emotion is more fulfilling than simple energy alone.

According to the *Codex*, the most intense emotion to feed off of is fear and the next is ecstasy either sexual or religious. Sadomasochism in the form of Vampire religious ritual provides a combination of all three emotions, hence it is an intense form of assimilating energy from another. Real Vampires retain a high status in the subculture and are well respected within the Vampire community.

Vampire Role Players

- Vampire role players take on a role/character/ personality/alter ego in a Vampire role-playing game and then act it out either on the Internet or among a group in real life.
- Role-playing games are extremely popular among juveniles and young adults.
- Games are based on occult ideologies and inspire acts of violence that are described in the role-playing game.
- Games inspire players to join Vampire religious groups whose theologies are strikingly similar to the game.

Vampire Role Players

Role-Playing Games evolved from war games and military simulations and go beyond typical board games, video games and Internet games to constitute a form of improvisational theater. The participant takes on a role/character/ personality/alter ego in a fantasy world and then acts it out either on the Internet or among a group in real life. Role-Playing Games are extremely popular among juveniles and young adults who are typically above average in intelligence, creativity and imagination. They have been the subject of intense debates since the 1970s with the extreme popularity of the game "Dungeons and Dragons."

Role-Playing Games center on an alternative fantasy world that players enter as actual characters. The characters have specific attributes, a variety of weapons and special skills. Some games are led by a game master or storyteller who determines the starting point of the game and guides the course of activity through traps and other situations. Controversial issues concerning Role-Playing Games such as "Dungeons and Dragons" continue to be the subject of many disputes. In 1985, Dr. Thomas Radedki, a psychiatrist at the University of Illinois School of Medicine, argued that the game caused young men to kill themselves. Radecki documented 123 cases of homicides and suicides attributed to "Dungeons and Dragons" and testified as an expert witness in eight murder trials in which the game was implicated. "Radecki claimed brutal murders, rapes, and crimes have been patterned after characters players concoct in the game. He cited one example in which a nineteen-year old Utah boy choked, raped and sadistically disposed of a fourteen-year old girl. Radecki surmised that the murderer/rapist, who slaughtered evil female Dungeons and Dragons characters to survive in the game, was unable to distinguish fantasy from reality when he committed the heinous crime."[1]

The debates about the influence of Role-Playing Games on violence were at their peak in the 1980s — the same time when allegations of Satanic Ritual Abuse were being taken seriously. Unfortunately, in the 1990s, there was a backlash against both allegations claiming that Satanic Ritual Abuse and Role-Playing Games were part of a Satanic panic. Additionally, the huge amount of profits generated by the games silenced negative publicity and serious research, which resulted in the allegations being much more difficult to prove. Causal relationships of the effects of violence inspired by the media, games and music are notoriously difficult to establish and rarely hold up in court. Although at this time only a small percentage of crimes are committed due to violent influences of Role-Playing Games, there is no doubt that they are occurring. Role-Playing Games are the most dangerous of the interactive games because the player takes on an entire persona and experiences the attributes of the character. The threat is that an alienated, disaffected teenager gets a taste for power, revenge, violence and respect that he does not receive in real life and decides to remain in character even when the game is over.

The most popular Role-Playing Game since "Dungeons and Dragons" is focused on Vampires and is called "Vampire: The Masquerade." It is based on a virtual fantasy world called the World of Darkness where Vampires have control but vie for power among themselves. Published in 1991, "Vampire: The Masquerade" has tens of thousands of players and although it is a fantasy game, it is modeled closely on reality. Since the history of the Vampires is based on actual events in human history, the stories presented in the many books that accompany the game are quite plausible and although fictional are similar to the theologies of current Vampire religions.

Vampires in the game are known collectively as the Kindred who are descended from Caine — a reference to the Biblical Cain who, in Genesis, killed his brother and was afflicted with an undesignated curse. In the World of Darkness, Caine is cursed with eternal life and a craving for blood for his crime of killing his brother, Abel. After wandering in the wilderness for many years, Caine lived among mortals and created a number of Vampires by draining victims of their blood and filling them with some of his in a ritual known as the Embrace. These Vampires then created more of their kind through subsequent Embraces.

Caine's children inherited his blood thirst and Vampiric powers, however, with each new generation, the powers weaken until in the 21st century, the Vampires are in their sixth and seventh generations and are cautioned not to create more because their descendants will not be able to defend themselves. Interestingly, the fictional Vampire theology that interprets the Bible

Vampire: the Masquerade

- A popular role-playing game that focuses on Vampires and is based on the fantasy virtual world called the "World of Darkness."
- Vampires have control of the world but are vying for power among themselves. Stories are similar to the theology of current Vampire religions.
- One guidebook is especially pertinent to law enforcement because it provides specific details of gang warfare, including combat maneuvers, weapons and a section called Sect Justice where they advocate vandalism, torture, mutilation and murder.
- *Vampire: the Masquerade* is a virtual guidebook for gang activity.

to explain Vampire nature, origins and superiority is similar to white supremacist and occult religious groups that also interpret the Bible to explain their origins and superiority.

In "Vampire: The Masquerade," the Kindred get along for many years until the Inquisition where they are persecuted as heretics and infidels and almost entirely annihilated. To avoid total destruction, the remaining survivors had to conceal their vampire nature, hence the concept of the Masquerade where the Vampires pass themselves off as humans. The goal of the Masquerade is not only to remind Vampires to pose as humans but also to persuade humans that the Vampires have all been wiped out or never existed. During the Inquisition, most of the kindred joined together in an organization known as the Camarilla who recognize the authority of more powerful Vampires known as Justicers. Justicers discipline Vampires who bring unwanted human attention to them.

The Camarilla is made up of separate clans each with its own name, history and distinguishing characteristics. Some clans choose not to join the Camarilla but instead compete against it for control. Finally, internal struggles erupt within the organization. Since each clan has its own special qualities, role players choose which clan best matches their personality or a person they wish to be so that their character can be more realistic.

In the famous case of the Kentucky Vampire murder described in detail at the end of this chapter, Rod Ferral said he became interested in Vampire Culture through the game and was acting out a specific character in "Vampire: The Masquerade" when he tortured animals, started his own clan and eventually murdered two people.

In addition to the clans of the Camarilla, other opposing groups include those belonging to the Sabbat. The Sabbat clans are centered in the northeastern U.S. and are heavily involved in a power struggle for New York City. Unlike the Camarilla who attempt to solve problems through political influence, Sabbat clans opt for violence and force. The guidebook to the Sabbat is especially pertinent to law enforcement in that it provides specific details of gang warfare including combat maneuvers and weapons. A section titled "Sect Justice" advocates vandalism, torture, mutilation and murder. Another section of the book describes what is called a War Party where packs compete against each other for the privilege of killing the elder. Finally, specific blood rituals are held on particular dates and magical rites become increasingly dangerous at each level.

"Vampire: The Masquerade" is a virtual guidebook for gang activity. The clans in the book war with each other and all of them are at war with humanity. The very essence of the Vampire lifestyle is that it has to remain secret so that Vampires will not be destroyed by humans. The symbolism is obvious; humans represent the established society whose members, of course, are inferior to the Vampires. This allows alienated juveniles to indulge in a fantasy in which they are characters that have more power and control and are generally superior to everyone else. If there is still any doubt that "Vampire: The Masquerade" is potentially dangerous consider that the publisher decided to reduce liability in the event of future lawsuits by placing a disclaimer in every book stating, "This book uses the supernatural for settings, characters and themes. All mystical and supernatural elements are fiction and intended for entertainment purposes only. Reader discretion is advised."[2] In addition to the possibility of inspiring acts of violence that are described in the Role-Playing Game, "Vampire: The Masquerade" has even more potential for inspiring players to join Vampire religious groups whose theologies are strikingly similar to the imaginary World of Darkness. The players then advance from the fictional realm to become Real Vampires.

The Goth Movement

Most law enforcement agents were introduced to the Goth movement on April 20, 1999, when Eric Harris, 18, and Dylan Klebold, 17, killed 12 students and a teacher and wounded 23 others before shooting themselves at Columbine High School in Littleton, CO. Harris and Klebold were part of the Trenchcoat Mafia, a group of teenagers who were dabbling with the Goth movement.

The Columbine incident was not a true reflection of the Goth scene. Harris and Klebold were also fascinated with Satanism, violent computer games and Nazi culture. They chose Hitler's birthday as the day of the shoot-

The Goth Movement

- Goth is a counter-cultural movement, a rebellion against the establishment.
- Goths dabble in occult religions; some get involved in Satanism, Vampire religions or witchcraft.
- For many, the Goth movement is a phase they will grow out of; others may be recruited into one of the many organized occult religious groups.

Characteristics of Goths
- Juveniles
- Black clothing
- Black lipstick, nail polish
- Make-up that makes them appear pale
- Unusual hairstyles
- Tattoos, piercings
- Distinct musical styles
- Fascination with death

ing. They were initially identified with Goth culture because they dressed in black, listened to Marilyn Manson music and had a general philosophy of nihilism. The Goth scene is filled with juveniles and young adults who wear black clothing, black lipstick, nail polish and other make-up that makes them appear pale and have unusual hairstyles. Although Goths listen to distinct musical styles and are fascinated with death, immortality and dark emotions, they are generally nonviolent.

Goths constitute an integral part of Vampire Culture. Most teenagers who enter the Vampire Scene are first introduced through the Goth movement. Juveniles and young adults who feel alienated or self-impose their alienation embrace this dark subculture. For many, it serves as a response to not fitting in or being the target of bullies. It is essentially a refuge that provides a sense of community and belonging with others who feel they do not fit in. Others enter the movement because they are attracted to the music, the rebellion and the opportunity to be different. Essentially, Goth activity is a counter-cultural movement that expresses an explicit nonconformist attitude against the dominant establishment.

The terms *Goth* and *Gothic* have always been associated with mystery, darkness and fear. Goths originally referred to an ancient European tribe famous for bringing about the fall of the Roman Empire. Due to their history of pillaging and looting, the term *Gothic* became associated with being barbaric, uncivil and cruel. During the Renaissance, Italian scholars believed the classical arts were corrupted by the savage Goths who influenced a style of medieval architecture prevalent from the 12th to 15th centuries. Gothic architecture is characterized by ornate cathedrals with pointed arches, flying buttresses and statues of gargoyles that reflect the intense mysticism of the Middle Ages. In the late 18th and early 19th centuries, the term was applied to a genre of literature. Gothic novels were typically frightening stories set in castles with ghosts and supernatural events.

Today the term *Goth* refers to a subculture that began in the late 1970s. There is no single definition of *Goth*. Goths have disputes among themselves as to who is a true Goth and who is what they term a poseur. The Goth movement originated in London as a musical style when bands famous for advocating anarchy, despair and futility played at a nightclub called the Bat Cave. The style died out for a few years and then reemerged in the late 1980s in the United Kingdom and the United States with bands like Nosferatu, Mortal Coil and Marilyn Manson. Vampire imagery is frequently found in Goth band names and lyrices such as Type O Negative, Vampire Slave and Blood Flag. The Goth music scene became the basis for a distinct view of the world and soon evolved into an entire subculture.

In addition to being famous for wearing black clothes, Goths accessorize with chains and symbolic jewelry such as ankhs, crosses and daggers. Pierced body parts and anything that looks nonconformist is prevalent in Goth fashion. Dark clothing combined with pale make-up and black lipstick presents an overall image of death. Goths dabble in occult religions; some become involved in Satanism, Vampire religions or witchcraft. For many, the Goth movement is a phase they will grow out of; others may be recruited into one of the many organized occult religious groups.

Although Vampire Culture and the Goth movement support each other, they differ in the degree of commitment expected of members. Goths are dabblers and the Goth scene introduces juveniles and young adults into the blood rituals, sadomasochism and sexual bondage traditions of the Vampire and Fetish Scenes.

Blood Rituals

Blood is intrinsic to Vampire Culture. As described in Chapter 1, blood is extremely significant in religious ideology. There are specific rituals, attitudes and prohibitions on the use of blood in almost every society. Whether animal or human, blood historically is the mandatory substance for religious ritual and sacrifice is the ultimate religious experience. Symbolically, blood represents both purity and impurity, the sacred and the profane, life and death.

Throughout history and across cultures, people attributed sacred and magical qualities to blood, and blood rituals entailed everything from drinking blood, pouring it on the body and a variety of uses in ceremonies. In some cultures, it was believed that drinking the blood of a victim would endow the drinker with the victim's strength. Similarly, drinking the blood of an animal was believed to endow the drinker with the animal's qualities, hence the myth about Vampires having the characteristics of a bat. Blood has

---

Blood Rituals

- Throughout history and across cultures, people attributed sacred and magical qualities to blood.
- Blood rituals entail everything from drinking to pouring on the body and a variety of uses in ceremonies.
- In some cultures it was believed that drinking the blood of a victim would endow you with the victim's strength.
- Similarly, by drinking the blood of an animal you would acquire its qualities.
- For Modern Vampires, the use of blood is what separates the dabblers from the Real Vampires.

---

always held a prominent position in Vampire history, myths and symbolism, particularly since Vampires were traditionally bloodsucking creatures. For Modern Vampires the use of blood is what separates the dabblers from the Real Vampires.

In Vampire Culture, the use of blood is commonly referred to as blood sports, blood play, blood lust and blood fetishism and is an expression of sexual, spiritual, recreational or artistic activities that involve cutting the body and drinking blood. Blood rituals in the form of sacred acts of worship are fundamental to Real Vampire religious beliefs. Blood sports in the form of recreational and/or sexual activities are some of the most dangerous aspects of Vampire culture and are noticeably increasing in popularity.

Blood play involves cutting the body and having another person lick or suck the blood from the cut. Cutting is most often done by using a surgical scalpel or fine razor blade to make shallow cuts in the top layer of the skin. At many Vampire nightclubs, it is not unusual to see a group of people cutting each other and sucking each other's blood in what is referred to as a feeding circle. Blood play is frequently intertwined with sexual activities and becomes an integral part of the shared intimacy. Occasionally, blood sports entail using a syringe to draw blood and then imbibing it or sharing the blood with a partner. Essentially, blood sports include any sadomasochistic practice that involves blood and encompasses all forms of body mutilation such as self-scarring, play-piercing and cutting.

Katherine Ramsland, author of several books of Vampire fiction, entered the world of Real Vampires as an investigative journalist and wrote a non-fiction book titled *Piercing the Darkness: Undercover with Vampires in America Today*. In her 1998 book, she describes in nauseating detail many instances of blood rituals and sexual sadism and even provides an exhaustive descrip-

Blood Play

- The use of blood is commonly referred to as blood sports, blood play, blood lust and blood fetishism.
- Blood sports encompass all forms of body mutilation such as self-scarring, play-piercing in addition to cutting.
- Blood play involves cutting the body then having another person lick or suck the blood from the cut.
- Cutting is most often done with a surgical scalpel or fine razor blade making shallow cuts in the top layer of the skin.
- Occasionally, blood sports entail using a syringe to draw blood and then drinking it or sharing the blood.
- A group of people cutting and sucking each other's blood is referred to as a feeding circle.

tion of necrophilia. The events were related to her either through interviews with Vampires or she actually witnessed them.

Ramsland described a blood ritual involving a male and two females that she witnessed in a New York City apartment. "I smelled burning incense and saw a small glass container filled with dark liquid being heated on the stove. Several hypodermic needles lay on the counter nearby. One of the women, a blonde, who had streaked her long hair with ribbons of crimson, sat on a bed, leaning forward with a towel over her breasts. There was a scar on her shoulder that looked like a brand. Her back was bare, and the other woman had drawn several lines across it with a surgical blade. Blood ran in streams from these cuts toward a towel that was fast turning from white to red.... He wiped one of his fingers across DiDi's back and held it up covered in crimson. With a smile he put it into his mouth."[3] Every imaginable and unimaginable activity that entails blood occurs on a regular basis in the Vampire and Fetish Scenes.

To fully comprehend blood play, self-mutilation and masochism found in the Goth, Vampire and Fetish Scenes, it is important to have an understanding of how it evolved from movements in the art world and popular culture. Many expressions of the aesthetic are manifested in blood and flesh. The most familiar examples are evident in the current popularity of tattooing, piercing, branding and body modifications. These comprise the basic prerequisites for entry into the worlds of Modern Primitives, Vampire Culture and the Fetish Scene. These highly ritualized subcultures evolved out of various aesthetic styles such as Happenings, Body Art, Performance Art, Ritual Art and the Goth Movement.

Body Mutilation as Art

- Blood play, self-mutilation and masochism found in the Goth, Vampire and Fetish Scenes evolved from movements in the art world and popular culture.
- The goal of these artists is personal transformation and attempts to reclaim the spiritual.

Popular Culture:
- Tattooing
- Piercing
- Branding
- Body modifications

Art Movements:
- Viennese Actionism
- Happenings
- Body Art
- Performance Art
- Ritual Art
- Modern Primitives

Originally the goals of these artists was personal transformation and attempts to reclaim the spiritual. The result was unconventional forms of the sacred manifested in contemporary blood rituals found throughout the Vampire Scene.

Beginning in the 1960s and throughout the 1970s, several European artists performed ritualized violent actions that focused on the body. The most famous of these was a circle of Viennese artists that included Hermann Nitsch, Gunter Brus, Otto Muehl and Rudolph Schwartzkogler. Their work influenced many American artists in the 1990s and became known as Viennese Actionism. Nitsch conducted a series of performances titled "Orgies–Mysteries Theater" that frequently entailed dismemberment of animals, large quantities of blood and traditional religious symbolism. A 1974 performance titled "48th Action" at the Munich Modernes Theater involved the disembowelment of a slaughtered lamb whose entrails and blood were poured over a nude man, while the drained animal was strung up over his head.

Art historian Roselee Goldberg describes Nitsch's performance in terms of ritual: "Such activities sprang from Nitsch's belief that humankind's aggressive instincts had been repressed and muted through the media. Even the ritual of killing animals, so natural to primitive man, had been removed from modern-day experience. These ritualized acts were a means of releasing that repressed energy as well as an act of purification and redemption through suffering."[4] Nitsch is still conducting his Orgies–Mysteries Theaters; however, now they last as long as 6 days and are often protested by animal rights activists.

The most controversial of the Viennese artists is Rudolph Schwartzkogler who participated in Nitsch's actions and created works that he referred to as "artistic nudes — similar to a wreckage" in which he performed self-administered mutilations. He died violently on June 20, 1969, prompting several conflicting reports regarding the circumstances of his death. Art critic Robert Hughes, in a 1972 issue of *Time Magazine*, stated, "Schwartzkogler seems to have deduced that what really counts is not the application of paint, but the removal of surplus flesh. So he proceeded, inch by inch, to amputate his own penis, while a photographer recorded the act as an art event. In 1972, the resulting prints were reverently exhibited in that biennial motor show of Western art, Documenta V, at Kassel. Successive acts of self-amputation finally did Schwartzkogler in."[5]

American performance artist Chris Burden did not paint or sculpt a crucifixion; in 1974 in a work titled "Trans-Fixed," he had himself crucified to a car. In the 1970s, Burden's art performances also included having himself shot with a gun, punctured, burned and run over by a car. Burden's body became the ultimate sculptural material, the ultimate object.

Artist Gina Pane does art performances that consist of self-inflicted cuts to her body including her face. In 1971 she performed "Escalade Non-Anes-thesie" in which she climbed a ladder that had blades attached to the steps. In 1972, in a performance titled "The Conditioning" (Part I of "Auto Por-trait(s)," she laid down on an iron bed with very few crossbars that had 15 long candles burning underneath. Goldberg wrote that Gina Pane "believed that ritualized pain had a purifying effect and that using blood, fire, milk and the re-creation of pain as the elements of her performances she succeeded in her own terms 'in making the public understand right off that my body is my artistic material.'"[6] In 1974, in a performance titled "Psyche," Pane knelt in front of a mirror, put on make-up and proceeded to cut into her face with a razor blade. In 1975, in "Le Corps Pressenti," she made cuts between her toes with a razor blade so that the blood would create permanent stains on a plaster cast that her feet rested on.

Many body modifications in performance art parallel non-Western religious rituals of various cultures and eras and became known as the Modern Primitive Movement. "Performance artist Michael Journiac made a pudding with his own blood and offered it for consumption by his audience."[7] This is similar to the practice of auto-sacrifice by Aztec priests who drew their own blood as offerings.[8] "Australian artist Stelarc suspends himself in different environments by ropes attached to hooks driven through his flesh. Although he claims that these works are only involved with transcending normal human parameters including pain,"[9] they are reminiscent of rituals among some Plains and Northwest Coast tribal groups of North America.

Performance artist Fakir Musafar has made it clear that his intention is to perform live demonstrations of religious rituals and practices. Influenced by *National Geographic* and *Compton's Picture Encyclopedia*, "by the time he was twelve, Fakir had begun a systematic, personal exploration of virtually

Modern Primitives

- The Modern Primitive Movement is a term used in the art world to refer to visual artists who distort, manipulate, mutilate and mark their bodies as a form of religious ritual.
- The Modern Primitive movement blends tribal traditions with technology to combine magic and science.
- Modern Primitives maintain that their performances are an experience of spiritual transformation.
- Their performances are similar to the initiation, endurance and mystical rituals of non-Western religious cultures.

every body modification and ritual practice known to man."[10] A small sample of his performances include hanging by flesh hooks while performing an Indian O-Kee-Pa ceremony, penis stretching with weights while performing sexual negation rituals of the Sadhu of India, having 1-pound weights attached to his chest with fish hooks enacting mystical practices of the Sadhu of India, and corseting his waist enacting an initiation ritual of the Ibitoe. Musafar Fakir has performed rituals and body modifications for over 40 years. He is known as the father of the Modern Primitive Movement.

In an interview with Andrea Juno and V. Vale in a book titled *Modern Primitives*, British performance artist Genesis P-Orridge recounts one of a series of art performances called "Coum Transmissions." "Instinctively, without pre-planning, I started to do cuts — scrape my body with sharp nails (not razor blades; to me, that didn't feel ritualistic enough; it had to be a dagger or nail or implement).... I was pushing myself to the point of being declared near dead. At the last Coum Transmissions action in Antwerp, I started cutting a swastika shape into my chest about 9″ square with a rusty nail; then I turned it into a Union Jack [the British Flag], and then just scratched and cut all over the place."[11] After that performance he was rushed to the hospital where he had a near-death experience inclusive of astral projection.

Another example of a violent art performance is "Autopsy" by Sheree Rose and Bob Flanagan. Flanagan lies nude on an autopsy table while he is whipped, beaten, strangled, pinched with clothespins, has various objects inserted into his rectum and has his penis sliced with a knife. The title has obvious references to death. Although Flanagan does not speak during the performance, he related in earlier interviews how "frequent near death encounters modified his concepts of gratification and abstinence, reward and punishment, and intensified his masochistic drive."[12]

The rationale behind both Genesis P-Orridge's and Bob Flanagan's art performances is that they are a means of achieving spiritual transformation through imposed or self-imposed pain and violence leading to death-like conditions. The question remains: how does one distinguish these activities as performance art from other acts of sadomasochism? In response to a similar question, Genesis stated, "I've met genuine masochists and they're usually rather dull, because they don't give you any intellectual explanation at all, nor are they interested in one.... I'm interested in heightened awareness, and I'm interested in learning more and more — about not just myself, but what is possible through the achievement of — not early trance states, but altered states in the true senses."[13] This statement presents the conception of sadomasochism as a form of spiritual art.

Another example of an artist considered a Modern Primitive is Ron Athey who incorporates piercing, bloodletting and tattooing in his art events to create rituals of redemption. Athey is HIV-positive and a former heroin addict. In a 1993 performance entitled "Martyrs and Saints," Athey hung nude strung up to a column with long needles inserted into his head in such a manner as to represent a crown of thorns. His stated artistic intention is to achieve redemption through self-mutilation. He has performed at Fetish Scene clubs.

The recognition of these masochistic acts as a form of art by professionals in the art world has significantly contributed to legitimizing acts of sadomasochism, body modification, self-mutilation and blood play that are so prevalent in Vampire Culture.

The use of blood in performance art, blood sports and Vampire Culture is often extremely violent and similar to another religious concept, mortification. In a wide variety of religious traditions, mortification occurs in the context of initiation rituals. "The term mortification derives from the Latin *motificare* ("to put to death").... Some practices of mortification seem intended symbolically to assimilate the initiate into a death-like condition that is to precede an initiatory rebirth."[14] The practices refer to specific forms of bodily discipline ranging from sleep deprivation to ritual forms of abuse. Deprivations are ways of symbolizing death: the dead do not speak, eat, drink, or sleep.

Violent rituals can be seen as endurance tests that serve as rites of passage into adulthood. The significance is not the violent act, but the symbolic death and rebirth.[15] The concept of body modification as a form of modern mortification is consistent with the Goths' obsession with death and the Vampires' concept of immortality. From a psychological perspective, cutting, blood play and self-mutilation are viewed as forms of psychopathology frequently caused by childhood trauma. Although this perspective clearly has merit, it diminishes the significant religious aspects of these acts and does not explain the large amount of people without histories of being traumatized who engage in this behavior.

When positioned in the ideological context of performance artists and Modern Primitives, the motivation for blood rituals can be viewed as an attempt to reclaim the spiritual in a technological world. In brief, juveniles and young adults mutilate themselves in search of spirituality. The pain is perceived as a mystical experience. This is completely consistent with the concept of Christian mortification which is an element in the more general practice of asceticism. The concept is derived from the Pauline ideal of participation in the crucifixion of Christ by putting to death the desires of the flesh. This self-imposed martyrdom was a way Christians could recapture some of the self-sacrificing intensity of the early church. This included various degrees of self-inflicted violence, such as fasting, sleep deprivation, self-flagellation, the wearing of what is referred to as a hair shirt (a scourge worn as a belt against the naked flesh, the rope made more painful by being knotted or by the addition of metal nails). The goal of this self-infliction of pain was to experience ecstatic union with God.

In a book titled *Holy Anorexia*, Rudolph Bell described the life of Catherine Benincasa, one of the many medieval women who tortured themselves as a form of Christian mortification. From the age of 16 or so, she subsisted on bread, water and raw vegetables. She wore only rough wool and exchanged her hairshirt, the dirtiness of which offended her, for an iron chain bound so tightly against her hips that it inflamed her skin. For 3 years, she observed a self-imposed vow of total silence except for confession. Three times a day she flagellated herself with an iron chain. Each beating lasted one and a half hours and blood ran from her shoulders to her feet.[16] Catherine's religious devotions rewarded her with visions that led her to believe she experienced mystical union with God and she was subsequently canonized as a saint by the Catholic Church.

Five hundred years later we still have 16-year-olds self-inflicting pain in an attempt to connect with the spiritual. It is no coincidence that Goths and Vampires are obsessed with mystery, death and immortality; those are the very things that traditional religions explain. Vampire Culture is a countercultural movement arising because the established religions do not meet the needs of this generation and they are seeking alternative forms of spirituality. Although their motivations may be innocent, there are very real dangers in their activities.

The immediate and obvious dangers are blood-borne diseases and accidental deaths caused by sadomasochism gone wrong. A general principle for determining how deeply someone is involved in Vampire Culture or any other form of occult religion is the use of blood. Once blood is exchanged, imbibed, extracted or used in any manner whatsoever in ritualized activity, the person has now committed to that religion or group. Additionally, blood rituals are addictive — both psychologically and physiologically when a person experiences

Blood: Law Enforcement Issues

Immediate and obvious dangers are:
- Blood-borne diseases.
- Accidental deaths caused by sadomasochism gone wrong.

Blood rituals are addicting both psychologically and physiologically:
- Physically, when someone is experiencing pain, endorphins (natural pain killers) are released; however, eventually more pain is needed to achieve the same endorphin high.
- Psychologically, persons feel that without blood their vitality will diminish, magical powers will subside or they simply are not themselves. It is not unusual for participants of Vampire Culture who are in this situation to carry around vials of blood.

A general principle for determining how deeply someone is involved in Vampire Culture or any occult religion is their use of blood.
- Once blood is being exchanged, imbibed, extracted or used in any manner whatsoever in ritualized activity the person has now committed to that religion or group.
- Self-mutilation can escalate into sacrifice, blood rituals that entail harming others.

pain, endorphins (natural pain killers) are released; however, eventually more pain is needed to achieve the same endorphin high. Psychologically, people feel that without blood their vitality will diminish, magical powers will subside or they simply are not themselves. It is not unusual for participants of Vampire Culture who are in this situation to carry around vials of blood. The more insidious danger of blood play is that occasionally self-mutilation is not a sufficient mystical experience and can escalate into sacrifice, blood rituals that entail harming others.

Vampire Crimes in History

Due to the problem of defining Vampirism, it is difficult to classify Vampire crimes because they are not always distinguishable from serial murders or crimes that entail particular fetishistic behaviors such as drinking blood, cannibalism or necrophilia. However, certain crimes in history have been designated Vampire crimes. The following list of crimes attributed to Vampires appears in Gordon Melton's *The Vampire Book.*[17]

It is significant to point out that all the listed crimes were enacted by individuals who were obsessed with blood as opposed to crimes committed by a group with shared Vampire or Satanic religious beliefs. However, many of these crimes occurred because the perpetrators believed there were magical or mystical qualities to drinking blood, which designates them as occult crimes. The relevance of these crimes to law enforcement is that the Vampire Scene literally gives perpetrators their first taste of blood and sanctions the act as acceptable behavior that can conceivably escalate to the following types of crimes:

1500s — Countess Elizabeth Bathory was known as a vampire because she tortured and killed more than 600 women so she could bathe in their blood. She was tried in 1611 and sentenced to life imprisonment in solitary confinement.

1861 — Martin Dumollard of Montluel, France, was convicted of murdering several young girls whose blood he drank. He was executed.

1872 — Vincenzo Verzeni of Bottanaucco, Italy, was sentenced to life imprisonment in two cases of murder and four of attempted murder. He confessed that drinking the blood of his victims gave him immense satisfaction.

1897 — Joseph Vacher of Bourg, France, while on a walking tour through the country, killed at least a dozen people and drank their blood from bites in their necks. He was finally captured, convicted and executed.

1916 — After receiving notice that Bela Kiss, of Czinkota, Hungary, had been killed in World War I, neighbors searched his property and found the bodies of 31 individuals, all of whom had been strangled. Each corpse had puncture wounds in the neck and had been drained of blood.

1920 — Baron Roman von Sternberg-Ungern, a nobleman in post-revolutionary Russia, drank human blood on occasion, seemingly in connection with a belief that he was a reincarnation of Genghis Khan. For his habits (and other reasons), he came into conflict with the new government and was executed.

1924 — Fritz Haarman was executed in Germany for killing and cannibalizing more than 20 people; during the last several years he also began to bite and suck the blood of his victims.

1929 — Peter Kurten was arrested in Germany for killing nine people, mostly young women. He stabbed, mutilated and drank the blood of his victims until he was sick. He was executed in 1930.

1940s — In a home in London, John George Haigh killed his victims, drained their blood and then disposed of their bodies in a vat of sulfuric acid.

1947 — Elizabeth Short of Hollywood, California, was murdered and her body dismembered. Later examination indicated that her body had been drained of its blood before the dismemberment.

1959 — Salvatore Agron, a 16-year-old resident of New York City, was convicted of several murders that he carried out at night while dressed as a Bela Lugosi-style Vampire. In court, he claimed to be a Vampire. He was executed for his crimes.

1960 — Florencio Roque Fernandez of Manteros, Argentina, was arrested after being picked out of a line-up by 15 women who said someone had entered their bedrooms, bit them and drank their blood.

1963 — Alfred Kaser of Munich, Germany, was tried for killing a 10-year-old boy. Kaser drank blood from the boy's neck after stabbing him.

1967 — James Brown, an American seaman, was discovered aboard his ship sucking the blood from a fellow crewman he had murdered. He had already killed and drained another sailor. Brown was sentenced to life in prison where he killed at least two more people and drank their blood.

1969 — Stanislav Modzieliewski of Lodz, Poland, was convicted of seven murders and six attempted murders. One witness against him was a young woman he attacked, who pretended to be dead while he drank blood from her. Modzieliewski confessed to thinking that blood was delicious.

1971 — Wayne Boden was arrested for a series of murders that began in 1968. In each case he handcuffed the victim, raped her, and then bit her and sucked blood from her breast.

1973 — Kuno Hoffman of Hurnber, Germany, confessed to murdering two people and drinking their blood and to digging up and drinking the blood of several corpses. He was sentenced to life imprisonment.

1977 — Richard Chase began killing and drinking the blood of animals in 1974. By 1977, he went on a string of killings in Sacramento, California during which he mutilated his victims and drank their blood. He became known as the Sacramento Vampire. Chase was sentenced to death but committed suicide first.

1979 — Richard Cottingham was arrested for raping, slashing and drinking the blood of a young prostitute. It was later discovered that he had killed a number of women and in most cases, had bitten them and drank their blood.

1980 — James P. Riva shot his grandmother and drank the blood coming from the wound. He later said that several years earlier he had begun to hear the voices of a Vampire who eventually had told him what to do and promised him eternal life.

1982 — Julian Koltun of Warsaw, Poland, was sentenced to death for raping seven women and drinking their blood. He killed two of the women.

1984 — Renato Antonio Cirillo was tried for the rape and Vampire-style biting of more than 40 women.

1985 — John Crutchley was arrested for raping a woman. He held her prisoner and drank much of her blood. It was later discovered that he had been drinking the blood of more willing donors for many years.

1987 — A jogger in a San Francisco park was kidnapped and held for an hour in a van while a man drank his blood.

1988 — An unknown woman picked up at least six men over the summer in the Soho section of London. After she returned home with a victim, she slipped drugs into his drink. While he was unconscious, she cut his wrist and sucked his blood. She was never arrested.

1991 — Marcelo da Andrade of Rio de Janeiro killed 14 young boys, after which he drank their blood and ate some of their flesh.

1992 — Andrei Chikatilo of Rostov, Russia, was sentenced to death after confessing to killing some 55 people whom he vampirized and cannibalized.

1992 — Deborah Joan Finch was tried for the murder of a neighbor. She stabbed the victim 27 times and then drank the flowing blood.

The Fetish Scene

Vampires frequently attend Fetish Scene and Body Scene clubs which involve public sadomasochistic activities. It is at the numerous "Scene" clubs where the worlds of body mutilation, piercing, performance art, blood rituals, tattooing and all forms of bondage and violent sexual activity converge. The Fetish Scene refers to clubs where fetishism, sadomasochism and bondage/discipline are promoted. The Body Art Scene refers to body piercing, tattooing, Modern Primitives and other activities. Performance artists who use blood attend and perform at all these venues. The various Scenes, which are all fundamentally based on violent aesthetics, are not mutually exclusive and usually overlap.

The names of the clubs often appropriately reference historical predecessors. For example, a popular Fetish club in Brisbane and Townsville, Australia, is called the "Hellfire Club." In 18th and 19th century England, Hellfire clubs were places known for raunchy sexual activities and reckless excitement where hedonistic and occult activities were prominent. The original Hellfire Club was founded by Francis Sashwood in 1751 when he converted an abbey into a cult headquarters by decorating it in Gothic style and pagan statuary.

The Fetish Scene

- Vampires frequently attend Fetish Scene and Body Scene clubs that involve public sadomasochistic activities.
- **Scene Club Style:**
  - Leather clothes (S&M)
  - Masks
  - Latex clothing
  - Whips
  - Chains
  - Restraints

- **"Scene" Club Activities:**
  - Feeding circles (blood)
  - Blood rituals
  - Sadomasochism
  - Bondage & discipline
  - Performance artists
  - Body mutilation
  - Piercing
  - Tattooing

It was rumored that these clubs were linked to Satanism and witchcraft. Keeping with tradition, the contemporary Australian Hell Fire clubs provide members with an assortment of specially designed rooms, furniture and devices in which they can imaginatively experience pain/pleasure.

One of the most infamous clubs in London today is appropriately named "Torture Garden." Founded in 1990, it is currently Europe's largest Fetish/ Body Art club. Average attendance is 600 to 800 people, and special events attract as many as 2000. The club claims to be a major pioneer in the Fetish Body Art Phenomenon. It is a combination of a fetish, sado/masochist, body art, Modern Primitives, straight, gay, performance art, body ritual, fashion, techno/industrial/atmospheric music, multimedia, and cyberspace club.

The concept of the Torture Garden may initially be difficult to grasp. It encompasses the most extreme manifestations of body piercing, mutilation and ritual uses of blood in Western culture. Besides dressing in the latest leather sadomasochism designs, original accessories worn by patrons include catheter bags filled with blood and urine, medical bags filled with blood and air hoses when necessary. Every imaginable form of mask, chain, whip and sometimes even chainsaws and blowtorches are part of the festivities. The Torture Garden also has a manifesto that clearly demonstrates the anomalous nature of Fetish clubs. Its manifesto boasts:

> Torture Garden remains the most radical and alternative club, always on the cutting edge of the latest underground subculture.... Torture Garden is a world where the bizarre, strange and dreamlike become normal.... Torture Garden is the apotheosis of all antino-

mies.... The dissolution of all oppositions.... As you
mutate with Torture Garden, you reach new peaks of
pleasure and eroticism and are freed from the shackles
of social convention.... Torture Garden breaks taboos.... Torture Garden has established an international reputation for encouraging artistic experimentation
and transgression....[18]

Fetish Scene clubs are analogous to religious festivals and appropriately
correspond to Vampire religious beliefs. Festivals are ceremonies that have
religious significance and take place at regular intervals; essentially they are
religious holidays. Each religion has its own requirements for ritual celebration and they often include fasting, a series of performances or rites and have
symbolic meaning. Historically, festivals culminated in a ritual sacrifice.
Scene clubs are reminiscent of the Greek Dionysian festivals in which all
forms of sexuality, violence and desire were acceptable during the ceremonies.
Dionysian rites were famous for orgiastic and emotional rapture, dance and
violent abandonment very similar to what transpires at the Scene clubs.

Dionysian festivals are ritual enactments of the drama of Dionysus, the
god who represents orgiastic violence. During the festivals, all pre-established
laws and moral rules were suspended for the duration of the celebration. The
function of the festival was to contain potentially destructive urges by allowing people to occasionally indulge in them in a socially acceptable situation.
Essentially these festivals were attempts to regulate aggressive and sexual urges
so they would not erupt into uncontrollable violence.

Vampire religions, Satanism and Dionysian rites all recognize the dark
side of human nature, which is why they advocate indulging in sexual and
violent desires as opposed to repressing them. However, the fundamental
difference is that the Greeks limited indulgence in violent desires to the duration of the Dionysian festivals, whereas Goths, Vampires and Satanists observe
no such limitations. Blood sports, sadomasochism, sexual bondage and other
routine activities of the Fetish Scene are not simply a form of catharsis engaged
in only during festivals but constitute an entire lifestyle that advocates excess,
indulgence and instant gratification with little or no boundaries to contain
violence. Essentially, the Fetish Scene is a never-ending festival where there
are no laws, no morality and no limits on sexual or violent urges.

Contemporary Vampire Religions

Vampire religions are attempts to bring order, responsibility and meaning to
this violent subculture. Commonalities among the modern religious Vampire

Vampire Religions

Commonalities among Vampire religions include:

- Hierarchical structures
- Opposition to Christian tenets
- Occult magical ideologies
- Dark symbolism
- Blood rituals
- Strict codes of conduct
- Advocating the acquisition of personal and political power

- Similar to other organized religions; beliefs vary among different sects according to church leaders.
- Rivalry among the various groups is common, with each professing spiritual superiority over the other and claiming that it is practicing the one true faith.

groups include hierarchical structures, opposition to Christian tenets, occult magical ideologies, dark symbolism, blood rituals, strict codes of conduct and advocating the acquisition of personal and political power. Similar to other organized religions, beliefs vary among different sects according to church leaders.

Rivalries among the various groups are common, with each one professing spiritual superiority over the others and claiming that it is practicing the one true faith. Similar to other new religious movements, many Vampire organizations and churches have asserted that they continually experience various forms of persecution through media and film perceptions of Vampires. Some of the better-known Vampire religions are discussed below.

The Sanguinarium

One particularly large and influential Vampire group has an intricate network of members and is referred to as the Sanguinarium. The name is derived from *sanguis*, the Latin word for *blood*, and signifies how Vampires regard each other, as in *"of the blood."* The Sanguinarium promotes a common Vampire lifestyle comprised of specific customs, etiquette, aesthetics and ethical tenets. It is managed and maintained by Vampires for Vampires. Members congregate at Havens (Vampire nightclubs) and Courts, which are social events or town meetings held in specific geographic locations.

A sophisticated system of Courts and Havens exist throughout the U.S. and Europe. For example, the Court of Gotham includes all of metropolitan New York City and the following Havens: Long Black Veil, The Bank, Alchemy, Contempt and Mother. Another example is the Court of Lost Angels

The Sanguinarium

- Large and influential Vampire group with an intricate network of members.
- Members congregate at Havens (Vampire night clubs) and courts.
- A sophisticated system of courts and havens throughout the United States and Europe.

Hierarchical Structure:
- The **Legacy**, the inner circle
- The Sanguinarium Council or Council of Vampyre International Community Affairs **(COVICA)** board of directors
- "**The Three Pillars:**"
  - Fledglings
  - Calmae
  - Elders

which encompasses Los Angeles and southern California and whose havens include the Fang Club in Los Angeles, Bar Sinister, Coven 13 and Absynthe in Hollywood, Vampiricus and Release the Bats in Long Beach, Repent in Anaheim and many more. Currently, the Sanguinarium lists ten Courts on its website; each Court containing many Havens. This demonstrates that Vampire Culture is not a passing fad but an extensive, highly organized community whose members number in the thousands.

The Sanguine Ankh is the symbol (sigil) of the Sanguinarium and allows members to identify each other worldwide. It was derived from the ancient Egyptian symbol of eternal life and refers to the priest of the Egyptian god Horus' use of the bladed ankhs for bloodletting rites.

Sanguinarium Texts

Important texts:
- *The Black Veil*, a code of conduct.
- *The Vampyre Codex*, a spiritual understanding of Vampyrism.
- *The Sanguinarium Lexicon of Terminology.*
- *The Vampyre Almanac* is the official publication of the organization.

The code of conduct is enforced by the Elders in the tradition of the *Black Veil* and is comprised of thirteen ethical tenets that all members are expected to abide by.

The hierarchical structure of the Sanguinarium is referred to as the Three Pillars. The lowest level consists of Fledglings who are either new to the lifestyle, inexperienced or who are children of Vampire adults. They are signified by having no prefix before their name and no stone in their sigil. After a period of initiation, Fledglings can become Calmae, which signifies they are experienced members of the Clan, Coven, or Circle and they wear a red stone in their sigil. The highest level is that of the Elders who are the most experienced and influential members of the Sanguinarium. They consist of leaders and founders of Clans, owners of Havens and fangmakers (dentists who make permanent fangs for members), and they have a purple stone in their sigils.

Organization consists of a board of directors called the Sanguinarium Council or Council of Vampyre International Community Affairs (COVICA). Board members are designated as ministers and each minister has a specific function. The Legacy is the inner circle of the Sanguinarium.

Important texts include a combination of fundamental writings from member groups inclusive of *The Black Veil*, a code of conduct, *The Vampyre Codex*, a spiritual understanding of Vampyrism and the *Sanguinarium Lexicon of Terminology*. *Vampyre Almanac* is the official publication of the organization. The code of conduct is enforced by the elders in the tradition of *The Black Veil* and is comprised of 13 ethical tenets that all members are expected to abide by. The first and most important is Discretion (keeping sanguine secrets confidential among members), followed by Diversity, Safety, Control, Lifestyle, Family, Havens, Territory, Responsibility, Elders, Donors, Leadership and Ideals. The philosophy of *The Black Veil* encourages honor, respect, safety, chivalry and unity of those in the culture. Punishment entails excommunication from a clan for various lengths of time according to the violation.

The Temple of the Vampire

Currently there is only one international church authorized as a Vampire religion by the U.S. government. The Temple of the Vampire has been legally registered as a religion since December 1989 and has paved the way for other Vampire religious groups to be acknowledged as practicing authentic religions. Sacred rites of the Temple of the Vampire include magical rituals to achieve the traditional powers of the Vampire, contact with Undead Gods and eventually the holy act of Vampiric Communion.

According to the Temple, Vampirism is a supremacist belief that claims that Vampire members are the next stage in evolution and exist as predators of humans. The Temple also professes that Vampires created all the religions of the world to keep humans under control; Vampires are the rulers of the world and humans are nothing but sources of energy for the Undead Gods. This is evidenced by their Vampire Creed that begins, "I am a Vampire. I

The Temple of the Vampire

- Legally registered as a religion since December 1989.
- Millennial religion whose origin is explained in their sacred text, the *Vampire Bible.*
- A supremacist belief that claims that Vampire members are the next stage in evolution and exist as predators of humans.

Church Hierarchy (five levels of initiation classified as grades or circles):

- The Vampire Initiate
- The Vampire Predator
- The Priesthood of UR
- The Vampire Sorcerer or Sorceress
- The Vampire Adept

worship my ego and I worship my life, for I am the only God that is," and ends with, "Bow down before me." The Temple of the Vampire's religious philosophy is explained in its main texts, *The Vampire Bible* and *The Higher Teachings of Vampirism*. Church publications include *Bloodlines: The Vampire Temple Journal* and *Lifeforce: The International Vampire Connection to CABAL*, a monthly newsletter.

According to Temple theology, Vampirism is an ancient religion that distinguishes between Living Vampires and Vampires who have experienced physical death who then become known as the Undead Gods. Genuine Vampirism is the exchange of energy between the Living Vampires and the Undead Gods in a ritual that the Temple refers to as Communion. Through this Communion, a practitioner gets closer to the Gods, develops higher levels of Vampiric skills and ultimately achieves immortality by becoming an Undead God. Energy offered to the Undead Gods is collected astrally from sleeping human beings.

The Temple of the Vampire is a millennial religion whose origin and resurrection are explained in *The Vampire Bible*. In the beginning, humans and Undead Gods were in direct contact with each other and humans voluntarily served and worshipped Undead Gods until a group of renegade younger Undead Gods destroyed this spiritual connection. On some level, humans remember this primal connection and are waiting for the Gods to return. During what is referred to as "Harvests," humans channel their energy to the Gods, which is needed to sustain their magical deeds. In the "Final Harvest" that will occur at an indeterminate time in the near future, the Undead Gods will return to earth as the visible rulers, Temple initiates will reach immortality and humans will continue their mortal lives as servant to them.

The church is organized in five levels of initiation classified as grades or circles. The first circle is the Vampire Initiate who must read *The Vampire Bible* and test the teaching through personal effort. The second circle is the Vampire Predator who must testify to the truth of Vampirism as a personal experience and a workable personal philosophy. The third circle, the Priesthood of UR, is achieved by one who testifies to the reality of Communion with the Undead Gods as a personal experience and signs an oath pledging loyalty to the temple. The fourth circle is the Vampire Sorcerer or Sorceress. This circle requires a testimonial to the successful personal application of the Nine Laws of Magic. Finally, the fifth and highest circle is the Vampire Adept which requires a testimony to both the successful achievement of the Twilight Condition and a personal recognition of the Dragon Within. Membership information is available on the Temple's website.

The Vampire Church and Other Vampire Religious Groups

Another well-known religious group is the Vampire Church, which has an ecumenical philosophy. Its foremost stated purposes are offering a haven for Vampires, sharing with others of their kind and learning from one another. Unlike the elitism of many of the other Vampire sects, the church does not tolerate racism (among Vampires), welcomes diversity and has a goal of uniting all Vampires in a common bond.

The Vampire Church considers psychic attacks and forceful feeding as unethical and barbaric and they are not tolerated. The organization consists

---

Vampire Religious Groups

Vampire Church
- Ecumenical philosophy.
- Offers a haven for Vampires.
- Does not tolerate racism (among Vampires).
- Goal is to unite all Vampires in a common bond.
- Considers psychic attacks and forceful feeding as unethical.
- Organization consists of a church council chaired by the Church Elder.

Vampire Religious Groups
- Kheprian Order
- Sekhrian Order
- Lucifer's Den
- Society of the Dark Sun
- Order of the Vampyre
- Thee Empyre ov Nozgoth
- Temple of Eternal Night
- The Lilith Tradition
- Coven of Vampires
- Many underground and developing groups

of a church council responsible for all activities, projects, the website and general well-being of the church. The council is chaired by the Church Elder who is head of the council and founder of the church.

Other religious groups are the Kheprian Order, whose members are primarily scholar-monks and their sister house, the Sekhrian Order, whose members are mystics and scholars. Both orders follow the Sanguinarium *Black Veil* or what is also called "Rules of 13." The Kepherian Order is where the *Vampyre Codex* originated.

Several Vampire religious groups openly state that they practice the black arts or what is referred to as the Left Hand Path. Some of the better-known groups are Lucifer's Den, Society of the Dark Sun and Order of the Vampyre. Some of these groups also identify themselves as Satanic orders and their philosophies focus on individuality, self-preservation and personal empowerment. One particular Vampyre religious organization known as Thee Empyre ov Nozgoth is attempting to unite all Satanic, Left Hand Path and other occultist groups who follow the dark paths into a new alliance. Its stated goals are political as well as religious and include overthrowing Zionist majorities, creating a pure blood race and a promised land for the Vampire race. Although all Vampire religions are theologically supremacist, Thee Empyre ov Nozgoth is clearly a white supremacist occult religion.

Other Vampire religious groups include Temple of Eternal Night, The Lilith Tradition, Coven of Vampires and many other unpublished, underground and developing groups.

The Vampire scene may have originated out of myths and Hollywood but it has evolved into a serious lifestyle that meets all the criteria to constitute an authentic subculture. This is demonstrated by the thousands of members worldwide and the growing number of associations, churches and communities. One of the common goals of the various groups is to be recognized and respected as a valid religion. With this goal in mind, Vampires have set aside their differences to create an alliance referred to as the Council of Elders whose members consist of a veritable who's who of the Vampire community. The goal of this independent organization comprised of the elders of member houses is to communicate and discuss important issues concerning Vampires. The many dedicated Clans, Churches, Covens, Orders, Houses and Circles clearly demonstrate that Vampirism is not just a temporary passing fad, but a genuine new religious movement.

Vampire Cults

Similar to other new religious movements that embrace violent self-gratification ideologies, Vampire religions can erupt into situations that have criminal consequences. In January 1997, Jon Bush, a 26-year-old man who

Self-Styled Vampire Clan

- 16-year-old Rodrick Justin Ferrell was the leader of a Vampire clan composed of four other teenagers.
- He became involved with Vampires through the role-playing game "Vampire: the Masquerade."
- Rituals included cutting each other's arms with razors and sucking the blood.
- Heather Wendorf, the daughter of the clan's murder victims, participated in the "embracement ritual" where she "crossed over" into the clan by drinking the others' blood in a cemetery.

claimed to be a Vampire was sentenced to 26 years in prison in Virginia Beach for sexually molesting eight teenage girls he had invited into his Vampire family. He initially recruited high school boys and used them to enlist young girls into the group. The youngest girl in the group was only 13 years old.

Bush's 30-member Vampire family played one of the Vampire Role-Playing Games "Masquerade: Eternal Night" in which participants assumed the roles of ancient Vampires. Bush told the girls they could become Vampires by having oral sex or sexual intercourse with him or by letting him bite them hard just below their breasts. Bush was clearly a sexual predator who used Vampire Culture as his scam to deceive and control young girls who due to the popularity of the Goth and Vampire Scenes were readily seduced.

A more famous recent example is a self-styled Vampire clan in Kentucky whose members were arrested on November 29, 1996 for the murder of a Florida couple. This incident has been sensationalized in books, television, interviews and an HBO special entitled "Vampire Murders." Sixteen-year-old Rodrick Justin Ferrell was the leader of a Vampire clan composed of four other teenagers. Their rituals included cutting each other's arms with razors and sucking the blood. On the day of the murders, Heather Wendorf, the daughter of the victims, participated in an "embracement ritual" with Ferrell and "crossed over" into the clan by drinking each other's blood in a cemetery. Ferrell then became her sire. That evening Rod Ferrell bludgeoned Richard and Naoma Wendorf to death with a crowbar in their Florida home. The letter *V* (symbolizing *Vassago*, Ferrell's Vampire name) was burned into their bodies. Smaller burns on each side of the *V* represented the other members of the clan.

After pleading guilty to armed burglary, armed robbery and two counts of first-degree murder, Ferrell was sentenced to death in Florida's electric

Vampire Homicide

- Rod Ferrell bludgeoned Richard and Naoma Wendorf to death with a crowbar in their Florida home in 1996.
- The letter "V" was burned into their bodies, symbolizing Rod whose Vampire name was Vassago. Smaller burns on each side of the "V" represented the other members of the clan.
- Ferrell was sentenced to death in Florida's electric chair on February 27, 1998 but due to his age the sentence was later reduced to life in prison.
- Another teenage clan member Howard Scott Anderson is serving life in prison after pleading guilty to participating as Rod's principal accessory in the double murder.

chair on February 27, 1998. He is the youngest person on Florida's death row. Another teenage clan member, Howard Scott Anderson, is serving life in prison after pleading guilty to participating as Ferrell's principal accessory in the double murder. Anderson's plea bargain saved him from the electric chair.

Ferrell's attorneys portrayed their client as a troubled youth addicted to drugs and sexually abused by relatives. He became involved with Vampires through the Role-Playing Game "Vampire: The Masquerade" and was initiated into the scene by an older teenager, Steven Murphy (Vampire name Jaden), who subsequently testified at the trial that he

> initiated Rod into vampirism during a crossing-over ceremony in a Murray (Kentucky) cemetery that involved slashing their arms and sharing each other's blood, followed by a lengthy period of meditation. As the senior Vampire who initiated Rod, Murphy said he became the younger boy's sire and was responsible for his behavior. And although he explained the rules of vampire conduct to Rod, the witness said, his protégé violated those principles when he organized his own band of followers.... The Wendorf Murders were not vampiric, Murphy explained, because Rod didn't bleed the bodies. 'There was no bloodletting. He did not take from them.'[20]

This contradicted his earlier testimony that Vampires do not kill and are expected to show the highest admiration for life. If Vampires do not kill, there would not be any knowledge of distinctive Vampiric modus operandi. It was brought to the detectives' attention through John Goodman (vampire name Damien), a close friend of Ferrell, that Ferrell's motivation for the murders was that he was "possessed with the idea of opening the gates to Hell, which meant that he would have to kill a large, large number of people in order to consume their souls. By doing this, Ferrell believed he would obtain super powers."[21] Psychological justifications aside, Ferrell's immersion into the occult clearly demonstrates that he was thinking in religious conceptions of sacrificial murder.

This case is just one of many that entail magical thinking, blood rituals and murder. Violent Performance Art, the Body Modification and Goth Movements, Vampire Culture and the Fetish Scene literally set the ritual stage for sacrifice. Ritual murder is the epitome of Vampire Culture freed from ethical responsibility to society. What begins as artists experimenting with the use of blood and mutilation as a form of personal transformation escalates to an entire culture founded on the principles of a dark mythology manifested in orgiastic ritual. Once blood rituals turn participatory and new religions ideologically validate sacrifice, murder is justified in the minds of true believers.

References

1. Larson, B., *Satanism: The Seduction of America's Youth*, Thomas Nelson Publishers, Nashville, 1989, p. 201.

2. Rein, M. and Brown, S.C., *Vampire: The Masqurade*, White Wolf Publishing, Clarkson, GA, 1998, p. 18.

3. Ramsland, K., *Piercing the Darkness: Undercover with Vampires in America Today*, Harper Prism, New York, 1998, pp. 153–154.

4. Goldberg, R., *Performance Art from Futurism to the Present*, Harry N. Abrams, Inc., New York, 1988, p. 164.

5. Stiles, K., *Out of Actions between Performance and the Object 1949–1979*, The Museum of Contemporary Art, Los Angeles, 1998, p. 290.

6. Goldberg, R., *Performance Art from Futurism to the Present*, Harry N. Abrams, Inc., New York, 1988, p. 165.

7. Hewitt, K., *Mutilating the Body: Identity in Blood and Ink*, Bowling Green State University Press, Bowling Green, OH, 1997, p. 104.

8. Eliade, M., Ed., *The Encyclopedia of Religion*, Macmillan, New York, 1987, vol. 3, p. 60.

9. Hewitt, K., *Mutilating the Body: Identity in Blood and Ink*, Bowling Green State University Press, Bowling Green, OH, 1997, p. 105.

10. Vale, V. and Juno, A., Eds., *Modern Primitives: An Investigation of Contemporary Adornment and Ritual*, Re/Search Publications, San Francisco, 1989, p. 6.

11. Vale, V. and Juno, A., Eds., *Modern Primitives: An Investigation of Contemporary Adornment and Ritual*, Re/Search Publications, San Francisco, 1989, pp. 167–168.

12. Vale, V. and Juno, A., Eds.,*Modern Primitives: An Investigation of Contemporary Adornment and Ritual*, Re/Search Publications, San Francisco, 1989, p. 206.

13. Vale, V. and Juno, A., Eds., *Modern Primitives: An Investigation of Contemporary Adornment and Ritual*, Re/Search Publications, San Francisco, 1989, p. 169.

14. Eliade, M., *The Encyclopedia of Religion*, Macmillan, New York, 1987, vol. 10, pp. 113–114.

15. Eliade, M., *The Encyclopedia of Religion*, Macmillan, New York, 1987, vol. 10, p. 114.

16. Bell, R.M., *Holy Anorexia*, University of Chicago Press, Chicago, 1985, p. 43.

17. Melton, J.G., *The Vampire Book: The Encyclopedia of the Undead*, Visible Ink Press, Detroit, 1999, pp. 147–151.

18. The Torture Garden Home Page, manifesto section. http://www.ain-exus.com/torturegarden/manifesto1.html

19. Ramsland, K., *Piercing the Darkness: Undercover with Vampires in America Today*, Harper Prism, New York, 1998, p. 291.

20. Linedecker, C.L., *The Vampire Killers*, St. Martin's Press, New York, 1998, p. 262.

21. Linedecker, C.L., *The Vampire Killers*, St. Martin's Press, New York, 1998, p. 159.

Syncretic Religions 7

Syncretic belief systems are religions that have combined two or more different cultural and spiritual beliefs into a new faith. Santeria, Voodoo, Hoodoo, Palo Mayombe, Candomble and Shango are some of the syncretic Afro-Caribbean religions. Brujeria, a form of witchcraft, has distinctly Mexican cultural and religious roots. Afro-Caribbean faiths originated during African slave trading in the 18th and 19th centuries when owners imposed Catholicism on their slaves and forbid traditional religious practices.

In an attempt to maintain their cultural and religious beliefs, Africans disguised their religion by assigning each of their gods the image of a Catholic saint. The names of the religions correspond to the geographical locations where they evolved and the African regions from which they derived. For example, Santeria (the way of the saints), originally called Lucumi, emerged in Cuba and derived from the southwestern Nigerian Yoruba tribe. This new faith was eventually introduced to other Latin American countries and became known as Candomble in Brazil and Shango in Trinidad. Voodoo, often referred to as Hoodoo in the U.S., evolved in Haiti and originated in Dahomey, now the Republic of Benin, and was practiced among the Fon, Yoruba and Ewe tribes. Magic and the belief in supernatural intervention occupy a significant place in the worship of all occult syncretic religions.

Currently there are several million people living in America who practice some sort of Afro-Caribbean faith most of whom are not involved in criminal activities. However, it is important that law enforcers become familiar with syncretic religious practices because they incorporate animal sacrifice, human bones, require ritual items found in cemeteries and can mistakenly be considered a form of satanic worship. Another aspect of syncretic belief systems pertinent to law enforcers is that each of these religions allows for the possibility of the practice of black magic. Black magic is often used to curse, threaten and intimidate perceived enemies who often include criminal justice professionals. The dark side of Santeria is referred to as Palo Mayombe, which

Syncretic Religions

Religion	Country
• Santeria	Cuba
• Voodoo	Haiti
• Candomble	Brazil
• Shango	Trinidad
• Brujeria	Mexico

Black Magic Tradition
• Palo Mayombe

- Syncretic belief systems refer to religions that have combined two or more different cultural and spiritual beliefs into a new faith.
- Afro-Caribbean syncretic religions originated among the religious practices of the Yoruba peoples in southwestern Nigeria.

Altar and religious painting in a Voodoo Temple in Miami, Florida.

originated in the African Congo and utilizes demonic forces for malevolent intentions. Many criminals, especially drug dealers, practice Palo Mayombe to aid in the trafficking of illegal drugs and to bring harm to their competitors.

Santeria

Santeria combines the cultural and spiritual beliefs of the southwestern Nigerian Yoruba tribe with the religious practices of the Catholic faith and consists of using magical rituals to worship or satisfy a pantheon of gods and goddesses known as orishas. The Yoruba people comprised a large number of ethnic groups and at one time had a powerful and complex social structure organized into a series of kingdoms, the most important of which was Benin which lasted until 1896 when the Yoruba were dispersed by English colonists.

Like all other Afro-Caribbean belief systems, Santeria found its way to America through the system of slavery. As families were scattered, their religious practices were influenced by their new surroundings, with each tribe assimilating the customs, ideas and religious beliefs of the new land. This diversified the magic ceremonies and the rites of each tribe.

In Cuba, where Santeria developed extensively, the Yoruba became known as Lucumi, a term derived from the Yoruba word *akumi*, which refers

Santeria

- Santeria means "the worship of the saints."
- Originated through the system of slavery.
- Mixture of the African beliefs of the Nigerian Yoruba tribe with Catholicism.
- Developed extensively in Cuba where it was known as Lucumi.
- Several million practitioners with significant numbers in Florida, New Jersey, New York and California.
- Religious practices are diversified depending upon the culture it evolved in.

Santeria altar on the store counter in a botanica (religious supply store) in Miami, Florida.

to a native of the Aku, a region of Nigeria where many Yoruba originated. Cuban Lucumi were deeply influenced by Catholicism and identified their gods and goddesses with the saints of the Catholic faith; hence, the creation of Santeria. Santeria is a term derived from the Spanish word *santo* (saint) and literally means the worship of the saints. Santeria did not become a known element of American society until the Cuban Revolution of 1959. As Cubans fled their island, the initial wave of priests and priestesses of Santeria carried their orishas to another new land and during the 1980 Mariel boat lift, the second wave of Santeria followers entered the U.S. Consequently, Santeria practitioners have become a regular part of many urban American landscapes, with significant numbers of followers residing in Florida, New Jersey, New York and California.

Due to the growing population of Santeria practitioners many officers routinely discover the remains of sacrificed goats, chickens, roosters and other animals covered in sacrificial matter in areas such as cemeteries, beaches, near railroad tracks and other places that have magical significance to believers. Although it is illegal to discard animal corpses in public places, most of these cases are not indicative of violent criminal behavior but are remnants

Santeria: Law Enforcement Issues

- Officers routinely discover mutilated animal remains covered or stuffed with food.
- Remains are found in public places, on beaches, near railroad tracks, in cemeteries.
- Need to distinguish mutilated animals that were used in satanic rituals from acts of sadism.

Rule of Thumb:
- Santeria practitioners do not torture their sacrificial animals; they either slit the throat or break the neck. If an animal has obviously been tortured then it is either another occult tradition or an act of sadism.

(Top): Palo Mayombe cauldron ritually discarded on railroad tracks. (Bottom): The Palo Mayombe cauldron contained a human skull with religious beaded necklace still around the neck. (Photos courtesy of Detective Christine Kruse-Feldstein, Miami Dade Police Department Crime Scene Unit, Miami, Florida.)

of ritual ceremonies. A general rule of thumb for officers is that Santeria devotees do not torture their sacrificial animals and most often either quickly slit the throat or break the neck of an animal. If an animal is discovered that has obviously been mutilated or tortured, then it was done by a practitioner of one of the black magic traditions of Santeria, another occult religion or a non-religious act of sadism.

A basic knowledge of Santeria beliefs can assist officers in distinguishing between criminal violent crimes and typical Santeria worship. Knowledge of Santeria practices can also help officers avoid inadvertently offending practitioners or violating their rights during searches; for example, disturbing items without realizing that they constitute a religious altar, amulets, or other religious artifacts.

Santeria Religious Beliefs

Santeria is an earth religion, a magical religious system that has its roots in nature and natural forces. The beliefs and practices of Santeria involve a concept of power known as *ashe*, a term that describes the energy that permeates the universe. This is a cultural variation of the Melanesian concept of mana or the American Indian concepts of wakan and manitu. Ashe is manifested in persons, religious paraphernalia, invocations in the Yoruba language, the sacred stones, the herbs, the ngangas (sacred cauldrons) and almost anything connected with Santeria magic.[1]

Santeria Theology

- **Santeria** is a magical religious system that has its roots in nature.
- **Ashe** is a fundamental precept and describes the energy that permeates the universe; it is in everything, people, plants, stones, etc.
- **Eggun** is the term for deceased family ancestors and ancestor worship is central to the practice of Santeria.
- **Orishas** are the Santeria gods (saints).
- The foundation of Santeria worship is found in four natural elements:
  - *Water • Seashell • Herbs • Ritual stones (Otanes)*
- **Ebbo** is the concept of sacrifice, and offerings are made to the Orishas.

Santeria altar inside entrance to botanica in Bronx, New York. Every botanica has at least one altar; usually several will be found throughout the store.

Santeria Religious Beliefs

- Santeria spells, rituals and invocations are conducted to acquire Ashe from the gods.
- Ashe is the power to change things, solve all problems, subdue enemies, acquire love, etc.
- A person consults a priest and he ascertains what the god wants through "Diloggun" (the divination system known as the seashells).
- The orisha (God/Saint) determines what type of sacrifice (ebbo) is required to solve the problem. Ebbo can be offerings of food, flowers, candles or blood offerings.
- Ancestors must be periodically worshipped with offerings.

Altar containing offerings of flowers and a candle in a botanica in Miami, Florida.

Santeria is essentially based on natural magic and all of the basic elements of worship can be found in nature. The foundation of Santeria worship can be found in four natural elements: water, herbs, seashells and stones. Ritual stones, called *Otanes*, contain the spiritual essence of the Santeria gods and are kept inside decorative tureens whose color is indicative of a particular god. The power of the saints reside in the stones and the stones are not worshipped as religious statues who represent saints but as real living entities full of life and power. Worship of the otanes takes the form of elaborate rituals that follow an annual or monthly cycle. Some people "bathe" their otanes monthly while others "feed" their piedras (rocks) their favorite sacrificial animal on a regular basis.[2] Each time a food offering is made to a god, it is placed on a dish that is balanced on the top of an open tureen, the blood of animal offerings is poured directly on the stones in the tureen. At appropriate times the stones and tureen are cleaned and the cover is replaced.

The seashells, more commonly called cowries, represent the voices of the gods and are used in the divination system known as diloggun. Each god has his own set of 21 cowries which is kept inside the tureen with the stones. When a believer wants to speak to a specific god, he must reach inside the tureen, remove the shells and use them in the divination system. Water, another essential part of Santeria, is used in every ritual ceremony. Herbs are the fourth essential element in the worship of Santeria and every practitioner is a competent herbalist.[3] Over 500 different herbs have been given attributes and have dual purposes for healing and for magic.

The basis of many of the major spells of Santeria is herbs, plants, roots and flowers, each of which is believed to have a spiritual entity that guards it. Each root, flower, tree or plant is believed to be full of ashe (energy) and belongs to one of the orishas who must be asked permission whenever the plant is used. Additionally, Santeria rituals also require the use of sacrificial birds and animals. Each of the orishas is "fed" his or her favorite food or sacrifice in rituals referred to as ebbos.

The blood of roosters and goats is the most common sacrificial offering. Birds (pigeons, canaries, hens, etc.) are used in rubbing rituals where the client is cleansed — the function of which is for any negative feelings caused by evil is passed into the birds.[4] The magical practices of Santeria are a method for believers to gain control over their lives by invoking the proper gods who will effect changes. To truly comprehend this religion, it is necessary to understand that for Santeria believers, every aspect of human life is controlled by the pantheon of gods.

Santeria still retains the fundamental precepts of the ancient Yoruba tradition that includes the concepts of ashe and ebbo. *Ashe* is a Yoruba word that literally means *so be it* and is the symbol of divine power and energy. Ashe is the power of the Supreme God who created the universe and everything is made of ashe and through ashe everything is possible. The gods of Santeria are the repositories of ashe, the divine power/energy. Santeria spells, rituals and invocations are all conducted in order to acquire ashe from the gods. This energy or ashe is the power to change things, to solve all problems, subdue enemies and acquire love and money. Ebbo is the concept of sacrifice and is the way that the orishas are worshiped so that they will give their ashe. Every rite and spell of Santeria is part of the ebbo concept. Fortunately, sacrifice does not always require a sacrificial victim. Ebbo can be an offering of fruits, flowers, candles or any of the favorite foods of the orishas. Small offerings are referred to as addimus. Larger offerings are for bigger problems and when a blood offering is required it represents a serious danger or a significant event.

The orisha determines what type of ebbo (sacrifice) is required to solve a specific problem and the priest ascertains what the orisha wants by questioning him through the diloggun, the divination system known also as the seashells.[5]

Priests in the Santeria religion are known as Santeros (male) and Santera (female). They are also known by the Yoruba name *omo-orisha*, which means *child of an orisha*. There is a sophisticated hierarchy of Santeria priests containing 11 ranks, which is why followers are also referred to as Santeros and Santeras. High priests are known as Babalawos and they conduct sacrifices during initiation ceremonies and settle points of contention among Santeros.

One of the strongest precepts in Santeria is that the dead come before the orishas; hence, ancestor worship is central to the practice of Santeria. The dead in one's family, known collectively as eggun, must be fed periodically just as the orishas are given offerings. Water, coffee, bits of food, flowers and a candle are placed either on the bathroom floor or in another specific place in the house, often behind doors, as a method of honoring ancestors. "Therefore we have in Santeria a religious system that honors the ancestors and recognizes a direct contact between mankind and the forces of nature, which are seen as direct manifestations of God himself. This contact between God and mankind through nature is enforced through ebbo, sacrifice, for the purpose of receiving ashe, power."[6]

For practitioners of Santeria, Catholic saints are not simply representations of human beings who once lived and achieved sainthood; they are the embodiments of Yoruba gods. Ironically, the worship of saints in this manner is fundamentally anti-Christian in that it is a form of idolatry (worship of other gods). Santeria is a polytheistic religion that worships many gods and although believers may attend Catholic churches for an occasional mass, they could never be considered Christians theologically because a fundamental precept of Christianity is monotheism, belief in one God.

Some scholars argue that Santeria is actually a monotheistic religion, claiming that the orishas are not really gods, but the children of Oloddumare (God), and are worshiped as guardian angels. However, there is no disputing the fact that Santeria is deeply rooted in polytheistic African beliefs and worshipping statues as living forces is the very definition of idolatry, a violation of the first and second commandments in Judaism and Christianity.

Santeria is designated an occult religion, not simply for the reason that it is polytheistic but because it is based on belief in magic, the ability to effect particular results by means of supernatural powers.

The Santero is considered a man of knowledge and power who with the aid of the orishas can magically heal, improve finances, attract lovers, destroy rivals, etc. Although some spells entail harming enemies, the Santero is considered a white magician because his intention is to help solve human problems and achieve justice. Santeros do not make use of chaotic evil forces in their magic. Mayomberos or Paleros are practitioners of black magic who deliberately work with evil forces and are the most relevant to law enforcement. In order to comprehend the dark side of Santeria it is first necessary to have a basic understanding of the fundamental beliefs of Santeria.

In Santeria, faith is placed in the powers of the gods and goddesses and the power of the Santeros to bring about changes through the gods. In order for the gods to grant favors they must receive offerings that include everything from food, cigars, candles, incense to animal sacrifice. Typical Santeria altars entail statues of Catholic saints, food, flowers, cigars, rum, candles, glasses

Santeria Priests

Santeria (White Magic)	Palo Mayombe (Black Magic)
• Santeros (Male)	
• Santera (Female)	• Paleros
• Babalaswos (High Priests)	• Mayomberos
	• Deliberately works with evil forces.
• The santero is considered a man of knowledge and power.	• His intention is to harm or inflict misfortune.
• His intention is to help solve human problems and achieve justice.	• Many Mayomberos are first initiated into Santeria.
• He does not use the forces of chaotic evil in his magic.	

of water, candies, coffee and many ordinary everyday objects. Every practitioner of Santeria keeps a special place in their home for a 'boveda,' a special altar dedicated to the eggun (spirits of the dead), so the practitioner can properly worship their ancestors and be granted their protection.

To a practicing Catholic who first encounters a Santeria altar it appears to be nothing less than sacrilegious. In fact, for those who are unfamiliar with Santeria beliefs, bovedas can initially be interpreted as a form of witchcraft, Satanism or the religious manifestation of mental illness. However, historically and cross-culturally, making offerings to gods and dead ancestors in this manner is common practice. Gods are viewed as living entities who need sustenance; they need to be fed and in every religious tradition, blood is the most sacred gift one can offer.

When the Yorubas identified their gods with the Catholic saints, they become endowed with the supernatural powers of the African deities and each saint acquired specific attributes that control different aspects of human life. Each saint is identified with a force of nature and with a human endeavor. For example, Chango is the orisha (saint) who controls fire, thunder and lightning but also symbolizes raw power and control over enemies and general difficulties. Oshun symbolizes river waters but is also the patron of love, marriage, fertility and gold. She is the archetype of joy and pleasure. Yemaya is identified with the sea and is the symbol of motherhood. Ellegua is the god of the crossroads and controls change and destiny. These are just a few of the many saints of Santeria. Santeria faith is placed firmly in the powers of the supernatural saints in close alliance with the magical rituals of the Santeros.

Spells requiring the help of a saint must employ materials that are attributes of that particular orisha. For example, Chango is the god of fire,

Large Santeria altar containing statues, candles, cigars, water and food in New York City.

thunder and lightning and is most often used by Santeros to overcome enemies or to dominate a person. His symbols are a double-edged axe and mortar castle; his colors are red and white; his offerings are apples, bananas, red roosters and rams; and his equivalent Catholic saint is St. Barbara. Hence, if a gang member who practiced Santeria wanted to control his enemies through magic, he would either consult a Santero or conduct his own ritual worship of Chango using the items listed above and any additional or more specific objects that would be proper offerings. Conversely, if officers discover a crime scene that entails a mutilated ram, red roosters and a symbol of or an actual double-edged axe, it can be one indication that a person is being threatened. Knowledge of the particular spells of Santeria can be extremely useful to investigations that entail drug trafficking and Hispanic gangs because traffickers and gang members frequently are practitioners of Santeria or Palo Mayombe and often invoke spells for protection from the law and power over their enemies. Table 7.1 lists the attributes of the major orishas and their Catholic syncretisms.

Of the many deities belonging to Santeria, seven have been grouped into a special cluster known as the Seven African Powers. Although each is worshipped individually, together they are believed to be immensely powerful. The orishas that constitute the Seven African Powers are used by Santeros in very difficult cases and include Obtala, Eleggua, Chango, Oggun, Orunla, Yemaya and Oshun. As a group the Seven African Powers are believed to control every aspect of human life. The following brief description of each orisha demonstrates how together they hold so much power.

Obatala — Obatala is known as the King of the White Cloth and is a symbol of peace and purity. He is also the father of mankind and is believed to control the mind and all thought.

Table 7.1 Santeria Gods

Orisha	Saint	Function or Power	Force in Nature	Weapon or Symbol	Colors, Numbers, and Feast Days	Offerings
Eleggua	Anthony, Holy Guardian Angel, Christ Child	Messages; controls fate, the unexpected; justice personified	Corners, crossroads	Clay or cement head with eyes and mouth made of cowrie shells	Red and Black; 3; June 13	Male chickens, epos, rum, cigars, coconuts, toasted corn, smoked fish, opossum, toys, candy
Orunmila	Francis of Assisi	Divination		Table of Ifa	Green and yellow; 16; October 4	Kola nuts, yams, black hens
Obatala	Our Lady of Mercy, Holy Eucharist, Resurrected Christ	Peace, purity	Fatherhood, all white substances	Iruke: horsetail with a beaded handle	White; 8; September 24	Cotton, cascarilla, yams, white doves, coconuts
Chango	Barbara	Power, passion, control of enemies	Fire, thunder and lightning	Double-edged ax, mortar castle	Red and white; 4, 6; December 4	Apples, bananas, red roosters, rams
Oggun	Peter	Employment, war, hospitals	Iron, steel	Metal weapons and knives	Green and black; 7; June 29	Roosters, pigeons, green plantains, rum, cigars
Ochosi	Norbert	Hunting, jails	All game animals	Crossbows	Violet; 7; June 6	Roosters, pigeons

Table 7.1 Santeria Gods (Continued)

Orisha	Saint	Function or Power	Force in Nature	Weapon or Symbol	Colors, Numbers, and Feast Days	Offerings
Aganyu	Christopher	Control of enemies	Volcanoes	Axe	Red and green; 9; November 16	Roosters, plantains, unsalted crackers with palm oil
Babalu-Aye	Lazarus	Causes and cures illness	Smallpox, leg ailments	Crutches	Sackcloth; 17; December 17	Toasted corn, pigeons, all types of beans
Yemaya	Our Lady of Regla	Maternity, womanhood	The oceans	Seashells, canoes, corals	Blue and white; 7; September 7	Watermelons, sugar cane syrup, she-goats, ducks, hens
Oshun	Our Lady of Charity	Love, marriage, gold	Rivers	Fans, mirrors, boats	White and yellow; 5; September 8	Honey, pumpkins, white wine, rum cakes, jewelry, hens
Oya	Our Lady of La Candelaria	Protection against death	Wind, burial grounds, thunderbolt	Horsetail	Maroon and white; 9; February 2	Eggplant, hens, she-goats

Eleggua — Eleggua is a symbol of destiny and of perfect balance in nature where he can help his followers in their human endeavors or create havoc in a person's life if they behave improperly. His acts are always justified and he never acts irrationally. However, he is also a trickster who stands in corners and at crossroads and guards the home against dangers. Ellegua is the first of the orishas to be honored during the ceremonies of Santeria and the first to be fed.

Chango — Chango is the god of fire, thunder and lightning and is very feared and respected. He has a large following in Santeria and represents power in all its forms, whether it is procreative, authoritative, destructive, medicinal or moral. Chango's control over fire makes him the patron of firemen. He is invoked for works of domination, passion and many other endeavors.

Oggun — Oggun is the ironworker and patron of all metals; he is also the overseer of surgeons, police and soldiers. Oggun provides employment and protection against criminals but he is also said to be responsible for all car and railroad accidents and is a symbol of war. Oggun is feared and respected in Santeria and he is worshipped and propitiated to protect his followers from what he represents. Oggun also symbolizes the sacrificial knife and the act of slaying. He is not an evil entity; he is simply the archetype of the violent occurrences that result from man's weaknesses and lack of control.

Orunla — Orunla's greatest power is divination; he is the master of the past, present and future and is the African concept of time. Orunla is not used for spells or cures like the other orishas. His power is strictly that of divination. Orunla is consulted in important matters, particularly to determine an individual's patron saint.

Yemaya — Yemaya is the goddess of the seawaters and a symbol of maternity. She is one of the most revered and popular of the orishas in Santeria and her sacred stones are shells found by the seashore. Yemaya is a symbol of womanhood and is often associated with the moon.

Oshun — Oshun is the divinity of the river and the symbol of the river waters without which life on earth would be impossible. She controls love, marriage, children, money and pleasure.[7]

According to Santeria beliefs each person is assigned a particular orisha (saint) and given a particular destiny when they are born. That saint is their guardian angel and is central to all of that person's ritual offerings throughout their life. It is the responsibility of the individual to understand his destiny and to grow with it rather than be a victim of it. Proper worship of the orishas bring devotees to a complete fulfillment of their destinies. The fundamental basis of Santeria is a personal relationship with the orishas that will bring the believers happiness, success and wisdom. This devotion or ritual worship occurs in four principal forms: divination, sacrifice, spiritualism and initiation.

Santeria altar in center of botanica (religious supply store) in the Bronx, New York.

Santeria Rituals and Magical Practices

Santeria rituals are shrouded in a tradition of secrecy that was not part of the original Yoruba religion. Although the Yoruba were successful in hiding their orishas under the guise of Catholic saints, it did not take long for the Spanish settlers to realize what the slaves were doing. This resulted in severe persecution which forced the slaves to cloak their religion in secrecy. This secrecy, which never existed in Nigeria, is still observed by the practitioners of Santeria today and is one of the reasons the religion is often misunderstood and viewed as dangerous.[8]

Religious participation in Santeria occurs either as rites or ceremonials. A person performs a rite alone or in the company of a Santero. A ceremonial is a situation in which more than two persons are present and it is always conducted by a Santero. The Afro-Cuban rituals form a continuum from simple rites such as lighting candles, offering glasses of water to the dead and to the orishas, to ceremonials that include complex ritual performances with anticipated verbal and gestural magico-religious behavior.[9]

Santeria Rituals

- **Divination** occurs when orishas speak to human beings, diagnose their needs and "open their destinies to fulfillment."
- **Sacrifice** occurs when human beings give their orishas the ashe (power) that is the sustenance of life.
- **Spirit Possession** involves fully opening the channels of ashe when human dancers are possessed by saints or ancestors.
- **Initiation** involves ceremonial rituals that show to the devotee and to the community the depth of the devotee's commitment to the religion, the orishas and his or her mastery of the techniques of invoking ashe.

There are four general categories of ritual practices in Santeria: divination, sacrifice, spirit possession and initiation. Divination occurs when orishas speak to human beings, diagnose their needs and "open their destinies to fulfillment." Sacrifice occurs when human beings give their orishas the ashe (energy) that is the sustenance of life. Spirit possession involves fully opening the channels of ashe when human dancers are possessed by saints or ancestors. Initiation involves ceremonial rituals that show the devotee and the community the depth of the devotee's commitment to the religion, the orishas and his or her mastery of the techniques of invoking ashe.[10]

Initiation

Santeria is based largely on a progressive system of initiations by which the initiate gains not only the protection of the orishas, but also increasing knowledge of the various practices and beliefs of the religion. The most important religious ritual of Santeria is called the *asiento* (making of the saint). Before a person can participate in this formal initiation ceremony, various preliminary rites must be completed. The first rite toward becoming a Santero is known as *recibir los collares* (to receive the necklaces). Beaded necklaces known as *collares* are believed to protect their wearer against evil as long as they are worn.

The necklaces are made of alternating beads in the colors specific to each god or goddess. Before he makes the necklace, the priest invokes the proper saint and asks for the saint's blessing. When the necklace is ready, it is washed in a river; an offering of a chicken and honey is made to Oshun at the riverside. After returning to the house, the priest makes the proper animal

Santeria Initiation Rituals

Santeria is based largely on a progressive system of initiations.

- **Recibir los collares** (to receive the necklaces).
- **Initiation of the Warriors** (receives Eleggua and cauldron of Oggun).
- **Asiento (hacer el santo)** (making the saint).
  - Previous two culminate in the asiento.
  - The most important initiation.
  - The process takes 1 year and costs thousands of dollars.
  - Entails strict taboos, animal sacrifices and a variety of rituals.
  - Initiate must wear white clothing for 1 year.
  - Initiate must be educated in the knowledge of the religion.

Collares (Beaded Necklaces)

- The necklaces are believed to protect their wearer against evil as long as they are worn.
- The necklaces are made of alternating beads in the colors specific to each god or goddess.

- **Yemaya** — 7 white, 7 blue
- **Oshun** — all yellow or 5 amber, 5 red
- **Chango** — 6 white, 6 red
- **Elleggua** — 3 red, 3 black
- **Oggun** — 7 green, 7 black
- **Oya** — brown beads striped blue
- **Babalu-Aye** — all white striped blue
- **Orunla** — 1 green, 1 yellow
- **Obatala** — all white beads
- **Aganyu** — blue and brown beads

sacrifices and food offerings and the necklaces are placed in the *omiero,* a ritual liquid mixture used during initiations for 7 days. The necklaces are later presented to the initiate in a complicated ceremony that lasts several hours. The initiate must dress in white during and after the ceremony.[11]

The second initiation is the making of Eleggua in the initiation of the Warriors, which includes Ellegua, Oggun and Ochosi who are said to fight all the human battles faced by the initiate and to give him guidance in all his endeavors. The initiate is given an Eleggua, a cement head with eyes, nose and mouth made of cowrie shells that is ritually prepared and anointed by a high priest. At the same time the initiate receives Eleggua, he also receives the cauldron of Oggun with all the war implements of the god and of the two other warrior saints, Ochosi and Oggun, who together will fight to protect the initiate. After a person has received these two initiations, he is said to have acquired half of the major initiation known as the *asiento*.[12]

The initiate is now prepared for the prolonged and complex ceremony known as *asiento* or *hacer el santo* (making the saint). The process lasts about a year, costs thousands of dollars and entails strict taboos, animal sacrifices and a variety of ritual activities:.

> The initiate chooses his initiation padrinos (godparents) who will train him throughout the year. Although the training is always unique for each Santero due to the subjective and eclectic nature of Santeria magic, there are certain invariants. For example, the religious parapher-nalia and the sacrificial animals are mainly directed to-wards the orisha who is assigned to the initiate. The wearing of the necklaces (which has to be imposed before the initiation) as well as wearing white clothing for a year, shaving of the head, observing food taboos, spirit pos-session by the initiate's santo and a complete knowledge of the Afro-Cuban pantheon and its ritual cycle are all common features in the initiation process. In the final ceremony, at the end of a one-year period, the Santero is reincorporated in the cultural life of the group. All of the previous taboos are lifted and the person is recognized in his or her newly acquired role. From then on each year he or she will celebrate a "spiritual birthday" on that day.[13]

Divination

Central to the Santeria religion are various divination systems by which the priests ascertain the will of the gods to resolve the daily problems of believers. Divination reveals the sources of the problems of everyday life, for example, problems of health, money or love, and provides resolutions. The Santero uses a set of 16 cowrie shells known as diloggun to determine the best solutions to his client's problems.

The Babalowa (high priest) uses two forms of divination. The most common is known as the opele, a long chain with eight medallions made of coconut rinds. The other is used only during initiation rituals to determine who the ruling orisha of an individual is. It is called the table of Ifa and is a

Santeria Divination

Central to Santeria are various divination systems that the priests use to ascertain the will of the gods to resolve daily problems of believers.

- **Darle coco al santo**: four pieces of coconut cast on the floor
- **Diloggun**: sixteen cowrie shells
- **Opele**: long chain with eight medallions made of coconut rinds
- **Table of Ifa**: wooden tray sprinkled with powder and lines are drawn in it

wooden tray upon which the Babalowa sprinkles a secret powder known as yefa and then draws a series of vertical lines that he interprets. Both the Santero and the Babalowa share the most common of divination systems in Santeria known as *darle coco al santo*, which uses four pieces of coconut that are cast on the floor to determine the wishes of an orisha. The coconut is not used in consultations; it is only used to determine whether the orishas were pleased or displeased with their offerings and how the offerings should be disposed of.[14] A Santero may interpret the disposal of animals to occur in places he is familiar with and accounts for officers frequently finding sacrificial animals in the same vicinity. Since the system of divination is based on faith in the religion and trust in the Santero, this practice allows for the possibility of an unethical priest to victimize believers with their approval. For example, he may require large amounts of money to assist in matters of love or health or advise them in ways that will benefit him.

Spirit Possession

One of the most dramatic forms of devotion to the orishas is ceremonial spirit possession, which consists of possession by the spirits of the dead and the saints. At ceremonies called *bembes, guemilere* or *tambores,* drums are played to invoke the orishas to join the devotees in dance and song. These feasts are celebrated in honor of a saint and are held for various reasons such as thanking an orisha. However, the most impressive of these *fiestas de santo* are those held on the birthdays of the saints.

The feast dates of the orishas coincide with the birthdates of their corresponding Catholic saints and are listed in Table 7.1. During the celebration, if an orisha chooses, the god or goddess will possess the body of the believer. This is known in Santeria as *surbirse el santo a su caballo,* which literally

Santeria Spirit Possession

Ceremonial spirit possession consists of possession by the spirits of the dead and the saints.

- **Bembes, Guemilere or Tambores** are ceremonies (feasts) where drums are played to invoke the spirits.
- **Surbirse el santo a su caballo** (the saint climbs upon his horse), an expression for the god possessing the body of the follower.
- Once possessed the believer performs spectacular dances, delivers messages, advice and takes on the characteristics attributed to the deity who possessed him.
- A possessed believer loses all consciousness during the possession and his personality is replaced with that of the gods.

means *the saint climbs upon his horse.* The Santeria believer is known commonly as the horse of the saints; and the mind of the initiate is considered the seat of the saints. Once an orisha possesses a believer, the incarnated saint may perform spectacular dances and more importantly will deliver messages, admonitions and advice to individual members of the community.

Spirit possession is a common ecstatic experience for both initiated and novice Santeria believers. When a Santero becomes possessed by an orisha, he takes on the characteristics attributed to that deity. A possessed believer loses all consciousness during possession and his personality disappears and is replaced with that of the god. A truly possessed devotee feels no pain, can predict the future and often describes scenes taking place thousands of miles away. The participants will speak to the possessed person as if speaking directly to the orisha. Any healing or advice is given by the saints or the dead through their mediums. Experienced Santeros can tell if a possession is not genuine and any person pretending to be possessed is held in contempt by the priests. In Cuba, false possessions were punished with oddaniko, a severe beating with a leather crop; as a result, most possessions are considered genuine.[15]

Sacrifice

Animal sacrifice is one of the most controversial issues in the practice of Santeria. In addition to the rituals and crimes associated with black magic, animal sacrifice is the most relevant to law enforcement. Officers who are unfamiliar with the practices of Santeria are justifiably shocked when they

Santeria Sacrifice

Three basic types of sacrifice:

- **Despojos (ritual cleansings):** the animals take on the negative vibrations of an individual and cannot be eaten (usually disposed of outdoors).

- **Ebbo Offerings:** made to the Eggun or the Orishas; depending on the ritual, the meat is not always eaten.

- **Initiation Offerings:** the blood is always given to the saints and the meat is always eaten and is believed to be full of the energy of the gods.

discover dead animals whose heads are missing, drained of blood and stuffed with food items. This becomes even more disturbing when the carcasses routinely appear in cemeteries, woods, on beaches, along rivers or near railroads.

It is very important for law enforcement officials to determine whether such animals were sacrificed for the purposes of Santeria, worship of another occult religion or killed by disturbed individuals. It is essential that these types of crimes do not go unreported or be relegated to trivial incidents not worth following up on. If mutilated animals are not the result of Santeria rituals, then not only will the sacrifices continue but they can very easily escalate to humans. A general rule of thumb is that practitioners of Santeria will only sacrifice those animals associated with the orishas and most often include feathered birds or goats. If an officer discovers a sacrificed dog or cat then the case requires more attention. Animal sacrifices entailing cats, dogs or larger animals such as cows are indicative of Satanism, the practice of Santeria black magic or other occult religions and are often related to other crimes such as death threats, extortion, grave robbing, murder or suicide. The following description of Santeria sacrifices will familiarize officers with typical Santeria rituals so they can distinguish them from animal mutilations that are indicative of more violent crimes.

The three basic types of sacrifice in Santeria are ritual cleansings, offerings to the egun or the orishas and initiation offerings. Ritual cleansings known as *despojos* are when the animals are believed to take on the negative vibrations surrounding an individual and therefore cannot be eaten. During a ritual cleansing, the blood of the animal is offered to the saints and the remains of the animal are disposed of in accordance with the wishes of the saint. Other types of *despojos* include herbs used in purifying baths and rubbing rituals in which an individual has a variety of ritual items such as fruits, oils, herbs, etc. rubbed on him in order to remove negative influences and evil spirits. Cleansing rituals are best explained as cathartic techniques in which the bad feelings caused by the evil in the person are passed into the birds and the curative properties of the herbs pass into the consultant. Many of the sacrificed animals that are routinely found along beaches, rivers or railroad tracks are often the result of ritual cleansings that were ritually required to be disposed of in such places.

The other two types of offerings are those made to eggun and the orishas known as ebbos and initiation offerings. During initiation offerings, the blood is always given to the saints and the meat is always eaten because it is believed to be full of the energy of the gods; as opposed to ebbo offerings where the meat is not always eaten. Most of the animals used in ritual sacrifice are fowl and include male and female chickens, roosters, ducks, guinea hens and pigeons. They are known collectively as *plumas* (feathers). In her book titled *Santeria: the Religion*, Migene Gonzalez-Wippler, a Santeria scholar and practitioner, describes a typical Santeria sacrifice:

> The sacrifice of a chicken during a cleansing ritual entails the chicken's feet and beak first being rinsed with cool water so it is clean for the saint, then the priest asks the person making the offering to kneel in front of the vessel that holds the orishas' sacred stones and to pray for good health and whatever else they may desire. As he prays, the person holds the sacrificial animal in front of the orisha and asks the deity to accept the sacrifice. The priest must 'give coconut' to the Saint before he begins the sacrifice to determine whether the saint is satisfied with the offering, only if the orisha expresses gratitude for the offering and agrees to help the individual does the sacrifice take place. The priest says prayers and then passes the animal all over the supplicant's body, praying that the cleansing will bring blessings to him; as the priest prays the person must turn slowly around. The priest then sings and prays as he plucks some feathers from the chicken and his chants indicate that the saint is doing the killing not the priest.

> Fowls may be sacrificed either by tearing off the head with a swift wrist movement or by cutting off the head with a sacrificial knife. Doves or pigeons must be killed by tearing off the head. The one making the offering must hold the chicken by the legs and wings. The blood

is allowed to drip on the saint's stones or if it is an Eleggua, on the cement head that represents him. A circle of blood is also made around the vessel holding the saint's emblem. The Santero then opens a jar of honey and pours a thin stream over the stones and then takes a mouthful of rum and sprays the orisha and the bird with it.

During the entire ceremony, the priest chants special prayers honoring the saint who is receiving the offering. The carcass of the dead bird is initially placed in front of the saint and the priest takes the coconut rinds and asks the saint where the bird should be disposed of. The first place he asks is for the garbage pail because it is the easiest form of disposal. If the saint says no, then the priest continues to ask for different places; the most common places are the woods, crossroads, railroad or cemetery. The animal cannot be disposed of any other way than the saint proscribes.

When the ritual is over, the person ritually cleans up the items, places them in front of the orisha and the priest lights two white candles on a white plate to officially end the ceremony. The body of the animal is then stuffed with candies, coconut, toasted corn and treated with rum, honey and the smoke of a cigar, which is then placed inside the animal, pennies corresponding to the number of the saint are also placed inside the carcass which is then wrapped in a bag and taken to the place indicated by the saint.[16]

There are many variations of these rituals dependent upon the individual Santero, his choice of spells and his interpretation of the divination systems; however, it is not uncommon to find animals stuffed with food and other ritual items in outdoor isolated places.

Sacrifice is used in a variety of magical spells for very specific events. Practitioners can consult numerous spell books if they do not consult a priest. These books, very similar to recipe books, provide the ingredients, amounts and detailed directions for conducting rituals. The spells are most often arranged according to the desired goal. For example, recipes may be organized under headings such as love spells, overcoming enemies, acquiring money, protection against evil and help during court cases. In communities

Santeria Sacrifice

- Most of the animals used in Santeria sacrifice are goats or feathered birds.
- Fowl includes male and female chickens, roosters, ducks, guinea hens and pigeons. They are known collectively as "plumas" (feathers).

- Animal sacrifices entailing cats, dogs or larger animals such as cows are indicative of either Satanism, the practice of Palo Mayombe, other occult religions or disturbed individuals.

with large populations of Santeria and Voodoo practitioners, it is not unusual to find headless chickens on the doorways and steps of courthouses and government buildings where practitioners discard the sacrificed bird as part of a spell that will protect them from being found guilty. Some of the required ingredients include items such as dirt from police stations, jails, and cemeteries in addition to very specialized herbs and sacrificial animals. The instructions on the following pages are examples from spell books.

The ingredients for these spells are either acquired in nature or purchased from religious supply stores called '*botanicas*,' most often located in Hispanic neighborhoods of large American cities. However, the technology of the Internet has made it possible to order many of the items online. Botanicas sell everything from statues of the Catholic saints, candles, herbs, oils, and incense to a variety of animal products. Frequently the owner of a botanica is a practicing Santero and throughout the store customers will find a variety of altars.

Botanicas are also very useful when conducting investigations into Santeria-related crimes. The owners are familiar with their customers and can recognize the types of spells their customers practice by what they purchase. The owners also are the connection to the Santeria community and developing a good rapport with them can save the investigator a great deal of legwork. However, occasionally a botanica will serve as a front for illegal activities involved in the practice of Palo Mayombe and similar to occult shops, there may be a backroom or basement in which rituals are held. The types of ritual items sold indicate which stores are more likely to be involved in illegally obtaining and selling human remains. Botanicas that cater to Santeros as opposed to Paleros will not sell items related to Palo Mayombe and will be more likely to assist officers in investigations.

Amulet to Escape the Law

This a very famous and powerful amulet that allows an individual to escape the law or avoid legal problems. This amulet can also be used to win a court case.

INGREDIENTS

1. Earth of the Mountains ¼ oz.
2. Earth of the Crossroads ¼ oz.
3. Earth of Four Jails ¼ oz.
4. Earth of Four Police Stations ¼ oz.
5. Polvo De Venado ¼ oz.
6. Palo Jobovan
7. Palo Cocuyo
8. Medium Size Hollow Deer Antler
9. Black Rooster
10. One Dark Pigeon
11. Seven Multi-Colored Beads
12. One Cowrie Shell
13. Four Red Candles
14. Miniature Smooth Stone from the Monte

PREPARATION

1. Place all of the earths into a large bowl.
2. Add the Polvo De Venado to the earth mixture.
3. Add the one-inch Palo Jobovan and the Palo Cocuyo to the earth mixture.
4. Place the stone into the bowl with the other ingredients.
5. Salute your spirits.
6. Take a mouthful of rum and spray the ingredients of the bowl.
7. Light a cigar and blow smoke directly onto the ingredients.
8. Using the ritual sacrifice prayer, sacrifice the rooster and the pigeon.
9. Pour the blood over the mixture and the stone.
10. Place the candles around the bowl.
11. Light the candles in honor of the spirits.
12. Allow the stone and the other ingredients to feed on the blood for 24 hours.
13. After the 24 hours, take all of the ingredients and place them into the hollow horn.
14. Seal the amulet with cement or a strong rubber glue.
15. Place the Cowrie shell in the middle of the glue along with the seven different colored beads.
16. When the glue or cement has hardened, it is ready for usage.

This amulet should be kept in your pocket or purse. This amulet can be fed when you are feeding your spirits. The spirit of this amulet likes rum and cigar offerings. Do this about once a week to keep the spirit in your favor.

Magical spells and animal sacrifice are disturbing to persons unfamiliar with these practices but they are not as serious as animal mutilations that are indicative of Satanism and other occult religions. However, although animal sacrifice may be theologically benign, they officially constitute crimes

Ochosi for Protection

This Ochosi is used for protection of your home. This Ochosi should be placed near the front of the door to ward off your enemies and witchcraft.

INGREDIENTS

1. Seven lavender candles
2. Salvadera (Spanish herb)
3. Espartilla (Spanish herb)
4. Anisette liquor
5. Tobacco cigar
6. Seven rooster tail feathers
7. Romero (Spanish herb)
8. Rubber cement
9. Rum
10. Holy water
11. One large metal crossbow of Ochosi
12. Quinta Maldicion (Spanish herb)
13. Siempre Viva (Spanish herb)
14. Yerba De Sangre (Spanish herb)
15. Large strand of brown and green beads
16. Espanta Policia (Spanish herb)

PREPARATION

1. Completely cover only the arrow and the shaft with rubber cement.
2. Wrap the shaft with the strand of beads.
3. The shaft of the arrow should be completely covered with beads.
4. The beads should be in the pattern of one brown bead and one green bead.
5. Place the seven rooster tail feathers at the end of the shaft and fasten with glue and beads.
6. Allow it to dry.
7. After the crossbow had dried, place the holy water into a large white bowl.
8. Add the Espanta Policia, Salvadera, Romero, Espartilla, Quinta Maldicion, Siempra Viva and the Yerba De Sangre into the Holy water.
9. Mix the ingredients well,
10. Place the metal crossbow into the white bowl.
11. Pour the Anisette liquor over the crossbow.
12. Take some rum into your mouth and spray directly on the crossbow.
13. Do this three times.
14. Light the cigar and blow smoke directly on the crossbow.
15. Do this three times.
16. Place the seven lavender candles around the white bowl and then light.
17. Allow the candles to burn completely.

Allow Ochosi to remain for three days in the mixture.

Place over your front door.

Religious mural painted on the side of a botanica in the Bronx, NY.

Botanica for Santeria practice in the Bronx, NY.

Vandi Candle & Incense, manufacturer of Santeria religious supplies, in the Bronx, NY.

under most state statutes and local ordinances and represent continual problems for health departments, the ASPCA and animal rights groups.

The New York courts, in a case titled *First Church of Chango v. American Society for the Prevention of Cruelty to Animals*, 134 A.D.2d 971, 521 N.Y.S. 2d 356 (1987), affirmed, 70 N.Y. 2d 616, 521 N.E.2d 443 (1988), ruled that animal sacrifices were not protected, and could be prohibited under the New York State anti-cruelty law — that is a neutral, generally applicable statute. A later case concerning the practice of animal sacrifice went all the way to the U.S. Supreme Court *Church of the Lukumi Babalu Aye v. City of Hialeah*, 508 U.S. 520 (1993)) after a Florida Santeria church was prevented from conducting animal sacrifice. In 1993, the justices unanimously ruled in favor of the church, arguing that animal sacrifice is protected by the First Amendment. However, this historical decision providing rights for Santeria practitioners cannot accommodate all of the proscribed rituals that are in opposition to city health codes. For example, the ruling does not allow for disposing of animals in public places, which may be necessary according to a particular ritual. Essentially, Santeria sacrifice can never be completely reconciled with U.S. laws because it conflicts with health codes and interpretations of what constitutes cruelty to animals.

Additionally, sacrifice in the worship of the dark side of Santeria goes beyond basic problems for the health department and has been associated with more serious crimes such as grave robbing, drug trafficking and murder. Not only is the intention of the worshiper to cause harm, but the items required for particular spells can only be obtained illegally.

Altar centerpieces and ngangas for sale at a Santeria botanica in Miami, FL.

Catholic Saints and Santeria candles for sale at a botanica in the Bronx, NY.

Santeria botanica in the Bronx, NY.

"Iruke," horsetail with beaded handle for sale at a botanica in Miami, Florida.

Typical Santeria sacrifice containing chickens, corn, beans, pennies and other ritual items. (Photo courtesy of Bradford K. Varney, Pennsylvania State Constable, Bucks County, Pennsylvania.)

Voodoo

Voodoo is also known as Vodun, Voudou, Vodoun and Hoodoo and is derived from *Vodu*, a word that means *spirit* or *deity* in the African Fon language. *Voodoo* and its derivative *Hoodoo* originated as derogatory expressions to refer to systems of sorcery and magic or to specific spells or charms stemming from these systems. Since many American practitioners currently refer to their religion as Voodoo, that term will be used in this chapter.

In contemporary America, the Voodoo religion still sustains a serious stigma that originated from the many inaccurate and racist depictions in Hollywood films and the media in general. Voodoo is still ridiculed and certain Internet websites mock Voodoo magic. However, Voodoo is an established religion with as many as 60 million followers worldwide with large populations in New York, Miami and Montreal — cities with the greatest concentrations of Haitian immigrants. Similar to Santeria, Voodoo is a syncretic religion that developed as a response to the African slave trade; however, Voodoo evolved among the slaves who were taken to Haiti. Although some of the rituals and ceremonies of Voodoo are comparable to those of Santeria, the religions have marked differences. They originated from different African tribes and the rites varied with each tribe. Voodoo derived from the African

Voodoo

- Voodoo is also known as Vodun, Voudou, Vodoun and Hoodoo.
- Voodoo is an established religion with as many as 60 million followers worldwide with large populations in New York, Miami, Louisiana and Montreal.
- Voodoo derived from the African tribes of the Nagos, Ibos, Aradas, Dahomeans and others and evolved in Haiti.
- Same types of crimes as Santeria, animal sacrifice, etc.

Voodoo statues and assorted ritual items in a Haitian botanica in Miami, Florida.

Voodoo Theology

- Voodoo has many deities, known collectively as Loa and known either as Rada or Petro, each corresponding to a Catholic Saint.
- Rituals are similar to Santeria and include initiation, divination, sacrifice and spirit possession.
- Voodoo altars are for the worship of gods and are kept in small rooms known as badji.
- Male priests are called Houngan and female priests are called Mambo (white magic).
- Bokors, also known as Caplatas, practice black magic.

tribes of the Nagos, Ibos, Aradas, Dahomeans and others. Although they do share Yoruba and Kongo influences, the cultures they assimilated in were different; Haiti was under French influence during the slave trade while Cuba, Puerto Rico and the Dominican Republic were under Spanish rule.

Voodoo has a loosely organized priesthood open to both men and women. Male priests are called Houngans and female priests are called Mambos and they limit their practices to white magic, while Bokors, also known as Caplatas, practice what is referred to as left hand magic, black magic or evil sorcery. It is the image of the Bokor that usually provides the stereotypical portrayal of the practitioner of Voodoo spells that are supposed to cause death, illness or injury, to obtain riches, to bring bad luck to enemies or good fortune to a client and also to invoke the zombie, a corpse that has been raised from the grave to live again as a mindless slave.

Essentially, Haitian Voodoo is comprised of both good and evil uses of magic as utilized by the Houngan and the Bokor. The many different types of Voodoo rituals range from individual acts of piety such as lighting candles for particular spirits to large feasts sometimes lasting several days. Similar to Santeria, initiation, divination, sacrifice and spirit possession are fundamental Voodoo rituals.

The Haitian form of Voodoo has many deities, known collectively as Loa, who participate in ritualistic ceremonies in several different ways. Rituals are most commonly held to invoke a particular god who best fits the need of the moment and gods are known either as Rada or Petro. Rada and Petro spirits sharply contrast and the Rada spirits are known for their wisdom and benevolence while the Petro spirits are known for their power and Congo influence. Each Loa has its own attributes and form of worship. Table 7.2 describes the Voodoo pantheon of gods.

In addition to the attributes listed in Table 7.2, the Voodoo saints also have their own symbolic drawings called *veves* — line drawings that are most often drawn during ceremonies to worship a particular spirit.

Voodoo first came to the U.S. in 1803 when the prohibition against importing slaves from the West Indies was lifted to allow planters access to more labor. What began in Louisiana as the Haitian transplant of Voodoo eventually evolved into an American syncretism known as Hoodoo. This newer form of the ancient traditions developed differently in the U.S., supplanting many of its religious aspects with more cultural and medicinal aspects. Indeed, the Hoodoo leader, known as a Hoodoo doctor:

> ...is a maker of medicine, a treater of ills, and perhaps a historian.... He does not perform marriages, christen babies or bury the dead. For these functions there is the ordained minister of one of the established churches. Hoodoo doctors do conduct meetings, but never in a church or even a consecrated building as does the Haitian Houmfort, a Voodoo temple. They prefer the outdoors, with large trees for shelter where they can

Table 7.2 Pantheon of Voodoo Gods

Name	Corresponding Catholic Saints	Rites	Colors	Attributions; Habitation	Characteristics	Symbols	Offerings
Legba	Peter, Anthony	Rada	Red	Protector of the home; gates and crossroads	Interpreter of the lwa, keeper of the gates, crossroads and paths; rival of Dambala	Feeble old man in rags	Cassava, rice, green bananas, smoked foods, mottled rooster
Azaka	Isidore	Rada	Blue, red, green	Harvest; fields	Peasant lwa, cultivator of fields and agriculture; distrustful, sly, greedy; hates townspeople	Mabouya (small reptile)	Corn, bread, unrefined sugar, brandy
Gede	Expedit	Rada and Petro	Black, purple, white	Making or repelling spells; cemeteries, subterranean places	Lwa of the dead	Cadaver, black cross, farm implements	Black goat, black rooster
Baron Samdi	?	Rada and Petro	Black, purple	Cross at the entrance to cemeteries	Head of the Gede (lwa of the dead)	Tall; black clothes	Salted herring, black goat, black hens
Dambala	Patrick	Rada	White	Wealth, luck, happiness; springs and rivers	Principle of goodness	Snake, rainbow	Everything white: hens, rice, milk, eggs

Table 7.2 Pantheon of Voodoo Gods (Continued)

Name	Corresponding Catholic Saints	Rites	Colors	Attributions, Habitation	Characteristics	Symbols	Offerings
Ayida Wedo	Our Lady of Immaculate Conception	Rada	Blue, white	Wealth, luck, happiness; springs and rivers	Wife of Dambala	Snake, rainbow	Everything white: hens, rice, milk, eggs
Ezili	The Virgin Mary	Rada	Blue, pink	Love; river banks	Mulatto, coquette, sensual; beauty and grace, luxury, pleasure; promiscuous	Heart, mirror	Toiletries; rare and refined dishes, rice, chicken
Ogou Feray	James the Greater	Rada	Red	Fighting against miserable conditions; Calabash tree, bamboo	Warrior and soldier	A saber driven into the earth	Red rooster, bull
Agwe	Ulrich	Rada	White, green, pink	Protection of navigation, and shipping; fishing, sea fishing	Mulatto, fair skin, sea-green eyes; naval officer	Boat, oars	White sheep, hens; fine drink; champagne
Simbi	The Magi	Petro	Black, gray	Gift of clairvoyance; springs, caves, mountains	Guardian of springs and ponds	Pond	Black or gray animals; pig, goat, guinea fowl, turkey, hen

expound, undisturbed, their different theories of the
supernatural in their own ways.[17]

It would be incorrect to state, however, that Hoodoo practitioners use
only white or positive magic; clearly some Hoodoo rites in various urban
locations have invoked evil spirits, exacted discomforting curses and mapped
out the deaths of enemies. There is currently no data available that discloses
the degree to which practitioners may or may not be involved in criminal
activity directly connected to their belief in Voodoo.[18] However, the same
types of crimes, i.e., animal sacrifice, extortion, grave robbing, etc. that apply
to the worship of Santeria also occur in the practice of Voodoo.

Brujeria

Brujeria is not only the Santeria term for witchcraft but also refers to a
religion that has distinctly Mexican cultural and religious roots. Brujeria is
the practice of witchcraft and involves the use of magic to appease and control
the gods/spirits specific to the Brujeria religion. Brujeria combines many
cultural and ritualistic traditions of ancient Aztec myths, European witchcraft
and Cuban Santeria with the religious traditions of the Catholic faith. The
roots of this syncretic belief system can be traced to the mid-16th century
when according to Mexican religious legend the Virgin Mary appeared to an
Indian convert and informed him that she wanted a church constructed on
the spot. Subsequently, the Shrine of Our Lady of Guadalupe was built.

The Aztecs, who for many centuries had worshipped the pagan goddess
Toantzin, almost immediately disguised their goddess in the safety of Guad-

---

Brujeria

- Brujeria is a religion that has distinctly Mexican
  cultural and religious roots.
- Brujeria is the practice of witchcraft and combines
  ritualistic traditions of ancient Aztec myths,
  European witchcraft and Cuban Santeria.
- Brujeria evolved in the 16th century when the
  Spaniards designated Toantzin, an Aztec pagan
  goddess, a Roman Catholic and the former
  priestesses of Toantzin went underground
  becoming "brujas."

alupe, and in the process took the first step in creating Brujeria. When the Spaniards designated Toantzin a Roman Catholic and demanded Aztec allegiance, the Catholic priests were unaware that they had helped preserve the very paganism they had hoped to destroy. "By Christianizing Toantzin, they'd made it safe for nominally Catholic Indians to venerate her, with the provision that they call her Nuestra Senora de Guadalupe and attend Mass regularly." Subsequently, the former priestesses of Toantzin went underground becoming *brujas* whose native magic lay hidden under a veneer of popular Catholicism. Researcher Mary Virginia Devine describes how the brujas adapted to each culture with which they came into contact:

> The conversion of the northern tribes to Catholicism not only gave the brujas more clients, but also exposed them to the herbal lore of the Yaqui curanderas, thus helping revive the almost forgotten Aztec tradition of medicine. Contact with urban Latinos added European ceremonial magic ... to their system. And when the brujas left their homeland to settle in America's inner cities, they found a treasure trove of black folklore, Hoodoo and Voodoo, which they promptly incorporated into their teachings. By the 1950s, Brujeria had taken root in Chicano communities from Los Angeles to New York and from Tulsa to Detroit.[19]

In contemporary America, brujas practice a magico-religious system that centers around Guadalupe; the bruja (priestess) is her representative on earth. Brujas worship Her as an all-knowing and all-powerful goddess who grants believers every wish when propitiated according to the rituals of Brujeria. Such rituals constitute the magical nature of the belief system. The female bruja, usually working within the safety and serenity of her own home, conducts the rituals and rites of the faith as she sees fit. Brujeria followers who wish to use the bruja's services approach her with a particular problem and entrust her to create a spell to eradicate the problem. Her spell will involve divination techniques, and in some cases, tarot cards and increasingly more often in the U.S., astrological signs.

In essence, the bruja's services are enlisted to extinguish the deeds of two spirits: the *elementales* and the *diablera*. The elementales, nature spirits who cause problems "because their stupidity leaves them open to exploitation by devils" are of four types: gnomes (earth), undines (water), sylphs (air) and salamanders (fire). The bruja evokes a spell to make the particular elementales depart or, in the most serious cases when the spirit is working directly for the devil, to kill the elementales. The diablera, the evil spirit

Brujeria Theology

- Brujas practice a magico-religious system that centers around Guadalupe.The bruja (priestess) is Her representative on earth.
- Brujas worship her as an all-knowing and all-powerful goddess who grants believers every wish when propitiated according to the rituals of Brujeria.
- The brujas use divination to rid people of evil spirits: the elementales and the diablera.
- Most brujas are solo practitioners and their spells are kept in a *Libreta*, similar to a *Book of Shadows*. Most are written in nonacademic Colonial Spanish.
- A few practice together and the organizational structure of such groups is similar to the Witchcraft tradition, consisting of covens or confradias of thirteen of less.

who is directly under Satan's employ is the bruja's primary enemy. Diableras encourage promiscuity and homosexuality, inflict disease on people and cast evil spells on good people. It is the bruja's task to cast a spell to undo the diablera's hex.

The bruja's magical instruments and tools are very basic, originally designed for easy disguise in the event of a surprise visit from a Catholic priest. The necessary instruments are the *cuchillo*, a plain knife, and the wand which is most commonly a recently cut tree branch. The bruja's altar usually consists of a dresser upon which a white cloth is spread and several tools are placed: two long white candles and a candle holder; a votive candle, a glass for holy water; incense; and a statue of Guadalupe. The brujas' spells are kept in a *Libreta*, similar to a *Book of Shadows*, in which all their individual and collective secrets are written. Like Wiccan (neo-Pagan) practitioners, brujas do not share their spell books. Most spell books are written in non-academic Colonial Spanish or in a Tex–Mex dialect that borrows from American English.

Most brujas are solo practitioners; however, many meet for spiritual worship and a few practice together. The organizational structures of such groups draw heavily from the Witchcraft tradition and consist of covens or confradias of 13 or fewer people. Wearing white cotton robes tied with a white silk ribbon or a cord and a silver medal of Guadalupe, brujas gather for several ceremonies during which they pray to Guadalupe that their powers will be great and strong. They usually meet for 13 new moon ceremonies and several of the Wiccan sabbats.[20]

Palo Mayombe

- Combines the belief systems of the ancient African Congo tribes with Yoruba religion and Catholicism.
- Dark side of Santeria.
- Using magical rituals that manipulate, captivate and/or control another person.
- Priests of Palo Mayombe are known as paleros or mayomberos.
- Centers its rituals around the spirit of the dead instead of the orishas.

Palo Mayombe

Palo Mayombe is another syncretic Afro-Caribbean belief system that combines the cultural and spiritual belief systems of the ancient African Congo tribes with the religious practices of Yoruba slaves and Catholicism. Just as Satanism corresponds to the dark side of Christianity, Palo Mayombe corresponds to the dark side of Santeria. It uses magical rituals that manipulate, captivate and/or control another person most often for the practitioner's malevolent purposes.

Like the people from Nigeria, the Congo slaves were forcibly brought to the Caribbean and subsequently forced to adapt their cultural and religious beliefs to the dominant culture and Catholic religious tradition of the new land. Through the assimilation process, the Congo slaves also incorporated some of the beliefs, symbols and rituals of Santeria. The result of this particular syncretism was Palo Mayombe, derived from the Spanish *palo* meaning *wooden stick* or *branch* and referring to the pieces of wood practitioners use for their magic spells.[21] Priests of Palo Mayombe are known as Paleros or Mayomberos. Although the origins of the Mayombero and Santero share similar roots, there are two features that distinguish the rituals and beliefs of these different and individualistic belief systems.

First, although many Mayomberos are originally initiated into Santeria, very few Santerians also practice Palo Mayombe. In fact, most Santeria practitioners fear the Mayombero, claiming he practices a sinister form of Santeria, which they call brujeria, black magic or witchcraft. It is important to note that officers who practice Santeria should never be forced to investigate crimes associated with Palo Mayombe, because for them these crimes are not just spiritually offensive, but can be perceived as life threatening. Second, the

Palo Mayombe: Sacred Cauldron

Nganga contains:
- Wooden sticks (21).
- Various herbs, feathers.
- Animal bones (skulls or other bones of various birds).
- Small iron agricultural tools (rakes, picks, hoes, etc.).
- Sacred stones.
- A chain with a padlock will often be wrapped around it.
- Items that may be of special significance to the palero.
- Human bones (invariably a human skull).

rituals of Santeria most often focus magic on positive actions designed to improve one's personal position or please an orisha. Palo Mayombe, on the other hand, centers its rituals around the spirits of the dead, often using magic to inflict misfortune or death upon an enemy. In fact, the Mayombero does not use the orishas but rather invokes the evil spirit of one specific patron who resides in his nganga, the cauldron used during most rituals.[22]

Another very important distinction is that some practitioners of Palo Mayombe claim that although they evoke the spirits of the dead, their intentions are not to harm; rather they use Palo in particularly difficult cases because it works much faster and is more effective than Santeria rituals. These Paleros practice what is called *Christian Mayombe* because their sacred cauldrons are sprinkled with holy water, which differentiates them from practitioners of the dark side of Santeria. Although Christian Paleros work with the spirits of the dead, they only work with good spirits. Unbaptized Paleros work exclusively with the spirits of suicides, criminals and evil witches.

Palo Mayombe is the practice of malevolent magic in the context of myths and rituals of Congo origins and its magic is often accomplished with the use of human bones. Practitioners of Palo Mayombe specialize in accomplishing sorcery through the spirit of the dead. "The Palero is rayado, that is, cut in Palo. This means that the individual has had the initiatory designs of Palo cut with a razor on his skin."[23] The source of the Palero's power is the cauldron where the spirits of the dead reside. The African name for the sacred cauldron is *nganga*, a Congo word that means *dead, spirit* or *supernatural force*. Items typically found in the nganga include a human skull, bones, graveyard dust, crossroads dust, branches, herbs, insects, animal and bird carcasses, coins, hot spices and blood. The initiate in Palo is known as *Mpangui, Nganga Nkisi* or *Tata Nkisi*. The nganga does what its owners order it to do and working with it is referred to as *playing* with it.

When the spirit of the nganga carries out its owner's wishes, he or she gives it blood as an expression of gratitude.[24] The Paleros also serve their ancestors, all the dead and the spirits of nature. Chango is the orisha most often worshipped by the Paleros who call him Nsasi and claim he originates from the Congo. For personal gain or a fee, the Paleros will perform rituals to inflict mental or physical harm or even death on an individual. A Brujeria or Bilongo is a black magic spell that is achieved in many ways, as when a person is given a magical preparation in food or drink or when a spirit of the dead is sent with the intention of causing torment and misfortune to the victim. Other kinds of black magic include leaving animal carcasses (decapitated roosters, dead goats, human skulls, etc.) at the entrance of a business or home or preparing special dolls stuffed with ritual items (pendants, herbs, names of people, etc.) and kept at home.[25] Depending upon the circumstances, these rituals may be designated as harassment or as terroristic threats.

The forensic aspects of Santeria stem from the practice of Palo Mayombe because human bones are frequently found in a cemetery wrapped in plastic or burlap or in a shallow grave. When these are discovered, the forensic scientist must investigate to determine their origin, identification, and other information. Signs indicative of their ritualistic use include adherent wax, bloodstains, chicken feathers, and the association with the colors of one of the Seven African Powers (usually Eleggua) and the presence of pennies (often in multiples of seven).[26] The following is a detailed description of the Palo Mayombe rituals involved in making the sacred cauldron, as described by Santeria scholar Migene Gonzalez-Wippler. The application to law enforcement is clearly evident.

> The Mayombero waits until the moon is propitious, and then he goes to a cemetery with an assistant. Once there, he sprinkles rum in the form of a cross over a pre-chosen grave. The grave is opened, and the head, toes, finger, ribs, and tibias of the corpse are removed. The Mayombero usually knows the identity of the cadaver, which is known as kiymba. They are usually recent graves, as the Mayombero insists on having a head in which the brain is still present, or those belonging to very violent persons, especially those of criminals and of the insane, for the purposes of the Mayombero are generally to commit acts of death and destruction.... After the macabre remains are removed from their graves, they are wrapped in a black cloth and the Mayombero and his helper return to the witch's house.

Palo Mayombe:
Law Enforcement Issues

- Human skulls are used in the nganga.
- The cauldron is "fed" with blood.
- Human bones wrapped in plastic or burlap are frequently found in a cemetery or in a shallow grave.
- Graves are opened, and the head, toes, fingers, ribs and tibias of the corpse are removed.
- Animal carcasses (decapitated roosters, dead goats, human skulls, etc.) are left at the entrance of a business or home.

The Mayombero lies on the floor. His assistant covers him with a sheet and lights four tapers, which are placed on each side of the Mayombero's body, as if he were dead. On the blade of a knife he places seven small heaps of gunpowder, known as fula. The body of the Mayombero becomes rigid and then goes into convulsions as the spirit of the kiyumba takes possession of him. The assistant asks the spirit if it is willing to work for the Mayombero. If the spirit agrees, all the heap of gunpowder will ignite spontaneously and simultaneously. If the gunpowder does not burn, the answer is negative and the body remains must be returned to the cemetery. Once the spirit accepts the pact, the grisly ceremony is ended.

The Mayombero writes the name of the dead person on a piece of paper and places it at the bottom of a big iron cauldron, together with a few coins, which are the price of the kiyumba's help. The body's remains are added to the cauldron, together with some earth from the grave. The Mayombero then makes an incision on his arm with a knife that must have a white handle, and lets a few drops of blood fall into the cauldron, so the kiyumba may drink and be refreshed...After the human or animal blood has been sprinkled on the remains, the Mayombero adds to the cauldron the wax from a burnt candle, ashes, a cigar butt, and some lime.

Also added to the mixture is a piece of bamboo, sealed at both ends with wax, and filled with sand, sea water, and quicksilver. This gives the kiyumba the speed of the quicksilver and the persistence of the sea tide, which never rest and are forever in movement.

The body of a small black dog is also added to the cauldron to help the spirit "track down" its victims. Next to the dog, a variety of herbs and tree barks are placed inside the cauldron. The last ingredients to be added are red pepper, chili, garlic, ginger, onions, cinnamon, and rue, together with ants, worms, lizards, termites, bats, frogs, Spanish flies, a tarantula, a centipede, wasp, and a scorpion. After the nganga is ready, it is brought back to the cemetery where it is buried and left for three Fridays. Then it is disinterred and taken to the woods, where it is again buried for another three Fridays, this time by the side of a ceiba, or any other magical tree. At the end of this combined period of forty-two days, the nganga is taken home by the Mayombero, where he again gives it some fresh blood and adds some rum with pepper, dry wine, and water. The nganga is finished and ready to work.[27]

This description provides insights into the types of crimes that occur through the practice of Palo Mayombe. The illegal actions involved in the making of the sacred cauldron described above include cemetery desecration, theft of human remains and animal mutilation. However, much more serious crimes can occur once the Palero begins to use the nganga.

Human Sacrifice

The most recent case of human sacrifice in the worship of Palo Mayombe was discovered in April 1989 in Matamoros, Mexico. In this case a young American University of Texas student, Mark Kilroy, and several Mexican citizens were kidnapped and later ritualistically killed and sacrificed by orders of drug dealer and Mayombero, Adolfo de Jesus Constanzo.

Adolfo de Jesus Constanzo was a Miami-born career criminal and leader of the most violent cult in modern times. He practiced Palo Mayombe which was an integral part of his serious drug trafficking operation and was responsible for many incidents of human sacrifice; where his victims were slaugh-

Palo Mayombe: Crimes

- Illegal actions involved in the making of the sacred cauldron:
  - **Trespassing**
  - **Cemetery desecration**
  - **Theft of human remains**
  - **Animal mutilation**
  - **Threats**
- Officers who practice Santeria should never be forced to investigate crimes associated with Palo Mayombe because for them these crimes are not just spiritually offensive but can be perceived as life threatening.

Palo Cult: Matamoros Mexico

- Leader: Adolfo de Jesus Costanzos a.k.a. El Cubano (The Cuban) or El Padrino (The Godfather).
- High Priestess: Sara Villareal Aldrete (The Godmother) 24-year-old college student.
- Drug trafficking operation and human sacrifice.
- 23 (documented) ritual murders.
- Victims tortured, dismembered, hearts, brains and other vital organs removed while they were alive; others were skinned alive.

tered in meticulous and elaborate ceremonies. He was known to his followers as either El Cubano (The Cuban) or El Padrino (The Godfather).

Constanzo's ritual activities stretched from Mexico City to the impoverished areas around Matamoros, near the U.S. border. He and his many followers committed numerous sadistic murders. Although no final number of victims was ever agreed upon, 23 ritual murders were well documented. When the bodies of victims were dug up, which included at least 14 separate remains, some of the bodies had been beheaded and trussed with chicken wire; others were totally dismembered. Hearts, brains and other vital organs had been removed as victims were tortured and dismembered. At least a few of them were more than likely alive during the process; still others had obviously been skinned while alive. In a nearby shed, other decomposing human organs were found in blood-caked vats and cauldrons. The stench around the ranch, which became known as "Hell Ranch," was overpowering. Constanzo's biography demonstrates how the religious beliefs of Palo Mayombe were used to justify murder, achieve power, inculcate fear and intimidate competitors.

> Born in Miami on November 1, 1962, Adolfo Constanzo was the son of a teenaged Cuban immigrant and neighbors in Little Havana accused Aurora Constanzo of being a witch because people who angered her were likely to discover headless goats or chickens on their doorsteps in the morning. Adolfo's mother had introduced him to the Santeria cult around age nine, with side trips from Puerto Rico to Haiti for instruction in voodoo, but there were still more secrets to be learned, and in 1976 he was apprenticed to a practitioner of Palo Mayombe. His occult godfather was already rich from working with local drug dealers, and he imparted a philosophy that would follow Adolfo to his grave: Let the non-believers kill themselves with drugs. We will profit from their foolishness.
>
> He had also begun to display bisexual inclinations, with a strong preference for male lovers. A modeling assignment took the handsome young sorcerer to Mexico City in 1983, and he spent his free time telling fortunes with tarot cards in the city's infamous Zona Rosa. Before returning to Miami, Adolfo collected his first Mexican disciples, including Martin Quintana, homosexual psychic Jorge Montes, and Omar Orea, obsessed with the occult from age fifteen.
>
> In mid-1984, Constanzo moved to Mexico City full-time, seeking what his mother called new horizons collecting other followers as his magic reputation spread throughout the city. It was said that Constanzo could read the future, and he also offered ritual cleansings — for those who felt they had been cursed by enemies. Of course, it all cost money, and Constanzo's journals, recovered after his death, document 31 regular customers, some paying up to $4,500 for a single ceremony. Adolfo established a menu for sacrificial beasts, with

Palo Cult: Drug Trafficking

- Constanzo sold drugs using his connections with ranking law enforcement officers who were members of his cult.
- Constanzo was involved with the Calzada family, one of Mexico's dominant narcotics cartels. When they refused to make him a partner, he ritually murdered seven members of the family.
- Constanzo was hired to magically protect drug dealers making them invisible to the police and bullet proof against their enemies.

roosters going for $6 a head, goats for $30, boa constrictors at $450, adult zebras for $1,100, and African lion cubs listed at $3,100 each.

True to the teachings of his Florida mentor, Constanzo went out of his way to charm wealthy drug dealers, helping them schedule shipments and meetings on the basis of his predictions. For a price, he offered magic that would make dealers and their hit men invisible to police and bulletproof against their enemies. Smugglers drawn from Mexican peasant stock, with backgrounds in Brujeria, believed that he could accomplish this. According to Constanzo's ledgers, one dealer in Mexico City paid him $40,000 for magical services rendered over 3 years' time. At those rates, the customers demanded proof, and Constanzo recognized the seriousness of disappointing men who carried Uzi submachine guns in their armor-plated limousines.

By mid-1985, Adolfo and three of his disciples raided a Mexico City graveyard for human bones to start his own nganga, the traditional cauldron of blood employed by practitioners of Palo Mayombe. The rituals and air of mystery surrounding Constanzo were powerful enough to lure a cross-section of Mexican society, with his group of disciples including a physician, a real estate speculator, fashion models, and several transvestite nightclub performers. Members of his cult also included ranking law enforcement officers. At least four members of the Federal Judicial Police joined Constanzo's cult in Mexico City; one of them, Salvador Garcia, was a commander in charge of narcotics investigations; another, Florentino Ventura, retired from the federales to lead the Mexican branch of Interpol. In a country where bribery permeates all levels of law enforcement and federal officers sometimes serve as trigger men for drug smugglers, corruption is not unusual, but the devotion of Constanzo's followers ran deeper than cash on the line. In or out of uniform, they worshipped Adolfo as a minor god in his own right, their living conduit to the spirit world.

In 1986, Florentino Ventura introduced Constanzo to the drug-dealing Calzada family, then one of Mexico's dominant narcotics cartels. Constanzo won the hard-nosed dealers over with his charm and magical practices, profiting immensely from his contacts with the gang. By early 1987, he was able to pay $60,000 cash for a condominium in Mexico City, buying himself a fleet of luxury cars that included an $80,000 Mercedes Benz. When not working magic for the Calzadas or other clients, Adolfo committed drug crimes of his own, once posing as a DEA agent to rip off a coke dealer in Guadalajara, selling the stash through his police contacts for $100,000.

At some point in his odyssey from juvenile psychic to high-society witch, Constanzo began to feed his nganga with the offering of human sacrifice. No final tally for his victims is available, but 23 ritual murders are well documented, and Mexican authorities point to a rash of unsolved mutilation-slayings around Mexico City and elsewhere, suggesting that Constanzo's known victims may only represent the tip of the iceberg. In any case, his willingness to torture and kill total strangers, along with close friends, duly impressed the ruthless drug dealers who remained his foremost clients.

In the course of a year's association, Constanzo came to believe that his magical powers alone were responsible for the Calzada family's continued success and survival. In April 1987, he demanded a full partnership in the syndicate and was curtly refused. On the surface, Constanzo seemed to take the rejection in stride, but he started plotting revenge and on April 30, Guillermo Calzada and six members of his household vanished under mysterious circumstances. They were reported missing on May 1, police noting melted candles and other evidence of a strange religious ceremony at Calzada's office. Six more days elapsed before officers began fishing mutilated remains from the Zumpango River. Seven corpses were recovered in the course of a week, all bearing marks of sadistic torture; fingers, toes, and ears removed, hearts and sex organs excised, part of the spine ripped from one body, two others missing their brains. The body parts were used to feed Constanzo's nganga, building up his magical strength.

In July 1987, Salvador Garcia introduced Constanzo to another drug-running family, this one led by brothers Elio and Ovidio Hernandez. At the end of that month, in Matamoros, Constanzo had also met 22-year-old Sara Aldrete, a Mexican national with resident alien status in the United States, where she attended college in Brownsville, Texas. Adolfo charmed Sara noting with significance that her birthday, September 6, was the same as his mother's. Sara was dating Brownsville drug smuggler Gilberto Sosa at the time, but Adolfo destroyed the old relationship with an anonymous call to Sosa, revealing Sara's infidelity. With nowhere else to turn, Sara plunged full-tilt into Constanzo's world, emerging as the madrina, godmother or head witch of his cult, adding her own twists to the torture of sacrificial victims.

Constanzo's rituals became more elaborate and sadistic after he moved his headquarters to a plot of desert called Rancho Santa Elena, 20 miles from Matamoros. There, on May 28, 1988, drug dealer Hector de la Fuente and farmer Moises Castillo were executed by gunfire. On August 12, Ovidio Hernandez and his 2-year-old son were kidnapped by rival narcotics dealers, the family turning to Constanzo for help. That night, another

Palo Cult: Human Sacrifice

- People were tortured, murdered and buried at Rancho Santa Elena (Hell Ranch) near Matamoros, Mexico.
- April 1989, kidnapped and sacrificed a popular pre-med student from Texas who was on Spring Break (Mark Kilroy).
- Police discovered Constanzo's nganga filled with blood, bones, a human brain and many other ritual items in Rancho Santa Elena.
- Police uncovered Kilroy's body and 22 others.

human sacrifice was held at Rancho Santa Elena to magically protect them, and the hostages were released unharmed on August 13, Adolfo claiming full credit for their safe return. In November 1988, Constanzo sacrificed disciple Jorge Gomez, accused of snorting cocaine in direct violation of his ban on drug use.

A month later, Adolfo's ties with the Hernandez family were cemented with the initiation of Ovidio Hernandez as a full-fledged cultist, complete with ritual bloodletting and prayers to the nganga. Adolfo also used human sacrifice as a method to eradicate his rivals and he sacrificed competing smuggler Ezequiel Luna at Rancho Santa Elena, on February 14, 1989; two other dealers, Ruben Garza and Ernesto Diaz wandered into the ceremony uninvited and were also murdered. Additionally, Adolfo sometimes demanded a sacrifice on the spur of the moment, without rhyme or reason and on February 25, Ovidio Hernandez provided his own 14-year-old cousin, Jose Garcia, who was then ritually murdered.

On March 13, 1989, Constanzo sacrificed yet another victim at the ranch, gravely disappointed when his prey did not scream and plead for mercy in the approved style. Disgruntled, he ordered an Anglo for the next ritual, and his followers abducted 21-year-old Mark

Kilroy outside a Matamoros saloon and murdered him in another sacrificial ritual. Kilroy's disappearance marked the beginning of the end for Constanzo's cult. A popular pre-med student from Texas, Mark Kilroy was not some peasant, transvestite, or small-time pusher who could disappear without a trace or investigation. With family members and Texas politicians applying pressure, the search for Kilroy rapidly became an international incident. By late March 1989, Mexican authorities were busy with one of their periodic anti-drug campaigns, erecting roadblocks on a whim and sweeping the border districts for unwary smugglers. On April 1, Victor Sauceda, an ex-cop turned gangster, was sacrificed at the ranch, and the spirit message Constanzo received was optimistic enough for his troops to move a half-ton of marijuana across the border 7 nights later. And then, the magic started to unravel.

On April 9, returning from a Brownsville, Texas, meeting with Constanzo, cultist Serafin Hernandez drove past a police roadblock without stopping, ignoring the cars that set off in hot pursuit. Hernandez was a true believer and actually thought he was invisible to the police and he was surprised when officers trailed him to his destination in Matamoros. Even so, the smuggler was arrogant, inviting police to shoot him, since he also believed the bullets would merely bounce off. They arrested him instead, along with cult member David Martinez, and drove the pair back to Rancho Santa Elena, where a preliminary search turned up marijuana and firearms. Disciples Elio Hernandez and Sergio Martinez stumbled into the net while police were on hand, and all four prisoners were interrogated through the evening, revealing their tales of black magic, torture, and human sacrifice with a perverse kind of pride.

The next morning, police returned to the ranch in force, discovering the shed where Constanzo kept his nganga, brimming with blood, spiders, scorpions, a dead black cat, a turtle shell, bones, deer antlers ... and a human brain. Captive cult members directed searchers to Constanzo's private cemetery, and excavation began, revealing 15 mutilated corpses by April 16. In addition to Mark Kilroy and other victims already named, the body count included two renegade federal narcotics officers, Joaquin Manzo and Miguel Garcia, along with three men who were never identified.

The hunt for Constanzo was on, and police raided his luxury home at Atizapan, outside Mexico City, on April 17, discovering stockpiles of gay pornography and a hidden ritual chamber. The discoveries at Rancho Santa Elena made international headlines, and sightings of Constanzo were reported as far away as Chicago, but in fact, he had already returned to Mexico City, hiding out in a small apartment with Sara Aldrete and three other disciples. On May 6, neighbors called police to complain of a loud, vulgar argument in Constanzo's apartment, some say, accompanied by gunshots. As patrolmen arrived on the scene, Constanzo opened fire with an Uzi, touching off a 45-minute battle in which, miraculously, only one policeman was wounded.

When Constanzo realized that escape was impossible, he handed his weapon to cultist Alvaro de Leon Valdez, a professional hit man nicknamed El Duby, with bizarre new orders. As El Duby recalls the scene, "He told me to kill him and Martin [Quintana]. I told him I couldn't do it, but he hit me in the face and threatened me that everything would go bad for me in hell. Then he hugged Martin, and I just stood in front of them and shot them with a machine gun." Constanzo and Quintana were dead when police stormed the apartment, arresting El Duby and Sara Aldrete. In the aftermath of the raid, 14 followers were indicted on various charges, including multiple murder, weapons and narcotics violations, conspiracy, and obstruction of justice.

In August 1990, El Duby was convicted of killing Constanzo and Quintana, drawing a 30-year prison term. Cult member Juan Fragosa and Jorge Montes were both convicted in the Ramon Esquivel murder and sentenced to 35 years each; Omar Orea, convicted in the same case, died of AIDS before he could be sentenced. Sara Aldrete was acquitted of Constanzo's murder but sentenced to a 6-year term on conviction of criminal association. Sara Aldrete claimed throughout the arrest and trial that she had been held against her will by Constanzo and knew nothing of the cult's activities. She was nearing the end of that sentence, in 1994, when her long-delayed trial on multiple murder charges brought another conviction and a 60-year prison term.

Police in Mexico are still uncertain of Constanzo's final body count. In June 1989, Martin Quintana's sister told police that Adolfo's first madrina was still at large, practicing her blood magic in Guadalajara. And from jail, before he died, Omar Orea said, "I don't think that the religion will end with us, because it has a lot of people in it. They have found a temple in Monterrey that isn't even related to us. It will continue."[28]

Unfortunately, in the brief decade since this cult was discovered, many scholars have published articles refusing to acknowledge the ritual murders as human sacrifice and relegate the deaths to a form of sadism. "Matamoros, many scholars of Afro-Caribbean belief systems assert, was an aberration involving an especially deviant personality who used his involvement with and knowledge of Palo Mayombe for his own economic, criminal, and psychological needs. To these scholars, Constanzo was yet another true criminal involved in spiritual ritualism. Others believe that Mark Kilroy was a human sacrifice murdered because Constanzo's true belief in Palo Mayombe required his death; for these adherents, what happened in Matamoros could and does happen across the nation."[29]

Essentially it is difficult, even for well-educated, good intentioned persons to recognize religious violence for what it is. Although it may be easier to comprehend brutal crimes as a form of psychopathology or as a method of achieving one's goals, to conduct a comprehensive investigation, these murders must be viewed in the context of the belief system they were perpetrated in. Scholars, psychologists and experts can sort out the motivations later.

Currently, there is another case of ritual murders occurring in Juarez, Mexico where approximately 320 young women have been raped, mutilated and murdered since 1993. Their bodies have frequently been found dumped near the border of El Paso, TX. Unfortunately, because the women who were between the ages of 13 and 19 were all poor and held menial jobs, their deaths have not been properly investigated. These murders are currently being attributed to one or more serial killers; however, in light of the incident in Matamoros, it is also quite feasible that another Mexican religious cult could be ritually murdering young women.

References

1. Martinez, R. and Wetli, C., Santeria: a magico-religious system of Afro-Cuban origin, *Am. J. Soc. Psychiatr.*, 2, 1982.

2. Martinez, R. and Wetli, C., Santeria: a magico-religious system of Afro-Cuban origin, *Am. J. Soc. Psychiatr.*, 2, 1982, p. 3.

3. Gonzalez-Wippler, M., *Santeria: The Religion*, Llewellyn Publ., St. Paul, MN, 1996, pp. 21–22.

4. Martinez, R. and Wetli, C., Santeria: a magico-religious system of Afro-Cuban origin, *Am. J. Soc. Psychiatr.*, 2, 1982, p. 3.

5. Gonzalez-Wippler, M., *Santeria: The Religion*, Llewellyn Publ., St. Paul, MN, 1996, pp. 4–6.

6. Gonzalez-Wippler, M., *Santeria: The Religion*, Llewellyn Publ., St. Paul, MN, 1996, p. 6.

7. Gonzalez-Wippler, M., *Santeria: The Religion*, Llewellyn Publ., St. Paul, MN, 1996, chap. 3.

8. Gonzalez -Wippler, M., *Santeria: The Religion*, Llewellyn Publ., St. Paul, MN, 1996, p. 3.

9. Martinez, R. and Wetli, C., Santeria: a magico-religious system of Afro-Cuban origin, *Am. J. Soc. Psychiatr.*, 2, 1982, p. 4.

10. Murphy, J.M., *Santeria: An African Religion in America*, Beacon Press, Boston, 1988.

11. Gonzalez-Wippler, M., *Santeria: An African Magic in Latin America*, New York, 1992, p. 32.

12. Gonzalez-Wippler, M., *Santeria: The Religion*, Llewellyn Publ., St. Paul, MN, 1996, p. 16.

13. Martinez, R. and Wetli, C., Santeria: a magico-religious system of Afro-Cuban origin, *Am. J. Soc. Psychiatr.*, 2, 1982, p. 4.

14. Gonzalez-Wippler, M., *Santeria: The Religion*, Llewellyn Publ., St. Paul, MN, 1996, p. 17.

15. Gonzalez-Wippler, M., *Santeria: An African Magic in Latin America*, New York, 1996, p. 61.

16. Gonzalez-Wippler, M., *Santeria: The Religion*, Llewellyn Publ., St. Paul, MN, 1996, pp. 156–158.

17. State of California Office of Criminal Justice Planning, *Occult Crime: A Law Enforcement Primer*, Sacramento, 1996, p. 11.

18. State of California Office of Criminal Justice Planning, *Occult Crime: A Law Enforcement Primer*, Sacramento, 1996, p. 11.

19. State of California Office of Criminal Justice Planning, *Occult Crime: A Law Enforcement Primer*, Sacramento, 1996, p. 14.

20. State of California Office of Criminal Justice Planning, *Occult Crime: A Law Enforcement Primer*, Sacramento, 1996, p. 14.

21. State of California Office of Criminal Justice Planning, *Occult Crime: A Law Enforcement Primer*, 1996, Sacramento, p. 12.

22. State of California Office of Criminal Justice Planning, *Occult Crime: A Law Enforcement Primer*, 1996, Sacramento, p. 12.

23. Gonzalez-Wippler, M., *Santeria: The Religion*, Llewellyn Publ., St. Paul, MN, 1996, p. 239.

24. Gonzalez-Wippler, M., *Santeria: The Religion*, Llewellyn Publ., St. Paul, MN, 1996, pp. 239–240.

25. Martinez, R. and Wetli, C., Santeria: a magico-religious system of Afro-Cuban origin, *Am. J. Soc. Psychiatr.*, 2, 1982 p. 4.

26. Martinez, R. and Wetli, C., Santeria: a magico-religious system of Afro-Cuban origin, *Am. J. Soc. Psychiatr.*, 2, 1982 p. 5.

27. Gonzalez-Wippler, M., *Santeria: The Religion*, Llewellyn Publ., St. Paul, MN, 1996, pp. 244–245.

28. Serial Killers Central, biographies, Adolfo de Jesus Constanzo, www.angelfire.com/oh/yodaspage/adofo.html

29. State of California Office of Criminal Justice Planning, *Occult Crime: A Law Enforcement Primer*, Sacramento, p. 32.

Ritualistic Crime Scenes 8

An alleged ritualistic crime scene should initially be handled like other crime scenes, however attention to specific clues will help determine whether the crime was the result of organized religious beliefs or individual ritualized activities. The symbols, forensics and artifacts found at the scene can help the investigator determine if the crime was conducted by an individual or member(s) of a group, identify the type of religious ritual, which establishes motivation, and determine whether that belief requires additional similar rituals that can signify future crimes.

This chapter contains lists of crime scene clues, symptoms of ritual and sexual abuse, symbols, alphabets, books, candles, and calendars that can assist in crime scene identification. In addition, there are suggestions for compiling a search warrant, conducting an occult-related investigation and a strategy for a ritualistic child abuse investigation with alleged occult links. Finally, there are examples from actual crime scenes to illustrate the variety of symbolic evidence uncovered in ritualistic crimes. It is important to note that some ritualistic crimes are conducted by individuals who mimic media depictions of the occult but are not involved in any organized group or follow any established belief system. However, if a crime scene indicates a particular religion, it will be useful to read the pertinent chapter in this book for more detailed information.

Crime Scene Clues

Ritualistic Crime Scene Clues in General (Chapters 5, 6 and 7)

- Mockery of Christian symbols (inverted cross, vandalized Christian artifacts)
- Use of stolen or vandalized Christian artifacts

- Candles or candle drippings
- Unusual drawing, symbols on walls and/or floors (pentagrams, etc.)
- Nondiscernible alphabet
- Drawings of occult symbols
- Animal mutilations including removal of specific body parts (anus, heart, tongue, ears, etc.)
- Use of animal parts (feathers, hair, bones) to form signs and symbols on ground
- Absence of blood on ground or in animal
- Altar containing artifacts (candles, chalice, knife, etc.)
- Effigies like voodoo dolls stuck with pins or otherwise mutilated
- Bowls of powder or colored salt
- Skulls with or without candles
- Robes, especially black, white, or scarlet
- Rooms draped in black or red
- Occult books on Satanism, magic rituals, etc.
- Calendars with peculiar days marked
- Computer used to visit occult sites
- Handwritten occult essays or diaries
- Animal or human body parts found in refrigerator

Ritual Homicide Investigation (Chapter 10)

- Location and position of the body
- Missing body parts
- Cannibalism or absence of blood in victim or at scene
- Decapitation, mutilation or removal of specific organs (head, heart, tongue, tibia, eyes, fingers)
- Location of stab wounds/cuts
- Branding iron or burn marks
- Wax, powders, oils on or around the body or crime scene area
- Human or animal feces consumed or found on victim
- Indications of bloodletting
- Stomach contents analyzed for urine, drugs, wine, potions, etc.
- Any sign of semen on or in the cadaver
- Evidence that the hands or feet were tied or shackled
- Any jewelry, charms, amulets, stones on, near or inserted in the cadaver

Clues Unique to Satanism (Chapter 5)

- Animal and fowl mutilations including the removal of specific organs (genitals, anus, heart, tongue, ears)

- Altar upon which stones or other implements are placed
- Occult writing; Biblical passages (sometimes written in blood)
- Circle on the ground (approximately 8 to 9 feet in diameter, may contain a pentagram)
- Symbols: inverted cross, pentagram (single point down signifies Satan), 666 (sign of the anti-Christ), NATAS (teen symbol for Satan) etc.; nondiscernible alphabet
- Goat's head (real or mock) symbolizes the devil
- Black candles and incense
- Robes, detached hoods
- Inverted cross, serpent, serpent with horns
- Skull with eyes hollowed out; red stones, rubies or candles placed in the sockets
- Tattoos (pentagram, goat's head)
- Human cadavers and/or body parts
- Human or animal blood
- Wax drippings on the cadaver and/or in body orifices
- Positioning of bodies (north indicates Satan's supremacy)
- Slashes or cuts in patterns on cadaver

Clues Unique to Santeria and Brujeria (Chapter 7)

- Coins in multiples of seven
- Sea shells
- Corn kernels
- Pieces of fruit (coconut, oranges, apples)
- Mutilated and beheaded chickens, hens, cows, goats, roosters (heads torn off)
- Scarves or pieces of clothing in specific colors (determines which saints are being worshipped)
- Necklaces in specific colors (also determines saints)
- Dolls with pins or strange symbols or writing
- Head of homicide victim missing from the scene
- Herbs, roots, flowers
- Parts of celba tree, or palm and cedar
- Animal blood and/or feathers
- Body oils
- Iron tools and objects
- Catholic saint statues
- Goblets of water

Clues Unique to Palo Mayombe (Chapter 7)

Sacred cauldron (nganga) containing:

- Human bones (invariably a human skull)
- Wooden sticks (21)
- Various herbs, feathers
- Animal bones (skulls or other bones of various birds)
- Small iron agricultural tools (rakes, picks, hoes, etc.)
- Sacred stones
- Often a chain with a padlock may be wrapped around the nganga
- It may contain other items that may be of special significance to the palero.

Clues Unique to the Goth, Vampire and Fetish Scenes (Chapter 6)

- Human blood (in vials)
- Hypodermic needles used to remove blood
- Razor blades
- Fangs (false teeth)
- Knives, swords
- Dramatic clothing, robes
- Metal claws that attach to fingers
- Whips, leather restraints, chains, sexual bondage items
- Unusual contact lenses
- Skulls, coffins and other gothic items
- Symbolic silver jewelry with precious stones

Symptoms of Ritualistic and Sexual Abuse

Although the symptomology of ritualistic abuse is a useful tool in assessing the type of trauma a child might have experienced, it is very important that it be placed in the proper perspective. Such a list can be very misleading and should not be presented as a guide for parents or professionals to use without some type of preface as to the timing and manner in which these "symptoms" manifest themselves. Prior to actual disclosure of the abuse, these symptoms are rarely present, or at best very subtly present, in a majority of the children.

Children who have been ritualistically abused are, for the most part, asymptomatic or the symptoms exhibited are consistent with developmental behavior and therefore easily dismissed by parents as well as pediatricians. The degree and intensity as well as the combination of behaviors are important factors when interpreting these symptoms. It is very important that parents and professionals understand this issue. At this time, it appears much more difficult to identify children who have been ritualistically abused as opposed to those who have been sexually or physically abused. Children who have been identified as victims of ritualized abuse were usually being screened initially because "traditional" sexual or physical abuse was suspected. Ritualized abuse was not a consideration. It was only after the disclosure process began that the children started acting out and talking about bizarre activities.

There appears to be important differences in terms of treatment, impact, etc. between sexual and ritualized abuse. Awareness of the differences can help parents and professionals better understand what might have happened to the child.

Symptoms Specific to Ritual or Satanic Abuse

Disclosures

- References to people in costumes (robed figures – typically brown, black, white, red or purple) or scary costumes (monsters, ghosts)
- References to body painting

Physical Symptoms

- References to "my other daddy" or "my other mommy" or "my other family" (meaning at school)
- Marks on the child's body, unusual bruising, especially in patterns

Behavior

- Aggressive play that has a marked sadistic quality. The child hurts others intentionally and seems to derive pleasure from doing so. The child destroys toys.
- Mutilation theme predominates. Child acts out severing, sawing off, twisting or pulling off body parts. Aggressive words include *saw, cut, slice, chop.* Taking out eyes or removing other parts of the face and head are common themes.
- Making threats to others that seem outside the child's experience/exposure, e.g., to cut someone up with a knife, to burn the house down or to make them disappear.
- The child engages in play that is not appropriate to his experience, e.g., wedding, bondage or sacrifice.
- Words used to describe parts of the body, urine or feces that are not used at home.

- Preoccupation with urine and/or feces.
- Discussion of feces or urine on the face or in the mouth. Constant discussion of urine or feces at dinner table.
- Urine or feces strewn or smeared in the bathroom.
- Inability to toilet train a child because the child is afraid (as opposed to not being ready to be toilet trained or in a power struggle with parents). The child may reveal fear of having to eat feces after using the toilet.
- Bowel movements outside the toilet.
- Preoccupation with death. The child "practices" being dead; asks whether he or she will die at age 6 (the satanic number); asks whether family eats dead people. Questions are distinguished from normal curiosity about death by their bizarre quality.
- Over-reaction to the sight of blood.
- Preoccupation with the devil, magic, potions, supernatural powers, sticks, swords, wands and crucifixions. Questions about these topics in families who do not believe in or discuss them are significant.
- Odd songs or chants by the child that are sexual or otherwise bizarre or have a "you better not tell" theme.
- Numbers or letters always written backwards (as opposed to a child who may sometimes or often reverse numbers or letters).

Emotions

- Fear of bathrooms.
- Bathing problems. Child exhibits inappropriate fear of water.
- Fear that there is something foreign inside the child's body, e.g., ants, ice or a bomb.

Symptoms Indicating Abuse Other than Typical Pedophile Experience

Disclosure

- References to drugs, pills, candy, mushrooms, bad medicine or injections
- References to people at school who are not school personnel
- References to television characters as real people (this is because perpetrators take on names like Barney Flintstone so that the child's disclosures will be dismissed as television-inspired fantasies)
- References to sexual activity with other children at school

- References to pictures or films being taken at the school at times other than when school pictures would normally be taken. Peculiar descriptions or references to nudity, sexual acts, unusual costuming or animal involvement when discussing photography at school
- Statement that child witnessed sex acts
- Discussion of being taken to peoples' house or other locations (junkyard, church, hospital, another school) that are not normal school outings for which parents have given permission

Behavior

- Harming animals, or discussion of animals being hurt or killed
- Unusual reaction to having photographs taken, e.g., reluctance or striking a provocative pose

Emotions

- Fear of going to jail, being tied up or caged. References to police coming after the child
- Fear of ghosts and monsters. Child's play frequently involves ghosts and monsters
- Fear of 'bad' people taking the child away, breaking into the house, killing the child or the parents and burning down the house

Symbols

Symbols are the oldest forms of communication and have the power to inspire faith, fear, loyalty, obedience and aggression. Symbolism is fundamental to religious beliefs and images, statues and signs have been imbued with magical qualities throughout history. Indeed, it is the manipulation of symbols through religious ritual that comprises the basis of magical practices. Additionally, for centuries, people have fought and died under emblems, banners or flags that have symbolic significance. Members of gangs and religious groups still fight and die under emblems, banners and colors that have symbolic significance.

Essentially, symbols are not mere images but representations of everything that is held sacred by that group, so to defile an image is to offend the entire community of believers and can be considered an act of blasphemy, sacrilege and/or war.

Symbols can be found in the form of graffiti, as tattoos on perpetrators, written in blood, carved on victims and any other conceivable medium placed on any surface imaginable. Symbols, especially in the form of tattoos and other body modifications, frequently signify affiliation with a particular philosophy and/or organization. The very act of permanently marking the body demonstrates a serious commitment to a belief system and provides the person with a sense of belonging, pride and identity. By their very nature, symbols signify specific meanings and particular groups will either adopt historical emblems or often create their own unique image that has special meaning to them. Fortunately, for the purposes of investigation, certain images, geometric shapes, numbers and designs have collective recognizable meanings for all members of society and clearly indicate certain beliefs and practices. Gang investigators have long understood the value of symbols in identifying criminals.

Religious symbols are especially powerful and hold exceptional emotional and spiritual meaning for their believers. This is exactly why vandalism or destruction of religious images is particularly offensive and is often designated as hate crimes. Occult and white supremacist groups often demonstrate their hatred of Judaism and Christianity by attacking symbols, texts, artifacts and buildings that are held sacred to those religions. A significant aspect of magical thinking is the belief that you diminish the power of your enemies by desecrating their symbols. This is exemplified in many ways, from Satanists deliberately inverting Christian symbols in their rituals to Islamic fundamentalists burning effigies of the American president and burning the American flag. These iconoclastic acts go beyond just rallying members to a cause and are perceived as potent magical rituals.

Symbols also change over time; for example, the swastika was an ancient and widespread sun sign until 1920 when Adolf Hitler recognized its dynamism and put it on the Nazi banner as an emblem of Aryan racial purity. The swastika has symbolized white supremacy beliefs ever since. Most symbols have a long unique history and have been associated with various religious movements, magic or rituals in various eras. The pentagram is also an ancient symbol originating in Mesopotamia 4000 years ago. It served as the official seal of Jerusalem from 300 to 150 B.C. and in Greece, it was adopted by the Pythagoreans as an emblem of health and mystic harmony. The pentagram steadily acquired occult meaning and medieval sorcerers used it to conjure up supernatural powers. Today, the pentagram, depending on which direction it is placed, signifies Neo-Paganism, Satanism and the occult in general.

Recognizing symbols is one of the most important techniques for investigating religious violence. Ritualistic crimes are manifestations of religious beliefs which are universally expressed through symbols. Unlike other criminals, perpetrators of religious violence will not attempt to conceal symbols that may identify them for two distinct reasons: (1) members are exceptionally proud of their affiliations and it would be perceived as cowardly, shameful or disrespectful to deny membership in a group; (2) in terms of religious ritual, the magic would be ineffective if the symbol or markings were altered in any way. Identifying tattoos, markings, mutilations and graffiti at crime scenes and on suspects is a proven technique for investigating ritualistic crimes. It would be impossible to include all of the symbols that represent alternative and occult religions; however, the following symbols were selected because they are currently the most commonly found at crime scenes or are associated with particular violent religious groups.

White Supremacist Symbols: General Racist and Neo-Nazi[1] (Chapter 3)

Aryan Fist.

Confederate Flag.

Nazi Swastika with Iron Cross.

Skull and Crossbones.

Odin's Cross.

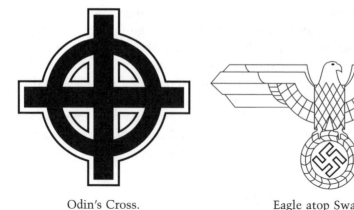

Eagle atop Swastika.

SS Thunder/Lightning Bolts.

Swastika Nazi Party Flag.

Variations of the Swastika.

Sturmabteilung (SA)/Stormtroopers.

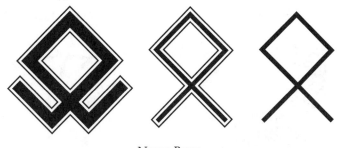

Norse Rune.

Sun Wheel (Black Sun).

Three-Bladed Swastika (Three Sevens).

White Supremacist Symbols: Skinheads (Chapter 3)

Hammerskin (Hammerskin Nation).

Fourth Reich.

Boot (racist and nonracist skinheads).

Skin Fist (racist skinhead).

Crucified Skinhead.

Chelsea (female skinhead).

W.A.R. Skins.

Peckerwood (Wood).

White Supremacist Symbols: Racist Extremist Groups (Chapter 3)

Ku Klux Klan (KKK).

American Front.

NAAWP (National Association for the Advancement of White People).

The Nationalist Movement (Victory Flag, Battle Flag).

The Order

Hammerskins (Hammerskin Nation).

National Alliance.

Stormfront.

American Nazi Party.

Aryan Nations.

World Church of the Creator (Creativity Movement).

White Aryan Resistance.

Phineas Priesthood.

White Supremacist Symbols: Prison Tattoos (Chapter 3)

Elbow Web (Spider Web).

Shamrock (with AB, Aryan Brother-hood).

NLR or Nazi Low Riders.

Occult Symbols (Chapters 5 and 6)

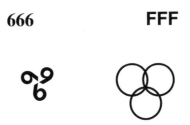

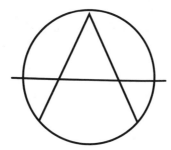

The Mark of the Beast (Rev. 13:16-18). Four different ways that refer to the "Mark of the Beast" or Satan. Note that the letter "F" is the sixth letter of the alphabet.

Anarchy. The symbol of anarchy represents the abolition of all law. Initially, those into punk music used this symbol, but it is now widely used by heavy metal followers.

Horned hand. The horned hand is the sign of recognition between those who are in the occult. It may also innocently be used by those who identify with heavy metal music

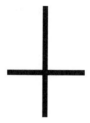

Anti-Christ. The upside down cross is a blaspheme of the Christian cross.

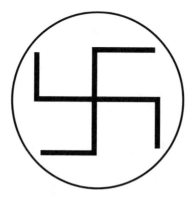

Swastikas. The "swastika" or "broken cross" is of ancient origin. Originally, it represented the four winds, four seasons and four points of the compass. At that time, its arms were at 90° angles turned the opposite way as depicted here. It turned in a clockwise direction, showing harmony with nature. The "swastika" depicted here shows the elements or forces turning against nature and out of harmony. The Nazis, SWP groups and occult groups use it in this manner.

Cross of Nero. This symbol represented peace in the early 1960s; but now, among the heavy metal and occult groups, it signifies the "Cross of Nero." It shows an upside down cross with the cross member broken downward — "the defeat of Christianity."

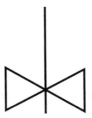

Anti-Justice. The Roman symbol of justice was a double-bladed ax in upright position. The representation of "anti-justice" is inverting the double-bladed ax.

The Inverted Cross of Satanic Justice. Often found carved into a victim's chest. When used in such a case, the victim is usually a traitor. It is also used as a backdrop near a "Baphomet" for curse and compassion rituals. The center vertical line indicates man's present. The horizontal line indicates eternity, past and future. The arch indicates the world. The inverted cross appearance symbolizes the epitome of anti-Christian theology.

Triangle. A triangle may vary in size, but is generally inscribed or drawn on the ground and is the place where a demon would appear in conjuration rituals.

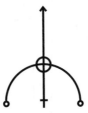

The Sexual Ritual Symbol. This is used to indicate the place and purpose. It is often carved into stone or painted on the side of the road to show present use of the location.

Circle. The circle has different meanings, one of which is to symbolize eternity. Another is that of protection from evil without and to contain power within. When used for ritual, it is 9 feet in diameter.

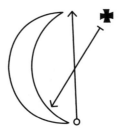

Talisman. The talisman or amulet is an object with drawing or writing inscribed in it of a god's name or image of a supernatural power. The majority of these are listed in the "Lesser Key of Solomon."

The Blood Ritual Symbol. This symbol represents human and animal sacrifices.

Ankh. The Ankh is an ancient Egyptian symbol for life. The top portion represents the female and the lower portion the male. This symbol had magical significance as an ancient Egyptian fertility symbol, symbol of life and worship to Ra, the sun god.

Pentagram. The pentagram, or with the circle, the pentacle, may be used in both black and white magic. Generally, the top point represents the spirit, and the other points represent wind, fire, earth, and water.

Cross of Confusion. The "Cross of Confusion" is an ancient Roman symbol questioning the existence or validity of Christianity.

Baphomet. The upside down pentagram, often called the Baphomet, is strictly Satanic in nature and represents the goat's head.

Here, the moon goddess Diana and the morning star of Lucifer are represented. This symbol may be found in both white witchcraft and Satanism. When the moon is turned to face the opposite direction, it is primarily Satanic.

Hexagram. The hexagram, also referred to as the Seal of Solomon, is said to be one of the most powerful symbols in the occult.

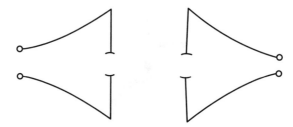

Trail Markers. There are many forms of directional trail markers which are employed by formal and casual occult groups alike. These markers indicate locations where occult activities may take place and how to get there. The markers depicted to the right show a small circle or starting place, then a direction to be taken. The rise or fall of the line show hills and valley type terrain. Other marker types could be a "pentagram" on the right or left side of a road, trail or even on a house or building. Markers may be very unique and only apply to one group.

N A T A S

N E M A

RED RUM

Backward Writing. Satanists are fond of writing words backwards. Here are several common examples.

Satanic Bible Symbol. This symbol is found in the Satanic Bible above the Nine Satanic Statements.

Baphomet. This is the sign of the Baphomet, a goat head inside an inverted pentagram within two circles.

Symbols of Lesser Demons from Ancient Beliefs (Chapter 5)

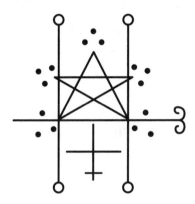

Astaroth.

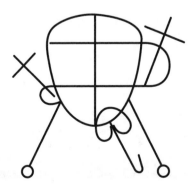

Baal.

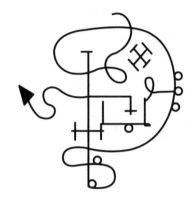

Asmodeus.

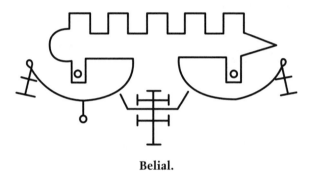

Belial.

Voodoo Symbols: Veves (Chapter 7)

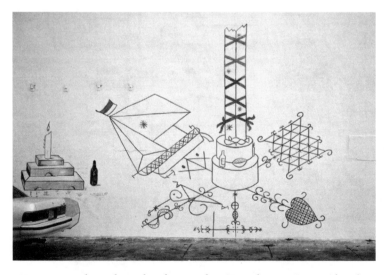

Veve painted on the side of a Voodoo Temple in Miami, Florida.

Veve (Voodoo symbol) painted on a Voodoo botanica (religious supply store) in Miami, Florida.

Palo Mayombe Symbols (Chapter 7)

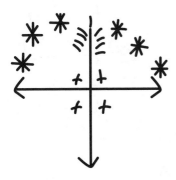

Francisco de Los Siete Rayos.

Los Espiritus Intranquilos.

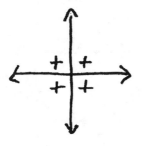

Zarabanda.

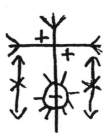

El Cristo Negro.

Santisima Muerte.

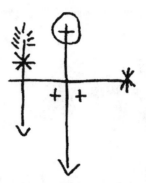

San Simon.

El Christo Re.

Madre de Agua.

Madre de La Luna.

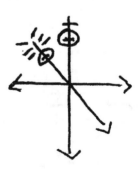

Mama Chola.

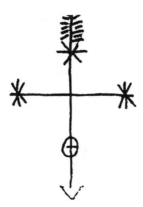

Santisima Piedra Iman.

Magical Alphabets

Alphabets are symbol systems. Symbols are used in combination with each other to create the words in a language. Alphabets, like symbols, have always been imbued with magical qualities. Magical alphabets are derivations of ancient languages that are attributed with mystical qualities. Occultists and religious fundamentalists use these languages because they are presumed to be intrinsically magical, to keep their personal rituals secret and to increase the potency of their spells.

Magical alphabets are frequently found written in a diary known as a *Grimoire* or *Book of Shadows*; however, they also appear in graffiti, as tattoos, on amulets and talismans, carved into candles and cut into victims. Fortunately, many occult spells are not only written in an ancient language but also in the perpetrator's own blood, which allows for precise identification. Many of these alphabets can be easily translated by using a simple letter equivalent; however, occasionally a perpetrator creates his own code or cipher in order to conceal rituals that entailed criminal activity.

If an investigator discovers a document or book that contains unusual writing, he should always have it interpreted to determine whether any crimes have been committed. University professors who specialize in ancient languages frequently donate their services to assist in criminal investigations. In almost all occult traditions, believers are ritually required to keep a diary detailing their magical practices, the purpose of which is similar to conducting accurate research: where the practitioner may want to repeat a particularly successful experiment at some time in the future, document his body of spell work and build upon his magical skills. These 'grimoires' not only comprise a strong piece of evidence in themselves but can also lead the investigator to forensic evidence such as bones, blood, weapons, etc. Every so often written documents containing occult language and/or symbols are sent to detectives, judges and other perceived enemies in order to threaten, curse and generally intimidate. In addition to being examined for typical forensic evidence, these letters or objects should be interpreted because the content may be evidence of terroristic threats or other appropriate charges. The following alphabets are the most commonly found in occult crimes and can be written as individual letters, words, sentences, paragraphs or entire books.

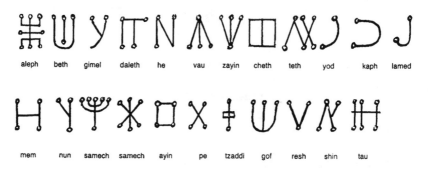

Malachim script.

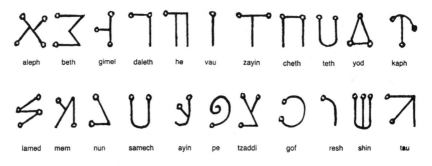

Celestial script.

Theban alphabet.

Hebrew alphabet.

Runes.

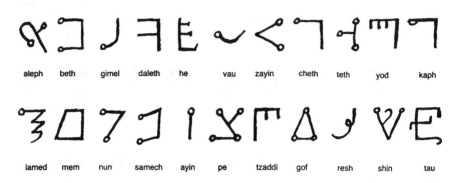

aleph beth gimel daleth he vau zayin cheth teth yod kaph

lamed mem nun samech ayin pe tzaddi gof resh shin tau

"Passing the River."
"Pafsing the River"

alpha beta gamma delta epsilon zeta eta theta

iota kappa lamda mu nu xi omikron pi

rho sigma tau upsilon phi khi psi omega

Greek alphabet.

ℵaleph	beth	gimel	daleth	he	vau	zayin	cheth	teth	yod	kaph

lamed	mem	nun	samech	pe	tzaddi	gof	resh	shin	tau	(z)

Writing of the Magi.

Beith (birch)	Luis (rowan)	Fern (alder)	Sail (willow)	Nion (ash)	Uath (hawthorn)	Dair (oak)	Tinne (holly)	Coll (hazel)	Ceirt (apple)
b	l	f	s	n	h	d	t	c	q

Muin (vine)	Gort (ivy)	nGéadal (reed)	Straif (blackthorn)	Ruis (elder)	Ailm (white fur)	Onn (gorse)	Úr (heather)	Eadhadh (poplar)	Iodhadh (yew)
m	g	ng	z/st	r	a	o	u	e	i

Éabhadh (aspen)	Ór (spindle)	Uillean (honeysuckle)	Ifín (gooseberry)	Eamhancoll (beech)	Peith (soft birch)
ea	oi	ui	io	ae	p

Eite (feather)	Spás (space)	Eite thuathail (reversed feather)

Ogham.

Enochian.

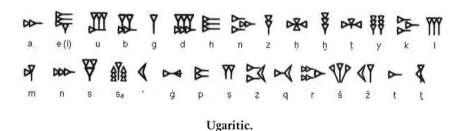

Ugaritic.

Aramaic.

يولد جميع الناس أحراراً متساوين في الكرامة والحقوق. وقد وهبوا
عقلاً وضميرا وعليهم ان يعا مل بعضهم بعضا بروح الإخاء.

Sample Arabic text.

Variety of magical alphabets.

Sacred Texts

Sacred texts are books or writings that contain the essential principles, beliefs, values, ethics, rules or theology of any organized group. These writings are often attributed to prophets who frequently are the current or recently deceased leaders of the group. Followers regard these books with the same respect and reverence that Christians hold for the Bible. Not only do these texts have great value for intelligence gathering, but when discovered at crime scenes and during searches, they clearly indicate affiliation with a group.

Unlike symbols that sometimes have a variety of meanings, sacred texts are not easily reproduced and in most instances can only be acquired through membership in a particular group. One example is the case of Buford Oneal Furrow, Jr. who opened fire at the North Valley Jewish Community Center in suburban Granada Hills, CA wounding five and shortly afterward murdering a Filipino–American postman. One of the first significant pieces of evidence found during a search of Furrow's van was *War Cycles/Peace Cycles*, a book by Richard Kelly Hoskins. This clearly indicated Furrow's affiliation with white supremacy and more specifically his goal of becoming a Phineas Priest, a concept put forth by Hoskins that entails murdering Jews and minorities.

Two other books frequently found during searches and at crime scenes are the *Turner Diaries* and *The Satanic Bible*. Unfortunately these books are so popular that they can easily be purchased in book stores. Although they do not have to be obtained through membership in a group, in the context of other evidence they clearly indicate affiliation with white supremacy or Satanic organizations. The *Turner Diaries* served as blueprints for numerous acts of terrorism including those of Bob Mathews' group (The Order), the Oklahoma City bombing by Timothy McVeigh, and for inspiring many individual acts of violence. *The Satanic Bible* is frequently found among items in perpetrators' homes who are involved in Satanic crimes. Investigators should pay particular attention to where books are found, i.e., a special place of obvious importance or reverence, hidden from sight or simply on a book shelf. They should note if any significant passages are highlighted, i.e., describing bomb making, overthrowing the government, killing minority groups, ritual sacrifice, child abuse, etc. If any manifestos, sacred tests, or occult doctrines are discovered during a search or at a crime scene, they should be viewed as having significant implications and should prompt further investigation into potential stronger ties to a related group or violent ritual practices in a particular religion.

Candle Magic

The most common form of religious worship entails the use of candles. Candles are sacred objects in both traditional and alternative religions and are an essential part of ritual worship. In occult religions, the making, manipulation and burning of candles constitute a form of sympathetic magic in which the goal is to influence people and events in a practitioner's life. Every attribute of the candle is significant for investigation. The shape, color, position at scene, objects attached to, markings inscribed on, oils anointed with and even where the candle drippings have fallen can indicate the group, ritual and the identification of the victim or future victims.

Most candles are purchased at occult or religious supply stores and are typically made of a blend of paraffin, stearic acid and a small percentage of beeswax. Very serious practitioners will make their own candles so they can be assured of 100% beeswax which is considered more potent for magical purposes. The most significant and immediately recognizable aspects of candles used for rituals are the color and the shape. Color plays an important role in magical rites with each color having a variety of attributes that are believed to emit individual vibrations and are used for specific spells. The shape of pre-formed candles are also indicative of specific uses. Although shapes and colors hold different meanings within different traditions, when viewed in the context of other ritual items found at crime scenes, it is possible to discern the type of spell work and the general intention of the practitioner from the shape and color of the candle.

Candle magic does not just consist of lighting particular candles. The use of candles is a ritual in itself and entails preparations such as anointing, inscribing and generally focusing energy onto the candle. Oils are specifically made for each intended use and are blended in certain ways according to magical specifications. There are a number of different candle-anointing oils on the market or the practitioner may use regular olive oil. Anointing candles is sometimes referred to as "dressing" them. It is believed that to achieve maximum effectiveness, they should be dressed by the practitioner himself so that he can concentrate on the purpose of the ritual and place his vibrations on the candle. The investigator may find an excellent set of latent prints on a magical candle.

Inscribing candles basically entails carving symbols or words that are relevant to the ritual into the candle. This frequently includes writing a person's name, birth date, astrological sign, etc. into the candle. The carving is done with an awl — a traditional magical writing tool that is the size of a pen or pencil and can be bought at both occult and craft stores. An inscribed candle can be an excellent piece of evidence because it may disclose a potential victim's name. However, names are usually written in one of the magical alphabets. When examining the candles for forensic evidence, take into consideration that it is also common for incense to be burned in the preparation of candles for rituals so that the smoke envelops the candle.

It is important to emphasize that all practitioners of occult religions practice candle magic and candles alone may not indicate criminal activity; they should always be viewed in the context of other signs of illegal activity. Although most candle magic ceremonies do not involve criminal behavior, similar to religious beliefs, certain candle ritual practices embrace the dark side of the religion and the goal of these rituals is frequently to harm others. Some of the candles used in harmful rituals will be immediately obvious; for example, some candles are used in the same manner as the Voodoo practice of sticking pins into a wax figure (not specifically a voodoo practice, but an act of black magic in any tradition). A popular book called *Practical Candle Burning Rituals* describes the ritual in detail:

> The practitioner takes a piece of wax, or clay, and proceeds to work it, forming it into the general shape of a human being. All the time he is working, the practitioner keeps his mind firmly on the intended victim. The figure may be basically very crude in shape, with no facial or body details — just a body, head, two arms and two legs, but the practitioner sees it as representing the victim. He sees the victim's face on the figure. He sees the details of his body, his stance, his gestures. To him it is the victim. If there is anything belonging to the victim that can be mixed into the wax it will help tremendously with the identification. Traditionally, nail parings, hair clippings, or the like are worked in. These create a tremendous bond between figure and victim.
>
> When completed, the figure must be named — a parody of baptism. It is sprinkled with salted water and then held in the smoke of incense while the practitioner names it for the intended victim. When that has been done, it may be wrapped in a clean white cloth and put on one side until needed. To actually work the malefic magic, the practitioner takes nine new, unused pins. He lays the wax effigy before him and taking the pins one at a time, jabs them into the figure with the wish that a particular thing shall happen. It is possible to purchase special figure candles, usually a red wax female and black wax male, from certain suppliers. These are candles in crude human form, with a regular wick running through them. They can be used as in the above described black ritual.
>
> Since such a candle is already formed, then it must have some object belonging to the victim attached to it, to personalize it. It must also, of course, be sprinkled, incensed and named. When the pins have been stuck

into such a figure candle and the curse is complete, the practitioner may light the wick and let the candle burn completely down. In this way, the curse is absolutely irrevocable.[2]

Although this ritual may sound ridiculous, it is a very common practice in occult religions and in the context of a crime scene can provide excellent forensic evidence. The following are descriptions of the symbolism of candle colors, types of candles and candle magic specific to the practice of Palo Mayombe.

Table 8.1   Symbolism of Candle Colors

Color	Attributes
White	Purity, truth, sincerity, spirituality, innocence, strength, power, respect, all that is good
Red	Strength, health, vigor, love, sex, fire, willfulness, power
Light blue	Tranquility, understanding, patience, health, inspiration, spirituality, devotion, happiness, kindness, peace, truth, wisdom
Dark blue	Impulsiveness, depression, changeability
Green	Finance, money, wealth, abundance, envy, greed, fertility, success, health, healing, luck, cooperation
Gold/yellow	Activity, attraction, persuasion, charm, confidence, success, unity, development of powers, concentration, evocation of spirits
Brown	Aggressiveness, balance, thrift, hesitation, uncertainty, indecision, neutrality, telepathic powers, study
Pink	Honor, love, morality, spiritualism; used by Wicca groups
Black	Evil, loss, discord, confusion, sadness, protection, repel black magic
Purple	Wisdom, dignity, honor, strength in business, business progress, power, tension, ambition, spirituality, psychic ability, strength
Silver/gray	Victory, good, conquest, power, cancellation, neutrality, stalemate
Orange	Joy, power, assertiveness, intelligence, cleansing, encouragement, adaptability, stimulation, attraction, friendship
Greenish Yellow	Sickness, cowardice, anger, jealousy, discord

Types of Candles

Novena Candles — Seven-day Novena candles are glass encased. As they burn, the flame rises in constant prayer asking for help. Many contain special prayers etched on the glass to aid in particular situations. Others have images of saints on the glass.

Altar Candles — These are two tall white candles that are always on the altar. They are placed at the two far corners and are always lit before any of the others.

Offertory Candles — These are the candles in the various symbolic colors dependent on the spell work to be done.

Astral Candles — These represent the practitioner and are determined on an astrological basis. A candle of the primary color may be used; or you may purchase astral candles that are made in two-color combinations.

Day Candles — These may be used in any of the rituals, depending upon the day of performance. Placed on the right front of the altar.

Cat Candles — The image of a cat has been used since Egyptian days. The color of the cat is significant. Black indicates luck; green-money; and red-love.

Cross Candles — Used as an altar candle and comes in many colors; colors are designated in each ritual.

Devil Candles — Symbol for use in exorcism rituals; considered as the evil within a person.

Figure or Image Candles — Made up as a male or female and used to represent the individuals involved.

Mummy Candles — Used primarily for power and success; shaped like a mummy (has other uses in Voodoo).

Seven-Knots Candles — A candle with seven knobs, comes in many colors; and is used for many purposes.

Skull Candles — Comes in all colors; used for all purposes and considered very strong. When used with a real skull, it is considered most powerful.

Reversible Candles — A specific type. Red interior with a black outer shell.

Double-Action Candles — Two-layered candle with two distinct colors; multipurpose.

Witch Candles — Used for power and love. Many colors.

Palo Mayombe Candles

Black Candles — Black candles are used for black magic and for strong spells of harm and destruction. Those working in Palo Mayombe light at least one black candle for the spirits twice a week. The candles are offered on Tuesdays and Saturdays.

White Candles — White candles are used to elevate spirits and for working with the light spirits of Palo Mayombe; offered to the spirits on Thursdays.

Red Candles — Red candles are used in Palo Mayombe spells of domination and to have victory over enemies; also used for love spells.

Crucifix Candles — Crucifix candles are used on spiritual altars for the Egun; red is used for love spells, black for spells of divine justice, white for healing and spiritual protection and green to open up the roads.

Seven African Powers Candles — Seven African Powers candles are a combination of seven different colors of wax. The world of the spirits is dark, but spirits are seen by spiritualists as rays of color. The spirits are particularly fond of these candles. A seven-day seven African Power candle brings blessings and supernatural powers from the spirits of Palo Mayombe.

Skull Candles — Skull candles are used when working with the spirits of Palo Mayombe. These candles may be placed near the cauldron of the spirit for spiritual communication. White skull candles are used for communicating with spirits of white light. This candle is also used to free an individual who is possessed by an unclean spirit. Black skull candles are used to communicate with the spirits of darkness and for spells of destruction.

Devil Candles — Devil candles are used when working with the powers of the dark or fallen angels. Red is for dominating an individual; black is for spells of destruction.

Gender Candles — Gender candles are used to make a man impotent or a woman infertile. These candles are also used to tie a lover down.

Black — Used to make a man impotent.
Red — Used to dominate or tie a man to you.

Gender Candles Female

Red — Used to make a woman infertile.
Black — Used to dominate or tie a woman to you.

Image Candle Male — Image candles are also used to dominate an individual. They are used in spells of harm as well as for love.

Red — Used to dominate a man.
Black — Used to cause or inflict harm.

Image Candle Female

Red — Used to dominate a woman.
Black — Used to cause or inflict harm.

Ritual Candles (Chapters 5, 6 and 7)

Novena candles in assorted colors for sale in a New York City botanica.

Skull, devil, cross, gender and figure candles.

Gender candles.

Sabbatic goat (Baphomet) candles.

Novena candles for specific purposes.

Figure candles.

Calendars

Another indicator of ritualistic crimes are the dates on which ritual violence or acts of terrorism occur. Since Christian Identity, Creativity, Odinism, Satanism, Santeria, Palo Mayombe and Vampire covens constitute organized religions, they practice specific rites on particular holidays. Originating from ancient agricultural timetables, neo-Pagan, Vampire and Satanic calendars celebrate the phases of the sun, the moon, the earth and the changing of the seasons.

Eight major holidays (sabbats) are common to both groups and many lesser holidays are celebrated including esbats (full moons). Cultural Spiritualist (Voodoo, Santeria, Brujeria) holidays concentrate on the worship of individual gods and often require animal sacrifice on those days. Occult holidays such as Samhain (October 31) are worshipped by many occult religions; however, the rituals are unique to each group and are useful methods of identification. For example, Traditional Satanic groups celebrate Samhain with an animal or human sacrifice, while Vampire groups hold huge gatherings at formal Vampire balls in cities across the country and engage in ceremonies entailing bloodletting and blood drinking. Dabblers in many of the occult groups choose Samhain, October 31, to hold their first blood sacrifice and many ASPCAs will not allow people to adopt cats the week before Halloween due to the large number of cats killed on that evening.

If a police department suspects occult activity in their jurisdiction, it is suggested that they patrol local cemeteries on the major occult holidays because cemeteries are very common places for rituals to be held.

In addition to general occult holidays, each group also has its own unique rites. For example, certain Satanic holidays require very specific types of violence ranging from sexual abuse to murder. Furthermore, the highest holiday for a Satanist is his birthday, which may be pertinent if a suspect's birthday coincides with the date of the crime.

In addition to religious holidays, terrorist groups celebrate dates that are significant to them such as founder's day, which is typically the birthday of the group's founder or the anniversaries of historical events that hold meaning to the group. April 19th has become a racist holiday for white supremacist and militia groups who have a tradition of marking anniversaries with violence. April 19, the date of the 1995 Oklahoma City explosion, was critical for several reasons:

April 19, 1775 — American Revolution began.

April 19, 1943 — Nazis burned the Warsaw ghetto.

April 19, 1985 — FBI raided Arkansas hideout of the Covenant Sword and Arm of the Lord, a white supremacist group.

April 19, 1992 — FBI aborted the first raid on Randy Weaver's cabin in Ruby Ridge, ID.

April 19, 1993 — Federal troops ended the standoff at David Koresh's compound in Waco, TX.

April 19, 1995 — Arkansas executed racial activist Richard Wayne Snell.

Due to the history of that date, law enforcement agencies are put on alert for potential terrorist attacks each year. April 20th is also a racist holiday. It is the birth date of Adolph Hitler and the shooters in the 1998 Columbine school massacre suggested they timed their violence in honor of Hitler's birthday.

Although calendar dates are excellent clues for an investigation, there are literally so many varieties of religious groups and holidays that every day on the calendar has meaning to one group or another. For that reason, calendar dates should always be viewed in the context of other symbolic evidence.

Occult Calendar (Chapters 5, 6 and 7)

Table 8.2

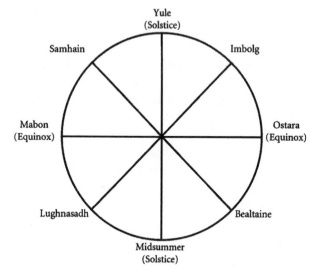

The Wheel of the Year.

The Greater Sabbats

Samhain (a.k.a. Halloween): October 31
Imbolc (a.k.a. Candlemas): February 2
Beltane (a.k.a. May Day): May 1
Lammas (a.k.a. Lughnasadh): August 1

The Lesser Sabbats[a]

Yule (a.k.a. Winter Solstice) December 21–23
Ostara (a.k.a. Spring Equinox) March 21–23
Litha (a.k.a. Summer Solstice) June 21–23
Mabon (a.k.a. Autumn Equinox) September 21–23)

[a] Dates vary each year.

Satanic Calendar (Chapter 5)

Table 8.3 Commonly Reported Satanic Holidays[3]

Date	Holiday
January 1	New Year's Day (a Druid feast day)
January 17	Satanic Revels
February 1 (or first full moon of Aquarius)	Imbolic
February 2	Candlemas
March 20–21 (sun's entry in Aries)	Feast Day Spring Equinox (called Alban Eiler by Druids)
April 19–26	Preparation for the sacrifice
April 30	Walpurgis Night (May Eve)
May 1 (or the first full moon of Taurus)	Beltane
June 21–22 (sun's entry in Cancer)	Feast Day Summer Solstice (called Alban Heruin by Druids)
July 1	Demon Revels
August 2 (or the first full moon of Leo)	Lammas (also called Lughnassadh, Lunasa)
August 3	Satanic Revels
September 7	Marriage to the Beast Satan
September 20–21 (sun's entry in Libra)	Midnight Host Fall Equinox (called Alban Elved by Druids)
October 29	All Hallows Eve
October 31 (or the first full moon of Scorpio)	Samhain (Halloween; start of the Celtic New Year)
December 22 (sun's entry in Capricorn)	Winter Solstice (called Arthuan by Druids; also called Yule)
December 24	Demon Revels
Person's birthday	Highest of all holidays

This is not an exhaustive listing of holidays for the various Satanic groups. Survivors report idiosyncratic variations and cult-specific dates (such as members' birthdays).

Racist Calendar (Chapter 3)

Table 8.4 Important Dates for White Supremacists[4]

Date	Holiday
January 16	Martin Luther King, Jr.'s birthday; also the birth date of Robert J. Mathews, leader of The Order, a white supremacist group dedicated to the overthrow of the U.S. government in the mid-1980s.
April 19	Known as Waco Day, when the FBI forcibly ended the Branch Davidian standoff; also the anniversary of the Oklahoma City bombing
April 20	Adolf Hitler's birthday
June 30	"Night of the Long Knives," when Hitler consolidated power by murdering rivals within his own party in 1934
August 17	Death of Rudolf Hess, Hitler's deputy Fuehrer, who was the longest imprisoned Nazi criminal convicted at the International Military Tribunal at Nuremberg in 1946
November 9 and 10	Anniversary of Kristallnacht ("Night of Broken Glass"), the 1938 pogrom when Nazi ordered gangs to burn down hundreds of synagogues, destroy property and attack Jewish civilians
November 25	A Declaration of War against the government of the United States was signed by members of The Order in 1984
December 8	Known as Martyr's Day; the date when Robert Mathews, leader of The Order was killed in a shootout with the FBI in 1984
February	Black History Month
June	Gay and Lesbian Pride Month
Memorial Day Weekend	Large Skinhead gatherings and concerts
Labor Day Weekend	Skinhead concerts and Stone Mountain Klan gathering in Georgia

Investigatory Strategies

Four primary keys to investigations that may contribute to a successful prosecution:

- Recognizing occult symbols and rituals at the crime scene.
- Compiling a comprehensive search warrant that may lead to further physical evidence.
- Conducting a carefully planned investigation of an alleged occult crime.
- Planning and implementing a specific investigation strategy for ritualistic child abuse crimes related to the occult.

Compiling a Search Warrant

Putting together a comprehensive search warrant that may provide badly needed physical evidence is essential to an occult crime investigation. Be sure to validate the need for every item prior to the search. Information on the religious beliefs and practices described in previous chapters is useful in justifying the need to search for particular items. While the following items should be included on a search warrant, it is again important to emphasize that when interpreting the actual occult connection between evidence that is seized and an occult crime, other professional expertise should be obtained.

Search Warrant Items

Clothing and Jewelry

- Black satin or velvet gloves
- Robes, detachable hoods
- Costumes and masks
- Martial arts clothing
- Medallions with Satanic symbols
- Large ruby or other stone rings

Games, Books, Wallhangings

- Occult games
- Occult books
- Handwritten diaries

- Writings in nondiscernible alphabet
- Posters of heavy metal rock stars, mythological beings, nightmarish pictures, or sadomasochistic sex

Weapons

- Heavy wooden staff
- Sword
- Knives or athame (a knife with a black or decorative handle)
- Bullwhip, cat o' nine tails, ligatures
- Martial arts weapons

Ritual Items

- Altar, wooden stand, marble slab
- Crosses
- Candles and candle holders
- Chalice, goblet, cruet
- Gongs, drums, bells
- Hair and skeletal remains
- Coffin, coffin nails
- Ashes from fire pits, fireplaces, wood stoves
- Phallus, serpent symbols
- Incense and incense burner
- Body paint; face paint
- Feathers
- Mirror
- Herbs, especially salt, bay leaves and garlic
- Caldron or iron pot
- Coins, statues, stones, jewels

Conducting an Occult-Related Investigation

After the law enforcement officer checks the crime scene for possible occult links and arranges for an occult-specific search warrant, he then must take careful investigative steps designed to build a clear case for the prosecution. Based upon information obtained from *Occult Crime: A Law Enforcement Primer* published by the State of California Office of Criminal Justice Planning, Sacramento, CA[5] and many law enforcers who investigated occult-related crimes, the following investigative guidelines, many of which are essential for any good investigation, are suggested.

1. Document all evidence as soon as it is received. Provide a detailed accounting of all that is reported.
2. Assign at least one investigator who is not a member of the investigatory team to act as a liaison with the media and general public. This investigator should exclusively handle the media, handle hot line tips and prioritize leads as they are received.
3. Involve the District Attorney in the early stages of the investigation. Realize that by including the District Attorney at the beginning, chances increase for a more successful prosecution.
4. Keep all investigative information confidential for as long as possible. It is especially important to keep materials confidential until the suspects have been identified.
5. Execute search warrants as soon as needed, but not short of probable cause. Be sure to validate the need for every item prior to the search; look for items associated with rituals and/or a belief system as described elsewhere in this book.
6. Keep the following in mind when examining the evidence: Can you determine if the crime involved ritual or violent, random acting out? Did the abuse fall into a particular ritualistic pattern? If ritual was involved, was it a part of a belief system identified with a particular group or was it an individualistic belief system? Is there any evidence of networking at any level?
7. Build the case on physical evidence.
8. Avoid denial. Do not be misled with the following types of thoughts: I do not want to be wrong and look like a fool; my supervisor is skeptical about whether the case can be solved, so I better drop it; the suspects are credible in the community, so they could not have committed the crime; or, we won't be able to convince a jury they did it; this case will make/destroy my career.

Planning and Implementing a Strategy for a Ritualistic Child Abuse Investigation with Alleged Occult Links

While some of the same investigative techniques are required of ritualistic child abuse cases with alleged occult links, several steps specific to ritual abuse are also recommended. Ritualistic child abuse cases bring special investigatory problems. The multiple-victim/multiple-suspect (MV/MS) situation forces the investigator to work with multiple child victims and to investigate multiple suspects. In addition, in ritualistic abuse investigations, an investigator cannot believe everything he hears.

Law enforcers have to corroborate everything they hear and need to particularly be aware of clinicians and psychologists whose intentions are good but they do not have to corroborate what their clients are saying from the law enforcement perspective. Finally, take into consideration that inadequate cooperation exists between investigators, therapists and the parents. To help counter the effects of these investigatory problems, the following procedural guidelines are offered:

1. Document all evidence as soon as it is received.
2. Work as a team in which the roles of each team member are clearly defined. Recognize that the perspectives of each team member will differ, but this is a positive rather than negative factor that encourages a broader base for sharing and analyzing information. The team should be open to new theories, should review the case every 30 days, and should not eliminate any factors unless they are conclusive. Teams should be comprised of individuals with knowledge of ritualized or serial abuse and should minimally consist of investigators, clinicians and child protection workers. The department psychiatrists may be called to testify in the event an officer's competence and religious beliefs are attacked by the defense.
3. Assign at least one investigator who is not a member of the investigatory team to act as a liaison with two groups: (1) parents, custodians and other interested parties and support groups and (2) the media and general public. When dealing with parents, the investigator should help find immediate therapeutic assistance for the victim. This will not only help the child deal with trauma but will help him become a more credible witness. Additionally the investigator must caution parents to avoid contamination; they may not question the victim but may document any unsolicited revelations. It will become the job of the investigating team to validate any such revelations if they are to become part of the case. When dealing with the public, only the designated investigator should handle the media and hot line tips and prioritize leads as they are received.
4. Involve the District Attorney in the early stages of the investigation.
5. Keep all investigative information confidential for as long as possible.
6. Execute search warrants as soon as needed, but not short of probable cause. Be sure to have the crime lab print victims as children touch everything. Look for false identifications and birth/death certificates; look for items associated with rituals and/or a belief system.
7. Follow careful, well-documented interview procedures. Keep in mind when designing the interview questions that you need to determine as best as you can if the abuse described by the victim actually oc-

curred or whether it may have been an illusion designed by perpetrators to frighten or discredit the victim.

Prior to questoning audiotape all interviews to maintain clarity about who first originated the information and to dispel the theory that the interviewer "suggested" certain things to the victim. Arrange to assess the victim's verbalization skills and plan questions accordingly. Arrange for a clinician to be present to monitor the victim's stress level; inform the parents that it may be necessary for them to leave the room. Select an interview location where the child will be comfortable.

Before beginning the actual questioning, it may be helpful to play with the child in some capacity that will help build some rapport. During the actual questioning do not wear your uniform. Use the victim's terminology. Do not ask leading or suggestive questions or those requiring "yes" or "no" responses. Listen carefully and do not interpret what the victim is saying; let the victim speak in the narrative to allow for continuity in the interviewing process and to avoid contaminating the interview's outcome.

8. Keep the following in mind when examining the evidence and interview results: Can you determine if the crime involved ritual or violent, random acting out? Did the abuse fall into a particular ritualistic pattern? If ritual was involved, was it part of a belief system identified with a particular group or was it an individualistic belief system? Is there any evidence of networking at any level?

9. Build the case on information obtained in the first few interviews which can be substantiated. Consider conducting a separate investigation for information and accusations gained from interviews for which there is no currently available evidence.

10. Approach day care center investigation cautiously. Check for prior licensing in and out of the state and conduct extensive background checks on the center and the teachers. Review field interrogation cards, premise location calls, property records, birth and death records.[6]

> Law enforcers face many legal, spiritual and emotional hurdles when confronted with an alleged occult crime. While there are no simple solutions for jumping over these hurdles, most criminal justice professionals recognize the answer lies somewhere within the educational realm. Indeed, law enforcers must clearly understand the belief systems of occultists and know when practicing such beliefs are within legally-protect-

ed Constitutional boundaries and when such practices step over the line into clearly criminal conduct.

Additionally, law enforcers must have a clear comprehension of the barriers they will face when investigating an alleged occult crime and must be able to formulate a plan for overcoming such obstacles. They must understand and be prepared to act upon orders to perform in any of the three capacities required of occult-related law enforcement: maintaining order through a protection role; providing services through a public relations role; and enforcing the law through an investigative role. And perhaps most importantly, those assigned the task of investigating an alleged occult-related crime must be prepared to recognize occult symbols and rituals at the crime scene or call for a professional opinion from another source; to compile a comprehensive search warrant that may lead to clear physical evidence; to conduct a carefully planned investigation in an alleged occult crime; and when ritualistic child abuse with occult-links is alleged, to plan and implement an investigation strategy specific to that crime.[7]

Crime Scenes (Chapter 5)

Youth Subculture Satanism

Graffiti, altar and symbols found in abandoned building. (Courtesy of Detective Douglas Fowler.)

Satanism (Chapter 5)

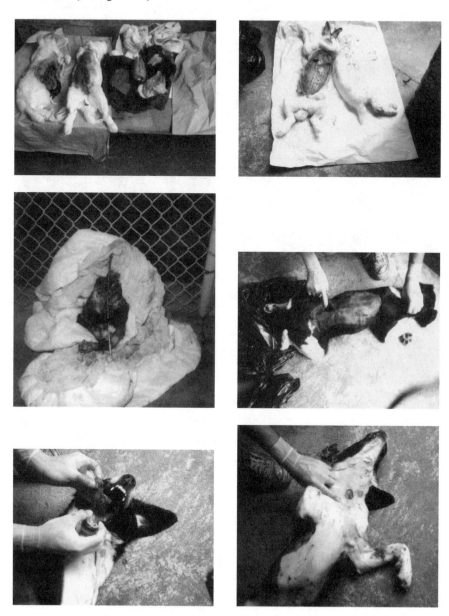

Animals that were tortured, mutilated and eviscerated. It is sometimes difficult to distinguish whether animals were mutilated due to Satanism or sadism. Black dogs are also frequently killed for Palo Mayombe rites. (Courtesy of the Animal Cruelty Section, Palm Beach County Animal Care and Control Division, West Palm Beach, Florida.)

Palo Mayombe (Chapter 7)

Nganga (sacred cauldron) containing 21 sticks, horseshoes, handcuffs, gun, money, letters, goat's head and other ritual items. (Courtesy of Ocean County Sheriff's Department, Criminalistics Investigative Unit, Detective William Poza-lante, Toms River, NJ.)

Palo Mayombe (Chapter 7)

Ngangas containing 21 sticks, human bones and a human skull. (Figures on the left courtesy of the Animal Cruelty Section, Palm Beach County Animal Care and Control Division, West Palm Beach, Florida.)

Palo Mayombe (Chapter 7)

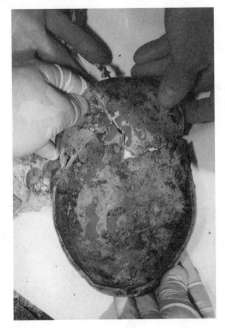

Palo Mayombe cauldron discarded on railroad tracks; contains blood, bones, human and animal skulls and iron implements. (Courtesy of Detective Christine Kruse-Feldstein, Miami Dade Police Department Crime Scene Unit, Miami, Florida.)

Santeria (Chapter 7)

(a)

(b)

(c)

(d)

(e)

(f)

Roosters, chickens and goats in sacrificial foods left in cemeteries, woods and along the beach. (Figures a through c courtesy of Ocean County Sheriff's Department, Toms River, NJ; Figures d through f courtesy of Bradford K. Varney, Pennsylvania State Constable, Bucks County, Pennsylvania.)

Self-Styled Satanism (Chapter 5)

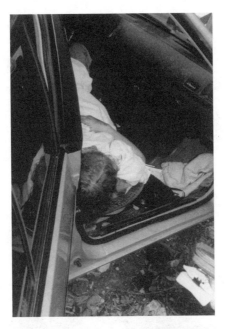

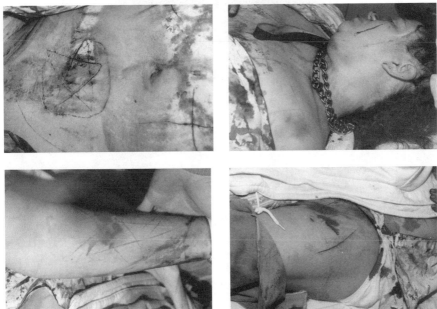

Satanic pentagrams cut into stomach and arms, chain tied around neck when victim was found in car in an isolated wooded area of Waco, Texas. (Courtesy of Detective James Blair, Waco Police Department, Waco, Texas.)

Self-Styled Satanism (Continued) (Chapter 5)

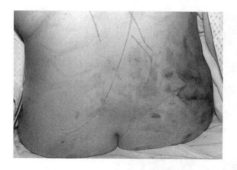 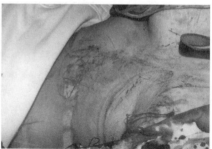

Cross was inserted into victim's vagina. The case turned out to be an incident of self-mutilation. (Courtesy of Detective James Blair, Waco Police Department, Waco, Texas.)

Traditional Satanism (Chapter 5)

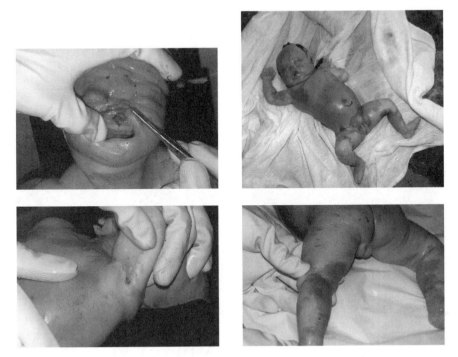

Autopsy of a 10-month-old female infant who was ritually tortured and murdered in a Satanic sacrifice. (Courtesy of Roger A. Forsthoff, Director of Forensic Laboratory, Hudson County Prosecutor's Office, Jersey City, NJ.)

References

1. Anti-Defamation League web site, Hate symbols database. http://www. adl.org/hate_symbols/default.asp

2. Buckland, R., *Practical Candle Burning Rituals*, Llewellyn Publ., St. Paul, MN, 1998, p. 173.

3. Sakheim, D.K. and Devine, S.E., *Out of Darkness: Exploring Satanism and Ritual Abuse*, Lexington Books, New York, 1992, p. 37.

4. Simon Wiesenthal Center, *Report: The New Lexicon of Hate*, Los Angeles, 1997, p. 21.

5. State of California Office of Criminal Justice Planning, *Occult Crime: A Law Enforcement Primer*, Sacramento, pp. 52–53.

6. State of California Office of Criminal Justice Planning, *Occult Crime: A Law Enforcement Primer*, Sacramento, pp. 52–53.

7. State of California Office of Criminal Justice Planning, *Occult Crime: A Law Enforcement Primer*, Sacramento, pp. 52–53.

Intelligence Strategies 9

Many highly respected government and private intelligence agencies monitor terrorist activities. They are variously referred to as antiterrorist organizations, counterterrorist organizations and watch groups and prior to September 11, 2001, they were subject to tremendous scrutiny and criticism for stigmatizing particular groups. Very few intelligence organizations monitor potential violence among occult religious groups. The few organizations that exist are extremely controversial, not taken seriously and consistently scrutinized for stigmatizing particular groups.

Although the threat of terrorism has become all too real for Americans, substantial denial concerning the existence of occult crimes continues. The combination of the lack of recognition, denial of occult violence among professionals, many groups' abilities to present themselves as law abiding citizens and their calculated manipulation of First Amendment rights makes intelligence gathering concerning violent occult religious groups an extremely difficult task. In addition to the sheer number of organizations, the illegal nature of their worship and the general social unacceptability of their ideals have forced many of the most dangerous groups underground. This is problematic in several ways: (1) there is no method of gathering empirical data to support claims of the existence of the more virulent groups; (2) the lack of evidence and extreme denial that these heinous crimes exist has created a backlash in which accusations of a "Satanic panic," "witch hunts" and "false memories" has led to the overturning of previous convictions; (3) the severe psychological damage done to survivors undermines their credibility as good witnesses and (4) the desire to categorize occult crime as a form of psychopathology as opposed to the perpetrator's rational choice (rational as in responsible frame of mind) interferes with the successful investigation, identification and prosecution of occult crime.

Furthermore, traditional intelligence operations and interrogation techniques do not work well in dealing with persons who practice nontraditional (terrorist and occult) religions because their worldview is based on values that are incomprehensible to most investigators, their philosophy often perceives law enforcement as persecuting them and their value systems are expressed in atypical behaviors.

In this chapter law enforcement issues and intelligence strategies specific to investigating religious violence will be addressed inclusive of the investigative advantages of understanding unfamiliar religious beliefs, particularly the significant concept of magical thinking. The variety of recruitment and indoctrination techniques, including Satanic Ritual Abuse, that have led to mass suicide, homicide and acts of terrorism will be described. Finally, suggestions for negotiations with groups that follow unknown religious practices and ideas for the prevention of religious violence will be recommended.

Law Enforcement Issues

There are specific practical, ethical, legal, tactical and spiritual issues that arise when investigating religious violence. The first and most immediate problem is the practical issue of distinguishing religiously motivated crimes from more typical crimes. The officer should always initially follow standard investigation procedures in order to rule out more typical motives such as disputes due to money, greed or relationships before religious beliefs or affiliations are suspected motivations. In many cases, symbolic evidence such as altars, pentagrams and ritual objects found at the crime scene or during a search obviously indicate ritualistic violence.

Law Enforcement Issues

- **Practical:** Distinguishing religiously motivated violence from more typical crimes or hate crimes.
- **Ethical:** Not letting your own beliefs interfere with investigation or protection role.
- **Legal:** Not violating civil rights, particularly First Amendment freedoms of religion and free speech.
- **Tactical:** Being morally and legally prohibited from penetrating a group due to highly secretive ceremonies that require all members to participate in violent rituals.
- **Spiritual:** Dealing with being spiritually, racially or nationally offended especially with more heinous occult crimes.

However, in some cases it can be difficult to distinguish typical hate crimes from occult crimes. For example, when a church or synagogue is vandalized, a closer examination of the evidence is needed to determine whether it is the work of a Satanist, white supremacist organization or individuals with their own agendas. Interpreting symbolic evidence found at the scene occasionally entails recognizing subtle distinctions. For example, Satanists will deliberately overturn crosses and specifically desecrate the holiest objects while white supremacists will use arson to destroy as much property as possible. Additionally, an investigation into a homicide of a minority or gay person may be an individual hate crime or the perpetrator may be a member of an organization. Identifying evidence such as books, symbols and artifacts found in suspects' homes as suggested in the previous chapter will assist in resolving these distinctions.

One of the most difficult ethical issues for law enforcement officers concerning alternative religious organizations is not letting their own beliefs interfere with their investigation or protection role. Many group philosophies entail overt racism, anti-Semitism, anti-Christian and anti-government beliefs. In addition, occult religions have rituals that entail desecration of sacred objects, animal mutilation, sexual abuse of children and ritual murder.

It is not surprising that a significant problem in investigating crimes that are spiritually offensive is that the law enforcer's own personal and spiritual belief system may inhibit an objective handling of the case. Officers frequently find it difficult to comprehend that such crimes are committed in the name of religion and not by persons who are mentally ill. It is important to understand that practitioners of religions such as Satanism are not mentally ill; they are making premeditated rational choices when they commit their crimes. Traditional behavioral analysis of a suspect may be helpful in some situations but it is equivalent to trying to make a square peg fit into a round hole. From a criminal investigative perspective, it is more useful to review evidence in the context of the perpetrator's belief system, which requires the officer to suspend personal judgments while working the case.

One of the many difficult duties that an officer is called upon to perform entails protecting the very groups that are frequently investigated for violent crimes. Many groups use legal protections afforded by the First Amendment freedoms of religion and expression to provoke controversy, recruit new members and bring attention to their cause. White supremacist rallies and marches are frequently violently protested by certain organizations and the general public, which unfortunately only serves to bring more attention to them and reinforce their belief that they are being persecuted by the government. Although many neo-pagan religious groups are clearly nonviolent, they are openly anti-Christian and many of their festivals, conferences and retreats are frequently protested by Christian fundamentalist organizations.

Both scenarios place law enforcement officers in the unpleasant role of protecting anti-Christian and racist groups. If an officer is assigned the task of keeping the peace during provocative rallies, the assignment should be viewed as an opportunity to get a first-hand look at the group's recruitment techniques, the tactics used to provoke protesters, the dynamics of their leader and, of course, an opportunity to identify members. Protests, violence, and arrests bring national media coverage to groups who then argue that they are the victims of a fascist corrupt government and intolerant society; as a result, they appear more principled, righteous and important to potential recruits and in the eyes of their followers. Considering these consequences, if protesters are arrested, it is worthwhile to check whether any of the protestors are connected to the group that held the event and were in the crowd with the sole purpose of instigating violence.

In addition to the ethical issues that make investigating religious violence so difficult, there are also tactical concerns. Many traditional occult groups conduct questionable rituals in which ceremonies are highly secretive and require all members to participate, therefore making law enforcers morally and legally prohibited from penetrating such groups. For an officer to infiltrate a group deep enough to collect valuable information he would most likely be required to participate in either sexual or violent rituals in order to convince the leader and other members of his commitment. Religious groups require complete immersion into their culture. Some of whom have used indoctrination techniques that were perfected on prisoners of war that would be difficult for even the best trained undercover agents to tolerate. Furthermore, leaders of religious groups are highly intelligent and experts in human nature; they are sophisticated con artists who not only attain their position by gaining people's confidence, but are skilled at discerning adversaries.

Finally, investigating occult crime is spiritually unnerving regardless of whether an officer is or is not actively religious. Crimes committed in the name of Satan and atrocities committed in the name of God affect our deepest emotions about the nature of evil. Even the most hardened detectives are uncomfortable and have nightmares when exposed to cases that involve sexual ritual abuse, torture and ritual murder. Although difficult and offensive, understanding the religious doctrines, beliefs and practices of violent religions from their theological perspective will greatly benefit the investigation, prosecution, negotiation and prevention of religious violence.

Investigating Religious Violence

There are many investigative advantages to understanding the religious beliefs of unfamiliar religions. Religious beliefs are essentially the philosophy of the

Investigating Religious Violence

Advantages are that Religious Beliefs Determine:

- **Investigative:** type of violence, offender characteristics, motivation, potential for future similar violence
- **Negotiation:** atypical responses to situations
- **Crime Scene:** place, date, weapons, objects, body disposal, symbolism
- **Victimology:** victim, potential future victim(s)
- **Forensics:** use of weapons, symbols, mutilations, sexual acts, body fluids (blood), signatures

group which inform you of what members hold sacred, what rules they live by, what violent activities are required of them and, more importantly, what they are willing to fight or die for. The beliefs specifically determine the type of violence, offender characteristics, motivation, potential for future similar violence, atypical responses to situations, choice of victim and potential future victims, place, date, choice of weapons, acts of mutilation, sexual acts, artifacts and symbolism found at the crime scene.

Even the most rudimentary knowledge of what a group practices can focus an investigation and provide important leads. The following strategies are suggested to assist in investigating religious terrorism and ritualistic crimes.

The most immediate task is to identify the organization, religion or belief system that is indicated through the symbolism and artifacts found at the crime scene, searches of suspects' homes, vehicles, etc. and interviews of witnesses. Crime scene information provided in Chapter 8 will assist in identifying the type of religion or organization. If it is discovered that a suspect is a member of an active group, one source worth pursuing is interviewing former members who are able to provide information on the religious beliefs, ritual practices, and organizational structure of the group and any illegal activities they may have witnessed. However, it is important to consider the circumstances in which former members left or were asked to leave the group and to take into account whether such witnesses hold grudges, vied for position in the group, etc. Although former members of alternative religions have consistently aided the police in investigations, there is a heated and ongoing dispute among religious scholars concerning the credibility of former members whom they refer to as "apostates."

Intelligence Strategies

- **Identify organization or belief** through crime scene, searches and interviews
- **Familiarize yourself with their beliefs:** check Internet for group web sites, read their recruitment materials, monitor their chat rooms
- **Suspend moral judgments:** do not apply your beliefs or your logic to theirs
- **Cross-reference for similar cases:** check geographic locations, important dates for that group
- **Consult intelligence agencies:** many government and private agencies may have valuable information available right on their web sites

Catherine Wessinger, a highly respected religious scholar, has made several negative accusations that one of the most significant factors in motivating law enforcement to use force against members of a religious group is information they receive from former members. As an example, Wessinger refers to the case of the Branch Davidians in Waco, TX where former members informed the police that followers viewed Koresh as God, that he was having sex with girls as young as 10 (one girl was 14 when she gave birth to his son), that Koresh would not submit peacefully to an arrest and that there was a high probability that there would be a group suicide. Unfortunately, all the informants' claims were accurate and their fears were justified.

Wessinger and many other scholars view the police acting on information from former members as a conspiracy to persecute religious groups in general and the Davidians in particular. She stated, "The typical tactic taken by apostates of exaggerating the facts and disseminating atrocity tales to magnify the dangers of the group had the effect of motivating law enforcement agents to use excessive force, which inevitably killed the children and young women who were supposedly in need of being saved from David Koresh."[1] These are the same academics who seem to believe that consulting them would have prevented the violence that occurred at Waco. Although religious scholars understand that knowledge of a group's religious beliefs is crucial for law enforcement, they do not fully appreciate the nature of violence. Academics can idealistically posit strategies but officers have to enter real scenarios that entail life and death situations. Information is one of the most valuable weapons officers can have and obtaining it from interviews with people who were members of or close to a group is certainly worth pursuing.

Although time consuming, it is essential that investigators familiarize themselves with a suspect's group or individual beliefs. Many individuals and groups have a web site that can easily be accessed on the Internet which provides detailed information on their philosophies, beliefs and rules of conduct. Some groups even advertise when and where they have ritual gatherings, festivals or meetings and post individual contact information such as e-mail addresses. Although members use aliases in the form of magical names, searching names on Internet providers frequently leads to their identification. Another very useful resource for information is monitoring either the group's chat room or chat rooms affiliated with that belief system.

Followers frequently discuss any related incidents especially if they appeared in the press. Depending on the length of the investigation, it may be useful to obtain the group's sacred books, which can easily be ordered through their websites or by mail and should be reviewed for any important dates or clues to potential violent events. The Internet is especially useful when investigating religious violence, and intelligence units should visit the websites of violent organizations on a regular basis.

Once an officer has identified a suspect's religion and has studied his occult or racist ideologies, it can be very hard to remain objective. The most difficult and important task that the investigator has to accomplish is to suspend his own moral judgment in order to apply logic to crimes that initially appear illogical, irrational and inexplicable. For example, it is not only illegal but morally reprehensible for adults to sexually abuse their own children; however, for some nontraditional religions sexual abuse is not only acceptable but required behavior. The initial response is to consider the abuse an act of pedophilia where the perpetrator achieves sexual satisfaction from children, but in the case of Satanic Ritual Abuse it is a required magical ritual, and for some millennial beliefs having sex with children is the result of the leader's interpretation of Biblical prophecy.

David Koresh, the leader and prophet of the Branch Davidians, had sex with and impregnated many young girls. Their parents were not only aware of his intentions but gave their daughters to him. The rationale was that Koresh was the messiah and had to produce 24 children who would become the wave sheaf of the future as prophesied in the Bible. The young women were considered by the group to be Koresh's wives and by producing children for David Koresh they were doing God's work. In their society, this was not viewed as child abuse but as a great privilege.

Once an investigator suspends traditional criminal behavioral interpretations (and revulsion) to view these acts from the religious perspective of the followers, strategies for negotiation, interrogation and investigation will be much more accurate and useful. This is especially relevant when interrogating suspects or interviewing witnesses who are members of alternative

---

Intelligence Resources

Available on the Internet:
- Regional Information Sharing System (RISS)
  www.iir.com/RISS/
- The Terrorism Research Center
  www.terrorism.com
- Southern Poverty Law Center
  www.splcenter.org
- Anti-Defamation League
  www.adl.org
- Emergency Response and Research Institute
  www.emergency.com
- Apologetics Index
  www.gospelcom.net/apologeticsindex/
- Institute for the Research of Organized and Ritual Violence
  www.ritualviolence.com

---

religions. Perpetrators of religious violence will not respond to questions accusing them of criminal activity but will be very responsive to questions concerning their religious practices and beliefs. It is imperative that officers realize that perpetrators of religious violence do not consider their actions to be criminal and are even capable of passing lie detector tests if the questions are not phrased in a manner that corresponds to their worldview.

It is important to take the time to cross-reference similar crimes by geographic locations, especially in situations where groups have member chapters in other states. It is also useful to cross-reference similar crimes by dates significant to the particular group. There may be related crimes that go unsolved because officers in other jurisdictions are unfamiliar with Satanic or occult groups. Since occult crime is not classified under any particular heading, incidents are frequently written up as gang crimes or relegated to domestic violence or nuisance reports.

Finally, it is very useful to consult intelligence agencies that may have valuable information concerning active groups. There are both government and private agencies that provide information to law enforcement agencies free of charge. An excellent resource is the Institute for Intergovernmental Research's Regional Information Sharing System (RISS), which is funded by the U.S. Department of Justice. RISS is comprised of six centers each covering various geographical regions that share intelligence and coordinate efforts against criminal networks that operate in many locations across jurisdictional lines. Some of the private terrorist watch groups that have information readily available on the Internet include the Terrorism Research Center which is dedicated to informing the public of the phenomena of terrorism and information warfare, the Emergency Response & Research Institute which provides 24-hour news, information, analysis and coverage of disasters and major emergency events. The Emergency Institute's web site is located at emergency.com and contains a counterterrorism operations page that lists a summary of worldwide terrorism events, groups and terrorist strategies and tactics and the Southern Poverty Law Center's intelligence project that tracks active hate groups in the U.S.

Another excellent resource is the Anti-Defamation League which maintains a terrorist organization database, state hate crime laws, hate symbols database and a law enforcement agency resource network. Unfortunately, the organizations that deal specifically with occult crimes are not as prevalent or well established. Some of the more objective ones include Apologetics Index whose web site contains a vast archive of articles, newspapers, commentaries and resources on religious cults, sects, new religious movements, alternative religions and religious practices and the Institute for the Research of Organized & Ritual Violence which specifically assists law enforcement agencies and criminal justice professionals on ritualistic crimes.

Magical Thinking

Do you believe in magic? The initial response to that question is usually "no"; however, we all engage in magical thinking in one form or another. Imagine for a moment a particular item such as a pen, pocket knife, tool,

Ritual altar items including pentagrams, Egyptian statues, chalices, etc. for sale at occult stores in New York City.

piece of jewelry or clothing that you always carry or wear. It would be upsetting to realize that you didn't have with you or worse, lost. Although the pens and other articles are everyday items, they have been imbued with special qualities and are consciously or subconsciously considered a form of luck or protection.

Think of how uncomfortable you would feel if you did not have your weapon on you; the attachment going beyond practical reasons. If that example does not resonate for you, imagine for a moment saying out loud that a close relative or friend is going to die, then immediately experiencing anxiety that the statement could possibly cause the death to happen. Frequently a person nearby will exclaim, "God Forbid," and if something positive is said they may exclaim, "From your mouth to God's ears." From a Western scientific worldview, attributing special qualities to inanimate objects and words is viewed as superstition. The objects that you would be upset about are essentially what practitioners of occult religions refer to as amulets and talismans and verbal or written expressions are the basis for magical spells and negative curses. In pre-technological societies when there were no explanations for natural events such as thunderstorms, earthquakes or even the daily rising and setting of the sun, everything was attributed to a variety of gods and if a tragedy occurred, it was believed that the gods were somehow offended. Early rituals and ceremonies were methods of appeasing the gods. The development of science and technology which provided logical explanations for natural events relegated magical thinking to the pejorative designation of mere superstition. However, we still retain the primal emotions that are the very foundation of our superstitious responses.

Understanding the concept of magic is crucial to investigating ritualistic crimes because perpetrators believe in magic; indeed, everything for them has magical qualities and making the proper offerings, spells and rituals is the only method of having any control over their world. The occasional anxious feeling that one experiences as a result of allowing superstition to override rational thought is a way of life for followers of occult religions.

The relevance of magical thinking for law enforcement is immense; it explains the psychology of the true believer who becomes a suicide bomber because he will immediately go to paradise, the Satanist who thinks sexual ritual abuse will increase his power, the Palo Mayombe practitioner who thinks he is supernaturally protected from the police and numerous other examples. Even nonviolent situations are relevant. For example, searching the home of a practitioner of Santeria and unknowingly disturbing an altar or investigating a mutilated animal left at a cemetery inadvertently insults believers who think that their worship has now been disrupted and their dead ancestors have been offended. Understanding magical thinking is especially pertinent in arrest situations because some followers actually believe that they are invincible and can even stop bullets. This was exemplified in the Matamoros, Mexico case described in Chapter 7. It is imperative that officers understand that magical thinking is universal and that although magic is associated with primitive cultures, it is dangerously thriving in the 21st century.

Magical thinking has been studied in the fields of psychology, psychiatry and anthropology. Essentially, scholars attribute magical thinking to primitive peoples who did not have explanations for the world or to a developmental stage in children whose cognitive abilities have not developed an understanding of the principles of cause and effect. The only explanation that is provided for adults who engage in magical thinking is that it is a form of psychopathology. In our scientific worldview we do not allow for the possibility of magic to exist.

This is the essence of the problem of investigating ritualistic crimes because a psychological behavioral perspective labels practitioners of magic as having obsessive compulsive disorder, personality disorder or schizophrenia and their crimes are relegated to the actions of psychopaths. This is a serious mistake, especially for prosecuting crimes, primarily because it provides an excellent defense for mental defect or insanity pleas, but more importantly, it does not allow for the possibility that these are rational logical actions taken by individuals who happen to hold worldviews that are different.

Heinous ritualistic crimes should not be rationalized but recognized for what they are — premeditated acts by sane individuals. Furthermore, labeling followers as psychopaths has very little value for investigating their crimes. If a perpetrator's beliefs require him to sexually abuse children in order for his magic to work, the investigator must determine what other criminal activities are part of his belief system, which could consist of anything from animal mutilation to homicide. However, if a behavioral scientist reviews the case from a typical psychological perspective, he may presume that the perpetrator is a pedophile who uses rituals as a method to rationalize his compulsion to seduce children. The behavioral scientist may recommend that the investigator look for other victims but significantly overlook the possibility that the perpetrator may have committed other types of violent crimes.

As with many other religious terms in this book, *magic* is a complex relative concept that is not easily defined. Religious magic is founded on the ideas of participation, contagion, contiguity and similarity. For the purposes of investigating religious terrorism and ritualistic crimes, it is most useful to focus on the concept of sympathetic magic, which is essentially based on the law of similarity and expressed in the magical principle that "*like produces like.*" When events cannot easily be explained by scientific principles of cause and effect but are merely correlated, they are perceived as related to each other either in the similarity between the two events; things involved in them or in the fact that the two events are occurring at the same time or same place (spatial and temporal contiguity). "Magical thinking is the belief that (a) transfer of energy or information between physical systems may take place solely because of their similarity or contiguity in time and space, or (b) that one's thoughts, words, or actions can achieve specific physical effects in a manner not governed by the principles of ordinary transmission of energy or information."[2]

In brief, magical thinking occurs when there is no clear explanation concerning causal relationships. The practice of magic is the ability to manipulate energy to bring about particular effects in accordance with the will of the magician (priest) through his manipulation of particular objects, rituals and ceremonies. Sympathetic magic, which is completely unscientific and a reverse reasoning of causal relationships, assumes that things act on each other at a distance through unidentified and inexplicable attraction. For example, in sympathetic magic it is possible to exert influence on someone through what is known as contagion. If you have items that have been in contact with a person such as clothing, hair and nail parings they can be used to cause things to happen to that person. Another example is the classic wax doll that is molded in the image of the person and through the likeness of the person whatever happens to the doll will also happen to the intended victim. In our Kodak-moment world, sympathetic magic is also worked frequently through photos or images of a person, which is exactly why some religions prohibit having their photo taken. They not only are concerned that their soul is being diminished but that it can be manipulated by others.

Another significant expression of magical thinking is known as *word magic* and the prime example is prayer. Followers of traditional religions pray with the hope that their words will intercede and effect changes. Followers of occult religions use words in a more deliberate and methodical manner to produce very specific results. This was described in Chapter 8 in the section on magical alphabets that are used in spells and rituals. In many religious traditions, names of deities are considered so sacred that the believer is not supposed to either know or utter it and a variety of euphemisms are used instead. In Satanism and the practice of other forms of black magic, it is essential to know the name of the spirit or demon whose power is being invoked. This can be very useful when investigating an occult crime for the reason that the symbol or writing can help ascertain the type of violence that occurred or will occur.

Also of relevance to the investigation is that in magical practices, if words are the main portion of the ritual, not reciting them correctly, omitting some and using others incorrectly may not only lead to the failure of the magic but even to the death of the magician. Deviating from the proscribed rituals

Magical Thinking

- Magical thinking is how pretechnological societies understood their world.
- Modern magic is the ability to manipulate events through one's will.
- Magical beliefs are expressed in:
  - Amulets
  - Talismans
  - Spells
  - Word magic
  - Rituals

FRIDAY 13TH

Superstition is a contemporary form of magical thinking

- **To investigate ritualistic crimes you have to suspend rational thought and engage in magical thinking.**

Superstitions concerning Friday the 13th and black cats are contemporary forms of magical thinking.

is unusual. Recognizing specific ritual incantations can be an excellent opportunity to identify individuals who have committed similar previous crimes or establish their membership in a particular group.

To investigate ritualistic crimes, an officer must enter the mind of the perpetrator, and in this case it entails suspending typical rational thought processes and engaging in magical thinking. Unfortunately, the investigations involve religions that embrace man's deepest, darkest urges — incest, blood rituals and sacrifice — the very impulses that mainstream religious morality has spent centuries suppressing. The most effective method of eradicating those urges was to relegate magic to mere superstition by not recognizing any form of thinking that cannot be explained from a rational scientific perspective. Followers of occult religions know that magical thinking is not taken seriously and use that knowledge to their advantage.

Recruitment Techniques

There are many misconceptions concerning the type of person who joins new religious movements. The most common misconception is that only people who are weak minded can be recruited into groups. Unfortunately, there is no single profile of who joins; in fact, surprisingly, many well-adjusted, high-achieving, intelligent people from intact families are successfully recruited.

Who Joins?

- No single profile.
- Many well-adjusted, high-achieving, intelligent people from intact families are successfully recruited.
- Between 1000–2500 cults in the U.S. alone, small to large.
- People between the ages of 18 and 30 especially vulnerable.

Predisposing Factors

Although there is no single profile for those who join cults, common factors include:

- **Vulnerability:** break up, family, school problems
- **Dependency:** ready to attach to anything
- **Naïve:** do not understand the true nature of these groups, very trusting
- **Disillusionment:**
  - no longer believe in...
                job, family, government, God
  - The Wizard of Oz is just a man behind a curtain

Members of the UFO religious group Heaven's Gate came from a variety of backgrounds and included college students, successful businessmen and children from wealthy families. Aum Shinrikyo members included many highly educated people, among them doctors, scientists, physicists and engineers. Adolfo Constanzo recruited everyone from local workers to drug dealers, who are not easily deceived. Depending on the philosophy of the group, members can come from all nationalities, races, social status or former religions.

Although there is no single profile certain predisposing social and emotional factors have been identified that indicate when people are most easily recruited. They consist of vulnerability, dependency, naivete and disillusionment. Although anyone at anytime can be persuaded to join, people are most susceptible to entering a group when they are vulnerable either from a tragedy, romantic disappointment, divorce, family or school problems or unexpected major changes in their lives. At a time when life decisions are made and there is a need to fill an emotional or spiritual void with either a new relationship, family or religion, many cult groups are more than willing to be substitute lovers, parents and priests. Other predisposing factors are dependency or the urgent need to attach to something new and naivete (being overly trusting and not understanding the true nature of these groups). Finally, the most significant factor that results in people joining new religious movements or terrorist groups is disillusionment. When a person is disillusioned he has suffered a significant disappointment and essentially has lost faith. The disappointment or loss of faith can be in anything important to him and which was held in high esteem such as a lover, job, family, government and God. In classical literature, this crisis is referred to as a loss of innocence and signifies a turning point in a person's life.

A variety of disillusionments occur throughout people's lives, beginning with finding out that the Easter Bunny and Santa Claus do not exist to questioning whether God exists. Charismatic leaders are experts at recognizing this time of soul searching and are skilled at taking advantage of the situation. Disillusionment not only occurs on a personal level, but also during social and political upheavals; for example, the tragedy of the World Trade Center left many people feeling vulnerable. Not only did many people return to church after the tragedy of September 11, 2001 looking to renew their faith, but many were recruited into a variety of occult and terrorist religions that were more than willing to offer solace and provide conspiratorial explanations to frightened people seeking answers.

Numerous statistics demonstrate that membership in new religions increase when times are unstable. At the end of 1999, there was a phenomenal

Recruitment Techniques

- **Breed a generation:** if you get them young you have a soldier for life (nursery schools)
- **Recruit high schools and colleges:** finding identity
- **Flattery:** subtle process of indoctrination
- **Sense of belonging:** identity
- **Overpowering techniques**: love-bombing, free meal, flirting (prostitution)
- **Distribution:** of money, medicine
- **Providing shelter:** alienating from family, friends
- **Slick advertising campaigns:** music, video games, posters

number of apocalyptic religions awaiting the end of the world, full of members who were disillusioned with mainstream religions, the government and fears of impending war and natural or man-made disasters.

Since younger people are still in the process of developing the skills to cope with disappointment, they are specifically targeted by terrorist and religious cults. Recruitment campaigns focus on high schools and colleges — the places where young adults are most impressionable and still forming their views about the world. They particularly focus on alienated teenagers who are seeking their identity and who desperately look for approval, a sense of belonging and a place where they feel valued and respected. Recruitment techniques are often a combination of affection and deception. Some of the standard techniques include flattery, distribution of money, food, medicine and/or providing shelter. More overt techniques include prostitution, having a female member seduce a young man until he follows her into the group. Members of many new religious movements will tell potential recruits whatever they think is going to gain their confidence, persuade them to join and have them commit to the cause.

Leaders of cult and occult groups are essentially con men playing a confidence game where the stakes are particularly high. Leaders of white supremacist terrorist groups target angry white men with recruitment campaigns that appeal to their resentment of controversial issues such as affirmative action, gun control, war in the Middle East and the economic crisis. The latest trend in recruitment is slick advertising campaigns that come right into homes via the Internet. Teenagers and young adults are exposed to racist music, posters, games and violent philosophies. Resistance Records, a renowned racist music company that promotes the ideals of the National Alliance has a website that offers hard-core violent records advertised as the soundtrack of the white revolution, Aryan Wear clothing, provocative posters and even a video game called "Ethnic Cleansing" that proudly claims to be:

> the most politically incorrect video game ever made.
> Run through the ghetto blasting away various blacks and
> spics in an attempt to gain entrance to the subway sys-
> tem, where the Jews have hidden to avoid the carnage.
> Then, if you're lucky... you can blow away Jews as they
> scream "Oy Vey!" on your way to their command cen-
> ter.... The Race War has begun. Your skin is your uni-
> form in this battle for the survival of your kind. The
> White Race depends on you to secure its existence. Your
> people's enemies surround you in a sea of decay and filth
> that they have brought to your once clean and White
> nation. Not one of their numbers shall be spared....[3]

The most proven technique that new religious movements and terrorists use for recruitment is to simply breed their own new generation. A person inculcated in a movement when young becomes a soldier for life. A fundamental principle of white supremacist and international terrorist groups is to raise children with their philosophy of hatred. It is also why so many anticult organizations are concerned about the issue of Satanic Ritual Abuse where traditional Satanists have been prosecuted for infiltrating nursery schools and day care centers. Alternative religions understand that they do not have enough members by only raising their own children, which is the most significant reason why they want to recruit young adults who will marry, reproduce and be able to inculcate children from birth. One of the reasons that al-Qaeda is so dangerous is that they are now on their fourth or fifth generation of raising soldiers in their religious war, while domestic terrorists are only on their second generation. The threat of violence and a self-fulfilling prophecy of a future race war multiplies with each new generation.

Indoctrination Techniques

After a person is successfully recruited into a group, the goal is then to keep him committed to the leader and the cause. This is achieved by sophisticated indoctrination techniques in which new recruits are subjected to contrived conversion and training methods that they are unaware of. This consists of a subtle process that begins with a positive approach that gradually escalates to the use of abusive behavior modification techniques. These methods include having ready-made answers foundational to the belief and supported by sacred literature being forced upon recruits, who are not allowed to question anything.

Membership requires unconditional surrender to the leader and the group's rules. An extremely important method is isolation; new members are consistently isolated from friends, family and any outside information and influences such as television, radio, newspapers, magazines, medical treatment, etc. Outside contact would be the equivalent of a "reality check" and would break the magnetism of involvement and the patterns of behavior. Leaders systematically process recruits away from their past lives by focusing on past deviant behavior such as drug use, sexual misdeeds, poor relationships, etc. This not only instills them with a sense of obligation, but also strengthens the idea that the new religion saved them and that they have no place to return to.

Groups also use a variety of consciousness-altering methods such as administering drugs and enforcing strict rituals as forms of asceticism that lead to restriction of reflective thinking and cognitive disturbances. This is

Indoctrination Techniques

- **Ready-made answers** and decisions forced upon recruits.
- **Unconditional surrender** is required.
- **Isolation**, eliminating outside information and influence (friends, family, media).
- **Consciousness altering methods** restriction of reflective thinking, thought stopping.
- **Process away from past lives**, focus on past negative behavior, sex, drugs, social hang-ups.
- **Constantly busy** and never alone, continual training, stifling resistance, inducing fear.
- **Asceticism/strict rituals** reinforce belief, violent initiations, constant repetition prayer, sleep and food deprivation.
- **Strong focus on the leader.**

achieved by a variety of established techniques such as keeping the recruits constantly busy and never alone either through training, Bible studies, violent initiations, sleep or food deprivation and repetitive actions. The goal is automatic submission to directives, stifling resistance and reinforcing the beliefs of the group and submission to the leader. This is similar to the dynamics that occur in severe domestic abuse situations where a woman is systematically isolated from her family, friends and becomes completely dependent upon her husband who slowly convinces her that she is worthless and her only value is obtained through him. Although she may be physically beaten on a regular basis, she will testify that she deserved it and that her husband loves her.

One of the biggest controversies surrounding new religious movements is the question of whether it is actually possible for groups or authority figures to influence and control the thoughts and behaviors of others. This is especially prevalent for prosecution issues where many former members claim that they were coerced into their violent acts and are not responsible for their crimes. The colloquial term for being indoctrinated into a group is "brainwashing," which was originally used to describe Chinese indoctrination techniques and soon after applied to Russian and Eastern European approaches, and finally became a popular term in American culture to describe everything from Madison Avenue advertising to federal investigations. The term is almost as controversial as the term "cult."

There are excellent philosophical and ethical arguments that brainwashing is a relative concept and indistinguishable from education and socialization that occurs in traditionally acceptable religions, schools and governments. Indeed, members of alternative religions consistently claim that the rest of society has been brainwashed by the media and government and that they are being persecuted for not sharing similar beliefs. This is exactly why intervening, investigating and prosecuting new religious movements is fraught with civil rights issues.

Although the concept of brainwashing may not be easily distinguished from ordinary education, it is clearly different from the concept of *coercion*. Coercion entails forcing a person to do something against his will either by physical violence, intimidation or threats. The problem of new religious movements is that members participate in their own victimization and are not aware that they are being deceived, coerced and intimidated. New religious movements operate successfully because at any given time members are not yet aware that they are being exploited or cannot express such an awareness because of uncertainty, shame or fear.[4]

One of the most significant legal problems for law enforcement concerning violent religious groups is that they have willing victims. How do you arrest, prosecute and convict leaders if their victims have been so inculcated into their beliefs that they testify that they have not been victimized? Freedom of religion allows people to participate in their own abuse. Fortunately, current laws prevent them from legally abusing their children. In an attempt to distinguish dangerous groups from nonviolent new religions, anti-cult scholars posited a more specific definition of the term "cult" that unfortunately was not universally accepted:

> **Cult (totalistic type)** — a group or movement exhibiting a great or excessive devotion or dedication to some person, idea, or thing and employing unethical, manipulative or coercive techniques of persuasion and control (i.e., isolation from former friends and family, debilitation, use of special methods to heighten suggestibility and subservience, powerful group pressures, information management, promotion of total dependency on the group and fear of leaving it, suspension of individuality and critical judgment, and so on), designed to advance the goals of the group's leaders, to the possible or actual detriment of members, their families, or the community.[5]

Whether it is referred to as persuasion, coercion, education, mind control, indoctrination, brainwashing, psychological operations or thought reform, they all refer to systematic attempts of manipulating human beings. There is numerous and credible evidence that brainwashing techniques have been developed by governments and tested on prisoners of war, military soldiers and unknowing victims. It is naïve to think that members of terrorist and occult religious groups would not employ this valuable knowledge to increase their numbers and attain their goals.

A classic example of the use of indoctrination techniques is the UFO religious movement Heaven's Gate founded and led by Bonnie Lu Nettles and Marshall Herff Applewhite whose activities culminated in a group suicide of 39 members. Applewhite and Nettles claimed to be extraterrestrial representatives of The Kingdom Level Above Human. They taught that human bodies were mere vessels, containers that would be shed when entering God's Kingdom, which in this case was a spaceship hidden behind the Hale-Bopp comet.

Heaven's Gate used a variety of successful recruitment techniques inclusive of newspaper advertisements, traveling through the country, posting fliers at colleges for meetings, establishing their presence on the Internet through their web site Heaven's Gate and by postings to various relevant newsgroups. At its peak, scholars estimate that there were between 200 to 1000 followers. During the 1970s, the group had a dramatic attrition rate until Applewhite instituted indoctrination techniques and claimed that the only way disciples would be ready to ascend to space was to renounce sex, drugs, alcohol, their birth names, all relationships with families and friends and to follow an intense regimen. Recruits had to follow detailed schedules that included mental and physical drills, experimenting with their sleeping patterns and their diets. They had thousands of rules to maintain the purity of their vehicles (bodies). Offenses included deceit, sensuality, breaking any instruction knowingly, trusting their own judgment or using their own mind, having private thoughts, having likes or dislikes, being vain about appearance and having inappropriate curiosity.

The discipline was shame based and during autopsies of members' bodies it was discovered that many of the men had been castrated through surgical removal of the testicles years earlier. A surviving member who ritually committed suicide shortly after explained that castration was a method of controlling sexual urges. The men and women wore their hair closely cropped and wore baggy clothing to avoid any sexual urges.

In the 1970s, the leaders offered what they called re-education classes at their camp called Central and followers had to check in with the leader every 12 minutes where they were assigned duties. During one 3-month phase, members had to wear hoods over their heads and could only communicate via written messages. In an interview, a former member emphasized that every thing was freedom of choice and said the group was very rights oriented. He did not take into consideration that under the severe restrictions group members did not have many choices to make and after years of having the group as their only family had grown very dependent on Applewhite.

Instead of writing suicide notes, members made a farewell videotape in which they were visibly happy about their choice to depart and acted as if they were leaving for a holiday instead of committing suicide. In fact, they didn't view their deaths as suicide but as a exiting to a higher level of existence. Although many new religious scholars claim that members remained in the group of their own free will and were not the victims of so-called brainwashing, in view of the years members spent denying their families, their bodies, and their total submission to Applewhite this should not be considered a voluntary mass suicide but nothing less than murder. A willing victim is a victim nonetheless. Ironically, Charles Manson was up for his ninth parole hearing at Corcoran State Prison the day after the bodies were discovered. He referred to the members of Heavens Gate as the "monks that just took their heads in San Diego." As the former charismatic leader of his own "family," Manson immediately appreciated the dynamics of the group.

As described in Chapter 2, the Japanese new religious movement Aum Shinrikyo (translated Aum Supreme Truth), founded in 1987 by Shoko Asahara not only escalated to the use of weapons of mass destruction but also entailed methods of indoctrination and coercion that led to the deaths of many members. Asahara insisted that his devotees practice an extreme form of asceticism or else they would not achieve salvation in the Shambhala millennial kingdom. His practice of asceticism in order to obtain salvation was so important to the group that it was necessary for everyone to undergo. It included fasting or living on a meager diet, being lowered into scalding or near-freezing water, being hung upside down or being given drugs such as LSD to stimulate altered consciousness. "Every member was encouraged to meditate and practice a variety of yogic disciplines, and the most committed disciples became shukkesha, renunciants. Becoming a renunciant meant cutting off all contact with one's family, turning over all property and assets to Aum, pledging devotion to Asahara, living communally and practicing rigorous asceticism. By these means, shukkesha believed they would develop superhuman powers of clairvoyance, levitation, and the ability to travel through the spiritual realms. The shukkesha aimed to become superhuman beings, the only ones who would not be destroyed in Armageddon."[6]

Members were convinced that society outside the Aum compound was under the influence of evil mind control and that Aum counteracted society's brainwashing with good mind control that taught supreme truth. Aum members listened for hours to audiotaped affirmations that said they should not doubt Aum because doubt is an illusion caused by earthly desire, etc. Asahara committed both accidental and premeditated murder and inflicted torture as methods of intimidating followers and dissuading defectors:

In 1988, Terayuki Majima died while being subjected to cold water submersion. Since Aum Shinrikyo had applied to become a legally registered religious organization, Majima's death was kept secret. Another member, Shuji Taguchi (25) was frightened by Majima's death, wanted to defect, and thus raised the possibility that he may report Majima's death to the police. Taguchi was murdered at Aum headquarters in February 1989. Taguchi was strangled, his neck was broken, and his body was burned in a metal drum....

On January 30, 1994 two former members, a pharmacist, Kotaro Ochida (29) and Hideaki Yasuda (26) sneaked into the Aum headquarters in Kamikuishiki to rescue Yasuda's ill mother. They were captured and brought into the presence of Shoko Asahara and his wife. Asahara gave Yasuda the choice of either killing Ochida or being killed himself. A plastic bag was placed over Ochida's head and Yasuda was forced to spray Mace into it. A rope was wound around Ochida's neck and Yasuda was made to strangle him. Yasuda was permitted to leave with instructions to tell his father that his mother was well and that Ochida had decided to rejoin Aum.[7]

In brief, members were severed from contact with their families, the outside world, and systematically indoctrinated into worshipping Asahara through the use of standard mind control techniques such as drugs, sleep and food deprivation, fear, physical beatings, isolation and constant reinforcement of new beliefs. Once inculcated into Aum Shinrikyo, members either willingly or out of fear for their lives followed the orders of Shoko Asahara.

In November 2001 John Walker Lindh, a 20-year-old American citizen was captured by U.S. forces in Afghanistan with a group of Taliban and al-Qaeda fighters who survived the bloody Mazar-e-Sharif revolt. Walker became known as the "American Taliban," and in a complaint filed in February 2002 in the U.S. District Court for the Eastern District of Virginia, Lindh was charged with the following crimes: conspiracy to murder U.S. nationals, conspiracy to provide material support and resources to foreign terrorist organizations, providing material support and resources to foreign terrorist organizations, conspiracy to contribute services to al-Qaeda, contributing services to al-Qaeda, conspiracy to supply services to the Taliban, supplying services to the Taliban and using and carrying firearms and destructive devices during crimes of violence.

On July 15, 2002, Walker pleaded guilty to two of the ten charges, serving in the Taliban army and carrying weapons in doing so. His agreement with U.S. prosecutors could keep him in prison for 20 years. In exchange, prosecutors agreed to drop other charges, including conspiracy to murder U.S. citizens that could have kept John Walker Lindh in prison for life. If John Walker Lindh's case had gone to trial, his defense would most likely have argued that he had been coerced into fighting for the Taliban and his confession would have been evidence of the degree to which he had been indoctrinated. His parents had immediately claimed in news reports that their son had been brainwashed. It is not a coincidence that the language used in Attorney General Ashcroft's statement to the press announcing charges against Lindh continually emphasized that Lindh made choices of his own volition:

> The complaint alleges Walker knowingly and purposely allied himself with certain terrorist organizations, with terror; that he chose to embrace fanatics, and his allegiance to those fanatics and terrorists never faltered, not even with the knowledge that they had murdered thousands of his countrymen, not with the knowledge that they were engaged in a war with the United States, and not, finally, in the prison uprising that took the life of CI agent — CIA agent Johnny Spann....

> The Department of Justice complaint based on Walker's statements in interviews states that on or about May 2001, Walker joined a paramilitary training camp run by the terrorist group Harkat ul-Mujahedeen. After his training was completed, he was given a choice to fight with the Harkat ul-Mujahedeen in Kashmir or join the Taliban to fight in Afghanistan. Walker chose to join the Taliban.... According to the complaint, when his al-Qaeda training was completed, Walker — again, by his own admission — chose to go to the front lines of the battle in Afghanistan....

> The criminal complaint filed today describes a series of crossroads John Walker Lindh encountered on his way to joining not just one, but two terrorist organizations. At each crossroad, Walker faced a choice, and with each choice, he chose to ally himself with terrorists. Drawn to South Asia, Walker chose to train with terrorists. Trained as a terrorist, Walker chose more advanced in-

structions from al-Qaeda. Schooled by al-Qaeda, Walker chose to fight on the frontlines with America's enemies. Our complaint, based on Walker's own words, is very clear: Terrorists did not compel John Walker Lindh to join them; John Walker Lindh chose terrorists....

Walker was blessed to grow up in a country that cherishes freedom of speech, religious tolerance, political democracy, and equality between men and women. And yet he chose to reject these values in favor of their antithesis, a regime that publicly and proudly advertised its mission to extinguish freedom, enslave women and deny education. John Walker Lindh chose to fight with the Taliban, chose to train with al-Qaeda, and to be led by Osama bin Laden. We may never know why he turned his back on our country and our values, but we cannot ignore that he did. Youth is not absolution for treachery, and personal self-discovery is not an excuse to take up arms against one's country. Misdirected Americans cannot seek direction in murderous ideologies and expect to avoid the consequences.[8]

The statement over-emphasizes that Walker was not coerced, indoctrinated or brainwashed and established the position for the prosecution if this case had gone to trial. A public trial that even hinted that al-Qaeda had successfully recruited a young intelligent American would have been a legal disaster, would provoke even more public suspicion and violence toward American Muslims and would most certainly have been a public relations nightmare for all involved.

Although the degree of Walker's recruitment into Islam is questionable, there is no doubt that he was systematically indoctrinated into al-Qaeda. Bin Laden immediately recognized the value of recruiting a young American and it is not surprising that he took the time to meet Walker. If Walker had not been captured at his young age, he could have easily risen in al-Qaeda ranks and as an American-born citizen who is not of Arabic descent, could have become one of their most dangerous spies.

When you examine the history of John Walker Lindh, he could be the poster child for recruitment and indoctrination techniques. He was born in Washington, D.C. in February 1981. His father, Frank Lindh, an Irish Catholic, worked at the U.S. Department of Justice by day and studied law at night until he graduated with honors and joined a law firm. When John Walker Lindh was 10, the family moved to Marin County, one of California's wealthiest counties. In California he attended what has been described as an elite alternative high school where students were allowed to shape their own studies. At the age of 15, John Walker Lindh was searching for a new personal religion and explored the religion of Buddhism as an alternative to Catholicism. At the age of 16, he became interested in Islam after reading the autobiography of Malcolm X. After using Internet chat rooms to speak to Muslims, he told his parents he wanted to convert to Islam and began attending a mosque.

As a Muslim John Walker Lindh met members of the Tablighi Movement (Preaching Society of Islamic Followers), which is a purist fundamental sect that directs Muslims to live life as the Prophet Mohammed did in the 7th century. He studied the Koran, adopted the name *Sulayman* and started wearing a long white robe and turban. After graduating from high school at a time when his parents were splitting up, Walker asked them for money so he could go to Yemen to learn the "pure" dialect of Arabic used in the Koran.

After a year in Yemen, John Walker Lindh returned to California and studied at a San Francisco mosque. Friends there said he seemed restless and no longer felt comfortable in the U.S. He returned to Yemen in February 2000 for additional studies, a few days before his 19th birthday. Walker told U.S. interrogators that in May he had joined a paramilitary training camp run by a Kashmiri militant group in Pakistan he then chose to join the Taliban, where he was sent for 7 weeks to an al-Qaeda training camp.[9,10]

If one reviews the predisposing factors for recruitment and indoctrination Walker was a prime candidate. He was a teenager who felt alienated from high school, he was searching for a new religion, he used the Internet where he was persuaded to follow up on his interest in Islam. He joined a fundamentalist Islamic sect that immediately gave him a new identity and a sense of belonging just at one of the most crucial times in his life (graduating high school and his parents divorcing), leaving him even more vulnerable to his new found religion and his parents unknowingly funded his trip to Yemen.

Once John Walker Lindh was in Yemen, isolated from his family, friends and American culture, it was not difficult for him to become immersed in the politics and culture of Islam. When he returned to the U.S. a year later, although his friends recognized that he had changed they did not understand the seriousness of the situation. Walker felt even more isolated and returned to Yemen to make his final commitment to the religion.

I agree with Attorney General Ashcroft's statement that, "Youth is not absolution for treachery and personal self-discovery is not an excuse to take up arms against one's country." However, I disagree with his statement that, "John Walker Lindh chose terrorists." John Walker Lindh chose Islam and the terrorists took it from there.

Satanic Ritual Abuse

Denial is not a river in Egypt.

- Many experts deny the existence of Satanic Ritual Abuse and attribute allegations to "Satanic panics," "false memories" and "witch hunts."

- Satanic Ritual Abuse is the most controversial subject in ritualistic crime.

- Different theoretical positions: psychopathology versus religious belief.

- Experts disagree on everything (especially in court).

Satanic Ritual Abuse

One of the most controversial and heinous crimes entailing systematic indoctrination techniques is Satanic Ritual Abuse. Although there are numerous psychological interviews, police reports and physical evidence of survivors of ritual abuse, the extreme denial of these crimes has made it almost impossible to prosecute offenders. For every anti-cult expert who testifies to the existence of traditional Satanists, there are 10 cult apologists who will testify that these are accusations of a "Satanic panic" or "witch hunts" and attribute them to false memories suggested to the victim by a psychologist with an over-active imagination.

Juries prefer to believe that atrocities such as torturing, impregnating and having sex with your own children in the name of Satan could not possibly occur and opt to believe the cult apologist experts' opinions instead of hard evidence. In an exceptional article on Satanic beliefs and practices, Martin Katchen and David Sakheim describe the indoctrination techniques used by traditional Satanists.[11]

> All "brainwashing" or "thought reform" appears to involve techniques that would result in the psychological destruction of the old self and the creation of a new indoctrinated self. It is very interesting to see how closely the descriptions of Satanic cult indoctrination follow the same type of course. Using the material presented by survivors undergoing psychotherapy, one can see the described atrocities as part of a larger psychological purpose, namely, to indoctrinate the person

into the group, to maintain membership and to separate the member from outside connections. Although most groups have such practices, those utilized by Satanic cults appear very similar to those utilized by other extreme totalist groups. Whether or not every report turns out to be accurate, it is helpful to understand how such experiences can be a part of a group's indoctrination.

As in the thought-reform methodology discussed by Robert Jay Lifton, most of the reported Satanic rituals are based around the theme of death and rebirth. There is the clear idea of killing off the old "good" self and finding or creating a new "evil" self. What typically seems to occur is that these attempts to destroy the old self end up creating what Lifton refers to as a "split personality." This is seen in the cult as possession by demons, but would be viewed from a psychological standpoint as the development of multiple personalities as a defense against the traumatic abuses. The cults will often deliberately encourage this dissociation, enabling cult members to keep the selves (and thereby the secret rituals) from being discovered. The "old self" functions in the normal world during the day while the "new self" is brought out for cult activities at night.

Many Satanic cult survivors describe specific death and rebirth rituals. These are usually very literal in nature, for example, survivors report being buried in the ground (sometimes in a coffin with a dead animal or person) after being severely abused. The reported abuse usually involves some type of mutilation that would result in severe hemorrhaging. After the injuries are inflicted, the survivor is then told that he or she (the old self) is going to die and be buried.

Rebirthing rituals also occur where the survivor's new self is "born into the cult." A number of survivors have described being placed inside a dead animal that had been cut open, and told that they were being "born unto Satan" as they were pulled out. The message to the child involved is that a new "evil" person is being developed (or found within) who will be able to be a part of the cult. The cults have ways of making the membership very concrete. Once a member, the child will often be branded, scarred, or tattooed with a symbol of the cult to permanently indicate the cult's "ownership" of that new person. Many survivors also describe rituals that parallel Christian rites such as baptism. In the Satanic version, the Christian symbolism is inverted. For example, instead of using "holy water," water is used that has been contaminated (e.g., by putting leeches in it). One survivor also reported having leeches put on her leg during such a ritual to represent "Satan's mark," as well as to transform her blood into "evil blood." Leeches and other such creatures (e.g., spiders, locusts, snakes) are used in these rituals because it is believed that they originate from the devil.

Survivors often describe what Lifton refers to among the thought-reform methods as a "fluctuation of assault and leniency," as well as "an assault on identity." The child in a cult situation is reportedly told that he or she is evil. There are many rituals and situations created to enforce this notion. For example, one patient described having "holy water" (likely some type of acid) thrown on her that burned her skin. This was done to "prove" to her that she was really evil. Victims are also deliberately shown that they can no longer trust their senses or previous notion of how the world works. This is accomplished in many ways; some of these involve the use of drugs; electric shock; hypnosis; torture; rape; humiliation; illusion; long periods of isolation (e.g., locked in a box or a closet); sleep, water and food deprivation; or being partially drowned or hanged by the hands or feet. This fostering of an alternative consciousness and confusion make it easier to put the child into a more suggestible state — what Lifton describes as "more readily influenced and are more susceptible to destructive and aggressive impulses arising from within."

As in other thought-reform approaches, one of the most important components is the establishment of guilt in the victim. Most cult survivors report having been forced to commit atrocities by the adults in the group who would then point out how evil the child must have been to have done these things. For example, the child is forced to hold a knife and stab something living. The adult then lets go of the child's hand, stands back and says, "Look at what you just did." In addition to various forms of physical violence, these activities can include forced sex with animals, or other children or adults or participation in pornography. Being forced to participate in rituals where other children are injured also undermines the child's sense of being a moral person. In addition the child is often told that because he or she resisted a cult request, someone else close to the child will be punished. Thus, even when the child resists what feels immoral or wrong, he or she is made to feel that another person is suffering because of his or her actions. This makes it feel like terrible consequences will occur whenever cult edicts are violated, despite internal feelings to the contrary. Thus, the only path to morality (and safety) is to follow cult orders and teachings.

Another essential ingredient in thought reform appears to be self-betrayal. The betrayal of the self occurs on many levels for cult members. Despite learning about religion in the outside world, the child is often forced to denounce and desecrate symbols of the church. This usually involves denouncing many of his or her own beliefs about morality as well as specific church teachings. Often survivors report being forced to engage in activities that are directly self-debasing such as "voluntarily" eating feces and human flesh, drinking blood and so on. They also report being betrayed by significant people in their lives, which leaves them with a sense of worthlessness. Parents and siblings are often reported to have been passive witnesses to tortures, leaving the child feeling that he or she must have deserved these since nobody stopped them.

Some survivors report having been stimulated sexually while forced to watch or participate in atrocities. This creates an additional sense that the body's reactions cannot be trusted. The confusion and shame inherent in feeling sexually excited during horrible events leads to further alienation from one's body. The child frequently blames him or herself for what occurs in order to hang on to some sense of perceived control amid overwhelming feelings of helplessness. Thus, the end result is a tormented individual who views him or herself as evil, culpable and dangerously out of control.

Dr. Lifton describes an event that he consistently saw in his observations of thought reform. He called it "the breaking point: total conflict and basic fear." Most cult survivors describe a similar experience. Usually the "breaking point" is deliberately induced by torture. Cult members beat their victims, fracture their limbs, and/or rape them repeatedly until they "brake." The most common "breaking" is psychological, through dissociation. Most survivors report psychotic episodes, feeling suicidal or experiencing delusions and hallucinations (some induced by involuntary drug use). Virtually every patient reports deliberately induced fear of annihilation.

Leniency and nurturance can be used as powerful compliance-inducing techniques. Many cult survivors report a sort of "good cop–bad cop" approach, in which one member of the cult acts as a nurturer after the tortures have occurred. This person appears to have the power to stop the abuse and to give back life. One patient reported that this "nurturant" person ended up with amazing power over her. She felt that she could not resist any of his requests, for he was the only one who could take away her terror.

In thought-reform methodology there is the creation of "a compulsion to confess." In the cults, this corresponds to the appearance of "a compulsion to accept the new teachings." There is no push in the cults to "confess," but rather to freely become a part of the group. The similarity lies in the spurious freedom of this commitment. One patient described a ritual in which she had to "voluntarily" sign "the book of names" for the cult. She was beaten and tortured until she was willing to do so. However, if there was any sense that she was only doing so to avoid further beating that was not acceptable. The signing had to be because she "wanted to."

"The channeling of guilt" is another technique mentioned in the literature on thought reform. The cult reverses "good" and "evil," but the process involved is essentially the same. Since the cult sees "evil" as a redeeming trait and "goodness" as a liability, the child typically begins to accept this way of thinking. He or she starts to believe that evil is powerful, that through evil one can accomplish whatever is desired. Thus, "good" begins to be condemned internally. The cults' standards of action become more and more accepted internally and become ego-syntonic. It is only safe to act and feel in ways the cult allows. Specific indoctrination to teach the child these reversals is reported very frequently. Physical abuse is presented as "a reward" and something that will give a child special powers. The child is told that the more he or she can endure, the stronger person he or she will be. Specific language reversals are also taught, such as that "hate" means "love" or "evil" means "good" and vice versa. Usually, personalities develop that internalize the aggressive, tyrannical parts of the cult, as well as specialized language and symbols needed to make the internal corrections necessary to avoid the wrath that inevitably occurs if the cults' standards are violated. Thus, the child in the cult environment develops an identification with the aggressors.

The cults also have specific rituals that reinforce, internalize and concretize this sense of guilt. Some patients actually report being forced to eat an eye and then being told that it will always watch them and will tell the cult if they violate the rules. Other patients discuss what has been termed "magical surgery" in which the

child is rendered unconscious and upon awakening is
convinced that he or she has undergone a surgical procedure in which a bomb, a monster, a snake, or Satan
himself has been placed inside of him or her. The child
is told that the intruder will squeeze internal organs or
that the bomb will explode if the cult is ever betrayed.
The child is also told that even thinking of telling someone about it will start the process. Of course, this cap-
italizes on the child's own physiological reaction to the
fear of telling. An increase in heart rate or tension in
the stomach will be interpreted as a sign that the snake
or the bomb is working. Thus, even the child's physi-
ology is turned against him or her. Many patients also
report that the cult has told them that it has spies
everywhere. There is a strong sense that no one can be
trusted and that anyone could be a cult member who
could trick them into betraying the cult and then turn
them in.

Part of the reeducation involves "loading the language." In such situations words and images take on
tremendous significance. This is obviously true in
magic where symbols and words become charged with
power. In Satanism, because of the paradoxical nature
of its reality, language can often be loaded with reversal of the usual meanings. For example, "God" will
mean an object of derision or an enemy. "Good" and
"evil" will have multiple meanings. Often special
names will be given to the member that are only for
use in cult activities. Thus, participants must either
learn a high degree of dissimulation or a high degree
of dissociation in order to respond correctly to outsiders in social situations when words with loaded
meanings are used. This clearly serves to further split
cult members from outsiders by making communication that much more difficult. In addition each cult
or coven maintains its own "book of Shadows" or
grimoire in which it codifies its rituals, often in secret
languages or alphabets such as Theban or Enochian.
Part of the reeducation involves teachings about the
outside world. For example, the cults try to point out
the inconsistencies of church teachings, much as the

communists pointed out logical inconsistencies in the prisoners' views about religion and morality. The cult will portray the forces of "good" being at war with the forces of "evil" and that both sides are equally dangerous to the other. However, they claim that the forces of evil will win because they are not held back by rules of morality. Many patients report having heard numerous stories about brutality committed in the name of religion. The clear message is that everyone is violent despite what they preach. Thus, the important thing is to be on the side with the power, the side that will win. It is not difficult to confuse a child. The child's previous notions of what is good become unclear. The child begins to feel a part of an inevitable process whereby "evil will come again to rule the earth." The choice is to be part of it or to be left behind and be killed.

The cults do not only try to convince members to show loyalty to the group by appealing to notions of logic or correct action. They also utilize very direct forms of blackmail. They may threaten members who have been previously forced to participate in pornography, murder, or other crimes. Members are reminded that they are equally in danger of society's wrath if the actions are revealed. There can also be threats toward family members or threats to reveal evidence of compromising activities (such as film showing the member having sex with an animal). Physical threats are commonplace. For example, one patient reported being forced to witness the tongue being cut out of a live cow. She was then forced to wear it around her neck and was told that if she ever talked about the group, the same would happen to her tongue. Many patients report being personally threatened or being forced to witness a childhood pet being killed as an example of what could happen to them if they ever betray the group. Thus, patients usually continue to demonstrate a tremendous sense of fear that the cult has the power to retaliate toward them and will do so. This is especially the case early in treatment when they begin to discuss what has occurred, since talking about cult activities is a major violation of the cult's rules.

As the new cult member develops and passes through the various rituals he or she acquires a place of increasing status in the cult. Some cults have positions determined from birth, but even in these, the novitiate gains more and more privileges and suffers less and less abuse by moving through the various entry rituals. As the new member becomes more involved, he or she begins to reap the benefits of membership financially, interpersonally, and in terms of feeling power over others. Clearly, feeling harmony with the group contrasts starkly to the earlier terror and confusion. The person is almost continually reminded that he or she will never fit into the outside world after having had such experiences. The clear message is that the cult is the only place where he or she belongs.

Just as the program of thought reform had specific stages, the satanic cults appear to have a series of rites of passage. The exact ages and corresponding rituals are not yet clear and may well differ across groups. However, it is clear that certain ages based on numerology appear to be selected for each of the types of initiation rituals. Various female patients have described an important ritual either at ages five to six or twelve to thirteen where they must give themselves to the cult. This is often described as a "marriage to the beast Satan" in which the young woman is raped by the men of the group and tortured. She is told that this insures her place in the group and guarantees her return to it as an adult. The ceremony typically involves the use of sacrifices and/or other activities far outside the realm of usual life. Another bonding ritual described by numerous survivors is the "satanic abortion" in which they are first impregnated by a member of the group and later forced to abort the fetus, which is subsequently killed and consumed by the group's members as part of a ceremony. Such extreme actions of course further split the person from the outside world and

> bind her to the cult, for she feels that no one else could
> accept or believe her afterward.
>
> The cult initiate is eventually given an important role
> in its functioning. Each member is reportedly
> groomed for a specific role, but as the process un-
> folds, the responsibilities and benefits increase for all.
> There is ultimately a sense of belonging and identifi-
> cation that can become so strong that the member
> will bring his or her own children to the cult to begin
> the process anew.[12]

It is important that people who claim to have been forced to participate
in the previously mentioned rituals or who fear for their lives are not
dismissed as mental patients. As bizarre as their allegations sound, it is
necessary to interview them and have them lead investigators to as much
physical evidence as possible. Attempts should be made to corroborate their
stories by visiting ritual sites and checking whether similar claims were made
to nearby police departments or in other locations where the group had
resided. Imagine being subjected to Satanic Ritual Abuse, escaping the
group, having the courage to report the activities to the police and then not
being believed. These allegations must be taken seriously because the consequences of not following through are devastating. In addition to revealing
a Satanic cult, one person could potentially help uncover a large organized
child abuse, pedophile and/or pornography ring.

Cases of Satanic Ritual Abuse have been referred to as multi-
offender/multi-victim cases, or as retired Supervisory Special Agent Kenneth
Lanning chose to call them multidimensional child sex ring cases. As a
member of the Behavioral Science Unit, Lanning was the FBI's authority on
ritual abuse for many years. Unfortunately his research into ritual abuse has
been extensively quoted by cult apologists and Satanists to support arguments
that Satanic Ritual Abuse does not exist and provoked accusations that he is
a Satanist who has infiltrated the FBI.[13]

Although I do not agree with many of Agent Lanning's views on ritualistic crimes, he has devoted his professional life and made important con-
tributions to issues of child sexual abuse and exploitation. Lanning's
perspective is consistent with current research in behavioral science which
prefers to relegate these crimes as forms of psychopathology. His goal was
to put forth an objective useful typology that minimizes allegations of Satanism which frequently contaminate and damage the prosecution potential of
ritual abuse cases.

Due to the fact that the criminal justice system needs to have scientific explanations for unspeakable behavior, Lanning has posited excellent suggestions for investigating child sexual abuse that are quite relevant for a successful prosecution. He emphasizes that the officer has to focus on physical evidence and the illegal activity regardless of the belief system. Lanning also prefers to refer to such cases as multidimensional child sex rings because that designation diminishes the highly charged emotions that are evoked, the definitional problems of ritualistic abuse and avoids media campaigns that have previously distracted and complicated investigations and prosecutions.

Negotiations

The United States counterterrorism policy is very clear: "First, make no concessions to terrorists and strike no deals; second, bring terrorists to justice for their crimes; third, isolate and apply pressure on states that sponsor terrorism to force them to change their behavior; and fourth, bolster the counterterrorism capabilities of those countries that work with the U.S. and require assistance."[14]

The U.S. policy on International Terrorism and American Hostages is: "The U.S. Government will make no concessions to individuals or groups holding official or private U.S. citizens hostage. The United States will use every appropriate resource to gain the safe return of American citizens

Negotiations

- Religious groups hold a nontraditional worldview. They do not recognize the authority of law enforcement.
- Religious groups do not respond with typical behavior; they have different values and priorities.
- True believers will fight and die for their cause.
- They consider their territory to be sacred space which they will defend till the death. Avoid confronting a group on its own ground.
- Need to understand their theology, symbolism, language. Even though they speak English they speak a different language.
- When getting expert advice from academics or other experts remember to get more than one opinion, they may have disinformation.

who are held hostage. At the same time, it is U.S. Government policy to deny hostage takers the benefits of ransom, prisoner releases, policy changes, or other acts of concession."[15]

These policies are appropriate and necessary to typical terrorism situations. However, religious scholar Jean Rosenfeld posited an excellent argument that hostage-taking incidents differ significantly from religious confrontations. In a presentation to the Los Angeles Police Department, Rosenfeld provided a brief description of millennial, apocalyptic and messianic groups' views of civil law and made the following points and suggestions for negotiating religious confrontations.[16]

- A religious confrontation always involves more than one person unless that person is acting on behalf of a religious community or group that acknowledges him or her as a member who is fulfilling the group's imperatives.
- Contrary to conventional wisdom, religious leaders are no more likely to suffer from mental illness than any other person. In certain studied cases (e.g., Jonestown, Aum Shinrikyo) in which a leader's mental state deteriorated, movements did engage in violent acts. However, the data do not yet support the assertion of a causal relationship between a leader's mental illness and violence or terror. In other words, there is no reason to assume that the leader of a new religious movement is "wacky."
- Religious groups regard perimeters as sacred boundaries that they will defend to the death. If possible, avoid confronting a group on its own ground or forcing it into an enclosure.
- Religious standoffs always involve an ultimate concern — that which members live by and profess willingness to die for — that must be taken into consideration in crafting a peaceful resolution.
- Even when religious groups use English, they speak a different language from the rest of society. They attach an unfamiliar set of meanings to words that seem familiar.
- Because they occupy sacred space in a different world, religious communities adhere to divine commands over and above the ordinary rules and mores of society.
- Because religious groups regard their laws as divine commands that take precedence over human laws, negotiators should take these laws into consideration during negotiations.
- Religious groups engage in highly organized behavior motivated by imperatives that outsiders are not familiar with or do not value; thus, their behavior does not necessarily conform to psychologically defined categories of basic human drives and needs.

- Religious groups may endure greater hardships and bear a higher casualty rate than non-religious groups because they believe that whatever happens is the will of God.
- Negotiators may use an understanding of the group's worldview to craft a rational agreement that reduces tensions or resolves the confrontation or both. Accomplishing this requires a detailed knowledge of the group's worldview and a flexible approach to group demands.
- Thus, time is an asset in resolving a religious confrontation, unless the group has announced a specific date on which it expects God to intervene, in which case there may be cause for concern about group suicide or mayhem.
- The negotiation team should include world view translators who can listen to and understand the mythology, ultimate concern and language of the religious group. Worldview translators should maintain a neutral perspective or critical distance and be able to win the trust of the group.
- Religious groups vary greatly. Within the same group individuals may have different interpretations of events. A prophet or leader may not be certain of the exact meaning of his revelation from God. Strategies for the resolution of each critical incident should exploit the religious constraints and ambiguities within the group. It is essential to decode the symbolic expression of the group to work toward a resolution members will accept.
- A negotiation is likely to succeed in crafting a non-violent outcome insofar as it allows the group to maintain its dignity as well as its ultimate concern.
- Religious standoffs, by definition, do not include the taking of hostages. Children of the group should not be considered hostages in order to redefine the incident as a hostage incident. Persons or groups who do take hostages should be approached according to a hostage taking model, not a religious standoff model. (Disagree children should always be viewed as hostages.)

The main points in Rosenfeld's suggestions are that religious groups hold a nontraditional worldview; they do not recognize the authority of law enforcement; they do not respond with typical behavior; they consider their territory to be sacred space; and significantly they are true believers who will fight and die for their cause. For example, one of the miscalculations that occurred at Waco during the Branch Davidian siege was that officials assumed that if the children were in danger of being consumed by fire, etc. maternal instinct would cause the mothers to protect and escape with their children. Unfortunately, the Branch Davidian worldview was that they were in an apocalyptic war, representatives of Satanic Babylon (law enforcement agents) were at their doorstep and by dying with their children, they were actually saving their souls for all eternity.

In Jonestown, members of the Peoples' Temple committed the largest mass suicide (more than 900 people) by drinking grape-flavored cool-aide laced with potassium cyanide and tranquilizers. The parents gave the juice to their children first, before taking it themselves and the babies were killed by having the poison squirted into their mouths with a syringe. Fortunately, the Heaven's Gate group suicide did not include any children.

With this in mind, I disagree with Rosenfeld's opinion that children should not be considered hostages. If the situation has escalated to the point where there are law enforcement agents engaged in a siege or a standoff or in negotiation with a religious group, the children should always be considered hostages since they do not have any rights or voice in the community. Although I agree that experts or, as Rosenfeld describes them, worldview translators should be consulted, they should not personally interact with the groups, that requires law enforcement officers who are trained in rules of engagement and other tactical aspects of negotiation. When obtaining advice from academic or other experts, it is crucial to get more than one opinion because some academics are unknowingly deceived while studying and interviewing members of a group and could be passing on disinformation.

Gordon Melton, Director of the Institute for the Study of American Religion and one of the foremost leading scholars in new religious movements, consistently defends the rights of new relegous movements in interviews and in court. Melton defended both the People's Temple and Aum Shinrikyo. He went to Japan and held news conferences suggesting that the Aum Shinrikyo sect was innocent of criminal charges and were victims of excessive police pressure. Since some scholars take the position that even groups that commit violence in the name of their religion should be protected under the rights provided by religious freedom, it is extremely important to obtain advice from a variety of experts in the field.

Finally, if the situation presents itself and the leader does not have complete control over his followers, a useful strategy involves invalidating the authority of the leader (in the eyes of his believers), demonstrating flaws and inconsistencies in his beliefs and instilling doubts in members which may result in internal struggles in the group leading to a nonviolent resolution.

Prevention

After the formation of so many new religious movements in the 1970s, there were international concerns about the detrimental effects of these movements

---

Prevention

- Recognizing harms.
- Educating law enforcement, schools and the public on recruitment and indoctrination techniques and their subsequent harms.
- Using appropriate existing laws to investigate, arrest and prosecute leaders and groups.
- Making groups financially accountable for their victims and families of their victims.

---

on the well-being of their members, members' families and society in general. This has led to national and international conferences, resolutions and legislation in a variety of countries.

Currently, there is a fierce debate among religious movement scholars concerns anti-cult laws that have been enacted in Europe, particularly France. In May 2001, France's National Assembly approved the final version of a "religious cults" bill, known as the About-Picard bill, named after the French politician Senator Nicolas About and Catherine Picard, a member of the French National Assembly. Among other measures, the legislation gives judges greater authority to crack down on errant behavior of more than 170 religious groups designated as sects in France. The legislation was initiated after a series of murders and suicides in France, Switzerland and Canada by members of the apocalyptic religious group Order of the Solar Temple in the 1990s. The legislation's many critics claim the French parliament has gone too far and empowers the French government to dissolve an entire religious denomination or spiritual movement should any leader, director, officer or even a member of any one of their churches or groups accumulate more than one penal offense. It does not matter whether the offense was caused in the name of the association or not. Supporters of the new legislation argue it will not infringe on religious freedoms but it is merely aimed at protecting the rights of worshippers from groups who may prey on them.

The 1980s was the last time that it was politically acceptable in the United States to publicly acknowledge that new religious movements were dangerous and four states New York, New Jersey, Kansas and Nebraska attempted to pass legislation that entailed deprogramming laws, all of which were soon stopped by civil rights organizations. "Deprogramming" is the term used to describe an involuntary intervention whose goal is to deprogram the newly acquired beliefs of a person who was indoctrinated into a new religious movement. It is another controversial subject and is relevant to law enforcement because occasionally families would hire deprogrammers to kidnap their adult age children out of new religious groups, take them to an undisclosed area so that they could take as much time as needed to dissolve them of their cult beliefs and demonstrate to them how their own decision-making power had been taken away from them. Although families felt they had no other recourse to get their children back, kidnapping (even of your own child), of course, is illegal, and one of the reasons the four states attempted to pass bills that included among other things the right to appoint temporary conservators for persons over 16 years old who could remove individuals from a cult for a 45-day deprogramming period.

The person applying to serve as the conservator would have to prove to the judge that (1) the person in the cult has undergone a radical psychological change, evidenced by a list of symptoms such as dramatic weight change, etc.; (2) the group practices coercive techniques such as isolation from family and friends, food and sleep deprivation and unreasonably long work hours; and (3) the group uses deceptive practices in its recruiting. Senators opposed to the bill pointed out that the criteria outlined in the bill could apply to other organizations including the U.S. Marine Corps and argued that proving deception involves passing judgment on the beliefs of the group, which endangers religious freedom. Although the deprogramming laws were not enacted, fortunately, beginning in the 1990s, four states have passed ritual abuse laws: Idaho, California, Illinois and, as recent as last year, Massachusetts.

Additionally, the events of September 11, 2001 required the passage of many necessary anti-terrorist laws, most notably the USA Patriot Act, to deter and punish terrorists around the world and to enhance law enforcement investigatory tools. Similar to anti-cult legislation, the new laws are also coming under attack by civil rights organizations for violating First and Fourth Amendment rights. It is very difficult to pass legislation in the U.S. that is objective enough not to interfere with religious freedoms and specific enough to prevent harms caused by new religious movements. However, in an attempt to assist in investigation, prosecution and, most significantly, the prevention of religious terrorism and ritualistic crimes, the following suggestions are proposed: (1) recognizing harms, (2) educating law enforcement, schools and the public on recruitment and indoctrination techniques and their subsequent harms, (3) using existing appropriate laws to investigate, arrest and prosecute leaders and groups, and (4) making groups financially accountable for their victims and the families of their victims.

In addition to recognizing occult crime scenes and ritualistic abuse described throughout this book, it is important to also identify the harms specifically caused by new religious movements. An excellent report[17] arose out of a 1984 anti-cult conference The International Wingspread Conference on Cultism held at the Johnson Foundation Wingspread Conference Center in Racine, WI. The Wingspread Conference pointed out that cults cause concern because of their unethical and manipulative practices combined with their lack of consideration for an individual's needs, goals and social attachments. They pointed out more important concerns such as cult practices resulting in harm to individuals, families and society at large. The harms outlined in the Wingspread Conference over 25 years ago are not only relevant today, but foreshadowed many of the mass suicides, murders and irreparable damage that has occurred in subsequent new religious movements. In view of the fact that the first step to preventing religious terrorism and ritualistic crimes is recognition, the following is the list of harms put forth by the Wingspread Conference.

Cult Harms

Individuals and Families

- Mental or emotional illness, impaired psychological development, physical disease, injury, or death of cult members.
- Fragmentation of families.
- Financial exploitation of members and their families.
- Neglect and abuse of children, including deaths resulting from physical violence, profound neglect, or the denial of medical treatment.

Government and Law

- Infiltration of government agencies, political parties, community groups, and military organizations for the purposes of obtaining classified or private information, gaining economic advantage, or influencing the infiltrated organizations to serve the ends of the cult.
- Tax evasion.
- Fraudulent acquisition and illegal disposition of public assistance and social security funds.
- Violation of immigration laws.
- Abuse of the legal system through spurious lawsuits, groundless complaints to licensing and regulatory bodies or extravagant demands for services (such as those provided by the Freedom of Information Act) as part of "fishing expeditions" against their enemies.
- Pursuit of political goals while operating under the rubric of a non-political, charitable or religious organization.

Business

- Deceptive fund-raising and selling practices.
- Organizational and individual stress resulting from pressuring employees to participate in cultic "management training" and "growth seminars."
- Misuse of charitable status in order to secure money for business and other non-charitable purposes.
- Unfair competition through the use of underpaid labor or "recycled salaries" by cult-operated enterprises.

Education

- Denial of, or interference with, legally required education of children in cults.
- Misuse of school or college facilities, or misrepresentation of the cult's purposes in order to gain respectability.
- Recruitment of college students through violation of their privacy or deception, often with subsequent disruption of such students' educational programs or goals.

Religion

- Attempts to gain the support of established religions by presenting a deceptive picture of the cult's goals, beliefs, and practices; and seeking to make "common cause" on various issues.
- Infiltration of established religious groups in order to recruit members into the cult.

Although the Wingspread outline of harms is fairly comprehensive, it does not include a classification for certain major crimes such as fraud, rape, battery and murder which have been committed at the instigation of cult leaders or in cult settings.[18]

The second step in prevention is educating law enforcement, schools and the general public of cult-related public hazards, recruitment and indoctrination techniques. Many resolutions were adopted in the early 1980s to address the issue of cults. One resolution that focused on education was implemented in 1982 by the National Parent–Teacher Association (PTA). In addition to other forms of school violence, the PTA still recognizes the problem of cults and provides violence prevention kits for a variety of manifestations of school violence. The association's specific suggestions on cults proposed at the 1982 convention are still relevant:

> Whereas, various cults often recruit members by deceptive means; and whereas, cults often keep their members by using mind control and by alienating the members from their families; and whereas, many families have deep emotional scars caused by their children's dependence on cults; and whereas an awareness of the recruitment and retention techniques of cults could help prevent a young person's entry into cults, therefore be it resolved that the national PTA urges state PTAs/PTSAs and their units to hold education programs to inform families and youth about methods of recruitment, and techniques used to exercise control over members' thoughts and actions by cults; and be it further resolved that the national PTA provide a list of available resources to assist state PTAs/PTSAs and their local units in planning such programs.[19]

Since many groups specifically target high schools, providing information on new religious movements' recruitment techniques to administrators, teachers and parents is an excellent method of prevention.

The third step in prevention is using existing appropriate laws to investigate, arrest and prosecute members and leaders of alternative religions who are engaged in activities that are legally unrelated to their religious beliefs. Although there is no specific legislation that addresses new religious movements, existing laws may be applicable to the prosecution of particular members or group leaders inclusive of immigration laws, cruelty to animals, tax evasion, polygamy, hate crimes, ritual child abuse, involuntary servitude and, in specific cases, child custody laws.

After September 11, 2001, immigration laws have frequently been used to detain potential terrorists for questioning. Hate crimes (18 U.S.C. § 241, 18 U.S.C. § 245 and 42 U.S.C. § 3631) which are defined as violent and intimidating acts of racial, ethnic and religious hatred that interfere with federally protected rights, such as housing, employment, voting, and public services, can be applied to domestic terrorist religions. In a situation where a new religious movement has its members turn over their entire salaries to the group or they fail to receive earnings for their services under the pretext of the group theology, the leader may be able to be prosecuted for tax evasion or peonage and involuntary servitude (18 U.S.C. §§ 1581, 1584) which is use of force or threats of force to compel persons to perform work against their will inclusive of modern-day slavery or worker exploitation, usually involving migrants, foreign domestic workers and religious cults.

In some new religious movements, sexual mores are determined by the theology of the religion and in some cases, men, especially the leader, will have taken more than one wife. Although, in an attempt to avoid prosecution, men will legally marry one woman and in the eyes of the religion have ceremonies where they marry additional wives. In some cases, there may be an application of bigamy or polygamy laws. These laws were enacted in the 19th century and consist of the 1862 Anti-Bigamy Act, the 1874 Poland Act, the 1882 Edmunds Act and the infamous 1887 Edmunds–Tucker Act. However, it is easier to investigate cases of polygamy through welfare fraud since many of the illegal wives will claim that they are single mothers who are independently raising their children even though they are financially supported in polygamous marriages.

For occult religions that practice animal sacrifice, all states have laws that prohibit cruelty to animals. Many states give a special role to the Humane Society or Society for the Prevention of Cruelty to Animals where officers of these private associations are considered law enforcement officers and are empowered to seek and execute search and arrest warrants, search private property for evidence of cruelty to animals and arrest persons whom they have reason to believe have committed an offense involving cruelty to an animal. As described in Chapter 7, a case involving the practice of animal sacrifice (*Church of the Lukumi Babalu Aye v. City of Hialeah*, 508 U.S. 520, 1993) went all the way to the U.S. Supreme Court. This historical decision providing rights for Santeria practitioners can never be completely reconciled with U.S. laws because it conflicts with health codes and interpretations of what constitutes cruelty to animals.

In both occult and cult groups, situations may arise in which one parent who is not a member of a group does not want their child raised in a new religious movement environment. Their objections are that cult groups frequently provide home schooling, children only socialize with members of the group, they may be denied medical care, may be indoctrinated into theologies of hate and be ritually abused. Because the United States Supreme Court has not yet decided a case involving religious upbringing and custody, there is no uniform national law. Instead, the law varies from state to state. Most state courts apply one of the following three legal standards when deciding religion and child custody cases:

1. Actual or Substantial Harm. The court will restrict a parent's First Amendment or parenting rights only if that parent's religious practices cause actual or substantial harm to the child.
2. Risk of Harm. The court may restrict a parent's First Amendment or parenting rights if that parent's religious practices might harm the child in the future.

3. No Harm Required. The custodial parent's right to influence the religious upbringing of his or her children is considered exclusive. If the custodial parent objects to the non-custodial parent's religious activities, that's the end of it; the court will defer to the custodial parent's wishes.

In addition, when deciding a dispute about religious upbringing, courts may consider any oral or written agreements that the couple previously made regarding this issue. However, again, how courts treat these agreements varies by state.[20]

Finally, Massachusetts recently passed the following act that prohibits all forms of ritualistic abuse applying severe punishments. The act acknowledges the reality of Satanic Ritual Abuse, indoctrination techniques and all of the acts of murder, mutilation and ritual abuse described throughout this book and is an exemplary model for other states.

The Commonwealth of Massachusetts

In the Year Two Thousand and One.
AN ACT PROHIBITING CERTAIN RITUALISTIC ACTS.

Be it enacted by the Senate and House of Representatives in General Court assembled, and by the authority of the same, as follows:

Chapter 265 of the General Laws is hereby amended by inserting after section 43 the following three sections: —

Section 44. No person shall commit ritualistic mutilation, dismemberment, or torture of a person as part of a ceremony, rite, initiation, observance, performance, or practice.

Any person who commits, attempts to commit or conspires with another to commit a violation of this section shall be punished by imprisonment in the state prison for life or for any term of years.

Section 45. No person shall commit ritualistic physical or psychological abuse, including sexual abuse of a child or of a physically or mentally disabled adult as part of a ceremony, rite, initiation, observance, performance, or practice.

Any person who commits, attempts to commit or conspires with another to commit a violation of this section shall be punished by imprisonment in the state prison for life or for any term of years.

Section 46. Whoever commits any of the following acts upon, with, or in the presence of a child age 18 or under shall be punished by imprisonment in the state prison for not more than ten years, or by imprisonment in a jail or house of correction for not more than two and one-half years, and whoever commits a second or subsequent such offense shall be punished by imprisonment in the state prison for life or any term of years.

(a) Actually commits or simulates the killing of, or tortures, mutilates or sacrifices any animal or human being.
(b) Forces the ingestion, injects or in any other way applies the use of a narcotic, drug, hallucinogen or anaesthetic or mind altering substance for the purpose of dulling sensitivity, cognition, resistance, memory or to distort perception of any criminal or unlawful activity.
(c) In any way forces the ingestion of or external application of human or animal urine, feces, flesh, blood, body parts, body secretions, drugs or chemicals.
(d) Forces or entices the child to have sexual contact with another human or animal during a ritual ceremony, or rite or other related observance.
(e) Places a child in a coffin or grave.
(f) In any way threatens the child with death or serious harm to the child, the child's parents, family, friends or pets.
(g) Unlawfully dismembers, mutilates or incinerates a human corpse.
(h) Forces the child to be placed in areas in which the child will come close to or in contact with human body parts.
(i) Simulates the performance of surgery and placing imaginary foreign object within the child for the purpose of creating fear within a child.
(j) Forces a child to participate in any ceremony, observance, practice or rite, purporting to be a marriage to any deity or other person and following such ceremony, observance, practice or rite with sexual contact or torture.

No person serving a sentence for a second or subsequent such offense shall be eligible for furlough, temporary release, programs outside a correctional facility until such person shall have served three quarters of the total of all minimum sentences.

In prosecution under this section, it is not a defense that a child under the age of 18 will be deemed to have consented to the actions of the defendant.

The provisions of this section shall not apply to:

(a) The lawful agricultural, animal husbandry, food preparation or wild game hunting and fishing practices and specifically the branding or identification of livestock
(b) The lawful medical practice of circumcisions or any ceremony related thereto
(c) Any state or federally approved, licensed or funded research project

The fourth and final suggestion for prevention of religious terrorism and ritualistic crimes is to make individuals and organizations financially responsible for harms to their victims and victims' families. The Southern Poverty Law Center has won precedent-setting cases against domestic terrorist organizations by helping victims of racist violence sue for monetary damages, which has substantially impinged on their operations. Cases have included:

> In October 1988, a federal court jury assessed nearly $1 million in damages against two Klan organizations and 11 Klan followers who were responsible for a violent attack on an interracial group who marched in all-white Forsyth County, Georgia, on January 17, 1987.

> In 1988, Tom and John Metzger sent their best White Aryan Resistance (WAR) recruiter from California to organize a Portland Skinhead gang. After being trained in WAR's methods, the gang killed an Ethiopian student. Tom Metzger praised the Skinheads for doing their "civic duty." Center attorneys filed a civil suit claiming that the Metzgers and WAR were as responsible for the killing as the Portland Skinhead gang. In October 1990, a jury agreed and awarded $12.5 million in damages to the family of the victim, Mulugeta Seraw.

> Nineteen-year-old Michael Donald was on his way to the store in 1981 when two members of the United Klans of America abducted him, beat him, cut his throat and hung his body from a tree on a residential street in Mobile, AL. The two Klansmen who carried out the ritualistic killing were eventually arrested and convicted. Sensing a larger conspiracy and convinced that the Klan itself should be held responsible, Center attorneys filed a civil suit on behalf of Michael Donald's mother. In 1987, the Center won an historic $7 million verdict against the United Klans and all the Klansmen who had played a part in the lynching.

> On May 17, 1991, Harold Mansfield, a black sailor who served in the Gulf War, was killed by a member of a white supremacist organization called the Church of the Creator. After Klanwatch investigators documented the group's violent history, the Center sued and ob-

tained a $1 million default judgment against the so-called "Church."

In the largest judgment ever awarded against a hate group, a South Carolina jury in 1998 ordered the Christian Knights of the Ku Klux Klan, its state leader and four other Klansmen to pay $37.8 million for their roles in a conspiracy to burn a black church. A judge later reduced the award to $21.5 million.

In September 2000, the Center won a $6.3 million jury verdict against the Aryan Nations and its leader, Richard Butler. The judgment forced Butler to give up the 20-acre Aryan Nations compound that had served for decades as the home of a who's who of violent white supremacists.[21]

These lawsuits not only disrupt their operations through financial losses, but send a message that violent groups that may elude criminal prosecution will still be accountable for their crimes.

References

1. Wessinger, C., *How the Millennium Comes Violently*, Seven Bridges Press, New York, 2000, p. 95.

2. Zusne, L. and Jones, W. H., *Anomalistic Psychology: A Study of Magical Thinking*, 2nd ed., Lawrence Erlbaum Associates, Hillsdale, NJ, 1989, p. 13.

3. Resistance Records website.   http://www.resistance.com/ethniccleansing/index.htm

4. Galanter, M., Ed., Cults and New Religious Movements, A Report of the American Psychiatric Association, from the Committee on Psychiatry and Religions, American Psychiatric Association, Washington, D.C., 1989, p. 180.

5. Galanter, M., Ed., Cults and New Religious Movements, A Report of the American Psychiatric Association, from the Committee on Psychiatry and Religions, American Psychiatric Association, Washington, D.C., 1989, p. 169.

6. Wessinger, C., *How the Millennium Comes Violently*, Seven Bridges Press, New York, 2000, p. 134.

7. Wessinger, C., *How the Millennium Comes Violently*, Seven Bridges Press, New York, 2000, pp. 123–124.

8. U.S. Department of Justice website, transcript of John Walker Lindh press conference, January 15, 2002. http://www.usdoj.gov/ag/speeches/2002/011502walkertranscript.htm

9. Newshour Extra, American Taliban: John Walker Lindh, January 16, 2002. http://www.pbs.org/newshour/extra/features/jan-june02/walker_john_1-2.html

10. BBC News Americas Profile: John Walker Lindh, January 24, 2002. http://news.bbc.co.uk/1/hi/world/americas/1779455.stm

11. Katchen, M.H. and Sakheim, D.K., Satanic beliefs and practices, in *Out of Darkness, Exploring Satanism & Ritual Abuse*, Sakheim, D.K. and Devine, S.E., Eds., Lexington Books, New York, 1992, pp. 29–35.

12. Sakheim, D. and Devine, S., *Out of Darkness: Exploring Satanism and Ritual Abuse*, Lexington Books, New York, 1992, pp. 29–35.

13. Sakheim, D. and Devine, S., *Out of Darkness: Exploring Satanism and Ritual Abuse*, Lexington Books, New York, 1992, p. 110.

14. U.S. Department of State Counterterrorism Office website. http://www.state.gov/s/ct/

15. U.S. Department of State Counterterrorism Office website. http://www.state.gov/s/ct/

16. Rosenfeld, J., A brief history of Millenialism and suggestions for a new paradigm for use in critical incidents, a presentation to the Los Angeles Police Department, in *Millennialism, Persecution & Violence*, Wessinger, Ed., Syracuse University Press, Syracuse, NY, 2000, pp. 350–351.

17. West, L.J., Persuasive techniques in contemporary cults: a public health approach, in Cults and New Religious Movements, A Report of the American Psychiatric Association, Gallanter, M., Ed., from the Committee on Psychiatry and Religions, American Psychiatric Association, Washington, D.C., 1989, p. 173–175.

18. West, L.J., Persuasive techniques in contemporary cults: a public health approach, in Cults and New Religious Movements, A Report of the American Psychiatric Association, Gallanter, M., Ed., from the Committee on Psychiatry and Religions, American Psychiatric Association, Washington, D.C., 1989, pp. 173–175.

19. West, L.J., Persuasive techniques in contemporary cults: a public health approach, in Cults and New Religious Movements, A Report of the American Psychiatric Association, Gallanter, M., Ed., from the Committee on Psychiatry and Religions, American Psychiatric Association, Washington, D.C., 1989, pp. 173–175.

20. findlaw http://consumer.pub.findlaw.com/family/children/nolo/ency/ 7F24-EF5E-1495-441C-97E83C5961B7238E.html

21. Southern Poverty Law Center website, Center battles white supremacist groups. http://www.splcenter.org/legalaction/la-index.html

Symbolic Analysis: Ritual Homicide Typology 10

Analyzing ritual crimes not only entails all the forensic, investigation and legal issues associated with violent crime but also posits its own unique problems. As described throughout this book, problems arising from investigating ritualistic crimes are generally beyond most investigators' typical experience. Due to the lack of standardized categories, law enforcers cannot agree on the extent of ritualistic crime, the types of crimes committed by individuals and religious groups or the motives of the perpetrators.

Additionally, the study of ritualistic crime is in its infancy. There is little empirical data, no agreed-upon classifications or typologies, hence, ritual violence is not often recognized, reported or investigated accurately. Furthermore, training on ritualistic crimes is not readily available, and because interpretations of what constitutes occult crime differ, distributed information is frequently inconsistent.

In an endeavor to standardize ritualistic crimes in this concluding chapter I have focused on the crime of ritual murder to introduce a ritual homicide typology and a corresponding investigative method that I refer to as Symbolic Analysis. The primary goal of this classification system is to characterize various expressions of ritual homicide through the identification of the religion, rites, and intent of the offender(s) based on symbolic evidence, the sacred context of objects, ritualized behavior and forensic findings at crime scenes.

Symbolic Analysis differs from typical criminal profiling in that it is not based on psychological methodologies but instead is based on religious concepts.

The principal purpose of this ritual homicide typology is to assist law enforcement investigators in crime scene identification and criminal investigation to distinguish the subtle but significant differences in characteristics

Ritual Homicide Typology

- A classification system that is an endeavor to standardize ritualistic crimes.
- Symbolic analysis differs from typical criminal profiling in that it is not based on psychological methodologies but instead is based on religious concepts.

- The primary goal of this classification system is to characterize various expressions of ritual homicide through the identification of the religion, rites and intent of the offender(s) based on symbolic evidence, the sacred context of objects, ritualized behavior and forensic findings at crime scenes.

of offenses. Additional objectives are to standardize information and compile accurate statistical data on ritual homicides for the purposes of criminal analysis and empirical research. Another primary goal is to identify similar cases, to notify agencies involved of the similar cases and to recognize patterns of violence that may be specific to particular organizations. Finally, this proposed typology maintains the same standardized categories, terminology and crime analysis forms used in the Federal Bureau of Investigation's Violent Criminal Apprehension Program (VICAP) while expanding upon the FBI's National Center for the Analysis of Violent Crime's crime classification system. In this chapter criminal profiling and symbolic analysis will be described and contrasted. The FBI's crime classification system will be summarized and reviewed with particular suggestions for ritualistic crimes. Categories of perpetrators' methods and motives and classifications of ritual homicides will be introduced and explained in detail. Samples of the most relevant questions of the VICAP crime analysis report for recognizing ritual homicides and a crime classification sample work sheet are located at the end of the chapter.

Criminal Profiling

Profiling is an investigative technique that is considered a type of applied criminology. It is a relatively new forensic discipline and unlike latent fingerprints, ballistics, DNA and other forensic methods, it is not a science but an investigative tool. It is referred to by a variety of terms inclusive of offender profiling, criminal profiling, psychological criminal profiling, psychological profiling, criminal personality profiling, socio-psychological

---

Criminal Profiling

- Profiling is an investigative technique that is considered a type of applied criminology. It is a relatively new forensic discipline and unlike latent fingerprints, ballistics, DNA and other forensic methods, it is not a science but an investigative tool.

Also known as:
- Offender profiling
- Criminal profiling
- Psychological criminal profiling
- Psychological profiling
- Criminal personality profiling
- Socio-psychological profiling
- Behavioral investigative analysis
- Criminal investigative analysis

---

profiling and, most recently, behavioral investigative analysis or criminal investigative analysis.

Although its origins can be traced back to as early as the 19th century in the work of criminal anthropologists, profiling became a formalized endeavor when the FBI founded its Behavioral Sciences Unit in 1974. Howard Teten and Pat Mullany, who were applied criminology and hostage negotiation instructors at Quantico, initiated profiling in the Behavioral Sciences Unit. "From 1975–1977, Robert Ressler, Dick Ault and John Douglas joined the unit, took on various responsibilities, and eventually became instructors in all the various training programs in applied criminal psychology. Other instructors were Tom O'Malley and Dick Harper who both taught sociology and Jim Reese, an expert on stress. The FBI's VICAP team (computer reporting system) was founded in 1983 by Pierce Brooks and the National Center for Analysis of Violent Crime (NCAVC) whose primary mission is identifying and tracking serial criminals was founded in 1984."[1]

Additionally, in the late 1980s and early 1990s, academic criminologists started researching serial killers and began to conduct studies in profiling, offer college courses on serial killers and consulting with law enforcement agencies.

Due to the various methodologies and different approaches to profiling, there is no one agreed-upon definition. However, Howard Teten, who is now considered the grandfather of profiling, put forth the following definition: "Offender profiling is a method of identifying the perpetrator of a crime based on an analysis of the nature of the offense and the manner in which it was committed. Various aspects of the criminal's personality

Definition of Profiling

Howard Teten, the grandfather of profiling, defined it as:

- A method of identifying the perpetrator of a crime based on an analysis of the nature of the offense and the manner in which it was committed.
- Various aspects of the criminal's personality makeup are determined from his or her choice of actions before, during and after the crime.
- This information is combined with other pertinent details and physical evidence, and then compared with the characteristics of known personality types and mental abnormalities to develop a practical working description of the offender.

makeup are determined from his or her choice of actions before, during and after the crime. This information is combined with other pertinent details and physical evidence, and then compared with the characteristics of known personality types and mental abnormalities to develop a practical working description of the offender."[2]

The current FBI definition of criminal investigative analysis, a new term for profiling, is "an investigative process that identifies the major personality and behavioral characteristics of the offender based on the crimes he or she has committed. This process involves a behavioral approach to the offense from the law enforcement perspective as opposed to a mental health viewpoint. The law enforcement perspective focuses on the identification and apprehension of the offender while the mental health viewpoint centers on diagnosis and treatment."[3] Building upon Howard Teten's definition of profiling the following definition of symbolic analysis, an alternative form of profiling, is posited:

> Symbolic analysis is a method of identifying the perpetrator(s) of a crime based on an analysis of the symbolic nature of the offense and the ritual manner in which it was committed. Various aspects of the criminal's beliefs are determined from his or her choice of actions before, during and after the crime. This information is combined with other pertinent details and physical evidence, and then compared with the characteristics of known symbols, rituals and practices of

subcultures and/or alternative religions to develop a practical working description of the offender.

A primary goal in proposing symbolic analysis and the corresponding ritual homicide typology is to assist investigators and criminal investigative analysts. This does not require any additional effort in reporting or obtaining evidence but can be achieved by evaluating the same information provided in police reports, medical examiners' reports and standardized VICAP forms used for other methods of profiling. The ritual homicide typology contains categories that differ from the more common classifications of criminal investigative analysis in that it is not based on a behavioral psychological approach or on preconceived categories of personality and behavioral characteristics of the offender but on significant aspects of religious experience and phenomenology. The important difference is that psychological categories are fundamentally based on Western scientific values, paradigms and methodologies that are often significantly contrary to non-Western, non-scientific religious explanations for events. Symbolic analysis assists the investigator in shifting his frame of reference from a Western rational perspective to a magical religious perspective by providing suggestions for interpreting evidence based on knowledge of alternative religious ideologies, rituals and values.

Additionally, the ritual homicide typology is especially relevant to murders committed by members of organized groups or multiple offenders because it is based on established group beliefs and alternative value systems. The behavioral approach is more relevant to individual mass, spree and serial killers who have expressed ritualized behavior that may not be part of any established

---

Definition of Symbolic Analysis

- Symbolic analysis is a method of identifying the perpetrator(s) of a crime based on an analysis of the symbolic nature of the offense and the ritual manner in which it was committed.

- Various aspects of the criminal's beliefs are determined from his or her choice of actions before, during and after the crime.

- This information is combined with other pertinent details and physical evidence, and then compared with the characteristics of known symbols, rituals, and practices of subcultures and/or alternative religions to develop a practical working description of the offender.

religious theology. From the aspect of analyzing group conduct, symbolic analysis could be considered a form of criminal intelligence analysis which was originally developed to assist intelligence units deal with organized crime but was found to be extraordinarily useful in the management of other complex cases involving homicide, street gangs, economic fraud and political corruption. Although there are several definitions of criminal intelligence analysis in use throughout the world, one definition was agreed upon in June 1992 by 12 European Interpol member countries and later adopted by others. It reads:

> Criminal intelligence analysis is the identification of and the provision of insight into the relationship between crime data and other potentially relevant data with a view to police and/or judicial practice. Criminal intelligence analysis uses uniform techniques focusing on the development of hypotheses, reconstructing the course of individual criminal incidents, identifying a series of related crimes, understanding criminal networks and analyzing the scope of and patterns in criminal activity. Criminal intelligence analysis techniques provide a standardized approach yet offer flexibility that is limited only by the ability and imagination of the crime analyst. Existing and new techniques are constantly being developed in order to extend the range of investigations and projects on which they can work. In the 1990s, strategic forms of criminal intelligence analysis have been more fully explored and crime pattern analysis has also become a well-used method for policy making. As criminals move into different areas of crime and their methods become more sophisticated, it is important for law enforcement agencies to be able to adapt their own methods.[4]

Symbolic analysis and the corresponding ritual homicide typology have applications for both criminal investigative and criminal intelligence analysis. The typology can assist behavioral analysts in quickly recognizing that applying Western morality is ineffective in particular cases and can assist intelligence analysts to identify groups and patterns of ritual violence.

Since the categories proposed for the ritual homicide typology are consistent with the FBI's Violent Crime Classification System, the investigator or analyst is encouraged to follow the same ideal criminal profiling process described in the FBI's *NCAVC Crime Classification Manual* which includes the following seven steps:

1. Evaluation of the criminal act itself.
2. Comprehensive evaluation of the specifics of the crime scene(s).
3. Comprehensive analysis of the victim.
4. Evaluation of preliminary police reports.
5. Evaluation of the medical examiner's autopsy protocol.
6. Development of the profile, with critical offender characteristics.
7. Investigative suggestions predicated on construction of the profile.

The manual states that:

> A thorough and comprehensive victimology is essential to the process and the victimology report (the victim's personality, life-style, and history) usually has great bearing on the analysis. The FBI Special Agents who are criminal investigative analysts try to evaluate why this victim was attacked and if the victim was known to the offender. They also attempt to gauge the victim's risk level (i.e., how this person's life-style, personality, etc. may have increased [or decreased] his or her chance of becoming a victim of a violent crime). The victimology also gives the analyst an idea of how much risk the offender took by approaching the victim.[5]

Although the significance of forensic information is also emphasized in the behavioral science approach, the primary focus is on the victim because it draws inferences about the offender based on predominating patterns of criminal behavior. However, the primary focus when investigating ritualistic crimes is on forensic symbolic evidence because the categories proposed in the ritual homicide typology draw inferences about the offender based on predominating patterns of religious experience and alternative value systems. Although both approaches are based on the same information, the interpretations can produce significantly different offender profiles.

Washington, D.C. Serial Sniper Case Study

The victimology in the case of the serial sniper who terrorized the suburbs of Washington, D.C. in October 2002 did not fit into any known established patterns of criminal behavior. The classic profile of a serial killer is a person who chooses similar victims, cares about the particular people he kills, cools off between attacks and then feels compelled to kill again. The snipers' victims did not have gender, age or race in common and were apparently chosen at random.

Many criminal profilers speculated that the attacker was a white loner, between 25 and 35 years old, with military experience, who had lived a long time in the D.C. area, was alienated from society and enjoyed exercising the god-like power of life and death. Many forensic psychiatrists stated that the shooter was a narcissist who did not experience any empathy for his victims. Additionally, profilers almost unanimously said that it was unlikely that a terrorist group was behind the slayings, arguing that terrorists would have looked for bigger targets to make a political statement. Psychological profilers were unable to provide an accurate offender profile because (1) analysis is based on established major personality and behavioral characteristics, none of which were consistent with their knowledge of the salient aspects of the shootings, (2) the emphasis that is placed on victimology was ineffective due to the lack of commonalities among the victims and (3) the use of a deductive methodology that limited the interpretation of evidence.

For example, the assumption that the victims did not share any characteristics is based on pre-established categories such as gender, race, age, workplace, etc. However, an inductive methodology would question what they had in common without any preconceived categories and the victimology would then determine that there were commonalities, such as the fact that they were all Americans, all engaged in common American activities of pumping gas, going to restaurants, school, shopping, etc., activities that reflect American values.

Once interpreted from the perspective of the ritual homicide typology, the offender profile of the serial sniper is quite different from the psychological profile. For example, as previously described, the victimology from a psychological perspective does not view the victims as having anything notable in common, whereas a symbolic analysis immediately recognizes that all the victims were part of the same American culture, engaging in activities that are reflective of Western American values. A symbolic analysis also places much more emphasis on the symbolic evidence, particularly the tarot card which contained the writing "Dear Policeman, I am God." The placement of the card was analyzed in view of other historical precedents where cards were left at murder scenes. The leaving of calling cards or trademarks has a particularly long history in crimes and in war. For example, in the Vietnam War, it was believed by U.S. troops that their Viet Cong and North Vietnamese enemies were superstitious, and often U.S. soldiers left a playing card near the body of an enemy they had killed. The ace of spades was used by several famous units including the Air Cavalry and the 25th Division. Tarot death cards would also turn up on Viet Cong corpses.[6] The tarot card was also analyzed in its typical method of use, which is for divination, and profilers commented that it does

Serial Sniper Case

Psychological Analysis

- Victims have nothing in common.
- "I am God"; playing god, exercising the god-like power of life and death.
- A narcissist who doesn't experience any empathy for his victims.
- Tarot card "signature" represents transformation, used by snipers in Vietnam.
- Language in letter; "Word is bond," English as a second language expression for verbal agreement.

Symbolic Analysis

- Victims are all Americans engaging in common American activities (shared Western values).
- "I am God"; a member of a religious group or ideology where followers consider themselves gods.
- A soldier (religious zealot) who doesn't experience any empathy for his victims.
- Tarot card originated with 14th century Muslims; used regularly in Voodoo, Santeria, Wicca divination; symbols on card represent secret societies.
- Language in letter; "Word is bond" expression widely used by black Muslim supremacist group Five Percenters (Nation of Gods and Earths) who refer to themselves as gods.

not literally represent death but is generally interpreted by tarot specialists as a form of radical change or transformation. Symbolic analysis of the tarot card would have entailed all of the previous information but delves into much more specific detail. For example, there are several different types of tarot decks, some of which are specifically designed for particular occult groups. The specific death card chosen also contains detailed symbolism; for example, the death card with the skeleton on a white horse is holding a flag with symbols that are representative of secret societies and of course the origin of the tarot card itself can be traced to 14th century Muslims. Finally current religions that regularly use tarot in divination include Wicca, Santeria, Voodoo and other syncretic religions that are predominant among particular immigrant populations.

The writing on the card in the sniper case was almost unanimously interpreted as a way of taunting the police, gaining attention and as a method of playing God, with the implication that the killer gets to determine who will live or die each day. This analysis may very well be accurate, but it only provides a behavioral perspective and the contribution to the investigation is limited.

From a religious perspective, the statement "I am God" is extremely significant. A fundamentalist Muslim would never claim that he was God because the statement constitutes a form of idolatry and one of the most severe acts of sacrilege. This was recognized by some profilers who instantly ruled out international terrorism and subsequently all Muslim groups. However, a typology based on religious concepts would have immediately recognized that there are religions in which followers identify themselves as gods. Particular Satanic and Vampire religions have theologies where their members aspire to be gods, and one group, known as the Five Percenters or more specifically, The Nation of Gods and Earths, refer to all male followers as gods.

Another piece of evidence, the letter that was found sealed, wrapped in plastic and tacked to a tree in the woods behind the Ponderosa Steakhouse in Ashland, VA, on October 19th, where a 37-year-old man was shot and wounded provided many clues for investigators. The words written on the cover page stated, "For you Mr. Police, Call me God" and were surrounded by five stars. The letter was neatly printed in ink on lined notepaper and contained errors in grammar, syntax, and spelling, including omitted letters, words, punctuation and irregular capitalization. It contained phone numbers the sniper called in a half dozen unsuccessful attempts to contact authorities and listed account information about a stolen platinum visa card that the assailants wanted reactivated with $10 million dollars that they could freely access. The letter also contained writing that threatened, "Your children are not safe anywhere at any time." The body of the Ashland letter concludes with the line: "If we give you our word that is what takes place Word is Bond." The expression "Word is Bond" is widely used by members of the Five Percenters and is the name of a song by hip-hop musicians the Brand Nubians, who, like an assortment of other reggae and hip-hop musicians, are members of the Five Percenters, who are often considered the youth wing of the Nation of Islam. There are, in fact, a number of songs that contain the phrase "Word is Bond," including American hip-hoppers House of Pain and any number of songs by Five Percenter Busta Rhymes. In addition, the letter had five stars on the title page and the stars are similar to ones that symbolize children to followers of the movement. The phrase "Word is Bond" is similar to one used by Montgomery Police Chief Charles A. Moose during a media briefing late Wednesday, October 23, in which he tried to communicate with the sniper, "If you are reluctant to contact us, be assured that we remain ready to talk directly with you. Our word is our bond." Chief Moose's response indicates that he recognized the significance of the expression as a verbal agreement; however, his correction of the grammar indicates that the phrase in the letter was interpreted as a grammatical error or was written by someone for whom English was a second language and not as a common phrase among members of any particular group.

The several references to the snipers wanting to be referred to as God, the expression "Word is Bond" and the five stars are enough indicators to suggest looking into the history, practices and beliefs of the Five Percent group. The Five Percent or The Nation of Gods and Earths, founded in 1964 by Clarence Edward Smith Jowers upon his expulsion from the Nation of Islam, is a loosely knit organization made up mostly of African Americans. The name of the group is derived from the "Mathematics" of the Nation of Islam "Lessons" and is symbolic of members believing that they are the true five percent gods of the universe with the knowledge and wisdom to deliver the black man from the home of the devil. Five Percenters do not consider their beliefs a religion and teach Islam as a righteous culture for black individuals. They believe that a black man with the knowledge (the Five Percent) is a god of himself as well as his people and that the "eurogentiles" have deceived the whole world, causing it to honor and worship false gods and idols.

Understanding this philosophy is essential for those who encounter Five Percenters. In its hierarchy, a Five Percenter male is a god with the highest status, followed by black males in the masses, earths (Five Percenter females), black females in the masses, white males and white females. Some members do not believe they are accountable for the crimes they commit because of their status as gods or earths. Many members formed loosely organized sets that distribute drugs and commit violent crimes, including against each other. Some Five Percenters profess their beliefs through the lyrics of popular rap and hip-hop music.[7] Since 1995, prison officials have designated the Five Percenters as a racist group that poses a security threat and, in at least five states, as well as the Federal Bureau of Prisons, they have been segregated from the general prison population. This has initiated several lawsuits and stronger anti-government sentiments among members. Essentially the Five Percenters and the Nation of Islam are considered black supremacist religious groups and ironically hold many of the same anti-Semitic, anti-regulatory and anti-government beliefs as white supremacist groups. Just as Satanic metal music is indicative of Satanism and black metal (stomper) music is indicative of young white supremacists, particular hip-hop groups are indicative of young black supremacists.

When reviewing the evidence in reference to the ritual homicide typology and conducting a symbolic analysis in the D.C. sniper case, two different offender profiles emerge. The behavioral profile and symbolic profile both suggest an offender with military experience and a person who is alienated from society (members of alternative religions deliberately separate themselves from society). Other than that, the profiles have little else in common. The behavioral profile suggested a white loner between 25 and 35 years old who had lived a long time in the D.C. area and was not part of a terrorist organization while the symbolic analysis suggested a black man or men who are members of a new religious movement that identify themselves as gods, hold anti-American and anti-government sentiments, consider themselves soldiers for their cause and could possibly be domestic terrorists.

Serial Sniper Offender Profiles

Psychological Profile
- White loner
- Between 25 and 35 years old
- Military experience
- Lived a long time in the D.C. area
- Alienated from society
- Enjoyed exercising the god-like power of life and death
- A narcissist who didn't experience any empathy for his victims
- Unlikely that a terrorist group was behind the slayings

Symbolic Profile
- Black men (more than one offender)
- Military experience
- Member of alternative religious/political group
- Member of non-Christian religious group
- Member of religious group that identifies themselves as God (black supremacist group)
- Exposed to occult ideologies
- Familiar with hip-hop culture
- Anti-American, anti-government beliefs
- Possible member of domestic terrorist group or cell

John Allen Muhammad is a twice-divorced, 42-year-old Gulf War veteran who converted to Islam 18 years ago, was a member of the Nation of Islam and earned an expert marksmanship badge in the U.S. Army. Lee Boyd Malvo, is an 18-year-old (17 at the time of the shootings) Jamaican native who with Muhammad's assistance had been smuggled from St. Elizabeth, Jamaica, to Haiti and then onto a tugboat into Miami, where he and his mother illegally entered the United States.

At the time of this writing John Allen Muhammad and Lee Boyd Malvo have been accused in all 10 fatal sniper shootings in the Washington, D.C. area. However, they have been linked to 20 other shootings including 13 deaths in Virginia, Maryland, Georgia, Alabama, Louisiana and Washington, D.C. Malvo faces his first trial for the October 14, 2002 shooting of Linda Franklin, 47, in the Seven Corners area. The trial is set for November 10, 2003 and has been moved from Fairfax County, VA to Chesapeake County VA. Muhammad faces his first trial in the October 9, 2002 slaying of Dean H. Meyers, 53, in Prince William County, VA. Muhammad's trial is scheduled for October 14, 2003 and has been moved from Prince William County, VA to Virginia Beach.

It is no surprise that Malvo's lawyers' defense strategy is based on their claim that Malvo was indoctrinated by Muhammad. They intend to demonstrate that he falsely confessed to some of the shootings because he was controlled by the more worldly Persian Gulf veteran Muhammad. In a letter to Malvo's defense team, Fairfax County's chief prosecutor Robert F. Horan Jr. disclosed to the defense lawyers that there are six witnesses who say sniper suspect Lee Boyd Malvo was obedient to John Allen Muhammad, including one who thought Malvo "appeared to be indoctrinated or brainwashed." The letter also provided support for lawyers' theories that Muhammad helped Malvo become a better marksman at a Washington state shooting range and that the teenager played a violent video game in which "Muhammad would coach Malvo on how to shoot in the sniper mode." Malvo's attorneys revealed their theory of Muhammad's domination of Malvo in a June 2003 motion asking for 23 pages of interviews with witnesses who are supposed to have told police that Malvo was "under the spell" of Muhammad. Those interviews might show "the potential of false or exaggerated confession," defense attorney Michael S. Arif wrote, and "such evidence bears directly upon the role and relative degrees of culpability" of Malvo and Muhammad. Prosecutor Horan sent a letter to Malvo's attorneys, naming six men in the Bellingham, WA, area "who comment on the degree of 'obedience' shown" by Malvo in 2001, when Malvo and Muhammad lived in a homeless shelter there. Horan also summarized the witnesses' assessments of the relationship, saying they described Malvo in various ways, including "very obedient," controlled and "intimidated" and "appeared to be indoctrinated and brainwashed." Horan said all the men thought Malvo was Muhammad's son.[8]

Malvo clearly fits the criteria described in Chapter 9 as someone who was the victim of recruitment and indoctrination techniques. His background and vulnerability made him the perfect candidate. Muhammad recruited Malvo at the age of 15. Left alone for long periods of time, Malvo immediately bonded with Muhammad who gave him the name John and identified himself as his father. Muhammad employed standard indoctrination techniques such as isolation, beatings, food deprivation, and military training, interspersed with providing the only protection and love Malvo ever experienced from a male authority figure. Although Lee Boyd Malvo should be held accountable for his crimes, the defense attorneys have a compelling argument that he was indoctrinated by Muhammad.

As the trials unfold there will be additional background information that can be analyzed for a more comprehensive offender profile, at some point in time John Allen Muhammad may even disclose what his motives were, which may turn out to be as typical as displaced anger and greed or as sophisticated as an Islamic sympathizer and domestic terrorist, in either situation this case has demonstrated the flaws in the current profiling systems.

There are many instances in which psychological profiling has been crucial for solving violent crimes but this particular case clearly demonstrated that the current behavioral typology does not always apply. Studies have shown that FBI profiling techniques are of some assistance in 77% of cases, provide leads for stakeouts, solving cases 45% of the time and actually help identify the perpetrator (unsub, unknown subjects) in 17% of cases.[9]

Currently, there are other methods of profiling being researched and applied such as geographic profiling. Geographic profiling is an investigative methodology that uses a connected series of crimes to determine the most probable area of an offender's residence. The research is based on the assumption that criminals like all humans tend to follow patterns of movement around and through geographic areas. For example, people are more likely to carry out routine activities close to home, work or school or within a set distance from the commuting routes between those points (the principle of least effort).[10] The system produces a map of the most probable location of the criminal's center of activity, which in most cases is the offender's residence. Ironically, this method of profiling was also inadequate for the serial sniper case because the suspects had no permanent residence and were living out of their car. When John Allen Muhammad and Lee Boyd Malvo eventually profess their motives, there will be ongoing hypotheses of what events in their lives led them to commit such heinous crimes.

Since psychological profiling and the proposed symbolic analysis are concerned with different aspects of human experience it is quite possible that their motives could include all of the previously mentioned: displaced anger, greed, Islamic sympathizers and domestic terrorists. Although there may initially be different offender profiles, all forms of criminal investigative analysis, psychological, geographical and symbolic, are not mutually exclusive and when the information is combined can present a comprehensive portrait of the offender and a multifaceted perspective of the crime.

Crime Classification

The categories proposed for the ritual homicide typology are consistent with the FBI's Violent Crime Classification System, a 10-year project of the National Center for the Analysis of Violent Crime. The goals of the classification system included standardizing terminology within the criminal justice fields, facilitating communications within the field and between criminal justice and mental health, educating the criminal justice system and the public at large to the types of crimes being committed and developing a database for investigative research. In keeping with these goals the ritual homicide typology retains the same defining characteristics as the classification manual for categorizing crimes. They include victimology, crime scene indicators, staging, forensic findings and investigative considerations.

Essentially all information obtained from active cases will remain the same so that officers will not have to fill out repetitive forms, and cold cases already in the system can be re-examined from the new perspective of symbolic analysis. The following is a summary of the FBI's crime characteristics

Crime Classification

FBI Classifications	Crime Scene Indicators
• Victimology	• Number of crime scenes
• Crime scene indicators	• Environment, Place, Time
	• Number of offenders
• Staging	• Organized or Disorganized, Physical Evidence, Weapon
• Forensic Findings	• Body Disposition
	• Items Left/Missing

Forensic Findings
- Cause of death
- Trauma
- Sexual assault

inclusive of specific suggestions that apply to ritual crimes. A corresponding crime classification sample worksheet can be found at the end of the chapter.

Victimology

Victimology is the complete history of the victim and should include as much information as possible about the victim. This information is especially useful in leading the investigator to the offender's motive and evaluating why that particular person was targeted for a violent crime. Some of the more important questions concerning victimology are: Was the victim known to the offender? What were the victim's chances of becoming a target for violent crime? What risk did the offender take in perpetrating this crime?[11] In addition to typical motives for violent crimes, ritual homicide victims may be current or former members of a religious group, inclusive of their own children; enemies of the group (actual, ideological or perceived) or the victim may have been selected because of the ritual need of the offender or for the purpose of the ritual.

Crime Scene Indicators

"There are many elements that constitute the crime scene. Not all of these will be present or recognizable with every offense. The following sections describe the major points an investigator should consider when looking at the crime scene."[12]

Amount of Crime Scenes

The investigator has to determine how many crime scenes are involved with the offense. A crime may involve one site in which the death scene and the crime scene are the same or there may be multiple crime scenes in which contact, assault, torture, death and body disposal occurred in different places. The amount of crime scenes can vary dependent on the type of ritual homicide.

Environment/Place/Time

> The environment of a crime scene refers to the conditions or circumstances in which the offense occurs. Is it indoors or outside? Was it during daylight hours or in the middle of the night? Did it happen on a busy street or on a deserted country road? Answering these questions not only assists in defining the classification of an offense, but also provides an assessment of the offender risk. Gauging these risk factors usually offers insight into an offender's motivations and behavior patterns. An additional question concerning time is, how long did the offender stay at the scene? Generally, the amount of time the offender stays at the scene is usually proportional to the degree of comfort the offender feels committing the offense at that particular location.[13]

In ritualistic crime, locations are always designated as either a sacred (holy) space or profane (ordinary) space. Violence in the form of occult religious ritual must always occur in sacred space; even mass murders/suicides must occur in sacred space. Outdoor secluded spaces are typical of ritualistic crime scenes due to the nature-based ideologies of most occult religions. They also provide enough privacy to prolong torture and conduct rituals.

At outdoor crime scenes, the investigator should always remember to look up and around for trail markers, unusual tree markings or anything that will indicate a ritual site. At one crime scene that was in a deeply wooded area, a water bottle had been placed on a high branch as a marker pointing to the ritual site. Also, note anything that appears out of place; for example, at another wooded crime scene, a circle was made out of branches, covered by leaves and perfectly blended in the environment. Religious terrorists will choose a location that is sacred to the victims or symbolically representative of their enemies' ideologies as a form of sacrilege and to instill fear.

How Many Offenders?

The answer to this question helps the investigator determine whether the offense should be placed in either the criminal enterprise category or the group cause category of the FBI crime classification system; both groupings include multiple offenders. In ritual violence crimes can be committed by one or more offenders who may be members of a religious group, a terrorist cell, or by a lone offender who is following the ideology of a group. However, some lone offenders enact rituals that do not conform to those of any organized group.

Organized or Disorganized/Physical Evidence/Weapon

> The amount of organization or disorganization of a crime scene will tell much about the offender's level of criminal sophistication. It also will demonstrate how well the offender was able to control the victim and how much premeditation was involved with the crime. It should be emphasized that the crime scene will rarely be completely organized or disorganized.
>
> Another aspect of the crime scene examination concerns the weapon. Questions the investigator needs to answer about the weapon include the following: Was it a weapon of choice, brought to the crime scene by the offender? Or was it a weapon of opportunity, acquired at the scene? Is the weapon absent from the crime scene, or has it been left behind? Was there evidence of multiple weapons and munitions? Multiple weaponry does not always signify multiple offenders.[14]

Disorganized crime scenes will generally be indicative of dabblers and teenage offenders; they frequently leave trash, food, bottles, etc. in the woods near the ritual site. Members of an established group will be highly organized and the crime scene will be particularly clean, because it is sacred space, it would be treated with the same respect as the space around the altar of a church.

The weapon of choice for ritualistic crime is a knife; it would be magically ineffective to shoot someone in a ritual. A ritual knife (athame) is one of the most sacred items of the offender and would rarely be left at a crime scene unless the perpetrator was interrupted in the act and had recently fled the scene. Usually a ritual knife or sword is found during searches of personal areas or on the suspect.

Religious terrorists use multiple weapons inclusive of explosives, firearms and weapons of mass destruction — anything that will achieve the highest casualities or instill the most fear.

Body Disposition

Some of the typical questions concerning body disposition are: "Was the body openly displayed or otherwise placed in a deliberate manner to ensure discovery? Or was the body concealed or buried to prevent discovery? Did the offender seem to have no concern as to whether the body would be discovered or not?"[15] Questions concerning body disposition address homicides that involve the intentional arranging of the body in an unnatural or unusual position, where the body was left in a degrading position or in a location to convey a message. Body disposition is one crime scene indicator whose psychological and symbolic interpretations can substantially differ from each other. In ritualistic crime, the body may be positioned in a manner that holds specific magical meaning for the group, was a necessary function of the ritual and has nothing to do with avoiding discovery or leaving a message. For example, the Order of the Solar Temple, a new religious group involved in three separate incidents of mass suicides/homicides, arranged the bodies in a circular star formation based on their theology that they were making "transits" to the star Sirius. Also, in ritualistic crimes bodies or body parts may be buried for magical purposes that have nothing to do with eluding the police.

Items Left/Missing

"The addition or absence of items at the crime scene often will assist the investigator in classifying the offense. The presence of unusual artifacts, drawings, graffiti, or other items may be seen with offenses such as extremist murder or street gang murder and is especially prevalent in ritualistic crimes and religious terrorism. Additionally, a victim's personal belongings may be taken from the scene of a sexual homicide as so-called souvenirs (i.e., photos, driver's license, costume jewelry; all belonging to the victim) even though they have no monetary value".[16]

Items left or missing from the crime scene is another crime scene indicator that is particularly relevant to ritualistic crime and religious terrorism. Symbols and artifacts found at the crime scene can help the investigator determine if the crime was conducted by an individual or members of a group, identify the type of religious ritual and whether that belief requires additional similar rituals which can signify future crimes. Ritualistic crime scene clues, including artifacts, symbols, alphabets, books, candles and pertinent dates, are described in detail in Chapter 8.

Staging

Staging is the purposeful alteration of a crime scene prior to the arrival of the police. The two primary reasons for staging are to redirect the investigation away from the logical suspect or to protect the victim or the victim's family. There is rarely evidence of staging in ritualistic and religious terrorism crime scenes. Perpetrators of ritualistic crimes will not interfere with their ritual because in many occult traditions any alteration of the ritual is a form of sacrilege and renders the magic ineffective. Perpetrators of religious terrorism want to take credit for the damage they have caused and if they did alter the crime scene it would be more for the purpose of being recognized instead of not being discovered. If a ritual crime entailed staging it would be indicative of a criminal who is not a true believer and whose primary motive has nothing to do with a group belief system.

Forensic Findings

"Forensic findings include the analysis of physical evidence pertaining to a crime, evidence that is used toward legal proof that a crime occurred. The primary sources of physical evidence are the victim, the suspect and the crime scene. Secondary sources include home or work environment of a suspect. Medical reports provide important evidence and include toxicological results, x-ray films and autopsy findings. In homicide cases the forensic pathologist identifies and documents the postmortem findings present and interprets the findings within the context of the circumstances of the death."[17]

Forensic findings are especially relevant to ritualistic crimes due to the amount of trauma, the symbolic nature of physical mutilations and the prominence of pre- and post-mortem sexual assault. In religious terrorism, the use of explosives and weapons of mass destruction are common indicators.

Cause of Death

"The mechanism of death is often a determining factor when investigators attempt to classify a homicide. The victim of a street gang murder almost always dies from gunshot wounds. Explosive trauma is a frequent finding with many criminal competition and extremist murders. Strangulation is common to more personal crimes."[18] In ritualistic crimes entailing sacrifice, the cause of death will frequently result from torture, blood loss or dismemberment caused by knife wounds inflicted during a ritual sacrifice. Murders committed for the purpose of millennial group beliefs can entail everything from poison to immolation to gunshot wounds. Suicides and homicides committed for the purpose of religious terrorism commonly include explosive trauma or death from chemical, biological or incendiary devices.

Trauma

"The type, extent and focus of injury sustained by the victim are additional critical factors the investigator uses when classifying a crime. Overkill, facial battery, torture, bite marks, and mutilation are examples of forensic findings that often will lead the investigator to a specific homicide category and a possible motive for the offense"[19] Mutilation is extremely common in ritualistic crimes and includes symbols cut into the body, bite marks, particular forms of dismemberment and bloodletting. These and other forensic findings are listed in the Crime Scene Clues section of Chapter 8.

In religious terrorism, trauma is not only caused by typical explosive incidents but may also be caused by projectiles such as nails, bolts, spikes and steel balls that have been added to the explosive charges in order to increase the number of fatalities. Additionally, the latest trend in terrorism is to first saturate the nails and bolts with rat poison to create chemical weapons. Once the nails and bolts enter the body, the rat poison prevents blood from coagulating so that when physicians attempt to operate, they cannot stop the bleeding, which leads to more fatalities.

Sexual Assault

> Evidence of assault to the victim's sexual organs or body cavities has great bearing on motive and classification. The type and sequence of the assault is important, as well as the timing of the assault (before, during or after death). The investigator should remember that the apparent absence of penetration with the penis does not mean the victim was not sexually assaulted. Sexual assault also includes insertion of foreign objects, regressive necrophilia and many activities that target the breasts, buttocks and genitals."[20]

In ritualistic crimes and religious terrorism, motivations for sexual assault differ substantially from motivations for other crime classifications. In ritualistic crimes, sexual assault is perceived as a form of sexual magic and has less to do with the gratification of the offender than with achieving magical power and/or as an indoctrination technique. This is based on the magical concept that any form of severe extreme emotion caused by either torture or sexual pleasure will increase the magical power of the offender. In religious terrorism, sexual assault is used as a strategy of war to humiliate and demoralize enemies.

Investigative Considerations

Once the investigator has classified the offense (and thus the motive), the investigative considerations and search warrant suggestions can be used to give direction and assistance to the investigation. The FBI classification manual outlines the following 10 basic steps to a crime scene search:

1. Approach the scene
2. Secure and protect
3. Preliminary survey
4. Narrative description
5. Photograph scene
6. Sketch scene
7. Evaluation of latent fingerprint evidence and other forms of evidence
8. Detailed search for evidence and collection
9. Preservation and documentation of evidence
10. Final survey and release of scene

The forensic analysis of physical evidence of hair and fibers, blood, semen and saliva can provide the basis for critical testimony in court.[21]

Perpetrators Motives and Methods

The FBI typology has three categories of offender behavior at the crime scene: staging, modus operandi and personation (the signature). Staging, as stated earlier, is the purposeful alteration of a crime scene prior to the arrival of the police, and there is rarely evidence of staging in ritualistic and religious terrorism crime scenes. Method of operation or *modus operandi* is defined as the actions taken by an offender to perpetrate the crime successfully — a learned behavior that evolves as the offender becomes more sophisticated and confident.[22]

The FBI's crime classification typology refers to ritualistic motives and methods of operation as the signature aspect or calling card of the crime. Another term the FBI uses for the signature aspect is *personation*, defined as, "Unusual behavior by an offender, beyond that necessary to commit the crime. The offender invests intimate meaning into the crime scene (e.g., by body positioning, mutilation, items removed or left, or other symbolic ges-

Perpetrators

No standard typology currently exists for perpetrators of ritualistic crimes. The following categories are suggested:

- **Method of Operation**
  - Dabbling
  - Ritualism
  - Paramilitary

- **Motives**
  - True Criminals
  - True Believers
  - True Followers

These categories are not mutually exclusive.

tures involving the crime scene). Only the offender knows the meaning of these acts. When a serial offender demonstrates repetitive ritualistic behavior from crime to crime, it is called the signature. The signature aspect of a crime is simply repetitive personation."[23] Ritualistic crimes by their very nature entail personation. The premise that only the offender knows the meaning of his ritualistic acts is based on a behavioral approach that does not recognize unfamiliar religious rituals. If an investigator is aware of alternative religious practices, it is very possible that he will comprehend the meaning of the offender's signature.

Interpreting the signature aspect of a crime is precisely where symbolic analysis departs from behavioral analysis. Although the FBI's category of the signature aspect of a crime is useful in distinguishing ritualistic crimes from non-ritualistic crimes, it is not specific enough to distinguish between types of ritualistic crimes. Therefore, it is necessary to have additional categories to distinguish between ritual homicides. No standard typology currently exists for perpetrators of ritualistic crimes; however, building upon previous reports, the following categories for perpetrators' methods and motives are suggested. These categories are not mutually exclusive from each other or from the FBI's Violent Crime Classification System.

Methods of Operation

- **Ritualism** involves people who commit criminal activities characterized by a series of repeated physical, sexual and/or psychological assaults combined with a systematic use of symbols, ceremonies and/or machinations. The need to repeat such acts can be cultural, sexual, economic, psychological and/or spiritual.[24]

- **Dabbling** involves people who are intermittently and experientially involved in occult activities. While dabbling in supernatural belief systems involves non-criminal activity which stems from a vague, curious interest, some dabbling involves intense preoccupation that culminates in criminal behavior. Such perpetrators most often act alone or in small loosely organized groups. Dabblers usually make up their own belief system based upon some occult ideology and perpetrate criminal activity that conforms to that ideology.[25]
- **Paramilitary** methods of operation involve people who commit criminal activities characterized by highly organized, preplanned surveillance and military execution of violence combined with symbolism and/or a forensic signature specific to the group — "a style of operation that is characterized by the wearing of uniforms, the use of training compounds, a hierarchy of leadership based on rank and an internal code of discipline and conduct."[26]

Motives

- **True Believers** are religious practitioners who commit crimes because such acts fit into and/or are required by their particular belief system. These persons are involved in crime primarily because the ideology, rituals and tenets of their beliefs require them to do so.
- **True Criminals** are persons who use the occult as an excuse to justify or rationalize their criminal behavior. They are committed not to the belief system but to the criminal action. True criminals both dabble in the occult and are involved in rituals that fit their particular physical, sexual, psychological, social, economic and/or spiritual needs.
- **True Followers** are persons, most often young adults, who turn to the occult because of a deep sense of alienation from mainstream culture. Often inspired by music and film versions of the occult to shape their belief system and justify their criminal behavior. They are momentary true believers who have a strong desire for a sense of belonging and to feel valued.

Symbolic Analysis: Ritual Homicide Typology

The ritual homicide typology is based on the premise that the single most relevant factor in determining motive, method of operation, victimology and forensics of the crime is the sacred (holy) meaning held by the offender. Although the crime scene characteristics may resemble actions typical of sexual, personal cause or group cause homicide as described in the FBI

Ritual Homicide Classifications

FBI Typology	Ritual Typology	Media/Public
Sadistic Murder	Sacrifice	Occult Crime
Sexual Homicide	Ritual Murder	Serial Killer
Cult Murder	Millennial Murder	Cult Suicide
Extremist Murder	Holy War	Terrorism
Authority Killing	Iconoclasm	School Violence

classification system, in symbolic analysis the primary motive is based on the offender's necessity to ritually express his perception of the sacred.

These expressions of the sacred are grouped into five categories of ritual homicide and named for the religious concept that most accurately describes the offender's ritual actions. Each of these concepts are extremely sophisticated and not easily defined but their general meaning and application to crime scene identification is described.

- **Sacrifice:** In religious terms, sacrifice is an act of offering something as homage to a deity, especially the ritual slaughter of an animal or person. The offering (animal or human) will be carefully chosen to please the deity and the killing will always be in what is designated a holy place. In reference to crime scenes, the victim will have symbolic significance related to the type of ritual required for a particular outcome or holiday.
- **Ritual Murder:** In religious terms there is no distinction between sacrifice and ritual murder; however, there is a distinction between sacrifice and murder. Murder occurs outside of what is considered sacred. Ritual murder is a secular (non-religious) expression of ritual conduct. The psychological concept of ritual murder is more appropriate for this category and is defined as when a person is compelled to repeat particular behavior beyond the actions necessary to perpetrate the crime and invests intimate (sacred) meaning into the crime scene by body positioning, mutilation or symbolic gestures.
- **Millennial Murder:** Millennial murder refers to the religious concept of Millennialism and is often mistaken for the millennium, which simply means a thousand-year time span. Millennialism is defined as

any group that believes that the world will come to an end and that the true believers will achieve a condition of salvation and peace either on earth, heaven, outer space, etc. The distinction between the Christian concept of salvation and a new religious movement's concept is that for a new religious movement salvation will transpire in the near future and will only occur if the members follow the group's doctrine and the leader's prophecy. Typical crime scenes contain multiple offenders and multiple victims inclusive of members' own children and items that are symbolic for that group's doctrine.

- **Holy War** is initially similar to Millennial Murder, it is based on millennial religious beliefs; however, salvation cannot be achieved until there is an apocalyptic holy war between the forces of good and evil. Holy war is when homicide or suicide is prompted by a fervent devotion or a system of beliefs based on orthodox religious conventions. Followers of extremist fundamentalist religions hold a dualist worldview that requires them to participate in overthrowing the evil (Satanic) government by committing acts of religious terrorism. Crime scenes entail the use of explosives, weapons of mass destruction, guns and anything that will cause high casualties and/or instill the most fear.

- **Iconoclasm:** The definition of iconoclasm is the destruction of a sacred object, image or institution. In religious terms, iconoclasm refers to opposition to the veneration of images and an iconoclastic act is when idols (statues or images that are worshiped as gods) are destroyed. Iconoclasm also refers to attacking or overthrowing established or venerated institutions, practices or attitudes. In reference to crime scenes, the symbolism of the place and the victim has significant meaning to the offender. The violence is an act of rage, frustration and injustice and the offender's goal is to disrupt the sacredness and destroy the safety of the institution or place that "shunned" him.

These concepts have been placed into the context of ritual violent crime and have become the basis for the development of the ritual homicide typology. The need for this typology becomes evident when one considers that there is a common misconception that ritual murder is synonymous with sacrifice and that these concepts are often grouped together into the single designation of cult murder. The terms are frequently used interchangeably by scholars, law enforcement professionals and the general public. On the surface, there appears to be little or no differences, but from a forensic perspective they vary greatly and are highly significant.

An initial distinction between sacrifice and ritual murder is that sacrifice is sacred (holy) murder; hence, it is committed by true believers and the weapon will always be something that can ritually draw blood, most often a knife. The symbolic meaning of sacrifice is that it is a fundamental rite in the context of the belief system that sanctions sacrifice. Ritual murder is a secular (irreverent) crime entailing ritualized behavior generally committed by dabblers or true criminals and the weapon(s) are determined by the offender's personal preference. The symbolic meaning in ritual murder is a ritual interpretation of a personal belief system.

Millennial Murder is ideologically similar to Holy War, however, in Millennial Murder the violence remains internal to the group and manifests in mass suicide whereas in Holy War violence is turned outward toward society and manifests in mass murder (terrorism). Millennial Murder is group sacred murder, which often involves mass suicide of members and mass homicide of children and former members. Weapons can include poison, guns, immolation, etc. The symbolic meaning of Millennial Murder is that it is essential to achieving salvation in the context of the group's millennial belief system. Holy War is individual or group sacred murder that entails acts of terrorism inclusive of suicide bombings, shootings and weapons of mass destruction. The symbolic meaning of Holy War is that it is a response to interpretation of sacred literature and essential to eventually achieving religious salvation.

Iconoclasm is a secular (non-religious) category of individual and small group murder. Offenders are often juveniles and there are multiple weapons, most often semi-automatic guns, to inflict the most casualties. The symbolic meaning of iconoclasm is an act of blasphemy/sacrilege against the values/status/power of a predominant religion or religious-like institution.

Distinctions in the previously mentioned categories are crucial for inquiries, investigations and legal proceedings in regard to violent ritual crimes. Tables 10.1 through 10.3 provide common forensic findings, victimology, crime scene indicators, method of operation, motives of perpetrators and the symbolic significance of ritual homicides. All categories consist of premeditated crimes. Categories are not mutually exclusive and it is possible for one crime to fit into more than one classification. Table 10.1, Ritual Homicide Typology, describes methods of operation and motives, and introduces the five types of ritual homicide with corresponding examples. Table 10.2, Ritual Homicide: FBI Violent Crime Classifications, situates the five categories of ritual homicide to the closest related FBI classification systems. Table 10.3, Ritual Homicide: Symbolic Analysis, provides victimology, crime scene indicators, common forensic findings, symbolic significance and the probability of reoccurrence in the five categories of ritual homicide. The five categories are expanded upon following the charts.

Table 10.1 Ritual Homicide Typology

Method of Operation	Motives of Perpetrators	Types of Ritual Homicide	Examples
Ritualism: involves people who commit criminal activities characterized by a series of repeated physical, sexual, and/or psychological assaults combined with a systematic use of symbols, ceremonies and/or machinations. The need to repeat such acts can be cultural, sexual, economic, psychological and/or spiritual.	**True Believers:** are religious practitioners who commit crimes because such acts fit into and/or are required by their particular belief system.	**Sacrifice:** ritual killing as an offering, consecration, initiation or any other sacred act in its holiest sense. This act is required and/or fits into a particular belief system.	**Adolfo Constanzo, Matamoros, Mexico:** ritualism, true believer, sacrifice
			10-month-old infant: ritualism, true believer, sacrifice
	True Criminals: are persons who use the occult as an excuse to justify or rationalize their criminal behavior. They are committed not to the belief system but to the criminal action.	**Ritual Murder:** occurs when criminal conduct goes beyond the actions necessary to perpetrate the crime and some type of secular ritual behavior is expressed in the form of a "signature" or calling card.	**The Night Stalker:** ritualism, true criminal, ritual murder
Dabbling: involves people who are intermittently and experientially involved in occult activities. Dabblers usually make up their own belief system and perpetrate criminal activity that conforms to the ideology.			**Kentucky Vampire Clan:** dabblers, true followers, ritual murder; leader was true criminal
	True Followers: are persons, most often young adults, who turn to the occult because of a deep sense of alienation from mainstream culture. Often inspired by music and film versions of the occult to shape their belief system and justify their criminal behavior. They are momentary true believers.	**Millennial Murder:** when homicide or suicide is a response to a belief in a collective salvation or an actual or perceived threat of persecution that would interfere with achieving salvation.	**Branch Davidians:** ritualism, true believers, millennial murder
			Heaven's Gate: ritualism, true believers, millennial murder
Paramilitary: involves people who commit criminal activities characterized by highly organized, preplanned surveillance and military execution of violence combined with symbolism and/or a forensic signature specific to the group. The goal is to intimidate individuals, citizens or governments in furtherance of political, religious or social objectives.		**Holy War:** when homicide or suicide is prompted by a fervent devotion to a system of beliefs based on orthodox religious conventions. An act of destroying symbols of religious/political power and an attention-seeking act.	**Aum Supreme Truth:** ritualism, true believers, holy war; Shoko Asahara is also a true criminal
			World Trade Center Attacks: paramilitary, true believers, holy war
		Iconoclasm: when homicide is an act of destroying what a person holds sacred or idolizes. An act of destroying symbols/representatives of institutions that "shunned" or humiliated the offender and an attention-seeking act.	**Serial Sniper:** paramilitary, true criminal, iconoclasm
			Columbine H.S. Shootings: dabblers, true followers, iconoclasm
			Murder of Chiavenna Nun: dabblers, true followers, iconoclasm

Table 10.2 Ritual Homicide: FBI Violent Crime Classifications[a]

Ritual Typology	Sacrifice	Ritual Murder	Millennial Murder	Holy War	Iconoclasm
FBI Classification	Sexual Homicide 130		Group Cause Homicide 140		Personal Cause Homicide 120
Relevant Subcategories	Sadistic Murder 134	Disorganized Sexual Homicide 132	Cult Murder 141	Extremist Murder 142	Authority Killing 124
Victimology	The victim is often white female adults who are strangers, but multiple offenders may prey on men and children. Chosen through systematic stalking and surveillance. They are approached under a pretext, and a ruse may be employed.	Victim may be known to the offender because he often selects a victim of opportunity near his residence or employment. Victim is from same geographic area.	Occasionally cult murder is the result of members preying on a random victim. Most often the victim tends to be someone who is a member of the cult or on the fringe of membership. Generally, multiple victims involved.	Victim represents the antithesis of the offender's beliefs. Victimology depends on offender's doctrine. If multiple victims there will be similarities in race, religion, political beliefs, social or economic status. Also, ex-members or other threats to group.	Primary targets are people that the offender perceives are wronging him; secondary victims in place that offender associates with the symbolism of the authority.
Crime Scene Indicators	Multiple crime scenes: place of encounter, torture/death scene, and/or body disposal site. Weapons are brought to the scene then removed; use of restraints is common. Souvenirs are missing from crime scene.	The death scene and crime scene is often the same and displays symbolic quality of killing. Sudden violence to victim; depersonalization is present. Weapon is found at scene and left there. No plan to deter detection.	Crime scene may contain items that are symbolic, in the form of unexplained artifacts or imagery. Status of the body is dependent on purpose of killing. Murder to intimidate other members is concealed. Possible mass grave sites. Multiple offenders and victims.	Use of military tactics; the calling card of the group may be left at scene. Firearms and explosives are most often used; assault is generally a clean kill. Crime scene is low risk for the killer; risk is lowered by pre-planning and surveillance, high number of victims may indicate multiple offenders.	Offender is mission oriented; no intention to escape from the scene; may desire to die at the scene either by suicide or police bullets. Offender brings multiple weapons to scene, optimal lethality.
Common Forensic Findings	Bite marks and saliva on body, semen in body orifices, bruising or cutting of the sex organs.	Mutilation to the face and to specific body parts. Body parts may be missing from the scene. Sexual acts occur after victim's death and often involve objects inserted into body orifices.	Common forensic findings are wounds from firearms, blunt force trauma and sharp pointed objects. There may be mutilations of the body. Multiple weapons may have been used during a single event.	Forensics will reflect signature of the group, inclusive of bombing, dismemberment, decapitation, firearms, blunt force trauma, and more recently, weapons of mass destruction, suicide bombers.	The use of more than one firearm and often weapons are semi-automatic for quick firing. Various and numerous shell casings at scene. Wounds are severe and numerous.

[a] A category for occult crime was initially considered to be listed under Group Cause Homicide. Due to insufficient evidence, the FBI decided to omit the category which would have corresponded to Sacrifice. Satanic Ritual Abuse is classified under Multi-Dimensional Sex Rings, 318.01/02.

Table 10.3 Ritual Homicide: Symbolic Analysis

		Sacrifice	Ritual Murder	Millennial Murder	Holy War	Iconoclasm
Victimology		Victim selected according to the purpose of ritual; could be a stranger or member of the group.	Victim chosen according to the ritual need of the perpetrator; could be stranger or acquaintance.	Victims are members of the group, inclusive of their own children, so they can all achieve salvation.	Victim represents the antithesis of the offender's beliefs. Viewed as Satanic, heretics, traitors, etc.	Perpetrator will either know the victim or they are associated with place of humiliation. Feels the victim has hurt them.
Crime Scene Indicators	Weapon	Ritual knife (sometimes referred to as an athame).	Weapons vary according to the symbolic/religious manifestation of the perpetrator's beliefs.	Weapons include poison, immolation, overdose of drugs, gunshot, etc., often in a ritual setting.	Explosives, weapons of mass destruction, guns, anything to cause high casualties and/or instill fear.	Guns, automatic weapons; occasionally beating or stabbing.
	Date	Date coincides with an occult holiday, person's birthday, initiation or other symbolic date for group.	Date only significant if a pattern is detected that has meaning to the perpetrator; could be random or opportunity.	Date is highly significant and corresponds to group's interpretation of millennial goal and/or persecution.	Date may have significance to group but usually is random to instill fear or most opportune time.	Often occurs after a precipitating event, access to weapons, and sometimes occult or symbolic date.
	Place	Sacrifice will always be conducted in group's designated sacred space; often an isolated outdoor area.	Only significant if a pattern is detected that has meaning to the perpetrator; could be random or availability of victim.	Place is significant and has sacred meaning to the group; often occurs in or near the area where the group resides.	Places are highly significant and representative of enemies' values; also places that instill the most fear.	Place is highly significant. Usually where perpetrator felt humiliated and can disrupt security of others.
Common Forensic Findings		One or all of the following: mutilation, carving symbols into flesh, bloodletting, torture, cannibalism, sexual abuse and dismemberment.	One or all of the following: mutilation, carving symbols into flesh, torture, and dismemberment. Rape and sexual abuse are quite prevalent in ritual murder.	Mass suicide of members and mass homicide of children and ex-members. Type of violence is dependent on belief system and is often conducted in a ritual setting.	Reflects signature of the group inclusive of bombing, dismemberment, firearms, and more recently, weapons of mass destruction, suicide bombers.	Whatever will bring the most attention to the incident, usually killing as many people as possible, often with guns or brutally killing a significantly symbolic person.
Symbolic Significance		A blood ritual enacted to increase power and/or fulfill the requirement of the belief system.	The perpetrator enacts his own ritual which becomes the signature of the crime and has meaning to him.	A response to interpretation of sacred literature. Suicide will achieve salvation or take to next level/place.	A response to interpretation of sacred literature. Victims are perceived as evil and a threat to holiness.	Act of rage, frustration and injustice; the goal is to disrupt the symbols/place that caused alienation.
Probability of Recurrence		Sacrifice will occur each time it is required for ritual purposes.	High probability that ritual murder will escalate in violence and frequency.	A one-time incident and any members not present may commit suicide soon after.	Will continue to occur as long as group is in existence.	Usually a one-time incident by juvenile perpetrators who quickly confess or commit suicide at the scene.

Sacrifice

- **Ritual killing as an offering, consecration, initiation or any other sacred act in its holiest sense. Ritual murder is required and/or fits into a particular belief system.**

- Sacred category of individual or group ritual conduct.
- Victim can be a stranger or member of the group.
- Children of members and enemies are also victims.
- Multiple victims and offenders are common.
- Weapon most often a ritual knife.
- Symbols, artifacts found at scene and on victim.
- Crime scene is designated sacred space, often outdoors, possible mass grave.
- Body mutilation is common, draining of blood, cannibalism, sexual abuse and dismemberment.

Sacrifice

Sacrifice is a sacred (holy) category of individual and group ritual conduct. Sacrifice is always committed by a true believer, an occult practitioner who commits crimes because such acts are required or fit into his particular belief system. The victim, who could be animal or human, will be selected according to the purpose of the ritual. The victim can be a stranger or a member of the group. The crime can be conducted by a lone offender or by a group; however, the actual murder is generally enacted by one person (the designated High Priest). The death will occur in a designated sacred space, often an isolated outdoor area, determined by the group's doctrine. The date is often significant and may correspond to an occult holiday or a group holiday.

Sacrifice always entails a blood ritual and the most common weapon is a ritual knife. Depending on the group's doctrine, death may be slow and tortuous (most often with a human) or a quick slitting of the throat. A common forensic indicator of occult sacrifice is for blood to be drained from the victim. Other indicators are mutilation, carving symbols into flesh, cannibalism, sexual abuse and dismemberment.

The purpose of sacrifice is to increase personal power and/or fulfill the requirements of the belief system. Items required for the ritual are often related to other crimes such as trespassing, theft, extortion, vandalism, grave robbing, arson and possible kidnapping. Examples of sacrifice include a New

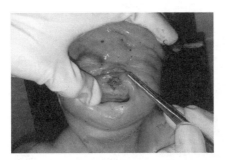

Autopsy of 10-month-old female infant (ritualism, true believers and sacrifice). (From Roger A. Forsthoff, Director of Forensic Laboratory, Hudson County Prosecutor's Office, Jersey City, NJ. With permission.)

Jersey case where a 10-month-old female infant was found floating in the Hudson River. The forensics indicated that she had been stabbed 37 times, her ears were mutilated, her voice box had broken from screaming, she had been drained of blood and an object had been inserted in her nasal cavity. Further investigation revealed that she had been the victim of a traditional Satanic ritual.

Another example of human sacrifice is the 1989 Matamoros, Mexico case described in Chapter 7 in which Mark Kilroy, a young American University of Texas student, and several Mexican citizens were kidnapped and later ritualistically killed and sacrificed by orders of drug dealer and Mayombero, Adolfo de Jesus Constanzo. Constanzo was responsible for at least 23 incidents of human sacrifice in which his victims were slaughtered in meticulous and elaborate ceremonies. When the bodies of the victims were dug up (which included at least 14 separate remains), some of the bodies had been beheaded and trussed with chicken wire; others were totally dismembered, hearts, brains and other vital organs had been removed as the victims were being tortured and dismembered. In a nearby shed, other decomposing human organs were found in blood-caked vats and cauldrons. According to the ritual homicide typology, in both examples the method of operation is ritualism, the motive is true believers and the category of ritual homicide is sacrifice.

Ritual Murder

Ritual murder is a secular (non-religious) category of individual ritual conduct and is often mistaken for sacrifice. Ritual murder involves people who commit criminal activities characterized by a series of repeated physical, sexual and/or psychological assaults combined with a systematic use of symbols, ceremonies and/or machinations. The need to repeat such acts can be cultural, sexual, economic, psychological and/or spiritual. Ritual murder can

Ritual Murder

- **Ritual murder occurs when criminal conduct goes beyond the actions necessary to perpetrate the crime and some type of secular ritual behavior is expressed.**

- Secular (non-religious) category of individual ritual conduct.
- The victim will be chosen according to the ritual need of the offender.
- Sexual assault (pre- and post-mortem), use of restraints and depersonalization (mutilation to the face).
- Mutilation of specific body parts. Objects often inserted in victim's body.
- Multiple weapons.
- Body parts and other souvenirs such as personal items may be missing.
- Signature or calling card (body positioning, mutilation, other symbolic gestures).

be committed by a true criminal or a dabbler and is generally the act of a lone offender.

Ritual murder occurs when criminal conduct goes beyond the actions necessary to perpetrate the crime and some type of non-religious ritual behavior is expressed in the form of a "signature" or "calling card." The victim is chosen according to the ritual need of the offender. Sexual assault, use of restraints and depersonalization are often present. Forensic findings often include mutilation to the face and specific body parts, objects inserted into victims' body orifices and sexual acts after the victim's death. Body parts or other souvenirs such as personal items may be missing from the scene.

The purpose of the ritual often fulfills a personal spiritual and/or sexual need of the offender. Offenders often make up their own belief system and perpetrate criminal activity that conforms to that ideology. Examples of ritual murder include the self-styled Satanist Richard Ramirez, dubbed "The Night Stalker," who in 1985 terrorized Los Angeles by breaking into people's homes, raping, torturing, mutilating and murdering his victims and, most notably, forcing them to declare their love for Satan. This case demonstrates the subtle differences between sacrifice and ritual murder.

Although Ramirez's murders entailed ritualism, they could not be considered actual sacrifices because they were not part of a Satanic ritual that fit into any particular Satanic religion. Instead they were expressions of his own Satanic beliefs, hence more specific to ritual murder where his "signature" entailed Satanic symbols. Additionally Ramirez's behavior was more indicative of a true criminal than a true believer.

Another example of ritual murder is the case of the self-styled Vampire clan in Kentucky who in 1996 murdered a Florida couple. Sixteen-year-old Rodrick Justin Ferrell was the leader of the Vampire clan composed of four other teenagers in which rituals included cutting each other's arms with razors and sucking the blood. Ferrell bludgeoned Richard and Naoma Wendorf to death with a crowbar in their Florida home. The letter *V* was burned into their bodies symbolizing Ferrell's Vampire name, *Vassago*. Smaller burns on each side of the *V* represented the other members of the clan. This case is clearly not representative of sacrifice because the victims were quickly bludgeoned to death in their own home instead of slowly tortured in a sacred space. Correspondingly, Ferrell was a true criminal who was dabbling in the occult; however, the other teenage members of the group can be designated as true followers who were also dabbling in the occult.

Millennial Murder

Millennial Murder is a sacred (holy) category of group ritual conduct. Millennial Murder is generally committed by a true believer — an occult/cult practitioner who commits crimes because such acts are required or fit into his particular belief system. However, the leader of the group may be a true criminal who uses the occult as an excuse to justify his abuse of followers.

Most often the victim will be a member of the group or on the fringe of membership. Children of members and enemies such as relatives of members are also victims. Multiple victims and offenders are common. The crime scene may contain items that are symbolic, in the form of unexplained artifacts or imagery. The place will have sacred meaning to the group and the date will correspond to the group's interpretation of its millennial goal and/or persecution. The status of the body is dependent on the purpose of the killing; i.e., murder to intimidate other members is concealed or possible mass gravesites. Common forensic findings are wounds from firearms, blunt force trauma and wounds from sharp pointed objects. There may be mutilations of the body. Multiple weapons may have been used during a single event. Also, mass murder/suicide can be by poisoning, drug overdose or immolation. The purpose of the ritual is a response to an interpretation of group doctrine and/or sacred literature that claims that death will achieve salvation or take participants to the next level, thus fulfilling the group's millennial goal and/or avoiding persecution.

Examples of Millennial Murder include David Koresh and the Branch Davidians who committed suicide in 1993 after a 51-day siege of their

Millennial Murder

- **When homicide or suicide is prompted by a fervent devotion to a system of beliefs based on unorthodox religious conventions and is a response to a belief in a collective salvation or an actual or perceived threat of persecution that would interfere with achieving salvation.**

- Sacred/holy category of group ritual conduct.
- The victim is often a member of the group or on the fringe of membership.
- Children of members and enemies are also victims.
- Multiple victims and offenders are common.
- Possible mass gravesites.
- Multiple weapons.
- Mass murder/suicide.

religious compound. Koresh considered himself the messiah and prophesized that Armageddon was near and continued to interpret scripture throughout the siege. Each and every action taken by the government held symbolic value for the Branch Davidians who literally believed that Satan was knocking at their door. The decisions Koresh made during the standoff essentially resulted in a self-fulfilling apocalyptic prophecy in which he and his followers died.

In 1997, Heaven's Gate believers opted to exit Planet Earth, which they thought was going to be destroyed, by leaving their bodies via suicide and beaming up to the mother ship that was behind the Hale–Bopp comet. Similarly, members of the Solar Temple chose to avoid the destruction of the world and decided to make transits, a mystical voyage, using group murder and suicide on three separate occasions in 1994, 1995 and 1997. All three cases exemplify ritualism as a method of operation, true believers (except for the members who were murdered because they chose not to commit suicide) and their apocalyptic theologies are all classic examples of Millennial Murder.

Holy War

Holy War is a sacred (holy) category of group or group-sanctioned ritual conduct. Holy War is always committed by a true believer, a religious soldier

Holy War

- **When homicide or suicide is prompted by a fervent devotion to a system of beliefs based on orthodox religious conventions or motivated by political doctrines that oppose the current government.**

- Sacred category of group or group-sanctioned conduct.
- The victim represents the antithesis of the offender's belief system and multiple victims often have similarities in race, nationality or religion.
- Victims also include persons who conflict with the group's objectives, informants, ex-members.
- Lone offenders, multiple crime scenes, confrontation site, death scene, burial site.
- Multiple offenders, crime scene is convenient and low risk, preplanned surveillance, use of military tactics.
- Calling cards or signature of the group will be evident.

who commits acts of terrorism because of his fervent devotion to a system of beliefs based on orthodox religious conventions. There are several types of victims targeted in Holy War; predominantly, the victim represents the antithesis of the offender's beliefs, therefore, victimology depends on this doctrine.

If multiple victims are involved, there will be similarities of race, religion, political beliefs, social status or economic status. The victim may be a victim of opportunity, a random target who just happens across the path of the offender at the wrong time, conversely, the victim may be targeted and die as a result of a premeditated, well-planned attack. Victimology also includes the victims who come into conflict with the group's objectives, this includes the informant, ex-member or any member who poses a threat to either the leader's control or the group's integrity.[27]

A paramilitary method of operation will be employed and could include the wearing of uniforms, the use of training compounds and the highly organized use of military tactics. There will often be multiple crime scenes: confrontation site, death scene and body disposal burial site. The calling card/signature of the group may be left at the scene. Multiple offenders will present evidence of different weapons and ammunition; the victim usually is well controlled, a significant number of victims also may be indicative of multiple offenders. If there are multiple offenders, the location of the crime

Tokyo subway, March 20, 1995 (paramilitary, true believers and holy war). (From Desmond, E. and Kunii, I.M., Prophet of Poison, *Time Magazine*, April 3, 1995, p. 29. With permission from Asahi Shimbun Publishing, Tokyo.)

scene may be one that is convenient and low risk for the killers. Offender risk is lowered by pre-planning and surveillance for both the assault and escape.

A lone offender may also demonstrate control and organization at the crime scene, depending on his level of professionalism. The forensics will often reveal the "calling card" or "signature" aspect of the group and can include bombing, firearms, and weapons of mass destruction or blunt force trauma from personal weapons (hands and feet).[28] The purpose of this type of ritual homicide is to overthrow the existing religious/political order to achieve political and religious goals.

Examples of Holy War include the September 11th attacks on America where over 3000 American citizens were killed. The suicide attacks on the World Trade Center and the Pentagon are considered a form of jihad by the perpetrators, as are all other acts of terrorism attributed to Islamic fundamentalists. Since suicide is religiously prohibited in Islam, suicide attacks have to be viewed as a form of sacred violence. Suicide in the cause of holy war is not only considered legitimate by the offenders but is also deemed one of the highest forms of self-sacrifice. Killing oneself for the glory of Islam is considered by extremist fundamentalists to be a supreme form of jihad and a type of terrorism that is allowed by the Sharia. It is not suicide (intihar), but martyrdom (istishhad), an act that will procure a special place in Paradise for the terrorist.

Another example of Holy War is the Japanese group Aum Shinrikyo whose apocalyptic beliefs led them to develop weapons of mass destruction so they could destroy the world and create Shambhala on earth. The most famous violent incident attributed to this group occurred on March 20, 1995 when five members boarded five subway cars at different stations in Tokyo at 8 A.M. and deposited plastic bags containing sarin gas on the floor, punctured the bags and immediately disembarked. The fumes of the deadly nerve gas injured over 5000 people and 12 people died. Although each of these religions are entirely different, they both exemplify paramilitary methods of operation, true believers' motives and they are both classic examples of the ritual homicide typology category of Holy War.

Iconoclasm

Iconoclasm is a secular (non-religious) category of individual and small group ritual conduct. Iconoclasm is an act of destroying what a person holds sacred or idolizes. In a political sense, an act of destroying symbols/representatives of religious institutions/power and an attention-seeking act. Iconoclasm is generally committed by true followers, most often young adults, who turn to the occult because of a deep sense of alienation from mainstream culture. Often inspired by music and film versions of the occult to shape their belief system and justify their criminal behavior.

They are momentary true believers. Offenders are also dabblers who are intermittently and experientially involved in occult activities. Dabblers usually make up their own belief system and perpetrate criminal activities that conform to their ideology. Primary targets are people who the offender perceives are "wronging" him; secondary victims happen to be in the place that the offender associates with the symbolism of the authority. The victims can represent the antithesis of the offender's beliefs and victimology depends heavily on the offender's doctrine. The offender is mission oriented usually with no intention to escape from the scene and may desire to die at the scene either by suicide or police bullets. The offender brings multiple weapons to the scene and the goal is optimal lethality.

The crime scene is usually a public place — the place of humiliation — and the location of the victim will indicate the motive. An ambush or blitz-style attack or long-range sniper attack is common because of the problem with victim control. Forensics include the use of more than one firearm and often weapons are semi-automatic for quick firing. Various and numerous shell casings will be found at the scene.

Wounds are severe and numerous and victims often suffer multiple wounds. Weapons of choice are often a firearm or a knife. An offender who adopts the method of operation of a group will also adopt their method of

Iconoclasm

- **When homicide is an act of destroying what a person holds sacred or idolizes. An act of destroying symbols/representatives of institutions that "shunned" or humiliated the offender.**

- Iconoclasm is a secular category of individual and small group ritual conduct.
- Primary targets are people that the offender perceives are wronging him.
- The offender is mission oriented, usually with no intention to escape from the scene and who may desire to die at the scene either by suicide or police bullets.
- The offender brings multiple weapons to the scene and the goal is optimal lethality.
- The crime scene usually occurs in a public place, place of humiliation.
- Forensics include the use of more than one firearm and often weapons are semi-automatic for quick firing.
- Wounds are severe and numerous and victims often suffer multiple wounds.

attack. The purpose of this type of ritual violence is to disrupt the symbols/ place that caused the offender's sense of alienation and injustice. Examples in this category vary and include the Columbine High School shootings in Littleton, CO where on April 20, 1999, Eric Harris, 18, and Dylan Klebold, 17, killed 12 students and a teacher and wounded 23 others before shooting themselves. Harris and Klebold were members of the "Trenchcoat Mafia," a group of outsiders who were dabbling with the Goth movement, fascinated with Nazi culture, learned to speak some German, were seen wearing Nazi symbols, and chose Hitler's birthday as the day of the shooting. It became evident after the investigations into these incidents that each of the perpetrators felt like outsiders, loners and misfits who were shunned from the school community. The individuals and community of students who rejected the teens were idolized by them, which is what made the rejection so much more devastating. Idolatry is characterized by the worship of sacred objects. Iconoclasm is the destruction of sacred objects; hence, killing what one worships can be considered an act of iconoclasm.

Another example of iconoclasm occurred in Chiavenna, Italy on June 6, 2000 where three teenage girls brutally murdered a nun, Sister Mary Laura

Manetti, after they had formed their own Satanic group which they said was influenced by the lyrics of heavy metal musician Marilyn Manson. In this case, the girls were reacting to their culture in which Catholic nuns are highly respected and representatives of a tradition they felt they were not accepted in. They embraced Satanism, the antithesis of Catholicism and by murdering Sister Manetti, they were simultaneously attacking the Catholic church.

In both cases the teenagers were dabbling in occult ideologies. In addition to being dabblers in the occult, the teens at Columbine also used a paramilitary method. Both groups were true followers who were influenced by media versions of the occult and committed acts of iconoclasm.

Another example of iconoclasm is the Washington, D.C. serial sniper case where John Allen Muhammad and Lee Boyd Malvo shot and killed 12 individuals for no apparent reason. Although their motivations are currently unknown and may initially appear to be greed, the fact that they chose to interact with the media and terrorize the entire Washington metropolitan area, the seat of government in America, indicates that they also felt shunned from society. They were attacking American values, aspects of which they obviously felt they were being deprived of. Their method of operation was clearly paramilitary. Their motivation is indicative of true criminals and their homicides were acts of iconoclasm.

VICAP Forms

The VICAP Crime Analysis Report Form was designed to collect information regarding the following types of crimes whether or not the offender has been arrested or identified: (1) solved or unsolved homicides or attempts, especially those that involve an abduction; are apparently random, motiveless, or sexually oriented; or are known or suspected to be part of a series; (2) missing persons, where the circumstances indicate a strong possibility of foul play and the victim is still missing; and (3) unidentified dead bodies where the manner of death is known or suspected to be homicide.

There are different versions of the VICAP forms that have been revised over the years. The original form contained 189 questions; and the more recent forms are a shorter version of the original. Due to the fact that many departments have different versions of the VICAP forms, the following excerpts refer to the content of the questions. The number and location of the questions differ on various forms. The following VICAP questions are particularly relevant for investigating ritualistic crimes:

- Was there writing or drawing at the crime scene (NOT on the victim's body)?

- If yes, indicate the location at the crime scene, the description of the writing or drawing and the instrument/tool used to write or draw at the scene.
- Was there writing or drawing on the victim's body?
  - If yes, indicate the location on the body, the description of the writing or drawing and the instrument/tool used to write or draw on the body.
- Was there evidence to suggest that a deliberate, unusual, or symbolic act or thing was performed at the crime scene(s) (such as defecation, unique objects placed at scene, foreign substance on body, etc.)?
- Were there elements of unusual or additional assault/trauma/torture to victim?
  - If yes, indicate what elements occurred (check all that apply and describe):
    - Body cavities or genitalia mutilated
    - Body cavities or wounds explored/probed
    - Body set on fire
    - Burns (cigarette, iron, etc.)
    - Cannibalism
    - Carving on victim
    - Evisceration
    - Hair cut/shaved
      - Head
      - Pubic
      - Other
    - Hanged
    - Kicked/stomped
    - Patterned injury
    - Shocked
      - Electrical
      - Stun gun
    - Skinned
    - Vampirism
    - Vehicular assault
      - Dragged by vehicle
      - Run over by vehicle
      - Pushed/shoved/thrown from vehicle
    - Whipped/paddled
    - Other
    - Unknown
- Were human bite marks identified on victim's body?

- If yes, indicate location of bite marks on body (check all that apply):
  - Abdomen
  - Anus
  - Arm(s)
  - Back
  - Breast(s)
  - Buttock(s)
  - Chest
  - Face
  - Foot/Feet
  - Genitalia
  - Groin
  - Hand(s)
  - Head
  - Leg(s)
  - Lip(s)
  - Neck
  - Shoulder(s)
  - Thigh(s)
  - Other (describe)
- Did the offender remove body parts?
  - If yes, describe body part removed, not recovered or recovered at scene or recovered elsewhere.
- Dismemberment method (check all that apply):
  - Bitten
  - Cut – skilled
  - Cut – unskilled
  - Hacked/chopped
  - Ripped
  - Sawed
  - Other (describe)
  - Unknown
- Is there evidence of sexual activity or attempted sexual activity with the victim?
- Type of sexual activity or attempt (check all that apply):
  - Vaginal
  - Anal
  - Victim performed oral sex on offender
  - Offender performed oral sex on victim
  - Foreign object insertion (see next question)
  - Digital penetration

- Hand/fist insertion
- Fondling
- Masturbation
- Post-mortem sexual activity
- Other (describe)
- Unknown
- If there was evidence of foreign object insertion, indicate the body orifice, the foreign object, and whether or not the object was still in victim's body when found.

Crime Classification Sample Worksheet

I. Victimology

Why did the person become the victim of a violent crime? About the victim

Life style
Employment
Personality
Friends (type, number)
Income (amount, source)
Family
Alcohol/drug use or abuse
Normal dress
Handicaps
Transportation used
Reputation, habits, fears
Marital status
Dating habits
Leisure activities
Criminal history
Assertiveness
Likes and dislikes
Significant events prior to the crime
Activities prior to the crime

II. Crime Scene

How many?
Environment, time, place
How many offenders?

> Organized, disorganized?
> Physical evidence
> Weapon
> Body disposition
> Items left/missing
> Other (witnesses, escape plan, wounded victims, etc.)

III. Staging

> Natural death
> Accidental
> Suicide
> Criminal activity (i.e., robbery, rape/homicide)

IV. Forensic Findings

A. Forensic analysis
> Hair/fibers
> Blood
> Semen
> Saliva
> Other

B. Autopsy results
> Cause of death
> Trauma (type, extent, location on body)
> Overkill
> Torture
> Facial battery (depersonalization)
> Bite marks
> Mutilation
> Sexual assault (when, sequence, to where, insertion, insertional, necrophilia)
> Toxicological results

V. Investigative Considerations

A. Search warrants
> Home
> Work
> Car
> Other

B. Locating and interviewing witnesses

References

1. History of profiling, North Carolina Wesleyan College Criminal Justice website. http://faculty.ncwc.edu/toconnor/401/401lect01.htm

2. History of profiling, North Carolina Wesleyan College Criminal Justice website. http://faculty.ncwc.edu/toconnor/401/401lect01.htm

3. Douglas, J., Burgess, A., Burgess, A., and Ressler, R., *Crime Classification Manual: A Standard System for Investigating and Classifying Violent Crimes*, Jossey-Bass, San Francisco, 1992, p. 310.

4. Criminal intelligence analysis, Interpol website. http://www.interpol./Public/cia/default.asp

5. Criminal intelligence analysis, Interpol website. http://www.interpol./Public/cia/default.asp

6. http://www.newsmax.com/archives/articles/2002/10/10/190358.shtml

7. http://www.usdoj.gov/ndic/pubs/669/overview.htm

8. Jackman, T., Disclosures May Help Malvo's Defense, *The Washington Post*, Thursday July 24, 2003, p. B01.

9. Teten, H., *Offender Profiling*.

10. Ron MacKay & Associates, Forensic behavioral analysis. http://www.comnet.ca/~fbamackay/geo.htm geographic

11. Douglas, J., Burgess, A., Burgess, A., and Ressler, R.,*Crime Classification Manual: A Standard System for Investigating and Classifying Violent Crimes*, Jossey-Bass, San Francisco, 1992, p. 8.

12. Douglas, J., Burgess, A., Burgess, A., and Ressler, R., *Crime Classification Manual: A Standard System for Investigating and Classifying Violent Crimes*, Jossey-Bass, San Francisco, 1992, p. 8.

13. Douglas, J., Burgess, A., Burgess, A., and Ressler, R., *Crime Classification Manual: A Standard System for Investigating and Classifying Violent Crimes*, Jossey-Bass, San Francisco, 1992, pp. 8–9.

14. Douglas, J., Burgess, A., Burgess, A., and Ressler, R., *Crime Classification Manual: A Standard System for Investigating and Classifying Violent Crimes*, Jossey-Bass, San Francisco, 1992, p. 9

15. Douglas, J., Burgess, A., Burgess, A., and Ressler, R., *Crime Classification Manual: A Standard System for Investigating and Classifying Violent Crimes*, Jossey-Bass, San Francisco, 1992, p. 9.

16. Douglas, J., Burgess, A., Burgess, A., and Ressler, R., *Crime Classification Manual: A Standard System for Investigating and Classifying Violent Crimes*, Jossey-Bass, San Francisco, 1992, p. 10.

17. Douglas, J., Burgess, A., Burgess, A., and Ressler, R., *Crime Classification Manual: A Standard System for Investigating and Classifying Violent Crimes*, Jossey-Bass, San Francisco, 1992, p. 16.

18. Douglas, J., Burgess, A., Burgess, A., and Ressler, R., *Crime Classification Manual: A Standard System for Investigating and Classifying Violent Crimes*, Jossey-Bass, San Francisco, 1992, p. 11.

19. Douglas, J., Burgess, A., Burgess, A., and Ressler, R., *Crime Classification Manual: A Standard System for Investigating and Classifying Violent Crimes*, Jossey-Bass, San Francisco, 1992, p. 11.

20. Douglas, J., Burgess, A., Burgess, A., and Ressler, R., *Crime Classification Manual: A Standard System for Investigating and Classifying Violent Crimes*, Jossey-Bass, San Francisco, 1992, p. 11.

21. Douglas, J., Burgess, A., Burgess, A., and Ressler, R., *Crime Classification Manual: A Standard System for Investigating and Classifying Violent Crimes*, Jossey-Bass, San Francisco, 1992, p. 11.

22. Douglas, J., Burgess, A., Burgess, A., and Ressler, R., *Crime Classification Manual: A Standard System for Investigating and Classifying Violent Crimes*, Jossey-Bass, San Francisco, 1992, p. 353.

23. Douglas, J., Burgess, A., Burgess, A., and Ressler, R., *Crime Classification Manual: A Standard System for Investigating and Classifying Violent Crimes*, Jossey-Bass, San Francisco, 1992, p. 251.

24. *Occult Crime: A Law Enforcement Perspective*, p. 25.

26. Douglas, J., Burgess, A., Burgess, A., and Ressler, R., *Crime Classification Manual: A Standard System for Investigating and Classifying Violent Crimes*, Jossey-Bass, San Francisco, 1992, p. 354.

27. Douglas, J., Burgess, A., Burgess, A., and Ressler, R., *Crime Classification Manual: A Standard System for Investigating and Classifying Violent Crimes*, Jossey-Bass, San Francisco, 1992, p. 151.

28. Douglas, J., Burgess, A., Burgess, A., and Ressler, R., *Crime Classification Manual: A Standard System for Investigating and Classifying Violent Crimes*, Jossey-Bass, San Francisco, 1992, p. 151.

Glossary

Agroterrorism: Terrorist attacks aimed at reducing the food supply by destroying crops using natural pests such as the potato beetle, animal diseases such as hoof and mouth disease and anthrax, molds and other plant diseases or chemicals that defoliate vegetation, such as Agent Orange, used in Vietnam.

Anthrax: An infectious and often fatal disease contracted from animals. Cutaneous anthrax is contracted through a break in the skin. Infection spreads through the bloodstream causing shock, cyanosis, sweating and collapse. Inhalation anthrax is contracted by breathing in anthrax spores, resulting in pneumonia, sometimes accompanied by meningitis, followed by death. Because its spores have a long survival period, the incubation period is short, and the disability severe, anthrax has long been developed as a biological weapon by several nations.

Antiballistic Missile: A missile for intercepting and destroying ballistic missiles.

Ballistic Missile: A guided rocket-powered delivery vehicle for use against ground targets. A large portion of its flight in a ballistic (freefall) trajectory. Ballistic missiles are an optimal delivery system for weapons of mass destruction because it is difficult to deter them.

Biochemterrorism: Terrorism that resorts to biological or chemical agents as weapons.

Biological Weapons Convention (BWC): Officially, the "Convention on the Prohibition of the Development, Production and Stockpiling of Bacteriological (Biological) and Toxin Weapons and on their Destruction." It was opened for signature by the United Nations on April 10, 1972 and went into force in 1975 but no formal verification procedure was established. Since 1991 an ad hoc group of signatory states has been developing a rolling text of a verification protocol to the Convention.

Bioterrorism: The use of biological agents such as bacteria and viruses in a terrorist operation. The most likely biological toxins terrorists might adopt are anthrax, salmonella, e. coli, hoof and mouth disease, the plague, smallpox, botulism and tularemia.

Blister Agents: These agents cause incapacitation rather than death. These are unlikely agents to be used by terrorists but might be used to injure many people and overload regional medical facilities. Lewisite or mustard gas are the best known of these.

Blood Agents: Blood agents are based on cyanide compounds. Hydrogen cyanide (AC) is a blood agent slightly more lethal than phosgene. Its rapid rate of evaporation makes it less a candidate for mass terrorism than for assassination.

Botulism: The botulinum toxin is extremely lethal and easy to produce. A small quantity of this toxin can destroy the central nervous system. Botulism may be contracted by eating contaminated foods or by absorbing the bacteria through cuts in the skin. Fewer than 200 cases are reported annually in the U.S. Intentional contamination of the food supply or aerosol dissemination of the toxin is the greatest concern of counterterrorists.

Chemterrorism: The use of chemical agents in a terrorist operation. The most worrisome chemical is the nerve gas sarin, used in the Tokyo subway attack that killed 12 but injured thousands. Chemical agents are far easier to store and transport safely. The most likely to be used are blister agents, choking agents, nerve agents and cyanide-based compounds.

Choking Agent: The chemical agents preferred in WWI have lost much of their destructive utility since the invention of nerve agents. Choking agents are lethal and are very easily obtained. Phosgene is a common industrial chemical that serves as a moderately lethal choking agent.

Cruise Missile: A guided missile that flies at a moderate speed and at a low altitude, following the terrain beneath it. The "Tomahawk" is a cruise missile.

Cyanide Agents: Hydrogen cyanide reportedly was used by Iraq in the war against Iran and against the Kurds in northern Iraq during the 1980s. The Nazis used a form of hydrogen cyanide (Zyklon B) in the gas chambers of their concentration camps. It is a colorless liquid that may be inhaled in gaseous form. Cyanide salts and liquid cyanide may be absorbed by the skin. Symptoms are dizziness, headache, palpitations and respiratory difficulty. These are later followed by vomiting, convulsions, respiratory failure, unconsciousness and death.

E-Bomb: An electromagnetic bomb that produces a high-power flash of radio waves or microwaves that destroys any delicate electronic circuitry it hits. It causes mass disruption without destroying life or property. An e-bomb could freeze transportation systems, wreck communication systems and destroy computer networks. The cost to a terrorist for an e-bomb with no bells or whistles: an estimated $400.

ICBM: Intercontinental Ballistic Missile. Ballistic missiles have no guidance system but are dependent upon their ballistic trajectory. ICBMs have long ranges (from one continent to another) but are expensive. However, it is possible to equip them with multiple warheads, each of which is guided to a different target. Four potentially hostile countries are currently developing ICBM programs: Iran, Libya, North Korea and Iraq prior to Operation Iraqi Freedom.

Information Warfare (IW): Warfare against the information systems of an enemy with or without destroying large physical assets, such as buildings. IW without destruction of large physical assets has the advantage of rapid reconstruction after the war. E-bombs would be a valuable asset in a targeted IW.

Iraq: Iraq launched 96 of its ballistic missiles, "Al Hussein," in the Gulf War. It is a modified Russian SCUD-B (surface–surface) missile with a range of about 650 km. Iraq has produced at least 80 "special warheads" for its Al Hussein missiles, 50 for chemical weapons, 25 for biological weapons, and 5 for trials. Sanctions were placed on Iraq after the Gulf War by the United Nations until it dismantled its biological and chemical weapons, but the UN observation team left the country before confirming compliance after a long series of delaying tactics by president Sadam Hussein. Saddam Hussein's lack of compliance concerning weapons of mass destruction directly led to the 2003 war Operation Iraqi Freedom.

Mustard Gas: Mustard agents are blistering agents because the wounds caused by these substances resemble burns and blisters. Mustard agents cause severe damage to the eyes, respiratory system and internal organs. Mustard agent was produced for the first time in 1822 but its harmful effects were not discovered until 1860. Mustard agent was first used as a chemical warfare agent during WWI. Victims continued to suffer with lung and eye injuries and pain 30 to 40 years after exposure.

Nerve Agent: The original nerve agents were insecticides developed into chemical weapons by the Nazi military during World War II. Now sarin, tabun, soman and a few others are the major chemical weapons currently stockpiled in several nations (including the U.S.). Nerve agents are hundreds to thousands of times more lethal than blister, choking and blood agents and are the most useful to terrorists because of the small quantity needed to inflict a substantial amount of damage.

P5:   The permanent five members of the UN Security Council: China, England, France, Russia, and the U.S.A.

Pakistan: Pakistan began its ballistic missile program with Chinese help and expertise but is now developing its own program. It currently owns approximately 120 ballistic missiles, some of which are capable of hitting anywhere in India, and is working on missiles with longer ranges.

Pathogen: Any agent or organism that can cause disease.

Plague: The pneumonic plague (more likely to be used by terrorists than bubonic) results in fever, shortness of breath and coughing with bloody sputum. It can lead to septic shock and death. This disease is usually carried by rodents and fleas but can be aerosolized and sprayed from crop dusters.

Proliferation: The spread of biochemical, nuclear and other weapons of mass destruction to countries not originally involved in developing them. "Primary proliferators" are the leading industrial nations, the U.S., France, Great Britain and Russia who originally developed nuclear weapons and biological and chemical warfare agents. "Secondary proliferators" are those countries that have developed indigenous programs and that now may or do sell their innovations to other countries or terrorist organizations. The U.S. government designates these countries to include China, Egypt, Iran, Iraq, Libya, North Korea, Russia, and Syria.

Radiological Weapon (Dirty Bomb):   A radioactive dirty bomb involves exploding a conventional bomb that not only kills victims in the immediate vicinity but also spreads radioactive material that is highly toxic to humans and can cause mass death, radioactive sickness and injury. Essentially, radiological dispersion devices are conventional bombs wrapped in radioactive waste that can easily be found in hospitals and industrial plants.

Salmonella: The symptoms of salmonella enteritis include muscle and abdominal pain, diarrhea, nausea, vomiting and fever. The symptoms usually are not fatal but dehydration resulting from the diarrhea is a complicating factor, and the disease could lead to meningitis or septicemia. Salmonella enteritis is the result of ingestion of contaminated food or water. The incubation period is 8 to 48 hours after exposure, and the acute illness lasts for 1 to 2 weeks.

Sarin: A colorless, odorless gas with a lethal dose of 0.5 milligram. It is 26 times more deadly than cyanide gas and is 20 times more lethal than potassium cyanide. A pinprick-sized droplet will kill an adult. The vapor is slightly heavier than air, so it hovers close to the ground. Under wet and humid weather conditions sarin degrades swiftly, but as the temperature rises, sarin's life expectancy increases regardless of humidity.

Smallpox: The first infectious disease afflicting humans that has ever been globally eradicated. Smallpox killed 300 million people in the 19th century. Human beings as a whole are extraordinarily susceptible to infection by smallpox right now, precisely because it has been eradicated. Within 48 hours, smallpox could travel from New York to Italy to Baghdad.

Syria: Syria has one of the largest ballistic missile arsenals in the Third World and the Pentagon believes that Syria has chemical warheads available for a portion of its SCUD missile force. It acquired its arsenal from Iran, Russia, China and primarily North Korea.

Tularemia: A highly infectious disease with symptoms that include high fever, pneumonia and pleuritis, it can cause respiratory failure and death. Because it is highly infectious, it is a possible terrorist bacteriological agent.

Weapons of Mass Destruction: Any weapon, nuclear, biological or chemical, that can kill large numbers of people. There are three types of delivery system usually considered for WMD: ballistic missiles, cruise missiles and combat aircraft.

Millennialism and Extremist Glossary (Chapters 2 and 3)[2]

Alternative media: Short-waveband radio, pamphlets distributed at gun shows, extremist magazines and Internet bulletin boards that provide information for far-right extremists. This underground information network is rarely encountered by the general public or mainstream journalists.

Alternative Religion: A term for non-mainstream religion.

Antichrist: A final world ruler who deceives the masses through the promise of a one world government resulting in world peace. His actual, hidden agenda opposes and attempts to suppress the true (often traditional) religion, particularly Christianity. In Dispensationalist doctrine, the Antichrist comes halfway through the tribulation.

Anticult movement: Experts and scholars who emphasize potential harms among new religious groups.

Apocalypticism: The belief in an approaching confrontation, cataclysmic event or transformation of epochal proportion about which a select few have forewarning so they can make appropriate preparations. From a Greek root word suggesting unveiling hidden information or revealing secret knowledge about unfolding human events. The dualist or demonized version involves a final showdown struggle between absolute good and absolute evil. In Christianity there are competing apocalyptic prophetic traditions based on demonization of liberation. Central to Christianity, the tradition also exists in Judaism, Islam, and other religions and secular belief structures. Believers can be passive or active in anticipation, and optimistic or pessimistic about the outcome.

ATF: The Federal Bureau of Alcohol, Tobacco and Firearms, considered to be government storm troopers by militiamen due to its role in the Waco, Texas incident.

Armageddon: The location in the Middle East where there is a final showdown between the Christian forces of good and the forces of evil commanded by the Antichrist. In popular usage refers to the final battle between good and evil.

Aryan Nations: Violent white supremacist group, originally based out of the Pacific Northwest now in Ullysses, Pennsylvania, that seeks to establish a white homeland.

Assault Weapons: Class of 17 semi-automatic weapons banned under President Clinton's Crime Bill. The ban boosted weapon sales and militia sign-ups nationwide.

Babylon: A symbol in Christianity of all that is sinful. A place designated as evil.

Book of Revelation: The last book in the New Testament describing the events of Jesus' second coming at the end of time; source of most "traditional" Christian apocalyptic beliefs.

Brainwashing: The colloquial term for being indoctrinated into a group is "brainwashing," which was originally used to describe Chinese indoctrination techniques and soon after applied to Russian and Eastern European approaches and finally became a popular term in American culture.

Branch Davidians: Considered martyrs by militia and white supremacist groups that hold anti-government beliefs.

Catastrophic Millennialism: Involves a pessimistic view of humanity and society — the world must be destroyed and then created anew. This will be accomplished by God (or by superhuman agents such as extraterrestrials) perhaps with the assistance of human beings. The millennial kingdom will be created only after the violent destruction of the Old World.

Charismatic Leader: Someone believed by the group to receive special revelation from an unseen source (such as God, angels, extraterrestrials); others will eventually claim charisma.

Chiliasm: The belief that the rewards of the saved will be enjoyed on this earth; the idea that collective salvation will come in this world. Chilia (1000 in Greek) stands for the years of Peace on Earth. Chiliasm sees the current system as hopelessly riddled with evil that must be radically transformed and encourages political activism; a.k.a. millennialism, millenarianism, millenarism (note spellings), see also, postmillennialism.

Coercion: Forcing a person to do something against his will either by physical violence or threat.

Creator: Members of the World Church of the Creator; adherents of the Creativity religion.

Cult: A politically incorrect and pejorative term used to refer to a religious group regarded as aberrant and dangerous.

Demonization: Portraying a person or group as totally malevolent, sinful or evil, perhaps even in league with Satan; acts as a form of dehumanization or objectification.

Dispensationalism: A theological system delineated most popularly in the *Scofield Bible* and followed by tens of millions of Christian premillennialists around the world. It includes distinct separation in God's plan of salvation between Israel and the Church, distinct historical ways and means of salvation, a literal interpretation of the Old Testament and an apocalyptic one of the New Testament that yields a pretribulational rapture of the Church.

Dualism: A form of binary thinking that divides the world into good vs. evil with no middle ground tolerated. A famous historic dualist movement was called Manicheaism.

Dualistic worldview: The world is seen as a battleground between good and evil, God and Satan, us and them. This produces conflict because it identifies particular groups as enemies.

Eschatology: The belief that God will bring an end to history and resolve the problem of evil with a Last Judgment; Biblical doctrines of these "last things." (The term also refers to questions of the afterlife and the fate of individual human souls.) Offers a dramatic solution to the problem of "God's justice" (theodicy).

Extreme Right: Militant insurgent groups that reject democracy, promote a conscious ideology of supremacy and support policies that would negate basic human rights for members of a scapegoated group.

False Prophet: A world religious leader who attempts to build one world religion, variously seen as Moon's Unification movement, world Communism, the New Age movement, or secular humanism. An ally of the Antichrist or False Messiah in the end times.

Four Horsemen of the Apocalypse: Signal the beginning of the Tribulations and God's judgment of the sinful. They represent the deceptive Antichrist seeking power (riding a white horse); war, revolution and civil strife (riding a red horse); natural disasters causing famine (riding a black horse) and pestilence and death (riding a pale horse). Note that at the end of Revelation, the real Christ returns riding a white horse. Some Christians dispute that the rider on the white horse is the Antichrist.

Hate Crime: A hate crime is a criminal offense committed against persons, property or society that is motivated, in whole or in part, by an offender's bias against an individual's or a group's race, religion, ethnic/national origin, gender, age, disability or sexual orientation.

Hate Group: The term "hate group" is used to describe any organization in any sector of society that aggressively demonizes or dehumanizes members of a scapegoated target group in a systematic way.

Identity Christian or Christian Identity: A U.S. derivation of the earlier British Israelism. It argues that the U.S. is the true Israel and white Christians are God's "Chosen People" of the Biblical covenant. Considers modern Jews and the state of Israel to be hoaxes. In its most virulent form, Jews are seen as agents of Satan, and people of color are considered "pre-Adamic" and thus pre-human.

Immanent Eschatology: Sometimes called preterism, it is the doctrine that everything necessary for salvation has already been accomplished, so there are no further prophecies to be fulfilled. In the theology of some churches, notably those of the Orthodox East, the "end" of history is held to be fully embodied in the liturgy.

Jihad: (Lit. "to struggle, exert oneself fully, give one's best effort") Military action with the object of the expansion of the house of Islam or the realm of peace where Islam rules (Dar al-Islam). The interpretation of jihad as an internal struggle comes from Sufi mysticism and remains a minority position within Islam, even at times considered un-Islamic.

Libertarianism: Political creed of many militia members, advocating the absolute minimum of government regulation along with a society ruled by a laissez-faire free market.

Mahdi: Messianic figure of Islam, one of the descendants of the prophet, who will usher in a reign of Islamic justice upon the entire Earth (Sunni). In Shi'I Islam, the Mahdi takes on a more supernatural cast — he has already been revealed, has gone into occulation and, therefore, can return at any time.

Messiah: An individual believed to be empowered by God (or a superhuman agent) to create the millennial kingdom. A messiah is always a prophet but a prophet is not always a messiah.

Messianism: The idea of a chosen one who signals salvation. A herald, prophet or avatar who announces access to secret or hidden knowledge or metaphysical revelation; claims to act on behalf of a greater spiritual power or public good; confronts leaders with accusations of tyranny, betrayal or corruption; and seeks to liberate the oppressed through the significant transformative renewal of the society or the arrival of a new metaphysical epoch. One of the most common ways that millenial beliefs manifest themselves socially, it often tends to devolve into megalomania, imperial pretentions and violence.

Millenarianism: A sense of expectation that a significant epochal transformation is imminent, usually involving apocalyptic events.

Millennial Goal: The ultimate concern of a millennial religion.

Millennialism: A sense of expectation that a significant epochal transformation is imminent, marking either the end of a thousand-year period or signaling its beginning, or both. Two major forms of millennialist response are passive waiting vs. activist intervention. It can involve varying degrees of apocalypticism.

Nazism and neo-Nazism: Nazism is the form of fascism developed by Adolf Hitler's National Socialist German Workers Party (Nazi Party) and the state it controlled in Germany and Europe from 1933 to 1945. Nazism was defined by a doctrine of Aryan racial supremacy, a program of German military conquest and systematic genocide against Jews and other people considered racial enemies or racially inferior. Neo-Nazism describes various post-WWII political doctrines openly or secretly derived from Hitler's ideology, including Christian Identity, National Alliance, Church of the Creator and others.

New Religious Movement: Politically correct term for non-mainstream religion (cult).

Nostradamus: A 16th-century prophet who utilized astrological charts and visions to write a prehistory of the world making predictions about events centuries in advance. The text, written in quatrains, is obscure and ambiguous. There are many published commentaries claiming to unravel their meaning.

One World Government: In the end times the Antichrist attempts to build a new world government.

One World Religion: In the end times, an ally of the Antichrist, the False Prophet, spreads a one world religion.

P.M.:   *Pontifex Maximus*; Latin for Supreme Leader; the Supreme Leader of The World Church of the Creator and Leader of all Creators of the World.

Patriot: Literally, the Founding Fathers, such as Patrick Henry, but in the current sense used as the term encompassing the militia culture. The Patriot Movement was reportedly launched by white supremacists in an attempt to clean up their image.

Postmillenialism: The belief that Christ will return after the establishment of the Millenial Kingdom, which arises from divinely inspired human efforts. In mild forms, blends with progressive reforms, in more extreme ones, with violent theocracies.

Premillennialism: The belief that Jesus will return before the beginning of the millennium and will be the impetus for the final battle between good and evil. It often includes apocalyptic expectation of Rapture, Tribulation, Antichrist, strong dualist tendencies and emphasis on preparation of self and missionizing.

Progressive Millennialism: Involves an optimistic view of human nature that became prevalent in the 19th century: humans engaging in social work in harmony with the divine will affect changes that non-catastrophically and progressively create the millennial kingdom.

Prophet: Someone who is believed to receive divine revelation from a normally unseen source such as God, angels, ascended masters or extraterrestrials. The prophet may announce the arrival of the millennial kingdom or the arrival of the messiah but does not have the power to create the millennial kingdom.

Protocols of Zion: Bogus book written at the turn of the century which outlines a Jewish conspiracy to control the world.

RAHOWA!:   Racial Holy War; the battle cry and greeting of white supremacists, especially Creators.

Rapture: In some Christian apocalyptic timetables, the idea that the collective salvation of the Christian faithful occurs through an ascension into heaven while Earth is purged of evil during the Tribulations through great punishment of those who rejected Christ in favor of sin. Whether or not Christians then return to an Earth purged of evil is in contention. Not all Christians believe in a literal rapture.

Religion: Ultimate concern, a comprehensive worldview that makes sense of the universe and of human existence. Religion explains where we came from and where we are going. Religion teaches followers its view of right and wrong.

Remnant: In some Christian apocalyptic timetables, the idea that in the end times or after the Tribulations there will still be a righteous remnant of faithful Christians.

Sect: Usually refers to a dissident group that has separated from another generally mainstream religion (often proclaiming its intent to recover principles and practices from an earlier time that the religion has drifted away from).

Signs of the Times: A phrase used to highlight the possibility that a specific worldly event may fulfill a Biblical prophesy and thus be a signal of the end times when faithful Christians are expected to engage in appropriate (and highly contested) preparations. Wars, earthquakes, comets, social unrest and examples of sinful immorality are commonly interpreted as signs. Christian Biblical prophesy in Revelation, Ezekiel, and Daniel generates contemporary interpretations.

Supremacy: A set of beliefs whereby one group is deemed superior to another and thus justified in assuming a dominant hierarchical relationship. Racism, sexism, and anti-Semitism are the major forms of supremacy in the U.S., but there are others based on ability, language, ethnicity, immigrant status, size, religion and more.

Survivalism: An apocalyptic view with both Christian and secular proponents who gather and store large supplies of food, water, medical supplies and usually weapons and precious metals in anticipation of an impending economic collapse, social unrest or the Tribulations. Sometimes survivalists withdraw to remote locations or form small communities for mutual self-defense. Some Christian fundamentalist survivalists believe that to avoid the Mark of the Beast they must live apart from secular society for a period of up to 42 months.

Theocracy: A system where the only appropriate political leaders are persons who see themselves as devoted to carrying out the will of God as interpreted by a common religion.

Tribulation: A period of great upheaval never before experienced on Earth. This is generally understood as a 7-year period during which the Antichrist will come to power under the false promise of world peace, while gradually instating a one world government (New World Order) that all must accept.

Ultimate Concern: A concern that is more important than anything else in the universe for the person (or the group) involved. The religious goal people want to achieve is a condition of permanent well-being (salvation). The ultimate concern may be heaven, the kingdom of God on Earth, escape from the cycle of rebirth or perfect happiness in everyday life.

White Supremacy: The term is used in various ways to describe a set of beliefs, organized white hate groups or a system of racial oppression that benefits white people. As an ideology, it is the belief that the socially constructed "white race" is superior to other "races." White supremacy is the most powerful form of racism in the U.S., and it has two major forms: racism by whites used to justify the oppression of people of color and the racialized construct of anti-Semitism in which Jews are claimed to be a distinct non-white race, and are then deemed a sinister race.

Xenophobia: Fear of or distaste for people, ideas or customs thought to be strange or foreign.

Islamic Glossary (Chapter Five)[3]

Al-Hakim Al_Shar'i: Religious authority, mujtahid.

Alhamdulillah: Praise be to Allah.

Allah: The name of the Creator of the universe.

Al-risalah Al-'amaliyyah: Practical treatise prepared by the jurist for the laity.

Asr: Late afternoon prayer.

Ayah: Verse of the Holy Quran.

Baligh: One who has attained the age of puberty.

Barzakh: Period between death and resurrection; purgatory; isthmus.

Bidah: Any innovated practices introduced in the religion of Islam. Considered heretical.

Bismallah: In the name of Allah, this statement is usually made by Muslims who are about to indulge in a lawful task.

Dajjal: Antichrist, the ultimate enemy of Sunni Islam who will overcome the entire Muslim world before being slain by Jesus at the end of time; thought to be Jewish. Has been identified in modern times with Attaturk, Nassar, Khoumeini, Israel, the U.S., various popes, the UN, etc.

Dawah: Propagation of Islam through word and action; calling the people to follow the commandments of Allah.

Deen: Usually translated as "religion." Deen is a comprehensive word that means a total way of life, following the commandments of Allah.

Dhikr: Mention of certain formulae like "subbban Allah."

Diyah: Indemnity or compensation for injury or death.

Dua Supplication: Invoking Allah for whatever one desires.

Eid al Adha: The feast of Sacrifice. This feast commemorates the Prophet Abraham's obedience to Allah by being prepared to sacrifice his only son Ishmael. A 4-day festival that completes the rites of pilgrimage and takes place from the 10th to the 13th of Duhl Hijjah (the last Islamic month).

Eid al Fitr: Three-day festival marking the end of Ramadan — the 9th month (the month of fasting)

Eid: Religious festival.

Fajr: Early morning prayer.

Faqih: Islamic learned man, a lawyer or theologian qualified to give religious verdicts.

Fasiq: A reprobate individual, neglectful and careless in his dress and behavior whose evidence is not admissible if he becomes a witness.

Fatiha: The opening chapter of the Qur'an. Fatiha should be read in every prayer.

Fiqh: Islamic positive law.

Ghusl: Full ritual washing of the body with water. Ghusl should be done after sexual intercourse, wet dreams, emissions, menstruation and childbirth.

Hadath: Condition requiring sudu' or ghusl.

Hadd al-tarakhkhus: Point away from the boundary of a city whose inhabitants cannot be seen. Some jurists consider it to be a point from where the city's call to prayers (adhan) cannot be heard.

Hadd: Punishment prescribed in textual sources (Qur'an and Sunnah) for certain violations.

Hadith: Sayings and traditions of the Holy Prophet Muhammad.

Hajj: Pilgrimage to the Holy city of Mecca performed in the last month, Dhu-l-Hijjah, of the Islamic lunar calendar.

Haram: Forbidden, prohibited. It is necessary to abstain from the acts which are harmful. If someone performs a harmful act, he will be punished either by the Islamic court or in the hereafter or both, for example, stealing or eating pork.

Hayd: Bleeding of a menstrual cycle.

Hijab: Veil worn by Muslim women for reasons of modesty and protection.

Hilal: Crescent.

Hukm: A judgment or legal decision by Allah. Order or command.

Husna: Kindness.

Ihram: State of ritual consecration to perform major pilgrimage (hajj) or minor one ('umrah).

Ihtiya Wajib: Precautionarily obligatory.

Ijma Unanimous: Consent of all learned men of Islam.

Imam: A person who leads the prayer and also a famous Muslim scholar.

Isa: Arabic word for Jesus Christ.

Isha: Night prayer.

Islam: Literally means "submission to the will of Allah."

Istihadah: Irregular bleeding other than the menstrual cycle.

Istihalah: Transformation; chemical change.

Istinqadh: Rescue, salvage.

Ja'iz, halal: Mubah permitted, allowed, lawful, legal. The acts or things that are permitted and lawful. There is no reward for performing it nor any punishment for neglecting it. Mubah is exclusively used for lawful things, not for permitted actions; an example, drinking tea.

Jahanam: Hell.

Jahiliyyah: Arabia in pre-Islamic times; adhering to makkan associationism.

Janabah: State after having sexual intercourse or ejaculation.

Jannah: Paradise.

Jibreel: Angel Gabriel.

Jihad: Means struggling one's utmost to be a better person in the sight of Allah and to establish Islamic way of life.

Jinn: A race of created beings that are made out of smokeless fire.

Juma: Friday, the Muslim's day of gathering or Friday noon prayers.

Jumu'ah: Friday.

Kaba: Holiest, and first shrine constructed for the worship of One God, Allah. Muslims face toward the direction of the Kaba, Mecca. Also spelled Ka'bah, Qa'ba, Qa'aba.

Kabirah: Grave or mortal sin (e.g., theft, homicide, adultery, false witness) which earns for its unrepentant perpetrator consignment to hellfire.

Kaffarah: Expiation, compensation, penalty.

Kair: Unbeliever who has rejected the truth of Islam.

Khalifa: A Muslim ruler of an Islamic state.

Khums: 20% tax levied on certain items.

Khutba: Sermon.

Kufr: Disbelief, infidelity, blasphemy.

Maghrib: Sunset prayer.

Mahram: One who falls within the prohibited degree for marriage.

Majhul al-malik: Unknown owner, derelict property.

Majlis: Assembly to commemorate religious events.

Makruh: Reprehensible, disliked, discouraged. It is used for the acts which are disliked but do not harm. If someone does a Makruh act, he will not be punished for it; however, if he refrains from it, then he will be rewarded. An example is eating before ghusl janabat.

Malaikah: Angels.

Marja: The high ranking mujtahid who is followed by the people. Literally, it means the point of reference. The high ranking mujtahids are called Marja' because they are the points of reference for the people in the shari'ah matters.

Maseeh: A title which means "anointed" or Christ title given to Prophet Jesus.

Masjid: Mosque; places of worship for the Muslims. In one sense the whole Earth is a Masjid for the Muslims, the dome of the heavens is the roof.

Miraj: The night journey of the Holy Prophet Muhammad (peace be upon Him) from Mecca to Jerusalem and then through the realms of the seven heavens.

Mu'min: Believer.

Muafiq: A person falsely pretending to be a Muslim.

Mufti: The independent jurist assigned to the task of giving free juristic counsel.

Muhammad: The name of the final Messenger and Prophet of God to humanity.

Muharram: The first month of the Islamic calendar.

Muhsanah: Literally, "protected;" name applied to a Muslim woman who is married or to the Muslim virgin or to a slave woman converted to Islam whose conversion makes marriage with her legitimate.

Mujahideen: Warrior for the cause of Allah.

Mujtahid: A religious scholar who is an expert of Islamic laws, the Shariah. Usually it is used for the high ranking mujtahids whose decrees are followed by the people.

Mukallaf: One who is competent to undertake religious obligation; religiously accountable.

Muslim: Literally means "submitting to the will," i.e., to the will of Allah, the Almighty.

Nadhr: Solemn vow, pledge.

Najasah: Ritual impurity.

Najis: Ritually impure; not equivalent to unhygienic or unclean.

Nifas: Bleeding of a woman after childbirth.

Non-baligh: One who has not attained the age of puberty.

Qada: Lapsed or due prayers, fasts, etc.

Qadar: Divine providence or God's disposition of any matter; divine decree.

Qasr: Shortened prayers of a traveler.

Qiblah: Direction in which all Muslims face when praying, which is the Kaba in Mecca, Saudi Arabia. The direction is north. East from New York.

Qiyas: To compare; Islamic jurisprudence's fourth foundation in which logical reasoning is used by learned men of Islam.

Quds: Jerusalem.

Qur'an: The last revelation of Allah given to humanity through his last Prophet and Messenger, Muhammad.

RAA: Abbreviation for Radiya Allahu'anhu.

Radiya Allahu'anhu Allah: Be pleased with him.

Ramadan: The month of Fasting, the 9th month of the Islamic calendar.

Riba: Interest, usury.

Riddah: Apostasy.

Ruku': Genuflection practiced in Salat or rite of worship.

Sa'y: Pacing back and forth seven times by a pilgrim between Safa and Marwah.

SAAS: Abbreviation for Salla Allahu alaihe wa Sallam.

Safar: Second month of the lunar year; tampering by pre-Islamic Arabs with the calendar for the purpose of prolonging or shortening the previous month (muharram) in which there is to be neither hunting nor war; also a disease thought to be contagious and consisting of a yellow worm in the digestive system.

Sahabi: Companion of Prophet, Muhammad.

Sajda: Prostration, as in prayer.

Salaam: Peace.

Salaat: Prayer.

Salla Allahu alaihe wa Sallam: May the peace and blessings of Allah be upon him. This phrase is recited whenever the name of the Prophet Muhammad (peace and blessing of Allah be upon Him) is mentioned.

Saum: Fasting.

Shaaheed: Martyr: martyred.

Shahada: The creed of Islam: "I bear witness that there is no deity worthy of worship except Allah, and I bear witness that Muhammad is the Messenger of Allah."

Shaitan: Satan.

Shar'i: Lawful, legitimate.

Shar'ia or Shari'at: Literally, the way. In Islamic terminology it means the laws of Islam, encompassing both the Quran and Hadith (the sayings of Prophet Muhammad).

Shawwal: Tenth month in the Islamic lunar calendar.

Shirk: Associating partners with Allah. The grave sin of shirk is not forgiven if a person dies in that state.

Siyam: Fasts.

Subhan: Allah means "Glory be to Allah."

Sunnat or Mustahab: Recommended desirable, better. It refers to the acts which are recommended but not wajib. If one neglects them, he will not be punished; however, if one performs them, he will be rewarded; for example, washing the hands before wudu'.

Sura: Chapter of the Quran. Quran has 114 suras or chapters.

Ta'zir: Discretionary punishment estimated by al-hakim al-shar'i or a judge that is not prescribed in the Quran or the Sunnah; chastisement.

Tahara: Purification of body, clothing and souls.

Tahir: Ritually pure; not equivalent to hygienic or clean.

Tamm: Complete prayers.

Taqlid: Emulating the opinions of a religious authority.

Taqsir: Cutting a piece of hair or nail by the pilgrim.

Tathir: Ritual purification.

Tawaf: Circumambulation around the Kaba.

Tawhid: The Divine Unity, in its utmost profound sense. Allah is One in His Essence and His attributes and His Acts.

Tayammum: Dry purification when water is not available or is detrimental to health.

Ulema: Scholars, learned men, wise men.

Ummah: People bound together by ideology.

Ummra: A pilgrimage to Mecca but not during the jajj period.

'urf: Convention, customary law.

Wajib: Obligatory, necessary, incumbent. An act which must be performed. A person will be rewarded for performing it and punished for neglecting it, e.g., the daily prayers.

Waqf: Property assigned for the service of Allah. An endowment.

Witr: A prayer which has an odd number of rakat (units); usually referred to the last prayer of the night after the isha prayer.

Wudu': Purifying with water before performing prayers.

Zakat: Wealth-sharing or institutionalized charity in Islam, consisting of an annual levy of $2^1/_2$% on appropriated wealth; third pillar of Islam after confession of faith and salaat.

Occult and Satanism Glossary (Chapter 5)[4]

Acolytes: Initiates.

Adept: One who is very skilled in magic or mysticism.

Altar: A table, shelf or platform set apart from the mundane and used excusively for religious rites and the ceremonial arrangement of sacred objects. Frequently made of found objects in nature such as tree stumps, mounds of earth or stone. In Anton LaVey's original Satanic religion, a nude worman was used as an altar.

Amulet: An object charged with power for protection or to avoid bad luck.

Animism: The belief that all things have souls or spirits.

Ankh: Egyptian symbol resembling a cross with a loop at the top. The ankh is a symbol of life, and often used to symbolize immortality.

Arcane: Secret, mysterious.

Asperge: Sprinkle with holy water for purification.

Athame: A ritual sword or dagger used by witches and magicians. Satanists use it for blood sacrifices.

Baphomet: Demonic deity represented by Eliphas Levi as a goat-headed god with wings, breasts and an illuminated torch between his horns, said to have been worshipped by the Knights Templars, depicted in the tarot as "The Devil" trump card. Popular image for Modern Satanists.

Bell: Often used as ritual tools. Rung to begin and end rituals.

Beltane: Celtic pre-Christian spring festival celebrated on May Day (May 1); one of the major Sabbats. The night before is called Walpurgisnacht and many occult crimes are committed in celebration of this holiday.

Bind: To restrain magically.

Black Magic: Use of power for evil purposes.

Black Mass: Satanic practice deliberately parodying the central ritual of Catholicism in which the host (representing the Body of Christ) is stolen from a church and desecrated. The ceremony includes drinking blood instead of wine, eating flesh instead of bread, reciting the Lord's Prayer backward and the alleged sacrifice of an infant.

Blood: Synonymous in magic with life-force; blood is used by some sorcerers and black magicians to inscribe magical names of power and to sign magical pacts with spirits; it is also consumed as a power-bestowing sacrament.

Book of Shadows, or Black Book or Grimoire: Magical diary containing personal spells, invocations and magical notes. Excellent piece of evidence when investigating occult crimes.

Cauldron: An iron pot or cup traditionally used to stir magical concoctions.

Celebrant: Presiding priest (Sacrifist).

Ceremonial Magick: Schools or methods of magick that place their emphasis upon long and complex rituals, especially of the Medieval and later European and Quabalistic traditions.

Chalice: A consecrated ceremonial cup.

Charm: Spoken or written magical words. Also objects carried for their magical powers or properties.

Circle: Typically measures 9 feet in diameter on the ground. Magic is done inside the circle for protection and concentration. In mythology, a symbol of totality and wholeness; and in Western magic, an important symbol used in ceremonial magic. Frequently found at crime scenes and can be made of dirt, sticks, powders, chalk, etc.

Cone of Power: The ritual act of visualizing a "cone of energy" and directing it toward whatever goal or task is at hand.

Conjuration: The act of evoking spirits by means of ritual formulae or words of power. In ceremonial magic, these spirits are urged to manifest within a triangle inscribed on the floor of the Temple (the triangle being a symbol of manifestation). Usually incense or smoke or some other "manifesting medium" is provided so that the spirits can be conjured to visible appearance.

Consecration: Sanctification or blessing. The act of setting apart the sacred.

Coven: An occult group; the ideal number in witchcraft is 13 but may range from 4 to 20 members; a group of witches who gather together to perform ceremonies at Esbats and Sabbats. Traditionally, the number of members in a coven has been assumed to total 13, but now it seems that covens do not necessarily have a specific numerical membership and groups gather in various numbers according to the nature of the rituals to be performed.

Crowley, Aleister: Probably the most famous — and notorious — occultist of the 20th century. Author of *Book of the Law*. Prophet of Ordo Templi Orientus. Author of *Magick in Theory and Practice* (1929).

Curse: Invocation of oath made with evil intent. Curses are associated with black magic or sorcery, are intended to harm or destroy opponents or property and often require the invocation of evil spirits.

Daemon: From the Greek *daimon*, a spirit, evil spirit or demon; also used as a term for beings at an intermediate level between God and people.

Degree: Ranking within organization.

Demoncracy: Worship of an evil nature.

Demonology: The study of demons and evil spirits, and the rites and superstitions associated with them. Usually associated with demonology or the gods of black magic and the Left-Hand Path.

Devil, The: The personification of evil called Lucifer or Satan in Christianity.

Directions, Four: In Western magic, the four directions are symbolized in ritual, representing the elements Air, Fire, Water and Earth, respectively.

Disciple: Lay member.

Divination: The magical art of finding out hidden information about past, present and future events.

Druids: Celtic priests in pre-Christian Britain and Gaul. Skilled in astronomy and medicine, they worshipped the sun and believed in the immortality of the soul and in reincarnation.

Elements: The four states of matter: solid (earth), liquid (water), gas (air), and plasma (fire).

Equinox: The time at which the sun crosses the Equator. This takes place on March 21 and September 22, and on these days the length of day and night are equal. Two of the eight occult holidays (Sabbats).

Esbat: Full moon coven meetings.

Esoteric: Term applied to teachings that are secret, and only for initiates of a group; mysterious, occult, "hidden".

Evocation: Calling something out from within. Invocation is calling something in from without.

Exorcism: A formal ritual of magical banishment; involves invoking the authority of a higher power to banish an unwanted entity.

Familiar: A non-human being, especially an animal, with whom one has an empathic psychic bond.

Goetia: Tradition of black magic, including incantations, ceremonies and techniques of sorcery, often provided practical instructions for contacting demonic spirits.

Great Beast, The: The name for the Anti-Christ in the Book of Revelation, and the name popularly associated with the magician Aleister Crowley.

Grimoires: Medieval collections of magical spells, rituals and incantations, which invariably claimed descent from classical Hebrew or Egyptian sources. Contemporary occult diaries.

Hand of Glory: Traditionally, a lighted candle positioned between the fingers of a dead person's hand — usually that of a criminal condemned to death. Today it is represented by a statue of the hand.

High Priest: Top leader — male gender.

High Priestess: Top leader — female gender.

Horned God: Symbol of male sexuality in witchcraft; part man, part goat.

Host: In Christianity, the sacred bread regarded as the "Body" of Christ in a communion service. It symbolizes Christ's personal sacrifice on behalf of humankind (from the Latin *hostia*, meaning "a sacrificial victim"). In various accounts of black magic and the Satanic mass, the host is desecrated.

Icon: A sacred image or representation.

Incantation: A hypnotic and sometimes rhyming chant used in spell casting.

Initiate: New member; one who has successfully passed through a ritual of initiation. In occultism, an initiate is regarded as one who possesses esoteric knowledge.

Initiation: A magical metamorphosis; a ritualized transformation experience that introduces one to a new level of reality. A rite of passage into a mystical society or religion.

Inverted Cross: Mockery of Christian cross.

Inverted Pentagram: Five-pointed star with single point downward.

Kali: Hindu goddess personifying the dark and terrifying forces of Nature. The word "kali" means black, and blood sacrifices are still made to her.

Key of Solomon: Title of a famous medieval grimoire published in two forms: The Greater Key of Solomon and The Lesser Key, or Goetia. The Lesser Key contains detailed commentaries on the nature of the spirits summoned in ceremonial magic, including those used in medieval witchcraft and necromancy.

Left-Hand Path: Practitioners of the occult who choose to work in dark magic.

Magic Circle: Circle inscribed on the floor of a temple for magical ceremonial purposes. Often 9 feet in diameter, believed to hold magical powers within and protect those involved in the ceremony from evil. Used as a focus of power for rituals; it is visualized as a doorway between dimensions.

Magic, White: Magic performed for a spiritual, healing or generally positive purpose, as distinguished from black magic which is performed for self-gain, to inflict harm or injury or for other evil purposes.

Magic, Black: Magic performed with evil intent. The "Black magician" or sorcerer calls upon the supernatural powers of darkness — devils, demons and evil sprits — and performs ceremonies invoking bestial or malevolent forces intended to harm another person.

Magician: A practitioner of magic.

Magick: Science/art causing change to occur in conformity to one's will. Technique of harnessing the secret powers of nature and seeking to influence events for one's own purpose. If the purpose is beneficial, it is known as white magic, but if it is intended to bring harm to others or to destroy property, it is regarded as black magic.

Mass: Ceremony.

Master: Top leader.

Medium: A person acting as a vehicle for non-corporeal entities by entering into a trance state and allowing his mind to be possessed.

Mentor: Senior brothers and sisters.

Minor Luminary: Lieutenants to leaders.

Missal: Book of rituals and teachings.

Monotheism: The belief that there is only one God that created and rules the universe.

Necromancy: Conjuring spirits of the dead to magically reveal the future or influence course of events. A ceremony in which the spirits of the dead are summoned to provide omens relating to future events or discover secrets of the past.

Necronomicon: Testament written by the "Mad Arab," Abdul Alhazred, in the 9th century A.D. Literally, *Book of the Dead*, or the *Book of Black Earth*, it serves as an amulet and a talisman against the Forces of Darkness. This is a sorcerer's handbook dealing with necromancy (communicating with the dead), invocations and conjuration of spirits and, among other things, magical formulas. This book is extremely popular and like the Satanic Bible frequently found at crime scenes.

Necrophilia: Sexual intercourse with the dead.

Neophyte: One who is a candidate for initiation.

Nudity: Believed essential to raising the forces through which magic works. Regarded by some occultists as sign of ritual equality and openness, nudity is also favored by ceremonial magicians who wish to dispense with cumbersome robes. Witches who perform their ceremonies naked are described as being "skyclad."

Occult: Latin for "hidden," it refers to practices and knowledge unpopular with modern science and religion; phenomena for which science has no theories or explanations; arts and sciences based on a different worldview than Christianity.

Pagan: One who is not a Christian, Jew or Moslem; practitioners of witchcraft and magic. The so-called New Pagans are dedicated to reviving the Old Religion and reestablishing the worship of Nature.

Paranormal: Unusual or supernatural; not explainable by current scientific methods.

Pentacle: A circle inscribed with a pentagram.

Pentagram: Five-pointed star with single point upward. The pentagram is an important symbol in Western magic and represents the four elements surmounted by the Spirit. It is regarded as a symbol of human spiritual aspirations when the point faces upward but is a symbol of Satanism when facing down.

Polytheism: The belief in more than one god.

Possession: An occurrence in which the personality is overwhelmed and replaced by a non-corporeal entity.

Precognition: Latin, foreknowledge. The ability to perceive events before they happen in contemporary time and space.

Priest: A man dedicated to the service of a deity; a member of a religious group who has achieved a higher sacred status.

Priestess: A woman dedicated to the service of a deity; a member of a religious group who has achieved a higher sacred status.

Right-Hand Path: Path taken in white magic. In mysticism and occultism, the esoteric path associated with spiritual illumination, and positive aspirations. It is the path of Light, as distinct from the so-called left-hand path of darkness that equates with evil, bestiality and black magic.

Rite: A ceremonial or series of acts.

Ritual: Tool to focus individual power of group members on a common concern or object. A prescribed form of religious or magical ceremony often designed to invoke a deity. Rituals are characterized by symbolic attire and formalized behavior and may involve imitating the deity in a ceremonial context in order to obtain supernatural power, spiritual illumination or other specific blessings from the god who is worshipped.

Ritual Abuse: Abuse that involves a series of repeated physical, emotional and/or sexual assaults combined with the systematic use of symbols, ceremonies or machinations.

Rose Cross: A golden cross with a rose at its center, it is the emblem of the esoteric order of the Rosicrucians.

Runes: Any of the various magical alphabets each letter of which contains an esoteric meaning.

Runestones: Magically charged stones marked with letters of a runic alphabet and used for divination by "casting the runes."

Sabbat: Significant holidays and celebrations, of which there are eight in the occult calendar.

Sacrifice: An offering made to a deity, often upon an altar. Sacrifices are performed ritually to placate a god and to offer blood, which is symbolic of the life-force and invariably associated with fertility. Some magicians believe that the ritual slaughter of a sacrificial animal or human releases life energy, which can be tapped magically and used to attune the magician to the god invoked in ritual. Sacrifices are also made so that the magician will acquire more power.

Sacrifist: Presiding priest — represents Christ.

Sanctum: Main ritual room.

Satanism: A religion that developed in reaction and as an opposition to Christianity.

Satanic Mass: In Satanism, a blasphemous ritual that parodies the Christian mass, invokes the powers of darkness.

Satanists: Practitioners of Satanic worship.

Scrying: Divination by gazing, as in a crystal, mirror, water, etc.

Seal of Solomon: A hexagram consisting of two interlocking triangles, one facing up, the other down.

Servers: Ritual assistants.

Shadows, Book of: In witchcraft, the personal book of spells, rituals and folklore a witch compiles after being initiated into the coven. The Book of Shadows is kept secret and traditionally is destroyed when the witch dies.

Skull: Human or animal used in rites.

Skyclad: Nude.

Sigil: A magical sign or cryptic device used to identify an entity.

Solomon: King of Israel. He was claimed to be the author of several magical grimoires including the Lesser Key of Solomon.

Sorcerers: Those who have made a pact with the devil.

Spirits: Discarnate entities, often the spirits of ancestors, who are believed to influence the world of the living.

Spiritualism: A religion based upon the belief in life after death and communication through mediums with the spirits of the departed.

Staff: A wizard's main implement. Made the same height as the wizard, it serves to contain, direct and focus magical energy. A wizard's staff embodies his personal mana and may not be used by anyone else.

Swiving: The ancient rite of copulation in plowed fields to increase their fertility by sympathetic magic.

Sword: In magic, a consecrated ritual weapon used for concentration and direction of energy.

Sympathetic Magic: The concept of Like attracts Like. Magic by association or imitation. The laws of sympathetic magic state that the effect resembles the cause.

Talisman: An object believed to hold magical powers.

Tarot: A set of 78 cards with illustrations into which are incorporated a vast amount of arcane symbolism. Considered by many to contain the sum total of all occult knowledge. The ancestor of our modern playing cards, the tarot is used today primarily for divination (cartomancy).

Thaumaturgy: The use of magic to effect changes in the reality outside the magician. The scientific and technical aspects of such workings; also known as sorcery.

Theurgy: The use of magic to effect changes in the magician's own internal reality. Magic used for self actualization. Focus is on prayers, invocations and meditations.

Wand: A consecrated short rod used ritually for concentration and direction of energy in circumstances where it would be inappropriate to use a blade.

Warlock: Male practitioner of Satanism. The term is also used to describe a sorcerer who is skilled in summoning supernatural evil forces and practicing black magic. Contemporary Wiccans use the term for an initiated Witch who turns against the Craft.

Wheel of the Year: The seasonal round of annual festivals, or Sabbats equated with the magic circle.

White Magic: Uses magical powers to do good.

Wicca: An alternative name for witchcraft. Practitioners of modern witchcraft continue to debate the origin of the word, which may derive from the Old English root *wt*, meaning "wisdom."

Witch: Female practitioner of Satanism or witchcraft; one who has been initiated as a member of a coven. Also a male practitioner of witchcraft.

Witchcraft, Modern: Neo-pagan movement. Witchcraft is the worship of the Old Religion and focuses primarily on the Great Goddess in her many forms: Artemis, Astarte, Aphrodite, Diana, Hecate. In modern witchcraft, the women rather than the men play the paramount role; members of the coven regularly meet at Sabbaths to perform seasonal rituals.

Wizard: From Anglo-Saxon *wysard*, "wise one." A solitary practitioner of magic and repository of arcane knowledge. Usually a specifically masculine term.

Vampire Glossary (Chapter 6)[5]

Astral Vampires: The disembodied spirits of living people who send them out to prey on others.

Baby Bat: A young newcomer to the Goth scene.

Banes: The mythical weaknesses of a vampire: garlic, faith, sunlight, holy water, etc.

Becoming, the or "Being Awakened":   The time when people realize their connection to the Vampire myth and begin to incorporate it into their life-style, thus becoming a Vampyre. This is similar to the "Dark Trick" or being "Embraced."

Blood Bond: A committed Vampyre relationship or marriage.

Bloodline: A family lineage of vampyres (a.k.a., "clan").

Blood Play: Also called blood sports and blood fetishism, it is a sexual, spiritual or expressive activity that involves cutting and blood. It is a form of sadomasochism and is sometimes associated with body art: tattoos, piercing, brands, decorative scarification, etc. Many but not all blood fetishists identify themselves as real Vampires.

Born Vampires: According to the culture, those who are naturally aware of their own Vampiric nature and realize it at an early age.

Brother or Sister: Familiar terms for Vampyres of the same clan to refer to one another.

Calmae: An experienced member of the vampyre scene or community.

Camarilla: A confederacy of vampire clans in the role-playing game "Vampire the Masquerade." The group formed to protect Vampires from destruction at the hands of humans by keeping Vampire existence and activities secret.

Changelings: Annoying mundanes who are interested but too young to join the scene, or who are too deep into fantasy.

Childe: A name used for a Vampyre who has been awakened into the scene by an older Vampyre.

Clan, Coven, Clutch or Circle: A small group of Vampyres who are bound together in bloodbonds, family-like bonds, friendships or companionship, much like an immediate family. Members of a coven do not have to be of the same clan.

Dhampyr: Those who were born sanguine or who Awakened on their own. Dhampir in legend is the child born of a Vampire and a mortal who can feel the presence of a Vampire and who make efficient hunters. Members among the clan of Lilith use this to refer to their newborn Vampyres.

Elder: A prominent member of the Vampyre Scene; someone who has founded a bloodline, or the leader of a clan.

Family Dentist: A fang maker who serves one or more clans or populations of Vampyres.

Fashion Vampires: According to the culture, dabblers who like dressing up and showing off.

Father or Mother: An Elder who is also a family dentist or a respected member of the community and who is seen as an advisor.

Fledgling: A childe Vampyre or someone new to the scene.

Garb: Historical or scene-specific clothing. Examples would be Medieval, Victorian, Edwardian, Fetish, etc.

Goth: Goth originally referred to an ancient European tribe famous for bringing about the fall of the Roman Empire. Today, the term Goth refers to a subculture that began in the late 1970s originating as a musical style. Goths are famous for wearing black clothes, pierced body parts and anything that looks nonconformist.

Haven: A Vampyre gathering place, usually a nightclub.

House: Another term for a family of Vampyres.

Incubae: Female demons of the famous myth of the European Middle Ages who attacked sleeping men at night and had sex with them.

Invisibles: Former members of the Vampire culture who have been expelled from the community.

Latent Vampires: According to Vampire Culture, those with a spark of Vampire nature inside them to begin with, but who need a ritual awakening or significant life experience to bring it out.

Made Vampires: Those who become Vampires through a ritual initiation.

Mradu: A sanguine scholar.

Mundane: A non-Vampire or non-scene-oriented person; also refers to people who do not have knowledge of or understand the Vampyre Scene. The slang for mundane is "Dane."

Necrophilia: Psychopathic condition involving an erotic attraction to dead bodies.

Nomaj: A sanguine astrologer or mystic. This is not a magician or sorcerer.

Porphyria: A disease that causes some of the classic symptoms of Vampirism.

Psychic Vampires: Those who derive pleasure or spiritual nourishment from draining others of psychic energy.

Regent: Influential leader of a Sanguinary responsible for overseeing the Black Veil, keeping peace and blessing havens.

Ronin: A Vampyre who is not a member of the clan or circle. In ancient Japan, Ronin referred to a Samurai without a Lord.

Sadomasochism: The pleasure some people derive from inflicting and/or suffering pain.

Sanguinarium: The "Vampyre connection" or a Vampyre Scene in a city, for example. It can also be specific to a group of sanguines in one domain such as the Gotham Sanguinary or the New Orleans Sanguinarium. The name of the largest Vampire Religious Group.

Sanguine: Real Vampire in the Vampire Culture; in Latin it means "blood." It is a term many Vampyres use to refer to one another as being "of the blood."

Sigil: The symbol of a clan or coven of Vampyres.

Sire: A Vampire who creates another Vampire through a ritual awakening.

Somnusium: To put one's sanguine nature to rest, such as taking a break from the scene or lifestyle.

Succubae: Male demons famous in the European Middle Ages who attacked sleeping women at night and had sex with them.

Swan (White):   People who cannot accept their lover's lifestyle and who consistently try to get them out of it.

Swan: A non-Vampyre/sanguine lover who is knowledgeable about the Sanguinary.

Swan (Black):   A mundane lover who accepts the Vampyre lifestyle but does not feel the draw to become sanguine.

The Kindred: Vampires and descendants of Caine (with an "e") in the role-playing game "Vampire the Masquerade."

Thrall: A specific term for a submissive who is devoted or committed to a master, much like a slave in the Fetish Scene.

Vampire: This spelling designates the fantasy aspect of legend, lore and myths referring to Vampires.

Vampirology: The study of Vampires; a subdiscipline of demonology.

Vampyre Connection: The sanguinarium, an informal network of organizations, businesses, clans and havens who cater to and make up the sanguinary.

Vampyre: A more familiar term for Vampires. This is the older Romanian spelling found in the 17th and 18th centuries and has been used by many Vampyre lifestylers to distinguish between the mythological Vampire and the Vampyre Scene. Refers to real Vampires.

Santeria Glossary (Chapter 7)[6]

Aberinku: Nonbeliever.

Aberínkula: Unconsecrated drums.

Abikú: A mischievous spirit who possesses a small child and sickens it until it dies.

Abo-Faca-Mano of Orúnla: An initiation conferred only upon men by babaloawos.

Abure: Brethren.

Acuaro: Pheasant.

Addele: The cowrie shells that are not read.

Addimú: Small offering to an orisha.

Afoché: Ritualistic dances played for tourists in Rio de Janeiro.

Agegun Oriṣa-Oko: Nigerian priestesses who become possessed by Oriṣa-Oko.

Ago: Ritual robes worn in Nigeria.

Agogó: A ritual bell used to call an orisha.

Agüan: Ceremony during which a person receives the initiation of Babalú-Ayé (Saint Lazarus).

Ahijado, ahijada: Godson, goddaughter.

Ajé: Witches.

Ajogún: Forces of evil.

Akpetebí: Handmaiden of Orúnla.

Akpwón: Singer during ritual drum playing.

Alabwanna:	The Lonely Spirit, Elegguá's mother according to a legend.

Alafin, Alafia, Alafina, or Alafina Crueco:	Titles of Changó.

Alagbaa:	Priest in charge of special ceremonies in Nigeria.

Alagbara:	Violent acts attributed to Oggún.

Albahaca:	An herb belonging to Obatalá used in the omiero and lustral baths.

Aleyo:	Outsider, nonsantero.

Alláguna:	An aspect or path of Obatalá.

Amuluo:	Sixteen-compound oddus of the divination systems.

Anamú:	A very powerful herb used in baths; feared by some santeros.

Añaqui:	Elegguá's mother according to a legend.

Ara orun:	A citizen of heaven.

Araba:	Chiefs of major towns in Nigeria.

Asentado en ocha:	Spanish for initiate of Santeria.

Asentar:	Literally, "to seat." In Santeria, it refers to the "seating" of an orisha inside a person's head during the kariocha initiation.

Ashé Orúnmila:	Sacred powder prepared by the babalawo.

Ashé:	Amen, power, blessings, energy. This dynamic concept has different meanings, among them charisma, luck, mana, spiritual force and fate.

Asiento:	The major ceremony of Santeria.

ASPCA:	American Society for the Prevention of Cruelty to Animals; it closely monitors the activities of the santeros.

Avatar, Avatares:	Paths or aspects of the orishas.

Awe Merin:	One of the divination aids.

Aye:	Another divination aid.

Ayugbona:	Assistant priest (priestess) to the padrino during the asiento.

Babalawo:	High priest of Santeria.

Babalocha:	A santero who has initiated other santeros.

Babalú-Ayé:	One of the most revered of the orishas.

Baba-Oru:	Ruling male orisha of a person, "heavenly father".

Bagan: A priest of Candomblé.

Bahia: A state of Brazil (São Paulo) that is Brazil's center of Candomblé.

Bajar a Orúnal: To bring down Orúnla in order to determine who is the ruling orisha of a person.

Bantu: One of the tribes involved in the sect known as Palo.

Batáa: The sacred drums of Santeria.

Bembé: Feast in honor of an orisha, usually involving the playing of batáa drums.

Bilongo: Black magic spell.

Botánica: Shop where Santeria religious supplies are sold.

Bóveda: The altar to the eggun, or dead.

Brujería: A magic spell; witchcraft.

Caballo: Spanish word meaning "hors"; used in Santeria to describe the omo while he or she is possessed (mounted) by an orisha.

Cabez grande: A leader, head of state or of the orishas.

Cabildo, cabildos: Temples of Santeria in Cuba.

Camino: Path.

Canastiller: The shelves where the tureens with the orisha's stones are kept.

Candomblé: Brazilian equivalent of Santeria.

Canto de puya: Chant used by the akpwón to needle an orisha to incite him or her to come to Earth.

Caracoles: Seashell divination.

Casa Branca: One of the most famous temples of Candomblé.

Casa de Santo: House of a santero.

Cascarilla: Powdered eggshell, used in seashell divination and in many of the spells and rites of Santeria.

Casilla: A medium.

Ceiba pentandra: Kapok tree, the sacred tree of Santeria.

Changó: Patron of fire, thunder and lightning and one of the most popular orishas.

Chivos capons: Neutered he-goats.

Clavos de Linea: Railway spikes

Cofá de Orúnla: Initiation conferred only upon women by the babalawo.

Collares: The necklaces, one of the initiations of Santeria.

Consulta: The consultation of a santero or espiritista.

Cuanaldo: Initiation wherein babalawo receives the sacrificial knife.

Cuchillo: Sacrificial knife.

Darle coco al santo: The coconut divination system.

Derecho: Ritual fee paid to an orisha.

Desenvolvimiento: Material and spiritual evolution.

Despojo: Ritual cleansing, usually involving herbs or other plants.

Dessounen: Rite that separates the "spirit" attached to an initiate just before or after his death.

Dida Obi: The kola nut divination system in Nigeria.

Diloggún: The seashell divination system.

Ebbó: Sacrifice, offering or spiritual cleansing.

Ebbochure: A small offering to an orisha.

Ebomin: Second-class priest of Candomblé.

Egba: Paralysis.

Eggun: The dead of one's family.

Egungun: Person possessed by an eggun.

Eledáa: The guardian angel.

Eleggua: Lucumi spelling for Elegbara, one of the names of the orisha Eshu. Arguably the most important orisha, the Lord of crossroads, the guardian of the gates; also, one of the warrior deities. Eleggua is the first orisha to be propitiated at Santeria rituals.

Elegun Changó: Priest of Changó.

Eleri-ipin: Orúnla's title as "witness of the ori," or guardian spirit.

Endiosado: A santero who thinks himself superior to others.

Epe: Curse.

Epó: Manteca de Corojo, palm nut oil.

Eriaworan: A divination aid.

Erindinloggun: Yoruba term for the seashell divination.

Eru Tuché: Seeds used in preparation of omiero.

Escoba Amarga: Ritual herb.

Eshu: Eleggua's name in Africa; one of the names of Eleggua in Cuba.

Espanta Muerto: Herb used in baths to dispel evil spirits.

Espiritism: Spiritism.

Espiritista: Spiritist.

Espiritu Travieso: A mischievous spirit.

Estera: Straw mat.

Eucharist: Holy communion.

Eupatorium Odoratum: Popular herb used in lustral baths.

Ewe: Herbs, plants.

Eya aranla: Music that is danced and sung by the participants at a drum party for the saints.

Eyerosun: Special powder used by the babalawo in the Table of Ifá.

Eyes: The "evil eye" is feared.

Fadela: Mixture of herbs and blood rubbed on drums for greater resonance.

Filho(-a) de santo: A santero or santera in Brazil.

Florida Water: An herbal liquid very popular in Santeria.

Fon: An African tribe from Dahomey.

Foribale: Genuflection in front of an orisha or elder.

Fuiri: One of the names given to the spirit living inside the palero's cauldron.

Fula: The piles of gunpowder used in Palo.

Fundamento de Santo: Initiation seen as a foundation of the asiento.

Gbaye-Gborun: Salutation to the babalawo; title of Orúnla.

Guano Bendito: Palms received at church on Palm Sunday.

Guardiero: A talisman or amulet, sometimes made out of a rail spike, used mostly to ward off evil.

Guemilere: Drum party in honor of an orisha.

Guerreros: A mid-level initiation in which the warrior orishas Eleggua, Ogún, Ochosi, and Osún are conferred.

Guiro: A type of drum party given to an orisha where only one drum is played accompanied by beaded gourds.

Ibeyi: Holy twins.

Ibo: An African tribe.

Ibochichi: Part of salutation to the babalawo.

Ico-Fa: Icofá, initiation given by the babalawo to women (Cofá de Orúnla).

Ifá: A name of the orisha Orula in Africa. Ifá is the ceremony in which a babalawo is created — making ifá.

Igbo igbale: Sacred groves in Nigeria where the eggun are invoked.

Iggi-Olorún: Name given by the Kongo to the ceiba ("house of God").

Ikin Ifá: Palm nuts used in Ifá divination.

Ikin: Palm nut.

Ikú acháan: Ritual staff used by the babalawo to invoke the dead.

Ikú: Death.

Ilari: King's messengers in Nigeria who were priests of Changó.

Ildé: Beaded bracelet; usually refers to the yellow and green bracelet conferred by babalawos as protective amulets to be worn on left wrist.

Ilé: "House," meaning the house of a priest or priestess and all those who belong to it.

Ile-Ife: Holy city of the Yoruba, thought by them to be where Creation began.

Ilé-Olofi: The church, house of Olofi (God).

Ilé-Olorun: The house of God; heaven.

Ilé-Orisha: House of an orisha.

Inafa: Collar de mazo; ritual necklace of the asiento made of many strands of colored beads.

Inle: An orisha identified with Saint Raphael.

Iré: Good luck.

Irofá: Deer horn used by the babalawo in the Table of Ifá.

Iroko: Sacred tree of the Yoruba, counterpart of the ceiba in Santeria.

Ironworker: Title given to Oggún.

Iruke: Scepter made of a horse's tail, used by Obatalá and Oyá.

Italero: Santero who is an expert in the reading of the seashells.

Itán: Major ebbó or offering in the iyanifá initiation.

Itótele: One of the batáa drums.

Itutu: Ceremony celebrated at the death of the santero.

Iyá: Mother.

Iyabó, iyawo: Novice; one who has been initiated a santero or santera but has not celebrated the first anniversary of his or her initiation.

Iyalocha: A santera who has initiated other santeros.

Iyá-Oru: Ruling female orisha of an individual; "heavenly mother."

Iyawó: Initiate after the asiento.

Jutía: Opossum, a staple powder used in Santeria.

Kadiempembe: Name given to the devil by the paleros.

Kariocha: Also known as "making saint" and asiento; the most important ceremony in Santeria in which the orisha is said to be installed — "seated" — in a person's head. After this ceremony the person is a fully initiated santero or santera.

Ketu: A city in Nigeria where Elegguá (Eşu) comes from.

Kilase: A type of offering to an orisha.

Kisengue: A scepter made of a human tibia used by the paleros.

Knife, the: The cuchillo, sacrificial knife.

Kolonia 1800: A staple cologne used in some Santeria spells and rites.

Kongo: An African tribe.

La Caridad del Cobre: Patron of Cuba and saint syncretized with Oshún.

La Colección: Collection of prayers used by the spiritists.

La Prendición: Part of the asiento ceremony.

Larde: Path of Changó.

Lariche: A part of the seashell divination.

Legba: Name given to Elegguá in Voodoo.

Letra del Año: Prognostications made by the babalawos at the beginning of each year.

Letra: Oddu or design in the seashell divination.

Libreta: Notebook received by the santero a year after his asiento containing prognostications of his future and prohibitions to observe.

Loción Pompeya: A cologne used by the santeros and spiritists during spells and rites.

Loiza Aldea: Town in Puerto Rico where many Yoruba descendants still live.

Los Guerreros: The Warriors; a major initiation wherein the initiate receives the protection of Elegguá, Oggún and Ochosi.

Lucumi: Religious, linguistic, cultural and ethnic identity of the Yoruba people and their descendants in Cuba.

Macumba: Spiritism in Brazil.

Macuto: A bundle, also a black magic spell.

Madrina: Godmother.

Mai de Santo: Brazilian santera.

Mama Ungundu: A name given by the paleros and the Kongo to the ceiba.

Manteca de Corojo: Palm nut oil.

Mano de Orúnila: Initiation given only to men by the babalawo.

Mariwó: Palm fronds.

Matanza: Sacrifice of the animals during the asiento.

Mayombero: Another name given to the palero who practices the regal mayombe, a type of Palo.

Medio asiento: Half of the asiento, the two initiations known as the Collares and the Guerreros.

Mediunidad Auditiva: Medium who can hear the spirits.

Mediunidad Clarividente: Medium who can see the future.

Mediunidad de Communicación: Medium through whom the sprits communicate with the living.

Mediunidad vidente: Medium who can see the spirits.

Meduinidad de Arrastre: Medium who can remove evil spirits.

Menga: Blood.

Minestras: Various mixed grains such as beans and corn.

Moforibale: The act of prostration in front of senior santeros as a sign of respect.

Montade, montado: "Mounted," said of a santero or santera when mounted — possessed — by an orisha.

Moyubbar: To pay homage to the orishas or to the dead during divination.

Moyumba: Litany to the ancestors recited before each Santeria ceremony.

Mpangüi: Title of the palero.

Mpolo Banso: Ashes.

Mpungo: One of the names given to the spirit living inside the palero's cauldron.

ñangale, ñangare: A special ceremony of sun worship conducted by the babalawo.

Ndoki: Evil witches.

Nganga: The palero's cauldron.

Nkisi, Nkita: Spirit living inside the palero's cauldron.

Nkunia Cas Sami: Name given by the Kongo to ceiba.

Nsasi: Name given to Changó by the paleros and Kongo.

Oba: Orisha said to be Changó's official wife.

Obatalá: Father of the orishas, creator of mankind.

Obi: In Africa it means "kola nut;" in Santeria it refers to the coconut, its oracle and its legend.

Ocha: An orisha that can be "seated."

Oddu: A design in one of the divination systems.

Ogún: Lord of iron; a very strong orisha; one of the warriors.

Olofi: Mankind's personal god.

Olokun: Immensely powerful orisha who lives on the bottom of the sea, sometimes thought to be a hermaphrodite. In Santeria, Olokun is thought to be an aspect of Yemayá.

Omiero: Herbal liquid vital to many Santeria rites.

Orisha: The deities or spirits that are the objects of active worship in Santeria.

Orula: Orunla, Orunmila: powerful patron of babalawos.

Oshún: Orisha of sensuality, owner of rivers.

Otán: Sacred stones of Santeria where the ashé of the orishas is deposited.

Padrino: Godfather; male sponsor.

Pai de santo: Brazilian santero.

Palero: Priest of Palo.

Palo Mayombe: A sect based on the beliefs and magical practices of the Kongo.

Panaldo: Ceremony conducted by the babalawo.

Pataki: Legend.

Pescado y jutia: Smoked fish and opossum in powder, a staple in Santeria.

Petiveria alliacea: One of the most important herbs used in Santeria.

Pimienta de guinea: Guinea pepper, popular in magic spells.

Pinaldo: Ceremony wherein the sacrificial knife is received.

Plumas: Fowls; feathers.

Prenda: The palero's nganga.

Quimbanda: The black magic aspect of Macumba.

Quita maldicion: Herb used to dispel evil spells.

Rayado: "Cut" in Palo.

Registro: The consultation conducted by the santero.

Regla: Region of Cuba.

Resguardo: Protecting talisman.

Sahumerio: "Smudging," where a specially prepared incense is used to dispel evil.

Sambia: (Nsambe):   God among the paleros and Kongo.

Santeria: Afro-Cuban religion in which the orishas, or deities of the Yoruba, syncretized with Catholic saints, are worshiped.

Santera, Santero: Santeria priest or priestess.

Santeros mayores: Elders of Santeria.

Sarayeyeos: Rubbing rituals used to rid a person of negative influences.

Siete Rayos: One of the names given to Changó by the paleros.

Spiritism: The practice of invoking the dead through prayers and rituals using several mediums.

Spiritualism: Demonstration by a medium of his psychic abilities to an audience for a fee.

Suyeres: Chants used during the asiento.

Table of Ifá: The main divination system of the babalawo.

Tambor: Drum; drum party for an orisha.

Tata: Father.

Tefar: To write or mark the oddus in Ifá.

Trono: The throne or display of the orishas' tureens during the tambor or the asiento.

Umbanda: The white magic aspect of Macumba.

Wanaldo: Initiation wherein the babalawo receives the sacrificial knife, known also as Cuanaldo.

Warriors, the: Initiation wherein the initiate receives the protection of Eleggua, Oggun and Ochosi.

Yefa: Powder prepared by the babalawo.

Yemayá: Orisha of the seven seas, one of the principal orishas in Santeria.

Yerbero: Herbalist.

Yewa, Yegua: The deity known as the devourer of the dead.

Yeza: The three tribal marks used by the Yoruba on each cheek; drawn in the color of the ruling orisha on the initiate during the asiento.

Yoruba: People of southwestern Nigeria whose magicoreligious practices are the basis for the Orisha Tradition in Santeria, Candomblé and Shango.

Voodoo Glossary (Chapter 7)[7]

Ago: Ritual exclamation meaning "Attention!"

Aizan Chiré: The ritualistic stripping of palms into fringes; occurs at the beginning of ceremonies. The operation is accompanied by songs and ends with the ritual baptism of the talisman.

Aizan: Fringe made with fibers of palm (*Oredoxia regia*); has the power to keep away evil. That is why the aizan is worn by initiates when they emerge from their period of retreat. The aizan is often hung on the lintel of humfo doors, on the poteaumitan or on other sacred objects. Sometimes it is used to cover offerings.

Arrêt or Arrestation: Magic charm to stop the effects of witchcraft or the hostility of bad spirits.

Assein: Iron rod topped with a little round platform. It is kept before the altar for holding candles. In Dahomey the asé are important cult accessories. They represent the ancestors.

Asson: Rattle of the voodoo priest or priestess; symbol of spiritual power, made of calabash covered with a net in which are enmeshed beads or snake vertebrae.

Assoto: Large, tall drum struck by several drummers who dance round it. Regarded as sacred; construction marked by long ceremonies.

Atutu: Ball of hot flour which initiates squeeze in their hands at the end of the bulé-zin; brings period of retreat to an end.

Bagi: Sanctuary room containing the altar to the loa.

Baka: Evil spirit; supernatural agent of sorcerers.

Bohun: Funeral rite which consists of hitting calabashes set over a bowl of water with sticks.

Boko: Derived from the Fon word Bokono (priest) the word is generally applied to hungan who practice black magic but is often used for a Voodoo priest. The boko is also a healer.

Borner: To restrain or "limit," to stop an evil loa from doing any harm to a person or a group of people.

Bosal: From the Spanish *bosal* which means "savage, untamed," this word is used of loa who appear for the first time in a person, or of hunsi who have not yet finished their initiation.

Bulé-zin: Ceremony in which earthenware pots in which offerings have been cooked are coated with oil and heated until the oil catches fire. The bulé-zin is a multivalent ceremony forming part of initiation, consecration and funeral ritual. The fire is supposed to heat the loa and give them more power.

Canari: Large pot which is consecrated and broken at funeral rites. Canari debris are scattered at crossroads. The cassercanari rites are widespread, particularly in the north of Haiti.

Caprelata: Magic charm.

Caprelateur: Magician who makes caprelata.

Caye-Mystère: House of spirits or loa. Synonym for humfo or sanctuary.

Connaissance: Knowledge of sacred lore which gives power to the hungan or the mambo.

Creole: Native to the country.

Croisignin: Literally, croix-signer; to "cross-sign." To trace with flour or any other substance a cross on any ritual object or person.

Dansé-lwa: The "fit of possession" in a voodoo ritual.

Djèvo: Initiation room.

Dyok: Evil eye.

Engagement: Pact which binds a person to a wicked spirit.

Envoi Morts: Sending of dead against a person in order to make him ill or cause his death. This form of witchcraft is also called expedition.

Escorte: Group of loa accompanying important loa. This word sometimes means a loa "family".

Ganmelle: Wooden trestle used for the preparation of "baths," or to hold food for loa.

Garde: Protective charm.

Gédé: "Spirits" of the dead.

Gros-Bon-Ange: One of the two souls that each person carries inside himself.

Habitant: Peasant.

Hungan: Voodoo priest.

Hungenikon: Choir master in a Voodoo society. The man or woman (also called reine chanterelle) who "launches" (envoie) the songs and stops them.

She helps the priest and takes his place when he is possessed or when for one reason or another he cannot conduct the whole ceremony.

Hunsi: Man or woman who has passed through initiation and who helps the hungan or mambo.

Hunsi-Kanzo: Hunsi who has passed through the initiation rites.

La Place: Title in a Voodoo society for the master of ceremonies. Armed with a sword or machete he leads processions, presents arms, pays homage to the loa and helps the officiant.

Lwa or Loa: "Spirit" of the voodoo religion.

Lwa-achté: Spirit purchased as insurance against misfortune.

Lwa-mèt-tèt: Protective "spirit" received at the time of initiation.

Lwa-rasin: "Spirit" inherited through the family.

Macoute: Satchel made of leaves of the Bourbon palm; part of a peasant's everyday equipment.

Mambo: Voodoo priestess.

Manger-Dyò: Offering used in consecration rites; consists of sweet potatoes, yams, malangas, cassava and ground maize mixed together and sprinkled with acassan and syrup. Used also for consecration are maize, grilled peanuts and lumps of cassave.

Manger-Guinin: Food offered to the rada-loa. The manger-guinin seems to be no different from the manger-dyò.

Manger-Loa: Ceremony intended to feed the loa in which animals and various foods are offered.

Manjé-lwa: Sacrifice in a Voodoo ritual.

Marassa: Divine twins.

Monter: This verb is used for a loa coming down into someone and possessing him.

Nom Vaillant: Ritual name for a hungan or mambo bestowed at the end of his initiation.

Ogan: Iron bell with external striker. The ogan can be a bit of metal which is beaten with a metal rod.

Oufò: Voodoo temple.

Oungan: Voodoo priest.

Ounsi: Voodoo initiate.

Owl: Bird associated in many cultures with evil powers, death and misfortune.

Pè: Brickwork altar in a sanctuary. On it are kept sacred pitchers, stones belonging to spirits, attributes of gods and accessories of hungan and mambo. Offerings for divinities are put on the pè.

Père-Savane: Bush priest.

Pèristyle: Humfo annex which looks like a big shed open at the sides. The scene of nearly all Voodoo ceremonies and dances.

Petro: Group of Voodoo gods and spirits.

Pittit-Fey: Petite-feuille, little-leaf member of a Voodoo society.

Placage: Union between a man and a woman recognized by public opinion, but not by law.

Placée: Common-law wife.

Placer-nam: Ceremony in which an object, notably a drum, is consecrated.

Point: Magico-religious term signifying "supernatural power," "magic power," "mystical effluvia." The "point" can be a charm and a spirit which executes the will of a sorcerer.

Poteau-Mitan: Post in the center of the peristyle regarded as the thoroughfare of the spirits. It is an outstandingly sacred object.

Po-tète: Pot containing hair and nail clippings of an initiate.

Pwen: "Supernatural" power of magical protective force.

Rejeter: The act of abjuring Voodoo practices or an abjurer of Voodoo.

Reposoir: Tree or any other place where a loa is supposed to live.

Roumbler: The calling of loa by beating drums.

Service: Ceremony in honor of Voodoo divinities.

Ti-bon anj: One of two spiritual principles of the individual, with gwo-bon anj.

Traitement: Cure undertaken with herbs and magic charms.

Ventailler: Ritual act by which birds are whirled round at arms' length.

Voodoo: Voudun, the Haitian religion based on the magicoreligious practices of several African tribes, such as the Fon, the Arada, the Yoruba and others.

Wanga: Evil charm.

Yanvalou: Dance which is carried out with the body sloping forward, hands on knees and shoulders rolling.

Zobop: Member of a secret society of sorcerers.

Zombi: Person from whom a sorcerer has extracted the soul and whom he has thus reduced to slavery. A zombi is to a certain extent a living corpse.

References

1. Many of the terms were found in Your Dictionary.com, The Global Language resource, Glossary of biochem terrorism http://www.yourdictionary.com/library/bioterrorism.html

2. Many of the terms were found in Center for Millennial Studies at Boston University, Apocalyptic Glossary: http://www.mille.org/welcome/glossary.html and Wessinger, C., *How the Millennium Comes Violently,* Seven Bridges Press, New York, 2000.

3. Parfey, A., Ed., *Extreme Islam,* Feral House, Los Angeles, 2001, pp. 313–316.

4. Some of the terms were found in Zell, O., Glossary of Witchcraft, Paganism and Occultism, in *Witchcraft, Satanism and Occult Crime,* Phoenix Publ., Custer, Washington, 1991; McCoy, E., *The Sabbats,* Llewllyn Publ., St. Paul, Minnesota, 1998, pp. 271–292.

5. Some of the terms are found in the *Vampyre Almanac,* Father Sebastion and K. Ramsland, 1998–1999 ed. and Stevenson, J., *The Complete Idiot's Guide to Vampires,* Pearson Education Co., 2002, pp. 299–302.

6. Some of the terms are found in Gonzalez-Wippler, M., *Santeria: The Religion,* Llewllyn Publ., St. Paul, Minnesota, 1996, pp. 315–329.

7. Metraux, A., *Voodoo in Haiti,* Schocken Books, New York, 1972, pp. 373–378.

Index